PATRONS AND DEFENDERS

INTERNATIONAL LIBRARY OF HISTORICAL STUDIES

VOLUME 1
Between Mars and Mammon: Colonial Armies and the Garrison State in Nineteenth-century India
Douglas Peers
1 85043 954 0

VOLUME 2
Empires in Conflict: Armenia and the Great Powers, 1912–1920
Manoug Somakian
1 85043 912 5

VOLUME 3
The Military Revolution of Sixteenth-century Europe
David Eltis
1 85043 960 5

VOLUME 4
Patrons and Defenders: The Saints in the Italian City-states
Diana Webb
1 86064 029 X

VOLUME 5
Independence or Death! British Sailors and Brazilian Independence, 1822–1825
Brian Vale
1 86064 060 5

VOLUME 6
Workers Against Lenin: Labour Protest and the Bolshevik Revolution
Jonathan Aves
1 86064 067 2

PATRONS *and* DEFENDERS

The Saints in the Italian City-states

DIANA WEBB

BLOOMSBURY ACADEMIC
LONDON · NEW YORK · OXFORD · NEW DELHI · SYDNEY

BLOOMSBURY ACADEMIC
Bloomsbury Publishing Plc
50 Bedford Square, London, WC1B 3DP, UK
1385 Broadway, New York, NY 10018, USA
29 Earlsfort Terrace, Dublin 2, Ireland

BLOOMSBURY, BLOOMSBURY ACADEMIC and the Diana logo
are trademarks of Bloomsbury Publishing Plc

First published in 1996 by I. B. Tauris
This paperback edition published by Bloomsbury Academic in 2021

Copyright © Diana Webb, 1996

Diana Webb has asserted her right under the Copyright,
Designs and Patents Act, 1988, to be identified as Author of this work.

All rights reserved. No part of this publication may be reproduced or
transmitted in any form or by any means, electronic or mechanical,
including photocopying, recording, or any information storage or retrieval
system, without prior permission in writing from the publishers.

Bloomsbury Publishing Plc does not have any control over, or responsibility for,
any third-party websites referred to or in this book. All internet addresses given
in this book were correct at the time of going to press. The author and publisher
regret any inconvenience caused if addresses have changed or sites have
ceased to exist, but can accept no responsibility for any such changes.

A catalogue record for this book is available from the British Library.

A catalog record for this book is available from the Library of Congress.

ISBN: HB: 978-1-8606-4029-2
PB: 978-1-3501-8357-5

Typeset by Monotype Baskerville by Lucy Morton, London

To find out more about our authors and books visit
www.bloomsbury.com and sign up for our newsletters.

CONTENTS

INTRODUCTION   1

PART I   Preliminary: The Cities and Their Saints before 1200

CHAPTER 1   Before the Commune   33
CHAPTER 2   Saints and Citizens in the Twelfth Century   60

PART II   The Cult in Action

CHAPTER 3   Saints and Statutes   95
CHAPTER 4   Building the Pantheon   135
CHAPTER 5   Rulers, Rites and Relics   198

PART III   Siena City of the Virgin

CHAPTER 6   The Virgin of Montaperti   251
CHAPTER 7   Virgin with Saints   276
CHAPTER 8   Advocates of Order   298
CONCLUSION   317
SELECT BIBLIOGRAPHY   323
INDEX   333

For A.W.W.

INTRODUCTION

I

At the end of the year 1400, Ser Luca Dominici, notary and chronicler of Pistoia, thus described the condition of Tuscany: 'This whole country is under tyrant lords, save for Florence and what the Florentines hold.'[1] In the course of 1399 Siena, Pisa and Perugia had submitted to Giangaleazzo Visconti of Milan, and Paolo Guinigi, who in September 1400 made himself *signore* of Lucca, was widely assumed to be the duke's client. Pistoia's vulnerability to a coup in favour of Giangaleazzo was now becoming a matter of urgent concern to the Florentines, who for much of the fourteenth century had exercised virtual overlordship over the smaller city. Diminished and impoverished by plague, not least by the savage epidemic which afflicted much of Italy in 1399–1400, Pistoia remained what it had always been: riven by faction. From the powerful fortress of Sambuca, the party-leader Riccardo Cancellieri held out a double threat to Pistoia and to Florence: he would yield Sambuca to Giangaleazzo unless the Florentines gave him their support. The time had come for the Florentines to assume total and direct control of Pistoia.

Ser Luca Dominici describes, from day to day, the process by which his city lost the last vestiges of its liberty. It was not just the comings and goings of Florentine troops and officials and the constant exaction of taxes that seemed significant to him. On 23 December 1401 he reported how it had been decided at Florence not only that the *anziani* (elders) of Pistoia should henceforth call themselves *priori* and *gonfalonieri* (standard-bearers) on the Florentine model, but that on the feast of St John the Baptist every year Pistoia must do as Arezzo did and send a *palio* (a length of fine cloth) worth one hundred florins to Florence.[2] Arezzo had been subjected to Florentine rule in 1384, an event which, more than any other until Pisa too succumbed in 1406, demonstrated Florence's advance to hegemony in Tuscany.

On 14 June in the fateful summer of 1402, as the rain fell incessantly and Giangaleazzo (soon to be lord of Bologna) loomed ever nearer, the Florentine priors wrote to demand that Pistoia should send the *palio* for the approaching *festa*. Defiantly Ser Luca reported: 'It was never agreed to here, and neither syndic nor *palio* was sent.'[3] The Pistoiese clearly understood that to send the *palio*, borne by an official representative of the city (the 'syndic') was symbolically to accept that they could no longer pretend to be anything but subjects of the Florentines. None the less, when in about 1409 Gregorio Dati wrote his account of the festivities of the Baptist at Florence, he listed Pistoia among the communities which sent a *palio*.[4]

Pistoia had subjects of its own, and that was another story. In July 1402 the Pistoiese prepared as usual to celebrate the feast of St James by bidding the subject communities of the *contado* to send their customary offerings. Several of the *podesterie*, notably Larciano, replied that they did not want to. At the request of the Pistoiese, the Florentine *capitano* and *podestà* issued instructions that they should do as they were told, to Ser Luca's warm approval. The *festa* itself was poorly attended, thanks to the weather and the state of emergency in the countryside. 'There was no one from the mountains,' reported Ser Luca, 'except some who came from Popiglio', and he lists a whole string of places which were unrepresented. More to the point, the men of Serravalle intimated that they did not want to offer the *palio*, but, 'seeing that the captain and *podestà* wished it, they offered it'.[5] Thus the Florentine officials delicately heaped coals of fire on the heads of the Pistoiese who had resisted sending the requested *palio* to St John.

Ser Luca Dominici thus describes how the feast of the patron saint was used by a dominant city as an occasion for the exaction of demonstrations of obedience from its subjects, which included its citizen population, dependent rural communities and even, as in this instance, other cities which had been reduced to subservience.

Such customs were universal among the Italian city-states.[6] The basic models for them can be seen in the homage traditionally rendered by the people at the major feasts of a church's patron saint, and in the payment of dues by episcopal tenants, which, like the cense-payments demanded by the communes, were often stipulated for the patron's feast-day. With the passage of time many episcopal tenants were subjected to the authority of the communes, and from the later twelfth century onwards surviving records of the submission of smaller communities, and also nobles, to the more powerful cities show them promising to render tribute at the church of the urban patron on his or her feast-day. By the latter half of the thirteenth century some city statutes included detailed regulations for this ceremonial, laying down the amount of tribute, in cloth, or in wax which was sometimes worked into large and elaborate candles, to be offered at the patron's altar by the representatives of subject communities and by the magistrates, guilds and individual adult males of the urban population. The celebration of the patronal festival thus expressed the urban government's authority both within and beyond the city walls.

II

In the early sixteenth century a humanist hagiographer, Giovanni Flaminio, thus described the urban patron saint:

> We can see that by a great gift of Heaven it has come about that every city has been divinely allotted some saint as guardian and protector. Rightly it awards him honour and worship at all times, but especially in uncertain or dangerous circumstances it has recourse to him as protector and defender. This is so well known in all cities that there is no need to give examples. For although it can be believed that all those blessed spirits which enjoy eternity with the angels care for Christians everywhere, it is none the less piously to be believed that there are very many of them who exercise a special care and protection over those places in which they were born, or where they lived for a long time, or suffered dire tortures and death for Christ, with happy results; or there are those, albeit foreign, whom the cities themselves have chosen as their patrons with a special cult and devotion.[7]

Such a being could trace his lineage to the Roman *patronus*, and it was, above all, the bishops, who preserved something of the traditions of imperial government, who interpreted the role of the patron saint to the communities under their charge. By a long early medieval process, this saint – often, but not invariably, the local or imported martyr whose relics were preserved in the mother church – came to be regarded as the patron not merely of the church and the diocese, but of the city conceived as a social and political community.[8] This process was usually controlled by the bishops, sometimes themselves writers, and formulated and publicized by other clergy who wrote within their sphere of influence or felt a personal and professional loyalty to a particular shrine. Did this clerical proprietorship of the saints exclude a lay shareholding?

Peter Brown has suggested that the 'ceremonial of the martyrs' in the west – as described by Gregory of Tours, and unlike its Byzantine counterpart – was 'the ceremony of the bishop and his shrine ... not the ceremony of a town'. The *adventus* of a saint's relics to a community attested to the personal merits of their recipient, usually the bishop. However, this had obvious relevance for his standing in the community: the ceremony incorporated 'the elements of heady enthusiasm and ideal concord ... acted out in such a way as to re-create and so re-embellish the precarious concord of the Christian community around its bishop'. Brown also observed that 'the western towns were already being pulled out of shape around their peripheral shrines'. In other words, the urban space in which the political life of the medieval city was going to be lived often had different focal points from those of the Roman town, and some of the differences resulted from the location of shrines which had, or came to have, significance for the whole community. Certainly similar processes were at work in the early medieval Italian city; we may not have a sixth-century Italian equivalent to Gregory of Tours, but Gregory the Great bears witness to the activities of several holy Italian bishops, and there seems no reason to suppose that conditions reasonably similar to those in Gaul did not obtain. Even if we are unable to discern the structure of the urban community in sociological detail, we can perceive that relics were potentially important for the bishop's relationship with that community.[9] The question before us is how soon its most prominent lay members identified themselves as stakeholders in the saint.

With the passage of time the Italian city began to deposit records that have rendered it much more visible to the historian. There is at least broad agreement about the chronology of the transformation of a society in which the bishop was frequently the most influential single figure, as landowner and wielder of public authority, to a society ruled by laymen, whether one or many. If for the early Middle Ages it can be asked what part, if any, the urban laity played in the management of the cult, the question to be asked for the period between *c.* 1000 and *c.* 1200 changes somewhat: at what stage can it be said that the ruling elements in the urban laity come to control the public cult and the process of relic acquisition on behalf of the urban community?

Richard Trexler has written of the 'predominantly private nature of relic acquisition in Florence before about 1300', and of the 'private' purchase of relics by merchants and clerics. Further: 'At this early point, relics obtained by the bishopric of Florence were not considered obtained by the commune; the two were separate entities, with separate patrons.'[10] Even if this is true, it is possible to discern already in the twelfth century, if not earlier, translations and acquisitions of relics which were unquestionably carried out with an audience of powerful laymen in mind, if not by laymen themselves. Furthermore, the activities of bishop and clergy, even when they were clearly not those of the 'commune', were equally clearly not 'private'. Nor should we beg too many questions about the relationships between the episcopal entourage, the lay nobility and the nascent *populus* in the prehistoric age of the commune. In the whole period down to the twelfth century, the problem is in fact largely one of visibility. The question is not so much whether there were laymen prominent and influential in urban government, and as such interested in the city's saints, but whether the interests and the vocabulary of chroniclers and hagiographers enable us to see them clearly, or at all.

In an age of fluid political and legal structures, often highly decentralized and localized, the saints, it could be said, symbolized power itself. Their role as defenders of rights and arbiters of disputes was particularly conspicuous in the monastic piety of the earlier Middle Ages. As far as the urban communities of that period were concerned, the bishop, as custodian of the city's principal relics, played the foremost role in controlling the supernatural power which the saints embodied and which, in an uncertain world, might need to be mobilized in the defence of the community against both the forces of nature and the dangers threatened by man. The fact that a number of sainted bishops themselves became urban patrons attests to this conspicuous role. It is arguable, however, that already by the twelfth century, when the urban laity began to appropriate the control of city government and with it, increasingly, control of the civic cult, the development of political and judicial institutions was beginning to modify the public role of the saints. Redress of grievance could be achieved (or at least sought) by other means.[11] Many of the uses of relics, admittedly, remained in essentials unchanged: neither the Florentine priors nor the dukes of Milan could make it rain. As symbols of political power, however, the saints would in future increasingly operate by conveying what Trexler calls 'authority and honour'[12] to those who were seen to control their cults, who venerated them publicly and saw to it that others did so too.

The enduring use of the vocabulary of patronage and advocacy kept alive the idea that the saints laboured with God for the earthly well-being of their cities. What follows is the story of how the laymen who ruled the Italian cities between the twelfth century and the sixteenth learned to speak this language; how the urban community, considered primarily as a political entity ruled by laymen, came to employ the saints for its own purposes. The patron saint symbolized the public power, and rulers could with propriety demand, in the saint's name, demonstrations of obedience that (as neither anointed monarchs nor consecrated bishops) they might perhaps not feel fully entitled to demand in their own right.

The saints most intimately involved in the protection of the city were often, but not always, the ancient patrons of the episcopal church. Such a patron might be one of the very greatest and most ancient of saints, like the Virgin at Siena, Parma and many other cities. He or she might be ancient, but more localized, like Geminianus of Modena, and in such a case it was likely that the relics had always lain either in the cathedral or in the saint's 'own' church elsewhere in the city. It was common for such a patron to share civic honours with the Virgin: at Milan and Verona, for example, the cathedral churches were dedicated to the Virgin, while the revered bishops Ambrose and Zeno, who were commonly regarded as the patrons of their cities, lay in their own churches on the margins of the old city centres. These were long-established patrons, whose sway was not disturbed by the development of the commune.

A variant pattern emerged when the commune adopted a distinct patron. At Florence, it was not the cathedral but the adjacent Baptistery which became the city's emblematic church. St James at Pistoia furnished an example of a different possibility: James had his own chapel within the cathedral of San Zeno, and his own office of works, and belonged to the commune rather than to the bishop. The cult of the Volto Santo at nearby Lucca has a similar appearance: the holy crucifix was located in a chapel in the cathedral of San Martino. Not until the fourteenth century did these communal governments publish statutes stipulating the payment of official civic homage to the titular saints of their cathedrals. This is not to say that the magistrates had not in fact previously attended celebrations which undoubtedly took place; only that, officially, these celebrations had been the sole concern of the ecclesiastical establishment. Some saints who were unquestionably regarded as civic patrons by virtue of their ancient connection with the cathedral church seem never in fact to have received statutory recognition.

There is a hint here of regional difference; the ancient bishop-saints of the northern plain, where episcopal power was generally more considerable than it was further south, tended to be adopted without demur by the communes.[13] The Venetian political community, however, by defining itself around the Doge, the Doge's church and the relics of St Mark, set a pattern which was followed, if not consciously imitated, by the Tuscan communes that have been mentioned. There were exceptions both north and south of the Apennines to what cannot be regarded as rules. In Tuscany, the already-established advocacy of the Virgin (as at Siena or Pisa) could hardly be improved on, and at Arezzo the ancient Bishop Donatus remained unquestioned patron, as Geminianus did at Modena. At Bologna in the thirteenth century, on the other hand, the ancient Bishop Petronius advanced, in an admittedly unusual development, to overtake St Peter, patron of the cathedral, and become the chief civic patron. Another northern city, Parma, where the Virgin was unquestionably supreme, adopted a lesser patron (St Hilary) in the later thirteenth century, perhaps to play a more narrowly political role than was thought befitting to the Mother of God. Almost everywhere, in the thirteenth and fourteenth centuries, there was a diversification and expansion of what Vauchez has neatly called the urban 'pantheon'. This development took place against a background of political instability and change, but the unchallenged position of the supreme patron at the centre of the pantheon can be seen as representing the continuity of civic identity through all vicissitudes. It is necessary to have at least an outline idea of what those vicissitudes were.

III

It is well known that already by the end of the thirteenth century, especially in the north Italian plain and in the Romagna, a region of small towns, rule by boards of magistrates in the name of the commune was giving way to rule by one man and his cronies, which, if successful, might result (as it did, for example, at Ferrara under the Este) in the establishment of dynastic succession. This process was not a simple, inevitable or smoothly continuous one. A number of cities – for example, Parma – oscillated for years in the later thirteenth and early fourteenth centuries between government *a comune* and effective despotism. A not dissimilar oscillation was experienced by the cities of the north-east (Padua, Verona, Vicenza, Treviso) after the tyranny of the da Romano brothers in that region ended in the late 1250s, but by the middle of the fourteenth century new despots had arisen – the Scala at Verona, the Carrara at Padua – and Venice was enjoying a first period of rule over Treviso, which in the meantime had been dominated for some years by the da Camino family. Venetian rule in the whole of this region became a permanent reality in the next century.

In Tuscany, where 'communal' institutions proved most enduring, Florence and Siena weathered the crises of the first half of the fourteenth century which forced them for periods of years at a time to vest titular authority in the hands of princes of the house of Naples, but Lucca, after the death of its native despot

Castruccio Castracani in 1327, became a political football, experiencing a rapid turnover of regimes until 1342, when Pisa established a control over it which lasted until 1369. Arezzo and Pistoia, as we have seen, were definitively under Florentine control by the end of the century, and Pisa followed in 1406. Native 'communal' institutions were, therefore, vulnerable not only to 'despots', native or 'foreign', but to the empire-building of neighbours which themselves retained 'republican' government. Since the twelfth century, all cities with the capacity to do so had been engaged on this aggrandizement, extending their authority over smaller towns and fortified places in their hinterland, and inducing rural nobles to accept subjection to the commune, although this subjection was often temporary and more in the nature of alliance. This territorial expansion, in the absence of any power capable of regulating it, inevitably led cities into conflict with one another. Siena's hopes of dominating southern Tuscany, for example, were repeatedly and successfully challenged by Florence: one clash between them, in 1260, played an important part in shaping the pious traditions which grew up at Siena around the patronal cult of the Virgin Mary.[14]

Power struggles between cities were accompanied by power struggles within them. Around 1200 many communes were appointing a *podestà*, an official first mentioned in the mid-twelfth century as an imperial representative; now, the *podestà* was an outsider, often a nobleman with legal or military experience appointed for a six-month term, who was intended to be a remedy for faction, the impartial director of the city's judiciary and its police forces. The *podestà* did not, of course, eradicate faction. In the mid- and later thirteenth century the pressure group known as the *popolo* – men of substance in urban life who were not regarded as nobles – laid claim, in many if not most cities, to a predominant share in political power. Their new prominence was promoted not only by social and economic change but, temporarily and paradoxically, by the apparent threat of the Emperor Frederick II to urban autonomy and the need of the papacy for allies against the Emperor and his local adherents, often identified as 'Ghibelline' nobles. The *popolo* appointed a *capitano*, who paralleled the *podestà* of the 'noble' commune. Simultaneously, the orders of friars were establishing themselves as a significant element in urban life, building bridges between the church and a laity which was not always unequivocally obedient to the directives of the ecclesiastical establishment. There were complex and often unstable local alliances of interests between and within social groupings, which involved and affected the interests of the clergy and the orders.

Frederick II's death in 1250 created a power vacuum at the head of Italian politics which was filled only partly by his bastard son Manfred, who ruled Naples and Sicily in the name, at first, of the Emperor's legitimate heir Conradin. The gap was for a time filled more completely by Charles of Anjou, younger brother of Louis IX of France, who was brought into Italy in 1265 by a French pope, Urban IV, and between 1266 and 1268 disposed of both Manfred and Conradin. For a while the new dynasty, installed on the throne of Naples, dominated the peninsula, a state of affairs which was not entirely to the liking of all the popes, nor to that of the cities, even if, like Florence, they called themselves Guelf. The revolt of the Sicilians against Angevin rule, which took place in 1282 and resulted in the separation of the island portion of the southern kingdom from the mainland, dented Angevin power, but by no means ended it. Meanwhile, the *popolo* set their stamp on the urban law codes which by 1300 were being produced in increasing numbers and complexity. Frequently, if with limited and transient success, they endeavoured to limit the influence of the nobles, who were deemed a factious and disorderly element in public life.

The *popolo* was not, however, hermetically sealed off from the magnate class, but linked with it by a hundred and one ties of neighbourhood, clientage, marriage alliance and business partnership, and the social and political aspirations of the more prominent *popolani* made them, too, factious and unreliable. Nor was the economic base everywhere sufficiently developed to produce a non-noble class which was even potentially self-sufficing. Most of the Italian cities were of modest size, markets for local agricultural produce, and best visualized, in Daniel Waley's lapidary phrase, as 'agglomerations of farmers and shopkeepers'.[15] For the majority of them, one variant or another of what we call despotism, the vesting of power in the hands of men with command of land, social influence and armed retinues, was a natural outcome. The attempts of two emperors-elect (Henry VII of Luxembourg between 1310 and 1313, and Louis of Bavaria between 1327 and 1329) to establish a meaningful imperial presence in Italy destabilized several local situations, but overall, if they had any lasting outcome, tended to confirm power in the hands of those towards whom it was already drifting.

By the later fourteenth century, the outlines of a consolidation of territorial spheres of influence around a handful of major centres were becoming discernible. In another half-century this development would produce a rough 'Italian balance of power'. The more southerly parts of the peninsula were occupied by monarchies. In 1282 the revolt of the Sicilian Vespers had put the King of Aragon on the island throne, leaving the mainland, with its capital at Naples, to one branch or another of the house of Anjou; in 1444 Alfonso V of Aragon reunited Sicily and Naples. A monarch of rather different type meanwhile endeavoured to stamp his authority on the amalgam of cities and territories which made up the states of the church. The absence of the popes from Italy for three-quarters of the fourteenth century increased their difficulties, and the authority of the papacy over the greater cities that supposedly formed part of its state, or over the tyrant-ridden Romagna, was frequently nominal before the sixteenth century. In this complicated situation, the greater cities of the 'papal state', such as Perugia or Bologna, experienced the mixture of periods of republican self-government and periods of effective domination by *signori* which characterized the history of many other cities.

In much of the northern plain, there was an ongoing contest for domination of a region divided by few natural barriers. The chief players were dynasties which, by 1300 or thereabouts, had established a fairly stable nucleus of power in one or more cities: the Scaligeri of Verona, whose authority extended at different times as far as Parma and even, briefly, to Lucca in Tuscany; the Este of Ferrara, who acquired possession also of Modena and Reggio, and were able to menace Bologna; and above all the Visconti of Milan. In 1398 Giangaleazzo Visconti received the concession of the title of Duke from the Emperor Wenceslas (who was then deposed by the electors for his pains). Giangaleazzo had established a sway which not only embraced most of the northern plain but, as we have seen, extended into Tuscany and even into papal Umbria. Before death removed him from the scene in September 1402, he had added the scalp of Bologna.

Giangaleazzo was able to exploit the fear and hatred of Florence which that city's Tuscan expansionism in the fourteenth century had raised up against it. By 1400 the Florentines ruled Arezzo, Pistoia, and a host of smaller cities in both northern and southern Tuscany. The death of Giangaleazzo enabled them, within a few years, to acquire Pisa. Cortona and Livorno followed in the next two decades, but a long-standing desire to subjugate Lucca, which issued in a war of conquest between 1429 and 1433, foundered on a diplomatic and military alliance between the Lucchese, the Sienese and Filippo Maria Visconti of Milan. Siena did not succumb to Florentine rule until 1555. Meanwhile, another republic had embarked on the enterprise of building itself an empire out of the ruins of Giangaleazzo's, before Filippo Maria could restore Visconti fortunes. Within a few years of Giangaleazzo's death, Venice ruled Padua, Verona, Vicenza and Treviso. Given the absence of natural boundaries already commented on, the Venetians thus became committed to a struggle with the Milanese over such Lombard outposts as Bergamo and Brescia. The Este of Ferrara and the Gonzaga of Mantua were the most prominent of the northern princely dynasties which had somehow to try to preserve their independence between the power blocs that had thus been created.

It is a point of cardinal importance – not least for the subject of this book – that throughout the confusing political upheavals, internal and external, experienced by so many cities between the mid-thirteenth century and the mid-fifteenth, the commune, and for that matter the *popolo*, continued to exist. The despot typically took a title such as 'governor, protector and defender of the city, commune and people of X'. (Such titles resembled rather closely, we may note, the titles that were accorded to the patron saints of the cities.) There were many variants, but all suggested that the city was a firm which, with many assurances of its future viability and integrity, the *signore* was taking over. The budding or established despot might keep offices such as the *podestà* and the *capitano del popolo* in being, naturally keeping the power of appointment in his own hands, or he might nominally hold them himself. The 'priors' or 'elders' who constituted the supreme magistracy of the commune, and often held office for a period of no more than two months, met a similar fate. Their function had been to oversee the operations of urban government and expenditure, to receive petitions and to submit legislation for the approval of the councils, very variously constituted in different cities, which represented the citizen body. Like these councils, they did not necessarily cease to exist under 'despotic' rule, certainly not all at once, although they would lose virtually all independent power of action. Even where despotism was avoided, as at Florence or Siena, power struggles within the ranks of those who considered themselves entitled to rule, and a keen sense of chronic insecurity, promoted a tendency to emasculate traditional institutions and to vest authority in *balìe*, special commissions with extraordinary powers which could be extended virtually indefinitely even in time of peace.

Given that the urban sense of identity remained irredeemably particularist, subjection to despotism was arguably less painful in itself than the loss of urban autonomy to a 'foreign' power, whether a despot or another republic. The native despot was a preferred solution, but with the expansion of dynastic territorial power, or that of Florence or Venice, it was not universally available. The Milanese could have a ruler from among their own, but the citizens of Lodi, Cremona or Parma could not. There was, however, little progress, before the sixteenth century, towards the creation of integrated territorial states. Dukes, despots and Venetians ruled their clusters of companies, appointing the chief executive but flattering and conciliating local elites by permitting them to continue to sit as directors, albeit acting under instruction.

A part of this process entailed the upholding of the civic cult. If the commune continued to exist under new management, so too the saint who (usually) had been its spiritual figurehead from the beginning must continue to receive what was due to him or her. Dominant cities were by no means always guiltless of appropriating relics from subject communities; but as a general rule, the extension of 'alien' rule over cities of any substance, although it might result in additions to the public cult, did not disrupt its core observances. The dukes of Milan indicated that saints who were dear to them should be venerated in their subject cities, and instituted celebrations which commemorated their conquests, but they also paid for the established civic celebrations; the Venetians did likewise. The Florentines were assiduous in exacting demonstrations of homage to their patron the Baptist from all their subjects, but they are also to be found, in the fifteenth century, legislating on the proper manner in which, for example, Donatus, the patron of Arezzo, was to be venerated. To these and other examples we shall return in due course.

IV

What we may call the 'civic cult' formed only a part of the routine that unfolded in a city's churches in the course of a year. The officiating personnel at celebrations of the patron saint or saints of the city were, of course, the urban clergy, who thus implicitly expressed their participation in the political community. Where a commune adopted the existing cathedral patron as its own, it was appropriating an existing ritual. The liturgical core of homage to the saint remained untouched, but the ancillary ceremonial, such as the processions which culminated in the offering to the saint, was amplified and adapted in various ways to the purposes of the commune. When honouring lesser patrons, or simply paying homage to the name-saints of local churches, the magistrates sent their offering, or sometimes went in person, to celebrations which would have taken place without them.

There were other occasions and ceremonies, already well entrenched in the practice of the early medieval church, with which the secular authorities might associate themselves, sometimes taking an important share of the initiative. *Inventiones* and *translationes* of relics were examples. These terms, which will recur frequently in this book, respectively denote the 'discovery' or rediscovery of a saint's relics, often a premeditated and carefully managed occasion, and the ceremony of removing relics to a new shrine. *Inventiones* generated their own descriptive topoi. It was commonplace, for example, to allege that the burial place of the relics had been so completely lost to view that only a dream or a vision brought it to light again. This had the effect of giving the *inventio* itself something of a miraculous quality, and reflecting spiritual credit upon those responsible for it (typically either the bishop himself or some simple and holy man). It was also, of course, common to discover that the corpse was incorrupt, and exuded a fragrance, the 'odour of sanctity', which confirmed the pedigree of the saint. More mundane modes of authentication included the discovery of inscriptions with the body. Where an *inventio* was not either genuinely or allegedly fortuitous, but premeditated, a formal 'recognition' (*expositio, revelatio*) of the relics, might be conducted, to demonstrate their authenticity and remind the community of their power. This was done, for example, when the relics of Geminianus of Modena were translated to his new shrine in the rebuilt cathedral early in the twelfth century, and the concerned involvement of the citizen body in the whole procedure is much stressed in the surviving narrative.[16]

An *inventio* often, if not invariably, led to a *translatio*, but 'translations' might equally well be the result of the acquisition of relics by any one of a number of methods. Theft (less commonly in the later Middle Ages),[17] gift, purchase, or a plea to the existing owner were all possible. Translations might take place over any distance, great or small: within the church where the saint was already buried, from one church to another in the same city, from countryside to town, from one region of Italy to another, or even from the other end of the Mediterranean. The anniversary of a translation was often (like the dedications of churches) formally commemorated in the liturgy.

The relics possessed or acquired by the city's churches took a significant role in the processions which played so important a part in urban religious life. Like crosses and images, relics were regularly carried in procession. Crosses, crucifixes, altarpieces and shrines were often, of course, by no stretch of the imagination portable. Stationary on an altar, all of them might constitute the destination of a pious journey. Anyone acquainted with medieval art, however, is aware of the wealth of forms which were produced specially for processional use. It was not uncommon (and this book contains several mentions of the practice) for a portion of a saint's relics, often the head or an arm, to be detached and enclosed in a suitable container so that they could be readily exhibited to the people and, at need, carried in procession. Fourteenth- and fifteenth-century chroniclers not infrequently give impressive lists of relics which accompanied processions held for a variety of purposes: to greet a new bishop, to pray for rain or an end to rain, to give thanks for victory or beseech God for peace internal or external. The arm of Geminianus of Modena, the head of Zenobius at Florence, the heads of Petronius and Dominic at Bologna, were only a few of those so used. While the saints could easily be depicted on banners, certain venerated images (most often of the Virgin) became indispensable parts of the processions held on really solemn occasions, and it was not unknown for such an image to be cut down by order of the civic authorities so that it could be carried. Thus these embodiments of the holy, as they were described above, emerged into the urban space and sacralized it; in the Corpus Christi processions which developed in and after the fourteenth century, the Sacrament, the Body of Christ Himself, was made visually available to the whole city. These modes of devotion unfolded against the urban backdrop, and the civic authorities were much more than passive partners in the direction of the spectacle. They instigated a whole range of processions in co-operation with the urban clergy.[18]

Much of medieval religion, like much religion at all times and in all places, was expressed in movement towards and between shrines. These were places where the holy existed in a greater concentration than elsewhere. Embodiments of the holy were displayed on the altar, or concealed beneath or within or behind it: relics, wonder-working or merely venerated images, the Sacrament itself. It was appropriate, and likely to be more effective, if supplications for deliverance, assistance or forgiveness, and thanksgiving for benefits received, were offered in this setting. At the most basic level this was the daily task of the clergy, who in the performance of the cult moved to and around and between altars, with or without an audience of the faithful. There were, however, many occasions, of which the festival of the civic patron was one, on which the ritual at the altar represented the culmination of a journey that was a great deal more than a Sunday-morning stroll. Journeys to shrines might be individual or collective; they might occur at regular intervals, or they might be exceptional and spontaneous; they might be voluntary or enforced by higher authority; they might traverse longer or shorter distances. Many might be describable as pilgrimages.

We perhaps tend to think of pilgrimage most readily as an individual, voluntary and long-distance activity, but it did not have to be any of these things. Pilgrims often travelled in groups; pilgrimage might be imposed as penance or punishment; and although the study of medieval pilgrimage has tended to focus on the great destinations, Jerusalem, Rome and Compostela, which attracted a long-distance clientele, by no means all (or even most) pilgrims arrived at their destination from far away. There is in fact a level at which pilgrimage is hard to distinguish from the recourse of local people to their neighbourhood shrine. A pilgrimage might be the result of a vow made in time of sickness or trouble: the votary undertook to go to give thanks and make an offering to the saint. A precisely similar vow could, however, bring the parents of a sick child, now cured, a hundred yards to the church, to present the child at the altar and to make an offering. Many collections of miracle stories go to great lengths to show how solicitous saints were for those who lived in the immediate catchment area of their shrines. Equally, it was a topos that a saint would often perform cures on behalf of suppliants, sometimes from implausibly far away, who had failed elsewhere, even at the greatest of shrines.

The stories told of the patron saints of the Italian cities show them functioning in both these modes, displaying their day-to-day concern for their constituents while also earning prestige for themselves and the church and city which claimed their relics by doing wonders before a wider audience. The same obligation rested on all the beneficiaries of their intercession: to come bodily to the shrine with the appropriate offering. The legal regulation of the patronal festival by the urban authorities was intended to ensure that this obligation to give thanks for benefits received by the whole city through the saint's intercession, day in, day out, was discharged by the urban community. The ceremonial was, of course, intended to be, simultaneously, a demonstration of obedience to the controlling authority which upheld and enforced the rights of the saint.

Where, however, were the boundaries of the community? It was not only in Italy that relics located in urban shrines attracted custom from a whole locality, or even a region, but the political relationship between town and country in the Italian setting made it a matter of especial concern to the civic authorities that the city's saint or saints should be seen to exert their spiritual authority over the whole area that the city claimed to rule. Both the citizens who dwelled within the walls and representatives of rural subject communities rendered a legally stipulated offering at the shrine on the patron's major feast-day. The former were organized into a procession, on the basis of either guild membership or neighbourhood, which traversed the city along a prescribed route. The latter were making a sort of enforced pilgrimage from their place of origin; their presence and their offering were formally registered. In both cases, there were fines for non-performance and incentives for informers.

A procession is a highly stylized journey, and shares a variety of possible symbolic meanings with pilgrimage: at a very basic level, both signify the journey of the human soul from the earthly to the heavenly city. Modern pilgrimages often culminate in a procession to or around the shrine, the 'real' journey merging into the ritual one. The journey, however long or short, is in itself important because it represents effort; the suppliant or penitent may hope to merit a hearing because he has had to put himself out, uprooting himself from his place of origin, to obtain it. It bears bodily witness to the faith. So, tradition has it that when, in 1260, the Sienese called upon the Virgin on the eve of battle with the Florentines, their ceremonial self-surrender to her was preceded by a penitential procession around the city. In 1399, when all over northern Italy bands of white-clad penitents besought Mary to intercede with her Son to avert the destruction of the world, processions held, in accordance with her instructions, from church to church, from shrine to shrine, from town to countryside and back, were an integral part of the devotion.[19] The processions and quasi-pilgrimages embodied in the patronal festivals of the cities expressed penitence and submission in a generalized, routinized form. The visible demonstration that their subjects had, willingly or unwillingly, made the effort and were there, satisfied the requirements of the city's rulers. They themselves also, of course, processed with their own more sumptuous offering.

In the earlier Middle Ages a rich interpretative literature had gathered about the processions of the church, written for the most part by men whose professional interest was in ecclesiastical rather than political symbolism, and who elaborated the supposed biblical antetypes of various processions in loving detail. Among these commentators was a north Italian bishop, Sicard of Cremona, who was actively promoting his city's saints at the end of the twelfth century and must have been very much aware of the civic context. For Sicard, as for others, the identification of the church with the celestial city was an interpretative commonplace; the word *civitas* is more likely to signify the heavenly Jerusalem than the real earthly city. However, the real city provided both the physical and the moral setting for the processional drama.

On Palm Sunday, for example, the entry of Christ into Jerusalem was re-enacted by the bishop, who ceremonially entered his own city, accompanied by the clergy, who went forth to meet him, and preceding the *populus*. Sicard speculated that there was another layer of meaning here: 'Perhaps we are recalling in this procession the procession of the children of Israel, who on this day crossed the Jordan with dry feet....'[20] While almost all processions might be held to make symbolic reference to the Christian people who had been prefigured in the people of Israel, some were conceived of more particularly as forms of intercession on behalf of the community in the here and now, and as such they should involve the whole community. The Major Litanies, held on St Mark's Day (25 April), were believed to have been instituted by Gregory the Great to repel plague from Rome; but like the Minor Litanies, instituted by Mamertus Bishop of Vienne in the fifth century to deliver his diocese from volcanic eruptions, and held before Ascension Day, they were also understood to be invocations of a springtime blessing on the year's crops. In these processions, Sicard commented, crosses were both carried and emblazoned on banners in recollection of Constantine's adoption of the emblem as the standard of the Christian army. Some churches, he said, had the custom of carrying a dragon 'with a long and inflated tail' ahead of the Cross and standards on the first two days of the Major Litanies; this dragon signified the devil, although it might be thought obvious that it also signified the plague which Gregory the Great had hoped to avert from Rome. On these occasions everyone, men and women, servants and maidservants, was bound to abstain from 'servile work' and to attend the procession, 'since as all have sinned all should petition for mercy'. Having made this stipulation, Sicard returned to the general significance of processions: 'It is to be noted that as in the Mass Christ's mission into the world is figured, so in our processions is denoted the return to our fatherland, and the solemnity of our processions parallels [*comitatur*] the egress of the people from Egypt in almost every particular' – a point which he then elaborates in detail.[21]

Another Christian ceremony which had replaced a pagan observance (as in fact the Litanies had done) was the feast of the Purification of the Virgin, known to the English as Candlemas. This had particularly well-understood antique and civic resonances. Sicard again gives an elaborate biblical interpretation: the participants were going forth, with Anna and Simeon, to meet the Lord. He also explains the significance of the candles, and even of the parts of the candle. Finally, he observes: 'Notice that the pagans at the beginning of this month purified [*lustrabant*] the walls of the city and dedicated them to Februus, that is to Pluto; this lustration Pope Sergius transformed into the present-day procession.'[22]

It was in the year of Sicard's death, 1215, that Odericus, a canon of the cathedral of Siena, composed his *Ordo Officiorum*. In his account of the ceremonies of the Purification, as elsewhere, he frequently followed Sicard word for word; but his special purpose was to describe how the ceremonies were conducted in his own city. After the blessing of the candles at the altar of the Virgin (the patron of Siena Cathedral) the bishop headed a 'general procession' with the canons and all the lesser priests of the city, 'and the people carry lighted candles in their hands'. The procession performed a circuit of the city, the singing accompanied all the way by a portative organ. At the Porta Pusterla the cantor began 'in a loud voice' the responsory *Civitatem istam*. On the return of the procession to the piazza in front of the cathedral, the bishop or the archpriest addressed a sermon to the people, as he did also at the end of the Palm Sunday procession.[23]

No reader of Odericus could be in any doubt of the Sienese clergy's consciousness of the civic dimension of the annual round. On the feast of St Agatha, for example, there was an old custom of holding a procession, with the Cross and a painted image of the saint, around the castle, 'for the preservation of the land and the liberation of the country' [*ad Terrae conservationem et Patriae liberationem*].[24] Relics were sometimes borne in the Litanies, with the Cross and the banners. Odericus describes the daily itineraries in minute topographical detail. On the first day, at the citadel of the old castle, the archpriest prayed for the city. The prayer [*Deus qui angelorum*] called on God, 'who visits holy Jerusalem with the protection of the angels', to extend his mercy to Siena, delivering it from all pestilence and infirmity, and conferring on it not merely *abundantia*, but 'mercy, justice and peace': 'May there be in it peace and charity everlasting.' The response called upon the Lord to embrace [*circumda*] the city, and his angels to guard its walls. On the third day, the participants performed a 'station' at the citadel, 'and those who are carrying the crosses and banners stop and there outside the gate the whole clergy and people wait, and when all are assembled the cantor, standing with two others on the threshold of the gate, sings three times *Dominus miserere*, and the chorus responds *Kyrie eleison*, and each time it is repeated more loudly. Then once again the bishop or archpriest says the prayer *Deus qui angelorum*.'[25]

While Odericus has a great deal to say about the liturgical celebration of the Feast of the Assumption, the chief feast of the cathedral's and the city's supreme patron, he was not directly concerned with the specifically civic processions and festivities which marked it as the greatest day in the civic calendar, whatever form they may have taken in 1215. He comments only that the cathedral on that day experienced a greater concourse of people than in the whole year; it was all the more essential for the clergy to be punctilious in the performance of their liturgical duty, imposing order where there might be tumult.[26]

Two hundred years later, an anonymous clerk of Parma revised the *Ordinarium* of the cathedral. He omits much of the interpretative detail that Odericus retained from sources such as Sicard of Cremona (he is, for example, much briefer on the subject of the Feast of the Purification), but he too gives illuminating information about the civic involvement in the ecclesiastical year. Writing in 1417, he was able to describe one solemnity which did not exist when Odericus wrote and which, in the course of the preceding half-century or so, had become a showcase for civic piety: Corpus Christi. The extent of lay involvement in the management of the procession is clear from his account. For example, he describes the order of the procession, but not the route that was to be followed through the city; this was to be decided by citizens named for the purpose.[27] Parma was another 'city of the Virgin', and here, as at Siena, the Feast of the Assumption was the great civic festival. Like Odericus, the anonymous author is concerned not with the civic processions, which were clearly in the hands of the secular authorities, but with what happened inside the cathedral. He noted, for example, that the *Vexillum Populi* (Banner of the People) was suspended by ropes from the apex of the vault over the choir, and remained there for three days together with all the hangings from the sacristy. He described certain offerings made at the Assumption – not because of their political significance, but because they were intended for the adornment of the cathedral and were under the control of the sacristan; the rest of the day's offerings went to the office of works 'in aid of the maintenance of the church' [*in auxilium ipsam ecclesiam conservandi*].[28] The *Fabrica*, as it is here called, or the *Opera*, as it was usually known elsewhere, was normally a body under lay control, which looked after the repair of the architectural fabric and awarded commissions for works of art. This was one of the many ways in which the laity impinged upon the day-to-day management of the local church.

V

I have not assumed, in any of what follows, that the Italian civic cults are automatically to be regarded as unique in Europe because of the unusual degree of autonomy enjoyed by the cities. Perhaps they were, but only a large-scale comparative study could establish the fact in conclusive detail. This book is not such a study, although it might be a contribution towards it. I would expect scholars expert in other areas of European sanctity – the cities of Spain, Germany or southern Italy, or cities north of the Alps – to see here things both familiar and less familiar. Sharon Farmer, writing about the cult of St Martin in medieval Tours, has illuminated just one example.[29] The burghers of the Châteauneuf at Tours tried, but failed, to throw off the authority of the canons of St Martin, who ruled them (with the backing of the kings of France), and therefore in large part dictated the terms on which the profits of the pilgrimage traffic, including such items as the income from taverns and the sale of wine, were divided. The burghers neither successfully appropriated St Martin nor installed a substitute as the emblem of the urban community. Many northern Italian cities were more successful in vindicating communal autonomy – in part because they were simply larger and richer, but in part also because of the absence of an effective central authority which, if it had so chosen, might have underwritten the authority of the clerical establishment. As a result, the manipulation of saints' cults by governments composed of laymen becomes visible.

As with other aspects of the history of the Italian city-states, there is on the one hand immense variety in the details which are specific to particular cities, even within the same region, with no two places evincing precisely the same pattern of development, while on the other there are very strong family resemblances, with parallel phenomena – and, indeed, cases of outright imitation – to be found everywhere. I have tried to discuss as many of the cities of northern and central Italy, over as wide a time-span, as I reasonably can. Inevitably I have been selective within that enormous potential geographical and chronological range, and have often simply followed my nose along trails which seemed to be of particular interest. Naturally, I cannot have mentioned every city or every cult that would have warranted inclusion; nor can a book as general in scope as this one hope to elucidate the networks of personal and political relationships, internal and external factors, which everywhere underlay the local pattern.

Many Italian cities had a 'sacred history' of sufficient richness to justify separate study. Siena, to which I have given a considerable amount of space, is only one of them. Venice, which has been much discussed,[30] I have largely left aside; and although I have things to say about Florence, I have not attempted to rework the ground surveyed, with rather different emphases and intentions, by Richard Trexler. This is essentially a work of synthesis, drawing on a miscellany of (mostly) printed sources: saints' lives and miracle collections, urban statutes and chronicles and record materials published by indefatigable hagiographers and Italian scholars of every century from the sixteenth to the twentieth. I cannot hope to have read all the voluminous scholarship that has clustered about even the saints and cults that I have mentioned, and my Notes indicate not everything that is relevant but the sources to which I am immediately indebted.

This material has been reinforced by selective research in,

principally, Siena, Pistoia and Lucca. If the Tuscan bias which is so familiar in Anglo-American historical writing on Italy is visible here, I must plead guilty, observing only that I was pointed in this direction when I wrote a doctoral thesis on Tuscan historiography in the first half of the fifteenth century. It was in the course of so doing that I encountered Ser Luca Dominici of Pistoia, Alessandro Streghi's vast verse chronicle of Lucca and his homage to saints Paulinus and Frediano, and Agostino Dati, the rather tedious humanist chancellor of Siena, who had much to say about his city's devotion to the Virgin and was a personal devotee of San Bernardino. Such figures reappear here, many years on, in a different framework.

The first two chapters essentially provide background. In a chapter which has no claims to be more than a preliminary sketch, I consider some of the pre-twelfth-century evidence for lay participation in the cult of saints, concentrating particularly on problems of terminology. The second chapter deals with the twelfth century, when an increasingly independent lay involvement in the urban cult is manifest, and the foundations of the patronal cults which are so abundantly documented in later centuries were laid. Chapters 3 to 5 constitute the central block of the book, and attempt to describe the civic cult in formation and in action.

Statute collections produced by the communes, the subject of Chapter 3, begin to survive in numbers from the early thirteenth century on. They furnish abundant information, though variable in quantity and value as between city and city, on the official cult. Chapter 4 is concerned with the various ways in which, from the thirteenth century on, cities built up their 'pantheon': a group of saints, additional and subordinate to the chief patron or patrons, who also received prescribed offerings from the officials of the commune or the guilds or both. One stimulus to this diversification was the incursion of the mendicant orders into urban religious life. Also important was the context afforded by the struggles of Frederick II with a succession of popes, and still more the introduction of the Angevins into Italy as champions of Guelfdom. It was in the later thirteenth century, in the aftermath of the defeat of the Hohenstaufen, that the practice of celebrating saints on whose feast-days victories or other notable events had taken place – the expulsion of a tyrant, the beginning or end of a regime –

became widespread. The saints to whom official honour was paid collectively identified loyalties and commemorated landmarks in a city's history. Bishop-saints were prominent among them. Some of these were well-documented historical figures, others were not; some (like Zeno, Geminianus or Ambrose) had been urban patrons for centuries; others (like Paulinus of Lucca, or, still more spectacular, Petronius of Bologna) emerged into the light of day in the communal period and rose to eminence, even pre-eminence, within the 'pantheon'.

Chapter 5 is an inevitably incomplete attempt to survey some features of the public cult in action in the later medieval centuries. There was an annual routine, which is described in record sources and often referred to by chroniclers and diarists; whether as a result of negligence, lack of funds, plague or warfare, however, it was not always perfectly observed, and the urban population was not always reverent or obedient. Saints' days had from the earliest times been occasions for fairs, markets, races and other entertainments; so they remained, in a context of multiplying secular festivities from which it is not always easy to distinguish them. Nor, of course, was the sacred routine itself entirely changeless. There were not only new saints to be celebrated, but devotions, notably the feast of Corpus Christi, which demanded and received regulation by urban governments. On the one hand the provision of bread and circuses, on the other a strong ceremonial emphasis on the majesty of rulership, mark the culmination of the process of appropriation of the cult which the communes had initiated in the twelfth century. It became ever clearer in the fourteenth and fifteenth centuries that so far as the rulers of the cities were concerned, whether they were despots or magistrates, the cult was intended to express their authority and status. The acquisition and advertisement of relics was part of the ruler's stock in trade, while regimes of all types favoured the use of effigies of the saints on their coinage.

The last three chapters form a section by themselves, and draw, by no means exhaustively, on the rich documentation of the public cult at Siena. Themes dealt with in Chapters 3 to 5 are elaborated here with specific reference to this one city. Siena was far from being the only city which claimed the Virgin Mary as its supreme patron, but the traditions which crystallized about her role in the Sienese victory at the Battle of Montaperti on 4 September 1260 had some unique features. We cannot know what really happened at Siena on the eve of the battle, when, it came to be believed, the citizens vowed the government of the city itself to the Virgin, but it is clear that the elaboration of the tradition into the form in which we now have it took place later, and may have owed much to the dangers and difficulties of the mid-fifteenth century. This tradition is the subject of Chapter 6.

The mendicant orders and their lay devotees in Sienese society were extraordinarily productive of saints from the later thirteenth century onwards, while the cathedral possessed its own, ancient, saints. In the course of the fourteenth century the civic authorities worked out a sacred routine, the subject of Chapter 7, in which honour was paid to a number of deserving saints, both ancient and modern, episcopal and mendicant. In the later fourteenth and fifteenth centuries, as Chapter 8 describes, Siena was assailed by recurrent internal dissensions and a progressive loss of power in the outside world, which had their effect on the cult of the Virgin and the tradition of Montaperti. The city had other spiritual compensations for its present difficulties, including the acquisition of two canonized saints, Bernardino and Catherine, in 1450 and 1461 respectively. With Ansanus and three other ancient martyrs whose relics were possessed by the cathedral, Bernardino and Catherine were accorded the official status of Siena's advocates in heaven – always, of course, under the supreme authority and direction of the Virgin.

It is important that I should make it clear what this book is not about. It is not a study of piety, if by piety the reader understands a more or less spontaneous interior state of religious devotion. At all times and in all places more saints were venerated, by groups and individuals, publicly and privately, than will find a place in these pages. My focus is on those devotions which were prescribed in laws made by laymen (who were never entirely removed from ecclesiastical influence) and those which, as described in the extant sources, seem to have had a particular political significance. The frontier between public and private devotion was, however, indistinct, and the authorities might promote personal acts of devotion for the public good. The Virgin was supreme patron of the tiny Umbrian city of Spello, which was, admittedly, subject to the papacy. According to the 1360 statutes, the *podestà* was bound to convoke all the clergy of the *terra* and 'request them with humble persuasions that every day in their churches, at the setting of the sun, they should ring their bells three times, with an interval, for lauds, so that each and every person can three times salute the blessed Mary, ever Virgin, saying "Ave Maria" '.[31]

The precise quality of the religious emotion felt by rulers or subjects in the Italian cities as they rendered their compulsory respects to the city's patrons is hardly possible to re-create. Unquestionably, however, the occasion afforded the rulers of the cities both the opportunity to display their own obedience to the heavenly powers (as prominent figures in procession and bearers of a handsome offering), and the power to exact demonstrations of obedience to civic authority: their authority, as symbolized in the altar of the saint.

I have, of course, incurred several debts in the course of more than a decade spent in working (somewhat intermittently) on this book. My employers, King's College London, kindly awarded me periods of leave of absence in 1984 (when I first began working on the idea) and then in 1991 and 1992, when I returned to it in good earnest. My thanks are also due to those colleagues who took over my teaching and administrative duties during these periods. My research was generously supported by the Wolfson Foundation in 1984 and by the British Academy in 1991; I must also acknowledge financial assistance from the School of Humanities at King's.

In Italy, I am particularly grateful to the staff of the Archivi di Stato at Siena, Pistoia and Lucca, for all their assistance. I owe a special debt to the staff at Pistoia who presented me with some of the archive's publications, and very useful they proved too. In addition, I am most grateful to Sig. Adrianno Tini-Brunozzi of the municipal archive in the delightful city of Spello, for making available to me a transcript of a large part of the city's fourteenth-century statute. In London, the resources of the British Library, the Institute of Historical Research, the Warburg Institute and the London Library have been equally indispensable. Some portions of the book first saw the light of day as seminar papers delivered at the Institute of Historical Research; my thanks to all those who made helpful comments on those occasions.

Finally, I record three personal debts. First of all I must pay tribute to Professor Nicolai Rubinstein, who supervised my Ph.D. thesis on Tuscan historiography, which in all sorts of ways, both direct and indirect, has fed into the present study. Professor Rubinstein did not succeed in making me a honorary Florentine, or the meticulous archival researcher that so many of the distinguished list of his research students have been, but what I do have in common with them is the fond recognition of his humane erudition and kindliness. Dr David d'Avray has undertaken the labour of reading the whole book and has favoured me with a great deal of encouragement, leavened with criticism of dangerous tendencies to reductionism. I hope I have done enough, in my response to his comments, to reassure him. I certainly think and hope it is a better book than it was before he read it.

My last acknowledgement is of assistance, moral and practical, given beyond the call of duty and over a period greatly in excess of ten years. It is a long time since my husband Tony coped with two small children and two lots of nappies while I voyaged to Italy; the two children are now teenagers, sceptical as only teenagers can be of the value of their mother's activities, but Tony continues to give me every support as well as sharing with me the enjoyment of Italian holidays. The dedication has to be his.

Notes

1. Dominici, *Cronache*, 1, p. 292.
2. Ibid., 2, p. 63.
3. Ibid., p. 105.
4. *L'Istoria di Firenze*, p. 93.
5. Dominici, *Cronache*, 2, p. 160.
6. For an introduction, the English reader should consult G. Chittolini, 'Civic Religion and the Countryside'.
7. *Chronica breviora faventina*, pp. 338–9:

Magno quidem ac caelesti dono factum cernimus, ut unaquaeque civitas sanctum aliquem protectorem suum ac tutelarem divinitum sortita fuerit, quae merito illum honore et cultu prosecuta semper quidem sed praecipue in rebus dubiis ac dificilibus custodem suum ac defensorem experiatur. Hoc autem adeo quidem cunctis urbibus notum est ut opus non sit exemplis uti. Nam licet credibile sit omnes illos beatos spiritus, qui sempiterno cum angelis aevo fruuntur christiani nominis ubique curam gerere, pie tamen credendum est, ex eorum numero quam plurimos esse, quibus praecipue locorum quorumdam cura sit atque protectio, in quibus vel nati sint illi ac diu versati vel felici successu pro Christo diros cruciatus ac mortem passi, vel quos etiam alienigenas ipsae civitates peculiari quodam cultu ac religione sibi patronos delegerint. Tales non paucos habet praeclara et vetus civitas Aemiliae Faventia, quorum describere vitam et res gestas propitio Deo decrevimus.

8. See, in general, A.M. Orselli, 'L'idea e il culto del Santo Patrono', in *L'immaginario religioso*.

9. 'Eastern and Western Christendom in Late Antiquity: a Parting of the Ways', *Studies in Church History* 13 (Oxford 1976), p. 1–24; reprinted in *Society and the Holy in Late Antiquity* (London 1982), pp. 166–95. See also 'Relics and Social Status in the Age of Gregory of Tours' (The Stenton Lecture, University of Reading, 1976), reprinted in *Society and the Holy*, pp. 222–50.

10. *Public Life in Renaissance Florence*, n.2, pp. 1–2.

11. As Patrick Geary has suggested in a different context: 'Humiliation of Saints', in *Saints and their Cults: Studies in Religious Sociology, Folklore and History*, ed. S. Wilson (Cambridge 1983), pp. 123–40 (originally published as 'L'humiliation des saints', *Annales* 34, 1979, pp. 27–42).

12. 'The Magi Enter Florence', p. 129. For a general survey, see Vauchez, 'Patronage des saints'.

13. I am grateful to Dr Edward Coleman for emphasizing this point in correspondence.

14. See below, Chapter 6.

15. *Medieval Orvieto* (London 1952), p. xvi.

16. Below, pp. 60–62.

17. For a fifteenth-century example of 'holy theft', see below pp. 227–30.

18. For an example of a contretemps involving the bishop of Florence on the occasion of a procession, see below p. 166.

19. D. Bornstein, *The Bianchi of 1399: Popular Devotion in Late Medieval Italy* (Ithaca, NY 1993). Chapter 1, 'The Religious Culture of Late Medieval Italy', can be recommended as an excellent introduction to the subject.

20. *Mitrale, seu de Officiis Ecclesiasticis Summa*, PL 213, col. 293.

21. Ibid., cols 367–9.

22. Ibid., cols 213–14.

23. *Ordo Officiorum*, p. 299.

24. Ibid., pp. 304, 117.

25. Ibid., pp. 208–19.

26. Ibid., p. 348.

27. *Ordinarium Ecclesiae Parmensis*, pp. 169–74. See further below, pp. 182–4, and for the feast in general, Rubin, *Corpus Christi*.

28. *Ordinarium*, pp. 183–5.

29. *Communities of Saint Martin: Legend and Ritual in Medieval Tours* (Ithaca, NY 1991).

30. For example, by H.C. Peyer, *Stadt und Stadtpatron*, pp. 8–62. See also E. Muir, *Civic Ritual in Renaissance Venice* (Princeton, NJ 1981); P. F. Brown, *Venetian Narrative Painting in the Age of Carpaccio* (New Haven, CT 1988).

31 Spello, Archivio Municipale, *Statutum Civitatis Hyspelli*, fol. 37 (Lib. I, cap. 22).

PART I

PRELIMINARY: THE CITIES AND THEIR SAINTS BEFORE 1200

CHAPTER I

BEFORE THE COMMUNE

Grégoire wrote that 'the hagiography of the early Latin Middle Ages almost never unfolds in an urban context; the space is that of the desert, even if at the gates of the city, or a space savage and free, a rural space, without limits....'[1] The devil was appalled to think that St Antony by ascetic practice might transform the desert into a city. The city was Christianized civilization, the desert was the devil's field of operations. This view expresses a deeply felt need for safety in numbers: men, feeling themselves to be few and weak, imagine their adversaries (in the hagiographical case, demons) to be numberless,[2] while the devil's fear is that the saint will somehow turn the tables. Yet the city has also, in the Bible and elsewhere, been the sink of iniquity, and in monastic literature this view sometimes merged with the classical pastoral convention, so that rural solitude signified peace, beauty and aptness for contemplation.

Here, however, we are concerned with the real rather than the metaphorical city. By the year 1100 writers who described life in the Italian cities were using a vocabulary which enables us to discern ranks within the urban lay population, and the emergence of social and governmental structures. The 'people' or the 'citizens' may be distinguished from 'knights' or 'nobles', and the greater among the 'people' from the lesser. There may be mention of 'consuls', whose existence has often been regarded as diagnostic of the existence of the 'commune'. The absence of a comparably differentiated terminology in an earlier period poses a basic problem for the historian in quest of social realities. The 'citizens' of the twelfth century had among their ancestors urban notables, often the tenants or in other ways the associates of bishop or count, and the word *civis* was used in texts of all kinds, narrative and non-narrative, throughout the early medieval period. Sometimes, however, especially before the later eleventh century and especially in narrative sources such as hagiography, it can be unclear whether it is in fact intended to have the more or less precise sociopolitical connotation which it might theoretically have. Like its relation *civitas*, the word often carried with it vague Roman or Augustinian associations, evoking the membership of an essentially otherworldly community.[3]

We must therefore look carefully, without entertaining great expectations, at the contexts in which persons called *cives* are mentioned. The words *plebs* or *populus* are not much more helpful; both commonly denoted the 'people' in their relationship either to the church in general or to a particular church, the laity rather than the clergy. They tend to appear as an undifferentiated mass, a faceless audience for manifestations of spiritual power, in need of pastoral care, easily led and not infrequently the perpetrators of disorder. Language is used to identify the leading and supporting roles in a spiritual drama rather than to describe social reality. In that reality, however, there were great laymen, princes, nobles, kinsfolk of the bishops, who could not and cannot simply be reckoned with the mass of the laity and who are, in fact, occasionally visible in the sources, co-operating with the clergy, even perhaps bullying them, in their task of presenting the saints to the Christian people. Such men had strong interests in urban property and politics, but cannot simply be described as an 'urban' laity. How (if at all) did those who described, and sometimes stage-managed, manifestations of the holy in early medieval Italian cities perceive the lay element, or elements, in their wider audience? Did they in fact see the city as a distinctive social environment inhabited by a distinctive public?

Early hagiography, in the sense of the description of the lives and deaths of saints, may well, as Grégoire suggests, set its scene in the wilderness (in imitation of the life of Christ himself) or just outside the city. The *inventiones* and *translationes* of long-dead saints, and the miracles which marked these occasions, are another matter. Whatever cities were like physically and socially, they were, in Italy as elsewhere in the Mediterranean world, the seats of the bishops who were most likely to seek to gather the saints to themselves and thus focus the devotions of the *plebs sancta*.[4] In 386 AD Ambrose of Milan performed one of the great archetypal translations of the early period, that of Gervasius and Protasius. At the time he was under siege by the Empress Justina, having refused to concede a church to her for Arian worship. Ambrose reported in a letter to his sister how he had addressed the people on the subject of the relics.[5] If Gervasius and Protasius came to light in the first instance to satisfy a practical need for the relics of martyrs, so that the bishop could consecrate his church 'in the Roman manner', as the people allegedly demanded, Ambrose clearly used them also to remind his audience more generally of its links with an already mythic, heroic Christian past. He stressed the historic continuity of the community, which was revealed and emphasized by the discovery of the martyrs. In their grand stature they recalled a heroic age [*prisca aetas*] and in the miracles which occurred after their discovery they restored the 'miracles of the olden time'. The city had rediscovered heavenly protectors whom it had always in fact possessed, but had forgotten. The Milanese were being urged to feel themselves linked to a holy past which was a source of irresistible spiritual power, and it was important that the saints whose *inventio* sparked this awareness should be native to the place. Ambrose pointed out, as a paradox in need of correction, that while the city had acquired the ownership of other martyrs, it had lost sight of its own. Milan did not in fact lack native saints and martyrs, but Ambrose, in the process of consecrating his basilica and enveloped in the crisis of his quarrel with the Empress, needed some new manifestation of the old and holy, specifically adapted to the Milanese situation.

The bishop's own motives are – in part, at least – clear enough, but we cannot penetrate very far into the nature of the community which he called his *plebs sancta*. To Augustine (in *Confessions* IX.7) God's purpose in revealing the whereabouts of Gervasius and Protasius was precisely to thwart the Empress, but, looking back as he wrote *De Civitate Dei* XXII.8, he also saw the practical value of the city of Milan as the setting for this miracle: 'It could come to the notice of a lot of people, because it is a large city, and the emperor was there at the time, and the thing happened with an immense number of people as witnesses, who were flocking to see the bodies of the martyrs Gervasius and Protasius.' Of the beneficiary of the major miracle inspired by the saints in 386 we know only that he was (according to Ambrose) a wool-worker and (according to Augustine) vowed to spend the rest of his life serving the basilica.[6]

Certainly this *inventio* attained great celebrity, and it was not the last in late-fourth-century Italy. In 395 Ambrose was himself subsequently responsible for the translation of the martyrs Nazarius and Celsus from a garden outside the city to the church of the Holy Apostles.[7] Invited to be present at the *translatio* of the martyrs Vitalis and Agricola, who had been found in the Jewish burial ground at Bologna, he then took some of their relics to Florence, where the *plebs sancta* of the church of San Lorenzo rejoiced at being thus fortified against the demons.[8] Ambrose's friend and correspondent Savinus, bishop of Piacenza, attained his greatest posthumous celebrity by discovering and translating to the basilica founded by his predecessor Victor the body of the soldier-martyr Antoninus. Bishop Victor, we are told, had prophesied: 'one greater than I will lie in this tomb'.[9] A recent holy bishop was improved on by a martyr of remoter antiquity. Savinus – who, like Ambrose, was much engaged in the contest against the Arians – may also have appreciated the value of novelty, and desired to establish for the *plebs sancta* of Piacenza a linkage with a holy past, real or imagined. This sense of linkage remained an important ingredient in the propaganda use of saints made by churches and urban governments in the centuries to come.

It was Alba Orselli's contention that, for both Ambrose and Augustine, the patronage of the saints extended over the people of a church rather than over an urban community as such.[10] The distinction, never a watertight one, becomes more difficult to make in later centuries. Bishops not only administered their dioceses and their lands from urban centres, but exercised power over the cities, their inhabitants and physical fabric. The pre-eminence of the city did not begin in the twelfth century, or even the eleventh; the bishop and his men were at the root of it.[11] The city, symbolically as well as actually delineated by its walls (for the upkeep of which the bishops of northern Italy were not infrequently responsible), possessed a more or less apprehensible identity even when settlement spilled beyond them. Things were a little different at the extremities of diocese or *comitatus*.¹² Here disputes over diocesan jurisdiction, which was ostensibly the bishop's concern, merged and overlapped with an essentially secular process of territorial self-definition. The bishops of Siena and Arezzo, for example, engaged in an exceptionally long-running dispute over the boundaries of their diocesan jurisdiction, and the laity can from time to time be perceived as involved in this contest. The patronage of a saint who dwelt on the contested boundary was (for at least part of the period) one of the matters at issue, and another patron saint became involved at a later stage.

We first have notice of the dispute in about 650 AD; Honorius III finally imposed silence on the Sienese in 1220.¹³ Among the seventeen churches in dispute between Siena and Arezzo were two which lay near the river Arbia, a few miles from Siena and only a third of a mile from each other. One became a parish church, Santa Maria in Dofana, while the other marked the burial place of St Ansanus, a martyr of the reign of Nero. In 714 the dispute was brought to the court of the Lombard King Liutprand. He ordered an investigation, from which it emerged that the contest over the church had already resulted in the murder by the Aretines of the Sienese judge (and brother of the bishop) Godebert. This in turn had created a feud between the 'inhabitants of the city of Arezzo' and 'the Sienese people'. It transpired also that Wilerat, the Sienese gastald (the king's local representative) had built, or completely rebuilt, the church of St Ansanus, which, it was claimed, the bishop of Siena had consecrated at the request of the bishop of Arezzo, as it was in the diocese of Arezzo. A committee of bishops appointed by Liutprand ruled in Arezzo's favour, but the Sienese gastalds were not prepared to give up. In 752 Pope Stephen II was told that the present gastald, Gauspert, had, without the knowledge of the bishop of Arezzo, translated the relics of Ansano from outside the church to an altar within, and had forced Ansfridus, bishop of Siena, to do the honours – or so the quaking bishop tried to claim, assuring the Pope that 'he would on no account have translated the body of S. Ansano and dedicated the altar, if the gastald Gauspert had not forced him to do so willy-nilly, in the presence of many men.'

It was never disputed that the churches at issue were in the 'county' of Siena, but traditionally they lay in the diocese of

Arezzo. So Stephen ruled once again in favour of Arezzo.[14] For a time, at any rate, the gastalds of Siena asserted authority over the relics of Ansano as a symbol of their wider struggle to render the diocese of Siena coterminous with its county. The relics continued to be mentioned in charters of Charlemagne and Louis the Pious to the church of Arezzo, then everyone seems to have lost interest in them. The churches were enumerated repeatedly in subsequent litigation, but the relics were not mentioned. The story of Ansanus was not, however, over, as we shall see in the next chapter.

St Donatus, patron of the church of Arezzo, had from time to time been mentioned by witnesses in the hearings of Liutprand, Stephen II and after, but only in so far as his name identified his church. Arezzo's second bishop, he was buried in a church built on the site of his martyrdom on a low hill, about a kilometre outside the city, and there the bishop and his canons had their residence.[15] From the ninth century the relics of Donatus were mentioned in the privileges of the Emperors for Arezzo. In 876 Charles the Bald declared that although the present site might be said to have been chosen by Donatus himself, it would be more fitting for the cathedral church to be within the city walls, as was normal elsewhere, and he granted the bishop the area of the ancient forum so that he could bring himself and his clergy into the centre of the Roman town. It is not clear whether there was at this date pressure from the Aretine laity to bring about this move, but this pressure was later manifested violently.

From this time on, in fact, the bishop and his clergy divided their functions and their residence between a number of sites. The baptismal church of St Mary, originally just outside the early medieval wall of the city, but well within the area of urban growth as Arezzo expanded from its hilltop nucleus down into the plain, increasingly became the focus of civic religion, and a detachment of canons resided there. The bishop himself moved his seat to the nearby abbey church of San Pietro (on the site of the present cathedral), while the old cathedral remained the repository of the relics of Donatus. In 1027–28 the old cathedral was sumptuously rebuilt on the model of San Vitale at Ravenna, and the relics of the saint were translated to a new shrine.[16] The account of the translation, which suggests a very clerical affair, with the *populus* appearing only as lookers-on, contrasts markedly with the narrative of the translation of Geminianus of Modena, less than a century later.[17] It was perhaps at about this time that the 'donation' of the centurion Zenobius, who had supposedly granted the disputed parishes to Donatus in gratitude for his conversion, was forged to support Arezzo's case against Siena.[18] From now on the saint was going to have a higher profile in the contest. The case received another hearing before Alexander II, but the records are lost; again the verdict went in favour of Arezzo. Gualfredus of Siena renewed the legal offensive and won a temporary ruling in his favour from Calixtus II in 1124, which was notified by the Pope to both the clergy and people of Siena. The Pope's death, however, left the issue open, and in 1125 Honorius II, reviewing the previous history of the case as far back as Liutprand, reaffirmed Arezzo's rights. If tradition is to be trusted, however, the Sienese had taken more than legal action under Gualfredus's leadership: they had removed the relics of St Ansanus from the church on the Arbia and installed them in the cathedral of Siena.[19]

The story of Arezzo and Siena, of Donatus and Ansanus, spans a long period and incorporates long silences, not least that of the tenth century. In northern Italy, however, the tenth century is not so silent that we cannot perceive its vital importance in the development of the cities, and the patronal cult was an ingredient of their life. For a generation from the last years of the ninth century, the contest for the kingdom of Italy which followed the breakdown of Carolingian authority, and the incursions of the mounted hordes of the Hungarians, combined to offer the bishops unprecedented opportunities and responsibilities. The Hungarian raids prompted a number of translations of relics inside the protective circuits of city walls, while the establishment of more settled conditions thereafter resulted in new suburban monastic foundations, sometimes redeveloping old sacred sites, and buttressed by new cults, mostly orchestrated by the bishop. In Golinelli's words, these foundations serve as 'an index of the progressive growth of the city, incapable from now on of containing within the walls of the preceding centuries a population which was increasing in numbers and political importance'.[20]

Outcomes, naturally, differed in different places. In principle, the bishop might have the initiative in the government of the city and the control of the cult, but local circumstances were not always favourable. They were not, for example, favourable to Rather, who, from being a monk in the neighbourhood of Liège, became bishop of Verona in 930 and in thirty-eight years was ejected from the see no fewer than three times.[21] He was an outsider, as the bishops of Verona customarily were from the eighth to the early twelfth century, but in addition he was clearly regarded as expendable, even when not actually as an enemy, by every ruler of northern Italy from Hugh of Provence to Otto I. He was also a zealot for the canonical rights of the bishop. On neither count could he stomach the cosy arrangements the cathedral clergy had made for the disposal among themselves of the revenues and property of the church. The picture he gives is of a state of things that is most familiar from the publicity it received a hundred years later during the 'Reform Movement'.

Rather complained that, with the backing of the count, 'all the clergy, knights, *coloni* and *famuli* were arrayed against him', and he could do nothing that needed doing.[22] The *coloni* and *famuli* were presumably peasant tenants and household servants and retainers of the nobility. Rather mentions no *cives*, no merchants or craftsmen, whether for him or against him. This is the more striking as we have a record of the *cives* of Verona, almost two centuries previously, opposing the bishop in a dispute over the funding of repairs to the city walls.[23] Rather, we may surmise, was simply not interested in the concept embodied in the word. Anyway, if we can believe his testimony that he met every possible obstruction when he tried to spend the appropriate portion of the church's income on rebuilding the churches of the diocese, devastated after the Hungarian raids, and when he tried to complete the cathedral and to spend on the church of San Zeno a gift of silver which Otto I had left him specifically for that purpose, it would seem that neither clergy nor laity, *cives* or otherwise, were zealots for the Virgin (patron of the cathedral church), or for San Zeno.[24]

Rather's only explicit reference to the cult of the saints and its public in the diocese of Verona comes from a curious work entitled *Invectiva de Translatione S. Metronis*, written not long after he had been restored to the diocese, after a long exile, in the wake of Otto I in 961.[25] Early in 962, it seems, the body of St Metro, of whom nothing is known except what Rather tells us, was stolen from the church of San Vitale, on the bank of the Adige. The opposition, obviously disgruntled that Rather had returned to the see, accused the bishop of negligence. It was his fault that the church had been so poorly guarded that the saint's precious body had been stolen. The burden of Rather's reply was, in effect, 'Much you care'. The church of San Vitale had apparently been converted into a military benefice sixty years before, and there was not even a priest in charge of it. Rather claimed that the clergy, custodians of Verona's long tradition of culture and learning, could not point to a written life of Metro, despite their professed reverence for the missing saint. Neither they nor their forebears had cared sufficiently to convert into verse or prose what, Rather said, 'the unlearned people recited [*plebs indocta canebat*]'. From this alleged oral tradition the bishop claimed to derive what he knew about Metro. Overwhelmed by an appalling sense of guilt, the saint had chained himself to a rock outside the church of San Vitale and thrown the key to the padlock into the Adige. There he remained in all weathers for seven years, until the bishop's fishermen caught a fish which had swallowed the key (not only a fairy-tale motif but one which appears in the legends of San Zeno himself). At this evident sign from heaven, Metro was released, received the Sacrament and died. His memory was devoutly cultivated by what Rather calls the 'common horde' [*vulgaris caterva*].

The bishop is clearly quite deliberately contrasting the irreverence and cynical hypocrisy of the literate clergy with the piety of the simple; but who exactly the simple were is left to our imagination, and perhaps they were more *topos* than reality. Rather, however, takes the opportunity to address to his readers what is in effect a sermon on the true meaning of the veneration of the saints. Whatever the outrage his opponents supposedly feel at losing Metro, the saint would not have gone had he not wished to; it is a 'praiseworthy theft' [*furtum laudabile*], if also a 'blameworthy loss' [*amissum damnabile*]. Perhaps Metro will be more venerated in his absence than he was when present; perhaps, even, the pious object of the theft was to elevate him to a more fitting position: 'For the *vulgus* more devoutly reverence the remains of a heavenly soul if they are not covered by the earth, but beautified by a shrine.'

By the tenth century, we can sense complex interactive processes at work between town and country, between the exercise of episcopal power and the growth of society. Hagiography, and perhaps more particularly translation narratives, can reflect, or refract, an awareness of real historical circumstances. So integral a part of the northern Italian imaginative experience did the Hungarian incursions become that a description of Modena appended to the *Vita Longior* of St Geminianus told how an invading horde entered the city but left it untouched through the good offices of the saint. In fact the Hungarians had left Modena to one side, behind its late-ninth-century walls, and sacked Reggio and the great monastery of Nonantola instead.[26]

In coastal regions the threat of Saracen piracy was more immediate. The sack of the church of Sant' Apollinare in Classe in the mid-ninth century supposedly brought about the translation of the saint's relics to the city of Ravenna. Even before this disaster, according to the author of the translation narrative, flood, the depredations of wild beasts and the inclement atmosphere had caused the progressive depopulation of Classe in favour of the city. The saint therefore permitted the Saracen attack so as to shame the inhabitants of Ravenna for their neglect of him. Once the *populus* of the city became aware of what had happened, they rushed to assess the damage, then held a council to deliberate on what was to be done. As a result of the translation, 'the martyr became more secure in the city, the city more secure in the martyr'.[27] Like the reputed removal of the relics of Prospero of Reggio from a suburban church threatened by flood to the security of the city late in the tenth century, this translation was disputed by interested parties in the twelfth.[28]

The absorption of relics into the city and the assertion of control over outlying shrines was not only prompted by external threat; it could be an important element in the exercise of episcopal authority, and therefore for the power of the city itself over its countryside. The point is well illustrated by the example of Parma. In the late ninth century the well-connected Bishop Guibold was a great acquirer of relics and rights over shrines. He allegedly brought the relics of the saints Giovanni Calybita and Cyriacus to Parma from Rome, and was confirmed in the possession of the ancient monastery of Berceto by a succession of claimants to the rule of Italy. Berceto, originally built by King Liutprand, contained the shrine of the Breton bishop Moderannus, who had supposedly brought relics of Remigius himself to the site. Guibold also sought and acquired rights over the shrine of San Nicomede at Fontanabroccola. Guibold died in 895; within a few years the incursions of the Hungarians resulted in the bringing of the relics of San Nicomede into the city.[29]

Sigifredus II of Parma, elected in 981, was another well-connected bishop, a member of the house of Canossa, with extensive patrimonial possessions in the *contado*. Otto II confirmed to him the rights and possessions of the *curtis regia* in Parma, including the *suburbium*.[30] This hint at the physical expansion of the city is supported by Sigifredus's own foundation of the monastery of San Giovanni Evangelista outside the walls. Among other 'suburban' possessions of the bishopric was the church of San Paolo, whither the relics of Santa Felicola were brought from Romolano on the river Enza in 983. In 1007 Sigifredus assigned to his chapter a share in the offerings rendered at shrines in the *districtus* on important feast-days, including those of Moderannus and Remigius at Berceto. He also reconfirmed to the chapter rights (which had fallen into disuse) to a share of the offerings made to St Donninus at his church on the site of his supposed martyrdom on the Via Emilia (or Strata Claudia) between Parma and Piacenza.[31] Disputes over this church and the settlement around it formed part of an ongoing battle over diocesan boundaries between Piacenza and Parma (like Siena, a relatively young see) and continued into the thirteenth century.[32] Bishop Ugo of Parma again confirmed the chapter's right to a share in the offerings at San Donnino in 1034–35, and Affò speculated that he might have instituted the fair of San Donnino which is mentioned in 1044.[33] A *passio* of the saint which clearly claims him for the bishopric of Parma may plausibly be assigned to this period.[34]

It was the purpose of the anonymous author to show an unnamed but 'venerable' bishop of Parma not only as instrumental in glorifying the saint and enlarging his church, but as acting, in so doing, as the leader of the whole community. The story follows a classic pattern. The inhabitants [*incolae*] are alerted to the presence of a martyr by an unearthly radiance about the place of his long-forgotten burial. They solicit the intervention of the bishop, who comes with his clergy to investigate. Excavation reveals the burial, identified by the odour of sanctity, and the bishop resolves, 'with the advice of the faithful there present', to build a church on the site. Throughout the narrative, the 'people' are almost invariably referred to as the *fidelis populus* or *populi fideles*. It is from this time that the place is referred to by the name of the martyr, and it becomes a focus of pilgrimage and miracle-working. The story so far has taken place in an unspecified past epoch. With the passage of time and the multiplication of the miracles, the 'faithful inhabitants' resolve to enlarge the church. They are, however, divided as to where precisely the martyr's remains are located. Now once again the bishop of Parma, to whom the place and the church belonged [*de cuius regimine et proprietate eadem et ecclesia et ecclesiae locus*], intervenes. For a while he delays taking action to find the remains, fearing that the devotion of the people will be diminished if they are not found, and at their insistence then proceeds to a happy conclusion, translating the relics 'to that place in which they are now venerably disposed'. The consequences were not only to the spiritual benefit of the local community. From that time forth the place grew in population; through the good offices of the saint and the benefit of his name it flourished in crops, livestock and trade, and – more important – flocks of pilgrims from many provinces who came to honour the martyr.[35]

Thus an awareness of growth in society at large could be associated with episcopal leadership of the local community, expressed in the propitiation of the saint who then exerts his beneficent influence. The involvement of the lay population in general is a trace element in such stories, but a few identifiable important laymen can be seen standing alongside the bishops. We have noted that the activist bishop Sigifredus II of Parma was in fact a member of the house of Canossa; subsequently both Count Bonifazio and Countess Matilda interested themselves in the cults of the hermit Simeon and the monastery of San Benedetto Polirone, outside Mantua, where he was venerated.[36] Bonifazio's interest extended to soliciting the canonization which was performed by Pope Benedict VIII, some time before 1023. An account of the supposed re-*inventio* of the Holy Blood at Mantua in 1049, seemingly written late in the century, garbled chronology by making Bonifazio, Pope Leo IX and the Emperor Henry III all present in the city for the event, and represented the inhabitants [*habitatores*] as resisting efforts to remove the precious relic to Rome; but we get no clear picture of these people.³⁷

Between Rather of Verona and his despairing efforts to finish the church of San Zeno with Otto I's silver, and the rebuilding and adornment of the same church in the early twelfth century, there intervened both the development of the commune in northern Italy and the 'Gregorian' reform movement. It was not only the non-noble laity who began to emerge into social and political prominence in this interval, but another class of men whose absence from Rather's Verona is striking when one reads of the turmoil of Milan or Florence a hundred years later: the monk-agitators of Vallombrosa, with their vivid presence in the streets of the city, or clerical rabble-rousers like Ariald of Milan, from the petty nobility in the neighbourhood of a great city, and his allies in urban society. Where, in Rather's world, were the new saints who would become such a feature of the Italian scene, eremitical and urban, not so very long afterwards?

Of course they grew out of the society of which his Verona formed a part, and, as he might have anticipated, largely in opposition to it. It is striking that the two most celebrated pioneers of the new eremitical orders in Italy were both members of the brawling nobility who pursued their blood-feuds into the streets of the burgeoning cities, and that both of them were said to have turned to the religious life precisely in order to escape involvement in feud. According to Peter Damian, Romuald of Ravenna was reluctantly involved in a feud between his father and a kinsman over the possession of a meadow, and, overwhelmed with guilt at merely having been present at the killing of the enemy, took refuge in the monastery of St Apollinare in Classe.³⁸ Giovanni Gualberto, pursuing the murderer of a kinsman to Florence and coming upon him in a place from which his adversary had no escape, had no choice, when he failed or refused to kill him, but to retire posthaste to San Miniato al Monte, where the crucified Christ above the altar signalled his approval of his action.³⁹ Now, as later in the Middle Ages, the nobility were the most promising recruits to sanctity; were they also the most enthusiastic of its spectators? Did other social groups yet possess a clear identity as an audience for sanctity?

Paolo Golinelli observes that the population of Reggio, as it appears in an eleventh-century collection of the miracles of San Prospero, is 'composed predominantly of *rustici*; the city was as yet too small and immersed in its rural surroundings to produce social entities sufficiently differentiated to be reflected in a hagiographical text'. Social realities did not yet compel a systematic adaptation of vocabulary.[40] Golinelli notes the appearance among Prospero's clients of some Tuscan merchants or 'businessmen' [*negotiatores*], whom the saint had delivered from shipwreck. Such persons were 'symptoms of a transformation of civic society', but harsh physical realities, such as recurrent flooding, would for the time being slow and limit economic growth at the most basic level, that of cereal production. Fine white bread, in this environment, could be seen as a sufficiently precious commodity for the compiler of Prospero's miracles to tell how an impious *paterfamilias* snatched some 'shining white loaves' from the women of his household, who had intended to offer them to the saint to be given in alms to the poor. (He ate them himself, with distressing results.)

The *Vita Longior* of St Geminianus of Modena, a text which probably belongs to the mid-eleventh century, a period of changes not yet fully accomplished, demonstrates both the nuances and the imprecision of the current vocabulary.[41] When the life of Geminianus, a fourth-century bishop, came to be written, probably not much before 900, it was modelled on that of another bishop-saint, Zeno of Verona. This first, short life was enlarged into the *Vita Longior*, which, as Golinelli observes, shows awareness of the different components of urban society. Geminianus, we are told, endeared himself to all the inhabitants and all the *suburbani* of Modena. Brought back into the city after his obligatory attempt to refuse election as bishop, he was greeted rapturously by 'all the citizens' [*cives omnes*] and agreed to serve – not out of ambition, but 'foreseeing damage to the real interests of the citizens, if they were subjected to the rule of outsiders' [*de re vera civium praecavens damnum, si dominio subderentur extraneorum*]. Geminianus was rightly sought after by the *populus mutinensis*; on his appointment the *cives mutinenses* greeted him with rejoicing, and the *plebs devota* gave thanks that they had been given such a pastor.

In this one passage of the *Vita Longior*, then, we find the phrases *populus mutinensis* and *plebs devota*, and several uses of the word *cives*. It was with the approval or assistance of the citizens [*faventibus civibus*] that Theodore, Geminianus's successor, built a basilica over his remains, to which the *plebs urbana et rustica* flocked and experienced miracles every day. On the first anniversary of the saint's death a large congregation assembled at the church, only to find itself cut off by a flood that rose to the level of the church's windows; but not a drop of water entered the church and the saint, when applied to in prayer, withdrew the waters and supplied a dry path, as for the people of Israel. The congregation is described in the course of this passage as 'a numberless horde of people' [*infinita populorum caterva*], as *populi*, as *cives* when, with the bishop, they hail the miracle, and finally as the *populus* for whom the 'dry path' is provided. The purely descriptive term *incolae* is also used.

If we consider the writings of Peter Damian, who also lived in the changing eleventh century and wrote about saints and miracles of both ancient times and his own day, we can see the risks of both over- and underestimating the political charge of his vocabulary. His sermons on Apollinaris of Ravenna are extremely rich in uses of the words *civis, civitas* and *urbs*, but they are overwhelmingly metaphorical.[42] The unreformed earthly city represents a hostile mass awaiting the healing touch of the missionary. Peter tells Apollinaris that there is a *multitudo populi* at Ravenna awaiting evangelization; Ravenna is a 'most unruly city' [*turbulentissima civitas*], while the saint is a 'citizen of the heavenly Jerusalem' [*civis supernae Jerusalem*]. The *cives* of the earthly city are as likely to be the 'citizens of this world' and to represent the internal enemies against which the ascetic must fight, such as pride and lust, as they are to be real people; the lonely struggle of the saint against the diabolic mass embodied in the *urbs* or *civitas* is heavily emphasized.

Apollinaris's fictitious status as a disciple of St Peter establishes a linkage between Ravenna and Rome, the model of the city that becomes truly a city through sanctification by its martyrs. Thus Ravenna:

> which was formerly a sanctuary of demons, through [Apollinaris] has become a capitol of celestial senators. For there the bodies of martyrs now rest, the relics of many saints are to be found. Before, evilly prolific, she produced in her children many offshoots for hell; now through the grace of God she has borne many citizens for heaven, so that it could deservedly be said to its people, 'Now you are not strangers and

pilgrims, but [fellow-] citizens of the saints and servants of God.' Rightly that spendid metropolis specially rejoices in the festivity of blessed Apollinaris, through whom, once profane and rustic, it has become priestly and royal.[43]

The same vision transpires from Damian's sermons on St Vitalis, who not only chose to be buried in Ravenna but made it known, in a dream, that his relics were not to be removed from the city. Vitalis is explicitly associated with Apollinaris; together they correspond to Peter and Paul, by virtue of whose merits Rome 'claims the principality of the whole world, and has become as it were the head of all other cities'. Thanks to Vitalis and Apollinaris, Ravenna 'has deserved to become the mother and mistress of all the surrounding cities'. Damian's reference is, of course, to Ravenna's metropolitan status in north-eastern Italy, not to the secular dominance of a city over its region.[44] Cityhood is altogether a spiritual rather than a sociological category.

Were Damian's urban references more concrete when he was writing about his own times? He tells a familiar type of story about the efforts of Ugo Bishop of Assisi (d. 1059) to bring the empty sarcophagus of the martyr Rufinus to his church within the city.[45] The actual relics of the saint had long since, for fear of pagan attack, been brought to safety and installed in a church of their own (not the cathedral, which was dedicated to the Virgin). The bishop, in compensation, wanted the sarcophagus for the 'mother church'. The *populus*, however, declared its opposition to any division between the martyr and his former tomb, and insisted that if the sarcophagus was going anywhere it was going to join the saint himself in his church. Of course the sarcophagus itself made the decision, refusing to be moved by any means to the cathedral, but it readily consented to be taken to the church of San Rufino – all of which went to show, as Damian observes, that *vox populi* equalled *vox Dei*: 'God was at one with his people [*pius Deus unum cum populo suo senserit*].' The only distinction he makes within the body of the 'people' is between the 'followers of the bishop' [*fautores episcopi*] and the 'remaining part' of the people [*reliqua pars populi*].

There was a sting in this particular tale. There was some uncertainty, in the absence of any 'historical monuments', as to when Rufinus's martyrdom should be celebrated, and it was customary just to keep the day of the dedication of his church. The bishop now opportunely discovered an account of Rufinus's martyrdom (*passio*), which enabled him to declare that the feast-day of the martyr was to be kept on 29 July. At once his opponents, so zealous a moment ago for the integrity of Rufinus's remains, alleged that this fabrication of a double festivity was burdensome to the people, a superstitious novelty, and prompted 'not by religious devotion, but by love of money'. The saint himself, however, was motivated throughout by a concern solely for the maximization of his own honour, and certain stiff-necked men who refused to observe the new day, 'and with their wives not only audaciously engaged in weaving but even freely applied themselves to rural pursuits, received their just reward and found their houses aflame with a fire which water could not extinguish'. They sought the martyr's forgiveness, and from that day forth on the feast of his martyrdom the people had flocked from all directions to his church.

Here and elsewhere in Damian's Rufinus stories the rural background is very evident. The saint releases a poor woman from the bullying of a landlord who seizes from her an ox and an ass which are the main means of her livelihood, and a *rusticus* whose cattle and other animals are seized by a band of twelve thieves gets them back again. Rufinus is brought within the walls of Assisi for safekeeping, but he serves the needs of what looks very much like an agrarian community. Damian's writings abound in reminders of the real nature of these little cities and their 'suburbs'. As a student of the liberal arts at Parma, he heard of a miracle which took place just outside the walls of the city to the west, at the church of Sts Gervasius and Protasius. On the night before their feast-day a man of the place got up early to take his cattle to pasture; a neighbour, observing his departure, insinuated himself into his bed, and deceived his wife into mistaking him for her husband. Somewhat unfairly, she later reproached her real husband for thus profaning the holy day; he protested his innocence and the offended couple laid their grievance before the whole *populus*, who were flocking to the church for lauds. The saints obligingly revealed the guilty party, who went into spectacular convulsions 'in the presence of the people' and expired.[46]

Damian sketches a mental world in which people's faith in their priests (and their saints) was dependent on their power to do certain things which needed doing in daily life – healing snakebite, expelling demons, keeping locusts and worm from the crops, finding lost children – and on God's willingness, which Damian insisted must be acknowledged, to operate for their benefit through clergy who might from any reformist standpoint be thoroughly disreputable.[47] In his account of the struggle at Assisi over Rufinus's sarcophagus – and, for that matter, over the institution of the martyr's feast – we can discern the outlines of the struggles between bishops and their local opponents such as took place in other Italian cities, but there is little that is distinctively 'urban' about the setting, and little in the vocabulary which is used that distinguishes the 'people' of Assisi from those of Florence or Milan. Damian and his fellow-reformers were familiar with real cities with turbulent inhabitants, and saw bad – or, at least, misguided – bishops everywhere being put to the test by their flocks. They were not, however, primarily interested in bequeathing to posterity a detailed profile of these 'citizens'. Contemporary usage often makes it difficult either to distinguish clearly those elements in the *populus* which we would like to be able to label clearly 'urban' or 'rural', or to distinguish groups within the 'urban' population. While preserving our awareness that cities were growing in Italy in the eleventh century, and that the groundwork for the 'city-state' and the 'commune' was being laid, we should be cautious about making distinctions which either may not have existed or may not have been clearly recognized by contemporaries, either in semantics or in actuality.

In the *Vita* of Ariald, the martyred Patarine priest of Milan, by the Vallombrosan Andrea of Strumi, the moneyer Nazarius is vividly portrayed as the type of man who was providing an audience for the new sanctity. He attended Ariald's first exhortation against unchaste priests and, when Landulf had spoken, called for silence and spoke himself:

> Who is not so stupid as not to see clearly that their life must be vastly dissimilar from mine, if I am to invite them into my home for a blessing, to feed them to the best of my ability and afterwards to kiss their hands and offer them a gift; and if I receive all the mysteries from them through which I hope for eternal life? But as we can all observe, their life is not only not cleaner, it is fouler.[48]

Here we have a classic expression of the core of the belief that the holy is something other, that it can be measured by its distance from the norm practised by *l'homme moyen sensuel*. The ideal is shown as appealing specifically to a member of what Lopez suggests we might call a bourgeois patriciate.[49] To Andrea, however, Nazarius is interesting principally as a *laicus* and a pious man, 'although married'; for Ariald, the *conjugati* constituted an order within the church.[50] Collectively we hear also of the *fideles* and the *cives Christiani*. Such terms indicate the viewpoint from which Andrea observed and classified his actors; he is not primarily interested in telling us whether Nazarius and his like occupied a particular place on the political map of Milan. He does, however, in at least one place describe the opposition to reform with some particularity as consisting of 'the greater part of the clergy and knights, together with many riff-raff from the lesser people' [*pars maxima clericorum et militum, necnon et multi de populo minore nequam viri*].[51]

Ariald appears to have been a man of some substance. His parents had rejected both pride (a vice to which only the well-born were entitled) and rapacity. His enemies on one occasion resolved to go and ransack a church he had built in his native place at his own expense, and to destroy the vines and chestnut trees in which, they said, he abounded. Of his named allies at Milan, two were clearly classifiable as urban nobility: the priest Landulf and his brother the knight Erlembald, who, like others of his kind later in the century and beyond, was persuaded to put off entering religion while he could fight the good fight out in the world. Landulf, indeed, was 'from the best people of the city in both rank and intellect' [*de urbanis excellentibus tam ordine quam ratione*], and he had the classic oratorical attributes of the highborn, being 'exceedingly powerful in voice and speech' [*nimis potens in voce et sermone*]. Nazarius, who put his household at Ariald's disposal, was from a different stratum, but Andrea does not explicitly tell us whether it was from this stratum, independent of the nobility, that Ariald's core support came.

We have already noted Andrea's brief characterization of the opposition to Ariald. If he was right, Landulf and Erlembald were taking arms against the majority of their class, and we are left to suppose that the 'good-for-nothings' were in some sense, however locse, the dependants of the knights. He does state, perhaps echoing Christ's words about bringing not peace but a sword, that the entire city was divided in the sense that households were divided against themselves on the issue of simony, while a series of episodes demonstrated, as the bishop's party sagely observed on one occasion, that mob violence could be whipped up on either side of the question.[52] Involved in this conflict was a contest for the patronage of St Ambrose, claimed by the old guard at Milan as the symbol of Milanese independence of the papacy, by the new as precisely the opposite, a figure who had always stood for Catholic unity under Rome. Ariald professed an intense reverence for the saints in general, and would send his hordes of followers away so that he could pay his devotions to Ambrose in the latter's church.[53] The attendance of 'all the citizens, of both sexes' with their candles at the feast of the translation of St Nazarius in May 1057 provided Landulf and Ariald, according to Landulf Senior, with an opportunity to whip up mob sentiment against unchaste clergy.[54] It does not tell us much about the lay element in Ariald's following that he presumed it to be 'illiterate'. In a sermon propounding the duties of the three orders in the church – *praedicatores* (the 'preachers', bishops and secular clergy), *continentes* (the professed religious) and *conjugati* (the laity, presumed to be married) – he expressed the view that *praedicatio* of a sort formed part of the duties of all three; the preaching of the *continentes* would be made more effective by their separation from the world, 'but even you, who are *idiotae* and ignorant of Scripture, must caution one another among yourselves against this evil in the common speech at your command [*communibus verbis quibus valetis*]'.[55] Presumably many of Ariald's following would in this sense have been *idiotae*.

Ariald's appeal was not solely to the townsman. He rebuilt the church called the Canonica, just outside the Porta Nova of Milan, and a multitude of worshippers flocked there 'not only from the city, but from villages and castles, until the church could not hold them all, big though it was'. Landulf Senior speaks of *suburbani quidam* in Ariald's entourage.[56] The fact that the old circuits of walls in no sense sealed off urban society from the countryside emerges again and again, especially from miracle stories in which movement towards the shrines which clustered around urban centres is an essential feature, whether in the form of relatively long-distance pilgrimage or of the shorter, almost day-to-day, recourse of the inhabitants of the surrounding countryside. One remarkable story among the miracles of Anselm of Lucca well illustrates both this point and the proposition that even a 'Gregorian' saint operated in a world of ancient superstitions and practices seemingly not in the least Gregorian.

Anselm died at Mantua in 1086. The nephew of Alexander II, he succeeded his uncle in the see of Lucca in 1071, and (although he accepted investiture from the Emperor, to his own subsequent regret) was expelled from it in c.1080 by forces similar to those which were opposing Ariald at Milan. A string of miracles, principally at his Mantuan shrine, is attested by his biographer, although some Lucchese miracles were clearly intended to dent the credibility of the imperialist intruder who had supplanted him.[57] The story on which we are focusing is described by the author as 'pleasing' [*jucundum*] to many people, as well as 'marvellous' [*mirabile*]. On the thirty-ninth day after the saint's death, an 'innumerable multitude of men' flocked to Mantua for the Gregorian litanies, bearing banners and holy relics, as was the custom. On their way they saw a great deer, and on the suggestion of one of their priests they began to invoke almighty God, praying that, through the merits of the saint to whom they were devotedly proceeding, he would concede the deer to them unharmed. She remained standing quietly as if fixed to the spot, and putting a rope around her neck they gently led her to the shrine of the venerable confessor. There was an incredible crush of people; some pulled out her hairs as evidence [*veritatis indicium*]; others were content to see; all were equally awestruck. The deer, however, was pregnant, and could not endure the pressure. When she reached the sepulchre, she collapsed. A little later, as she could not live, she was killed, her flesh was divided into parts and distributed with a blessing, and undoubtedly restored many invalids to full health. The near-sacrifice of a pregnant deer at the altar of a Gregorian saint is indeed a remarkable spectacle.[58]

The new order in the church was trying in the eleventh century to establish itself in power with the aid of the *populus*. At Milan, and also at Florence, we see with particular clarity that the promoters of the new order were quite literally and deliberately setting out to instil the fear of God into the people. Their eternal salvation was endangered, so they must be induced to believe, by their present worse than inadequate priests. In this context propaganda needs and traditional usage alike rather favoured the undifferentiated use of the term *populus*. It denoted God's people, whose fate as a whole, as a collectivity, was at issue. Yet the visibility of this *populus* in the religious setting is evidence for a social change to which the biographers of saints were in their own way intensely responsive. To Andrea of Strumi, introducing his life of Ariald, it seemed worthwhile, although the end of the world was nigh, to transmit to posterity knowledge of the new saints whose constancy was equal to that of the *antiqui*.[59] Those whom posterity were to remember as saints were winning recognition in the eyes of contemporaries for whom the idea of the saint was formed on an ancient pattern – for whom, indeed, the majority of those hitherto accepted as saints had lived and died in the first heroic ages of the church's history. The hour produced the men; the populace who were urged to join the struggle for reform were conditioned to expect manifestations of sanctity from the heroes of the struggle, while the new saints, to have an enduring effect on their society, had to render the services to its members that they expected of a saint and to identify themselves, or become identified, with their interests.

Among these interests, as the eleventh century turned into the twelfth, those of the men who ruled the cities were impossible to ignore. The cities, with their growing suburbs and enlarged circuits of walls, stood out in the landscape and constituted the centres from which townsman and peasant alike was ruled. The laymen who began to rule them in the course of the twelfth century were the political heirs of the bishop and his entourage. They were not infrequently to be found at odds with their bishops; but the role that they were now claiming to play committed them to an interest in the civic cult. They had to learn to share the public responsibility for obtaining celestial guarantees of the city's well-being; this and their increasing involvement, collectively, in the management of the fabric of the cathedral and other urban churches, and individually as patrons and benefactors of those same churches, meant a continuing involvement with the saints whose names were invoked and whose relics lay within the city and its locality. With the multiplication of new devotions and the complications of papal and peninsular politics, their successors had decisions to make as to how to adapt the civic cult to their needs, and to the needs of changing times.

Notes

1. R. Grégoire, 'Il contributo dell' agiografia alla conoscenza della realtà rurale', in *Medioevo Rurale: sulle tracce della civiltà contadina*, ed. V. Fumagalli and G. Rossetti (Bologna 1980), p. 347.

2. On demons as an invisible 'crowd', see the observations of Elias Canetti, *Crowds and Power* (revised Eng. transl., Harmondsworth 1973), pp. 50–51, 3.

3. For an example, see the discussion of Peter Damian, below, pp. 47–8.

4. For the bishop of Verona's role as custodian of the relics of the city's saintly protectors, see Miller, *The Formation of a Medieval Church*, p. 156.

5. Ep. 77 (formerly numbered 22), in *Corpus Scriptorum Eclesiasticorum Latinorum*, 82, *Sancti Ambrosii Opera Pars X, Epistulae et Acta*, 3, pp. 126–40.

6. Augustine, *Sermo* 286 (*PL* 38, col. 299).

7. Paulinus hints that here, as with Gervasius and Protasius, the community's memory was being jogged. The guardians of the place where Nazarius and Celsus were found said that they had been told by their kinsfolk not to desert it, for there was a great treasure buried there: *PL* 14, cols 40–41.

8. *Exhortatio Virginis* (*PL* 16), cols 351–4; Paulinus, *Vita*, col. 39.

9. The text, which is of much later date, is in *AB* 10 (1891), pp. 119–20.

10. *L'immaginario religioso*, pp. 107–8.

11. See, for example, the remarks, of C. Wickham, *The Mountains and the City* (Oxford 1988), pp. 144–5, 354–5. For the period between the ninth century and the twelfth in (especially) northern Italy, the writings of Paolo Golinelli are indispensable.

12. The word *comitatus*, indicating the sphere of jurisdiction of a count, gave rise to the later Italian *contado*, which will occur throughout this book, indicating the territory immediately dependent on a city.

13. The sources are to be found in Pasqui, *Documenti*, 1 and 2.

14. It was perhaps on this occasion that he gave the bishop of Siena the relics of the martyr Crescentius as a consolation prize, a probability arrived at independently by the present writer and by F.E. Consolino, 'Un martire "romano": Crescenzio', in *I Santi Patroni Senesi*, pp. 47–8.

The somewhat garbled text of the *translatio* of Crescentius (*Acta S* Sept. 4, pp. 351–3) dates it to the times of Ansfridus Bishop of Siena, Pope Stephen and King Charles I. The first two are, obviously, compatible with each other, but not with any King Charles. It seems most likely, if a rational explanation is possible, that the author got the king wrong, and confused Pepin with Charles the Great. The certain knowledge that the bishop and the Pope were in contact affords a plausible context for such a gift.

15. For the early medieval topography of Arezzo, see V. Franchetti Pardo, *Arezzo* (Rome–Bari 1986), pp. 13–27.

16. Franchetti Pardo, pp. 20, 27 n.26. As late as the early eleventh century the cathedral was referred to in the names of the Virgin and St Stephen as well as of Donatus, e.g. Pasqui, 1, n.63, pp. 87–8 (939); n.107, pp. 148–51 (1015) where St Hilarianus was also invoked. With the shift of episcopal and clerical activity nearer the centre of the city, the old cathedral site was increasingly often referred to as 'S. Maria in Grado', as when in 1050 Leo IX took the church under his protection, describing it as distinguished *inter alia* by Donatus's martyrdom (ibid., n.173, pp. 246–7).

17. The *translatio* has been published several times, e.g. by G. Cappelletti, *Le Chiese d'Italia dalla loro origine sino ai nostri giorni* (21 vols, Venice 1844–70), 18, pp. 93–6. For the *relatio* of Geminianus's translation, see below, pp. 60–62.

18. Text in Pasqui, 1, pp. 531–4.

19. See below, pp. 62–4.

20. *Indiscreta Sanctitas*, p. 79.

21. For the church of Verona in general, see Miller, *Formation of a Medieval Church*; for Rather and his works, see Reid, *Complete Works*, with full references to editions and literature. The quotations given here are in the present author's translation.

22. Reid, p. 226, translates 'all the clergy, nobles, farmers and serfs'.

23. *Codice diplomatico veronese*, ed. V. Fainelli (Venice 1940), pp. 205–8.

24. See e.g. the so-called *Liber Apologeticus* (Reid, pp. 498–505), and letters to Ambrose, chancellor to Otto I, and to the Empress Adelaide (ibid., pp. 524–5, 527).

25. Ibid., pp. 320–36.

26. Golinelli, *Indiscreta Sanctitas*, pp. 70–71. The *Descriptio* is in Muratori, II.2, cols 691–2.

27. *Spicilegium Ravennatis*, pp. 533–6: 'securior Martyr in Civitate, securior Civitas in Martyre suo redditur'.

28. See below, pp. 69–71.

29. Affò, *Storia di Parma*, 1, pp. 164–94. Present at Guy of Spoleto's coronation in February 891, Guibold brought the king's body back to Parma for burial before the altar of San Remigio in the cathedral. In 923 Guy's

widow Gertrude referred to the church at Fontanabroccola as hers (ibid., App. 48, pp. 329-30).

30. The grant was made 'cum edificiis et terris ac famulis nec non & rebus eorum in integrum et omne jus publicum et teloneum ac districtum civitatis ac ambitum murorum cum integro suburbio': ibid., App. 75, pp. 364-5.

31. Ibid., pp. 252-73 and App. 93, pp. 383-4. The church of San Donnino is the cathedral of what is now known as Fidenza.

32. In 1199 Parma joined forces with a number of allies to defend the place against a coalition headed by Piacenza and Milan (*Chronicon Parmense*, p. 7).

33. Ibid., 2, pp. 32-3 and App. 11, pp. 308-10.

34. Printed from an eleventh-century manuscript in *Chronica Parmensia*, pp. 471-6.

35. A similar association between a saint's relics and fertility and prosperity was claimed for Siena when the relics of Ansanus were translated to the city: see p. 63.

36. Golinelli, 'Culto dei Santi e Monasteri nella Politica dei Canossa', in *Indiscreta Sanctitas*, pp. 9-29.

37. Golinelli,' Istituzioni Cittadine e Culti Episcopali', in *Indiscreta Sanctitas*, pp. 84-8. The text, *De inventione et translatione sanguinis Domini*, is in *MGH SS* 15, pp. 921-3. There is in fact some indication that the cult of the Holy Blood at Mantua was associated with the imperial rather than the Canossa interest, and was de-emphasized by Matilda. Her own promotion of Anselm of Lucca may indicate an effort to establish, under dynastic auspices, the cult of a bishop-patron which the city lacked; the signs are that it was too obviously and closely associated with the Canossa interest to succeed as hoped, and Anselm did not displace the ancient patron of the cathedral, St Peter himself, at the centre of the patronal cult.

38. *Vita Romualdi* I, ed. G. Tabacco, *FSI* 94, pp. 14-15.

39. *Vita Sancti Johannis Gualberti*, ed. F. Baethgens, *MGH SS* 30. 2, p. 1080.

40. *Culto dei santi*, p. 105. Cf. the comment of Miller, *Formation*, p. 102: 'After 1000 ... many new groups emerged in Veronese society: merchants, urban functionaries, artisans, castellans, and affluent members of rural communities.' For the miracles of Prosper of Reggio, see A. Mercati, 'Miracula B. Prosperi'.

41. Text in Mombritius, *Sanctuarium sue vita sanctorum*, (2 vols, Paris 1910), 1, pp. 598-603. On the dating of the different versions of the *Vita*, see Golinelli, 'Istituzioni Cittadine', in *Indiscreta Sanctitas*, pp. 55-101. There can be no absolute certainty as to its date, and there has been argument as to the relationship between it and the *Vita Brevior*. A majority view appears to be that the longer version is an elaboration of the shorter,

which in turn is modelled on the *Vita* of San Zeno of Verona, imitating, for example, the story of how the saint cured an emperor's daughter who was possessed by demons. Golinelli (pp. 66–70, 88–90) is inclined to date the shorter life *c.* 900 and the longer to the middle of the eleventh century – that is, to a period before the turmoil of the investiture struggle. There is no mention in it of the decision taken, in 1099, to rebuild the cathedral and the shrine of the saint.

42. *Sermones* 30–32, ed. Lucchesi, pp. 172–83.

43. *Sermo* 30, p. 180:

> Quae enim erat daemonum antea delubrum, per hunc caelestium senatorum facta est capitolium. Ibi enim iam martyrum corpora requiescunt, ibi multorum sanctorum patrocinia reconduntur. Quae ergo prius, male fecunda, in filiis suis multas stipulas germinabat inferno, iam per Dei gratiam multos ciues parturit coelo. Ut iam populo illius non inmerito dicatur, *Iam non estis hospites et advenae; sed estis cives sanctorum et domestici Dei* ... Iuste ergo egregia illa metropolis B. Apolenaris festivitate specialiter gaudet, per quem, olim profana et rustica, facta est nunc sacerdotalis et regia.

44. *Sermo* 17, p. 91. Damian's emphasis on the presence of Vitalis in the city is to be seen alongside his doubts about the city's claim to Apollinaris; see below, p. 68.

45. *Sermo* 36, ibid., pp. 215–22.

46. *Opusculum* 26, in *PL* 145, cols 616–18.

47. See above all the *Liber gratissimus*, esp. cap. 18, 'Quod per indignos etiam sacerdotes exhibentur saepe miracula' (*MGH, Libelli de Lite* I, pp. 41–5).

48. *Vita Sancti Arialdi*, p. 1053. For a recent review of the sources and historiography of the *Pataria*, see P. Golinelli, *La Pataria: lotte religose e sociali nella Milano dell' XI secolo* (Milan 1984).

49. R. Lopez, 'An Aristocracy of Money in the early Middle Ages', *Speculum* 28 (1953) pp. 1–43. Nazario is mentioned pp. 41–2.

50. *Sancti Arialdi Vita*, p. 1056.

51. Ibid., p. 1057.

52. Ibid., p. 1065: 'popularis turba cito mutatur, et in diversas partes facile inclinatur'.

53. Ibid., pp. 1061–2. Ariald quotes 'noster patronus' Ambrose on the subject of simony, p. 1056.

54. *Mediolanensis Historie libri Quattuor*, ed. L. Bethmann and W. Wattenbach, *MGH SS* 8, p. 79; ed. A. Cutolo, *RIS* 4.ii, p. 91.

55. *Vita Sancti Arialdi*, p. 1056. On the whole subject of the written word and the reform movement at Milan, see B. Stock, *The Implications of Literacy* (Princeton, NJ 1983), pp. 151–240.

56. *Vita Sancti Arialdi*, p. 1058; *MGH SS* 8, p. 87; *RIS* IV.ii, p. 104.
57. On the sources for Anselm, see Golinelli, 'Una Agiografia di Lotta: Le "Vitae" di Sant' Anselmo di Lucca', in *Indiscreta Sanctitas*, pp. 117–55; E. Pásztor, 'Una fonte per la storia dell' età gregoriana: la "Vita Anselmi episcopi Lucensis"', *BISIMEAM* 72 (1961), pp. 1–33.
58. *Vita Anselmi Episcopi Lucensis*, ed. R. Wilmans, *MGH SS* 12, p. 26.
59. *Vita Sancti Arialdi*, p. 1050.

CHAPTER 2

SAINTS AND CITIZENS IN THE TWELFTH CENTURY

In twelfth-century sources, leading members of the urban laity are to be found involved in the cult of the saints in various capacities. They may be seen assisting at *translationes* or *inventiones* of interest to the whole community, and participating as spectators, and sometimes more, in contests between churches over the possession of relics. Sometimes they appear as the beneficiaries of a relic acquisition which may have been made with them principally in mind. As they progressively assumed the governing power in the cities, they moved also towards the position of themselves being relic acquirers, although they did not yet clearly have the initiative.

In 1099 the old cathedral of Modena was in ruins, and amid an apparent surge of popular enthusiasm a vow was made to rebuild the shrine of the saint. According to an account which, it seems to be agreed, was written very shortly afterwards, perhaps by the *magister scolarum* Aymo, there was a marvellous unanimity of clergy and people in this resolve.[1] Modena's recent ecclesiastical history had been chequered, like that of so many other cities just before and after 1100. The long-lived Bishop Eribert had been bishop already for thirty years when in 1084 he helped consecrate Guibert of Ravenna as antipope, and he lived on till 1094, overlapping with the 'Catholic' Benedetto, elected some time in the 1080s with Countess Matilda's blessing. Benedetto too was dead by 1097 and his immediate successor was short-lived, although Bishop Dodo was in place in 1100. The rebuilding of the cathedral, thus resolved upon during an episcopal vacancy, began under the watchful eye of Matilda and the expert direction of the architect Lanfranc, and the consecration was performed in October 1106 by Paschal II as part of the programme of restoring Catholic normality in northern Italy.

The author of the *Relatio* distinguishes between different elements in the 'people' which was, at least for the time being, so much in harmony with the clergy. There was unanimity between the citizens, the *prelati universarum plebium*, who were clearly not clergy and should probably be understood as the leaders of parish or neighbourhood societies,[2] and 'all the knights of the said church'. When the day came for Geminianus's relics to be moved, some (unspecified) people felt considerable grief and foreboding at this risky proceeding. Lanfranc, however, let it be known that he could not get any further until the relics were moved. A great assembly of local bishops, abbots and clergy, and such a 'gathering of knights (or nobles)' [*congregatio militum*] and 'assembly of people of both sexes' [*conventus populorum utriusque sexus*], took place that no one could move a muscle. An altercation now occurred between the bishops and the 'citizens and whole people' [*cives & totus populus*]. The bishops wanted to perform a ceremonial *revelatio* of the relics; the citizens totally rejected the idea. Appealed to for a decision, Matilda ruled that the consecration should await the coming of Pope Paschal. This meant a delay from May until October, when the Pope arrived in northern Italy. Further discussions then took place. The representatives 'of the knightly order' [*de ordine militum*] were insistent that the relics must be sedulously guarded lest in the course of the *revelatio* they be violated.

Although it is not spelled out, one suspects here not just superstitious dread of the consequences of meddling with the explosive charge of the relics but a lively suspicion, on the part of the laity, of how a bunch of bishops were likely to behave with a sumptuous saintly corpse exposed to view before them. The result was that six *milites* and 'twice six' *cives* took an oath, presumably to constitute a guard over the relics. Their motive was to ensure that Geminianus's patronage remained whole and entire on behalf of the city of Modena, and was not dispersed by opportunistic or impulsive gift-giving among the clergy. When the cover of the tomb was lifted and another cover found underneath, many thought that scrutiny should go no further, but the clergy were insisting on a transparent display of the authenticity of the relics. Buonsenior, the saintly bishop of neighbouring Reggio, and (interestingly) the architect Lanfranc manually performed the unveiling of the body, and from then on all was odour of sanctity and rejoicing. That the author of the *Relatio* should have made it his business to stress the concern of the laity with the honour and integrity of their heavenly patron should not surprise us; but if he had so chosen, he could have spoken of them simply as the *populus* or the *fideles*. That he did not, preferring the terms *milites* or *cives*, normally in combination, suggests that he was unselfconsciously reporting reality – indeed, a prevailing reality of the period.[3]

A similar outcome of social tensions was perhaps invoked in stone by master Niccolò in the 1130s when he carved the tympanum of San Zeno at Verona. Here the saint, in episcopal vestments, is depicted in an attitude of blessing. A group of *pedites* on his right bears a banner with a yellow cross on a blue ground, and the mounted *milites* are on his left. The accompanying inscription announces: 'The bishop gives the people an ensign to be prized, Zeno bestows the standard with a happy heart.'[4] Master Niccolò's San Zeno was aware of the role being played by the *pedites* in the military and political affairs of the city, and wished to advertise his awareness of his enlarged constituency. Geminianus and Zeno were established patrons; it was a matter now of bringing 'new' socio-political groups into a relationship with them.

Still in twelfth-century sources this sense of a lay presence is as often as not filtered through ecclesiastical preoccupations, and the terminology employed to describe it varies from the traditionally generic to the more or less specific. The story of how the relics of St Ansanus came to Siena from his church on the Arbia in 1107, for example, is supplied in *lectiones* for the feast of the translation, preserved in thirteenth- and fourteenth-century manuscripts.[5] It professes to tell how the military classes actively co-operated in the acquisition of the saint, and how all classes united in guarding and venerating him. The Sienese were alerted to an impending coup against the relics (undoubtedly by the Aretines, although no names are named), and decided to strike first. The clergy went forth in procession, but certain of the knights of the city went ahead and put the (still unnamed) Aretines to flight. The Sienese, we are told, acclaimed the 'return' of the martyr-evangelist: 'Come, father Ansanus, return to us, Lord, delay no longer in returning to your city.' The presence of many pilgrims (presumably on their way to or from Rome) in the hospital was opportune: many cures occurred, and pilgrims returning to their own country spread the word. It was in consequence of the pilgrimage traffic that resulted from Lombardy and northern Tuscany that the Sienese put the care of the relics on an organized footing. A fivefold division of the city was adopted and a rota established, 'so that the holy relics should never be without a numerous guard of clergy and people'.

Great stress is laid on the unifying force of this activity: 'To supply these vigils, the monasteries of monks and nuns, the *plebes* and *capellae* with their people, flocked with wholehearted devotion, according as they belonged to one of the five parts [of the city].' The bishop and his saints sought to exert an attraction over all the urban inhabitants, whose day-to-day loyalties and devotions would in fact be centred on their neighbourhood churches. In this unifying activity, too, the commune was the heir of the bishop, contending with the reality that the medieval city was a mosaic of local, private and sectional interests; for bishop and commune alike, the saint was the emblem of unity and of the authority to which they laid claim.

The saint brought to town had a further significance: his beneficent influence was transferred from the countryside to the city, and the fertility [*ubertas*] which had hitherto been 'lent' to the place where his body rested was translated with him into the city of Siena. It was therefore from this moment that Siena began to expand mightily in numbers of men and women, who successfully invoked their patron and triumphed in war. After three years of profitable vigils the relics were enclosed beneath a carved marble altar, but one of the arms was 'reserved' for use against fire and lightning. The utility of a portable relic for processional and emergency use is well attested elsewhere and at other times.

Just over a century later, in 1215, the canon Odericus compiled an *Ordo* of Siena Cathedral. He stressed the presence of Ansanus's relics, and regarded his cult at Siena as ancient.[6] The account just quoted of the alleged events of 1107 and after might be no more than a much later recension of a pious tradition of interest to the cathedral of Siena, and it is in fact hard to discern to what extent at this early date Ansanus was more than just one of the bishop's saints. The author, however, knew how to emphasize the civic role that he wanted it to be believed Ansanus had fulfilled; and the Sienese laity of course may well have been involved in the acquisition of the relics, whether it was really out of popular enthusiasm for the saint or simply by way of striking a blow in the ongoing battle with Arezzo.[7]

As we saw in Chapter 1, the bringing of saints from rural to urban shrines was nothing new, nor was the belief that the saint, as well as the city and its people, benefited from the move.[8] In about 780 Johannes, the new bishop of Lucca (who was later, probably significantly, to be credited with the miraculous acquisition of the Volto Santo), brought the relics of the African bishop-martyr Regulus to Lucca from their original shrine at Gualdo in the maritime regions of Tuscany, with which he had been familiar as a child. The translation narrative, which may well be associated either with the consecration of the new cathedral in 1070 or with the translation of the relics undertaken by Bishop Rangerius before 1109, recounts that an angel told Johannes that as Lucca was a metropolitan city [*provincia provinciarum*], it was befitting that Regulus should have his own burial place in the basilica of St Martin, which had been founded by San Frediano.[9] A language which associated the bishop as relic-acquirer with the benefits both received and bestowed by the city was now, in an age of growing cities, further developed.

Elsewhere in Gregorian and immediately post-Gregorian Italy, the gift or acquisition of new relics could highlight a struggle for power in urban society. In twelfth-century Ferrara there were peculiarly complex tensions not merely between clergy and laity, but between bishop and cathedral chapter, and between the lay nobility and the 'popular' forces, based on the neighbourhood societies, the *vicinia*.[10] The lay attendance at a council held by Bishop Landolfo in 1105 was distinguished into *proceres* (equated with what might elsewhere be called *capitanei*), *valvassores* (equated with *fideles*), *consules* and 'the chiefs of the people' [*maiores populi*, the representatives of the *vicinia*].[11] Between the middle of the eleventh century and the middle of the twelfth, the city and church of Ferrara witnessed a number of significant translations which represented moves in the bishops' struggle to maintain their own standing and that of their church in the face of competing forces. The cathedral, dedicated to St George, stood on the southern bank of the Po. From the late eleventh century it faced the competition in citizen esteem of churches, notably Santo Stefano, located in the developing city on the north bank. In 1135 a new cathedral was at last begun in this new centre.

The church of Ferrara had its own historic priorities, which complicated the politics of the Gregorian reform: the need to assert its episcopal status and to supersede, definitively, the more ancient see of Voghenza, and the desire to throw off the metropolitan authority of Ravenna. It was therefore hardly feasible for the clergy and nobility of Ferrara to buttress the authority of the antipope Guibert of Ravenna (Clement III, 1080–1100), whatever their desire, like their counterparts elsewhere, to resist reformist, 'Roman' influences. In 1071 the schismatic bishop Samuel installed relics of St Leo, supposed bishop of Voghenza, in the urban church of Santo Stefano, in token of Ferrara's supersession of the older see; two years later he gave half of the church and its possessions to the canons of the cathedral, who were frequently at odds with the 'Catholic' bishop, both now and later.[12]

These actions heralded a period in which the city was effectively withdrawn from obedience to Rome. Only in 1101 did Matildine forces restore Ferrara to Catholic obedience, and only in 1105 did Landolfo, the 'Matildine', 'Gregorian', or 'Catholic' bishop of Ferrara (1090–1139), receive consecration at Rome. If Samuel had had the backing of 'precommunal' forces, Landolfo was reliant on a *familia* with strong connections with the house of Canossa. In 1103, forces in the chapter hostile to the new bishop carried out a translation of their own, bringing the relics of St Romanus to the city.[13] In 1110 Landolfo installed the arm of St George in the cathedral, in what seems an obvious attempt to advertise the titular patron of the bishopric, and in 1128 he brought the crucifix of St Luke to the riverside church of San Luca.[14] Landolfo made it the objective of his long tenure of the see of Ferrara to attempt to build bridges between the disparate social forces at work in the city, as well as to restore the bishop's property rights in the diocese and his control over his tenants in chief. Towards the end of his episcopate he acceded to the pressure to move the cathedral into the centre of the city. With his death, it has been suggested, the attempt to hold the warring forces of clergy and laity in some sort of equilibrium broke down.

The 1140s were crucial years in the growth of communal autonomy. They probably also witnessed the composition in the new cathedral chancery of a forged privilege of Pope Vitalian and the Emperor Constantine IV, dated 657.[15] This not only firmly asserted the subjection of the church of Ferrara to the Roman see, but suggested that the Pope had instituted the commune of Ferrara. It was an intended blueprint for the co-operation, now rapidly eroding, between bishop and commune.[16] The commune, however, had the backing of the canons of the cathedral against the bishop. In 1143 Landolfo's successor, Grifo, presided over the translation of the relics of St Romanus from Rome to the monastery, in the heart of the city, which bore the saint's name. The relics, it was said, had come from Rome itself, and they were exhibited by the bishop to the people. This looks like an attempt to expunge the 1103 translation of the same saint from the record.[17] If the bishop was at odds with both his canons and the commune, the alliance of the latter may, paradoxically, have helped to ensure that, here as so often elsewhere in northern Italy, the bishop's saint, George, remained the chief patron of the city.[18] In 1173 the statutes of the commune were inscribed on the south front of the cathedral itself.

Arezzo was another city where shifting relationships between church and populace resulted in a relocation of the cathedral, but here the time-scale was longer. In 1084 Henry IV was induced to order the destruction of the wall around the episcopal residence, although he soon had it rebuilt. In 1111 Henry V sacked the town, ostensibly because the citizens had attacked the *episcopium*; Otto of Freising understood this to have been because they wanted to bring the cathedral into the city.[19] The issue had not yet been resolved when Arezzo's long-running dispute with Siena came up for a fresh hearing before Alexander III.[20] One witness, Baccalarinus, described simply as an Aretine citizen, recounted how when he was about fourteen or a little older, he had heard his father Guglielminus tell how Gualfredus of Siena had renewed the lawsuit against Arezzo. When things looked bad for the Aretine cause, an old man with white hair came up to Bishop Guido in the Lateran palace and asked him how the case was going. Guido replied that it was going badly, that he didn't know which way to turn. The mysterious old man told him to seek out the registers of Alexander II, in which the definitive sentence would be found. Then he vanished, and could not be found when the bishop sent Guglielminus to bring him back for further questioning. It was St Donatus, patron of the aggrieved Aretine church, all the time. The layman Guglielminus was sent to find and scrutinize the register: 'for my father,' says Baccalarinus proudly, 'was literate' [*erat enim pater meus litteratus*]. Thus the laity were involved as members of the bishop's entourage, as witnesses to the facts of the case, and as bearers of legend and makers of tradition.

In April 1203, Innocent III authorized the union of the cathedral with the monastic church of San Pietro.[21] The action was necessary 'for the peace of the city and church of Arezzo and the common utility' [*pro pace civitatis et ecclesiae Aretinae ac utilitate communi*], not to say 'to assuage discord and eliminate long-standing hatred' [*ad sedandam discordiam et inveteratum odium exstinguendum*]. The following year the Pope had to arbitrate in a dispute over the right to celebrate on the feast of St Donatus.[22] The Pieve had established a customary right to do so, and received both offerings and cense payments in the form of candles on this date. The canons now residing at San Pietro were disputing these rights, and the parochial prerogatives of the Pieve, apparently with citizen backing. The citizens (later referred to as 'nobles') who had in the past offered candles at the Pieve were claiming that they had done so not by way of cense but *de gratia*. Innocent pointed out that he had not actually transferred the cathedral to San Pietro, but had as it were opened a second branch there, and he decreed that the feast should continue to be celebrated at the old cathedral, where (as he pointed out) the saint's body lay, and at the Pieve (whose customary rights he was evidently not minded to disturb). The choice of attendance was up to the worshipper. He conceded baptismal rights to San Pietro, as part of the cathedral church, while refusing to withdraw them from the Pieve. Repeatedly and patiently the Pope drew analogies with his own practice as bishop of Rome. He did not celebrate the feast of the Apostles at St John Lateran, nor the feast of St John at St Peter's, 'although both are cathedral churches'; he performed baptisms at the Lateran, but the sacrament was available elsewhere in Rome.

The logical final step, uniting the Pieve with the cathedral, was not taken until May 1250, when bishop Guglielmino decreed the union, referring to continued discords about the celebration of the saint's feast.[23] In 1257 Massa Trabaria agreed to render to the commune every year *in festo beati Donati* a silken *pallium*, to be borne by a 'suitable envoy'.[24] By the early fourteenth century Donatus lay in a new shrine in the newly rebuilt cathedral on the site of San Pietro. Although the citizen body had been intensely interested in the location of the cathedral itself, and had appropriated the feast for its own purposes, the possession of the saint's relics seems not to have been controversial before the mid-fourteenth century. By this time the allocation of offerings as between the cathedral and the Pieve was the subject of statute law.[25]

Contests over the possession of relics did in fact take place within as well as between cities. They were contests, on the most basic level, for the offerings of the faithful, but also for prestige. Sometimes it seems that claims to the possession of whole bodies carried weight with the populace, or were believed to do so. Here different considerations might apply to a local patron who was assumed to be locally present in his entirety, and a great saint to whom there were well-known competing and superior claims. The Modenese *Relatio* strongly implies, as we have seen, that the laity wished to preserve Geminianus's patronage whole and entire for the church and the city by guaranteeing the integrity of the relics, and a similar concern seems to emerge from the narrative of the *inventio* and translation of Rufinus at Assisi in 1210.[26] The uncertainties of historical record made it possible for claims to be made which could be resolved only according to the particular exigencies of the local political situation. The extant narratives of such disputes usually invoke the *populus* as spectators or as partisans, but there remains the already familiar problem of putting flesh on the bones of these people.

At Ravenna, for example, it was believed that the body of St Apollinare had been taken from Classe to the ancient urban church of San Martino in Ciel d' Oro, which consequently became known as Sant' Apollinare Nuovo.[27] When, however, the abandoned church at Classe was taken over in 1137 by Camaldolese monks, they rapidly showed themselves either genuinely sceptical of the translation story, or unwilling to accept it.[28] In 1173 the monks mounted a full offensive to establish their ownership, obtaining papal backing for their cause. The story is told in a polemical tractate by Rodulfo, prior of Camaldoli.[29] For him the supposed tradition of Apollinare's removal to Sant' Apollinare Nuovo was a fabrication put about by the monks of that church to distract attention from the irregularities of their own life. He represented it as a quite cleverly contrived historical fiction, for the archbishop who had performed the translation was known to have been an active relic-collector. The custom, hitherto observed by the bishop and urban clergy of Ravenna, of going in solemn procession on the saint's day to celebrate mass at Sant' Apollinare in Classe, although perfectly intelligible as an act of public homage to his original burial place, was neatly transformed into an argument in favour of the continued presence of the relics at Classe: what other possible reason could there be for going there?[30]

In 1173 Alexander III sent his legate Hildebrand to investigate, with instructions to stage an *inventio* only if there were no other way of demonstrating to the *plebs* that Apollinare truly lay in the monks' church. The desired result was achieved, and the archbishop, a man of unimpeachable integrity who was to be blamed only for having believed the malign fabrications of the monks of Sant' Apollinare Nuovo, gracefully pronounced himself satisfied. The focus of the narrative is on the warring religious communities, but 'citizens' of Ravenna play supporting parts, arguing about the rights and wrongs of the case and obligingly experiencing miracles to attest to the authenticity of the claimed relics. An artisan of the city, significantly described as 'a simple and humble man' [*simplex & mitis vir*] reports how the saint himself had once described to him in a vision the wounds he had suffered on his legs when he was attacked on his way to Ravenna: when the relics were found, the scars on the leg-bones corresponded exactly. Here, as in earlier sources, the populace is only sketchily delineated; it appears in a supporting role, enacting a part dictated by the clergy.

A similar controversy had allegedly occurred thirty years earlier at Reggio Emilia, but the eventual outome was different, and, if Golinelli's arguments are sound, it may be possible to discern the lay backers of the ecclesiastical protagonists a little more clearly.[31] The relics of the bishop-patron San Prospero were brought within the walls of Reggio late in the tenth century, when the suburban basilica in which they had been deposited in the eighth century was threatened by flood. The bishop, having built a new church (San Prospero in Castello) not far from his cathedral to house the relics, established monks at the suburban basilica. The whereabouts of the saint seem not to have been controversial until the monks of the suburban monastery laid claim to him in a narrative which Golinelli dates to 1163–4.[32] Here they asserted that in 1144 Bishop Alberio (a Bolognese outsider) had staged a fictitious *inventio* of the relics at San Prospero in Castello. Grieved by this imposture, Abbot Amizo had urged him to come to the suburban church to see the truth. Alberio demurred, but offered to give the monks half of his relics, to dedicate both churches to the saint and to institute a double celebration, one to take place at the monastery and one at San Prospero in Castello.[33] Not seeing why he should be palmed off with half when he already had all, the abbot, with the backing of Achille Tacoli, the archdeacon and provost of San Prospero in Castello (which might at first seem rather surprising), sought the aid of the papal legate Cardinal Guido, who was at the time visiting the monastery of San Benedetto Polirone near Mantua. With the cardinal's support and that of the 'nobles and leading men' [*nobiles et proceres*] of the city, an *inventio* was staged at the suburban basilica, in which Archdeacon Achille was actively – indeed, physically – involved. Bishop Alberio yielded to superior force.

This alleged *translatio* has been described as 'highly suspect'.[34] The consensus of all the other evidence is that the late-tenth-century translation within the walls of the city had indeed taken place; and there is no extant legatine sentence or papal confirmation of the outcome, as there is in the (possibly equally suspect) case of Apollinare's relics at Ravenna. Golinelli suggests that the narrative was a 'pamphlet' written to back Achille Tacoli in the contest for the bishopric which resulted from the death of Alberio on 5 April 1163. He was a member of one of the powerful and predatory clans which had troubled the church of Reggio for generations;[35] as such he seems to have had the backing of other noble families such as the Manfredi, one member of which, Guido, supplanted Abbot Amizo in 1151, while another, Pizo, become the imperial *podestà* of the city in 1154. The 'nobles and leading men' of whose backing the monks boasted were, Golinelli suggests, men such as these, who, in a pattern to be found in other cities, had a particular interest in the monastery outside the walls, using it (and its property) both as a source of enrichment and as a *point d'appui* in the contest for dominance of the church and city.

Reggio had been notably pro-imperial, Bishop Alberio along with the rest; the schismatic Pope Victor IV was received in the city in 1161. In 1164 the Cardinal Guido who had aided and abetted the 1144 translation succeeded Victor as antipope, under the name Paschal III. By 1168, however, Reggio had joined the other cities of northern Italy in the Lombard League; and Golinelli speculates that the fact that Achille Tacoli, despite his powerful backers, lost the contest for the bishopric may not have been unconnected with a growing disillusionment with Barbarossa, his local noble supporters and his demands. The victorious contestant was the provost of the cathedral, Albericone dei Cambiatori, whose name suggests popular family antecedents. One of his first actions was to instruct Abbot Guido to refrain from further dilapidation of his monastery's property;[36] and in 1169 he received oaths of fealty and promises of good behaviour from the rural nobility.

The bishops of Reggio, in the later years of the century, were closely identified with the nascent commune. Their palace housed its deliberations, they represented the city on such important occasions as the negotiations at Constance, and (in 1182) the bishop himself was *podestà*. They had vindicated their possession of the city's heavenly patron, who unsurprisingly, as the thirteenth-century statutes attest, was also the patron of the commune. To underscore the point, the feast celebrated by the commune was the *dies natalitius*, 24 June, which was associated with the church of San Prospero in Castello rather than with the monastery.[37]

A not dissimilar *imbroglio* took place at Lucca a little later in the century. Here the relics of an ancient bishop-saint, San Frediano, were installed and venerated in the church which bore his name and which by 1100 was a centre of the reformed canonical life, on which Pope Paschal II drew for the reform of the community at the Lateran. Subsequent popes assigned other Lucchese churches to the care of San Frediano, and these signs of favour aggravated the jealousy of the cathedral clergy and others. From the beginning of the twelfth century there were indications of trouble within San Frediano's parish, which the cathedral canons seem, or so the popes suspected, to have abetted. From time to time there is a suggestion that the city officials were implicated, or at the least that they were not overzealous in doing the Pope's bidding.[38]

In a letter written to the canons of the cathedral on 8 January 1171, Alexander III retailed complaints he had received from the canons of San Frediano. They had been forbidden to proclaim publicly their possession of the body of San Frediano, and on pain of excommunication the citizens had been forbidden to attend at the church on major feast-days, as they had hitherto been accustomed to do. The Pope understood that what had stung the cathedral clergy into this action was the fact that on the day when the dedication of the cathedral was solemnly celebrated, the prior and canons of San Frediano had staged a rival attraction, the feast of Abraham. For the cathedral to lay claim to the body of San Frediano, however, was to impugn the actions of Eugenius III, who in 1147, in the presence of the previous bishop 'and almost the whole city', had himself 'elevated' the relics and consecrated the altar in which they were installed.[39] This slight Alexander could not tolerate, and he reminded the bishop and his party of the special regard in which the Holy See had always held San Frediano. The church was in no way to be defrauded of 'the accustomed veneration of the Lucchese people'; the cathedral clergy were no longer to celebrate Frediano's feast, or prohibit clergy or laity from visiting that church 'in the accustomed manner on major feast-days'. The Pope, for his part, had directed the prior and canons of San Frediano to remove their celebrations of Abraham to another more suitable day.

Here again the *populus* is visible as both audience and market for the public celebration of sanctity. Further adjudications on the various issues between the parties proved necessary: in April 1194, Celestine III referred to the 'scandal and contention' which had 'at one time' arisen not only between the churches but 'involving the whole city' [*de tota civitate*].[40] However, neither Frediano nor St Martin, patron of the cathedral, was destined to become the city's major patron. The warring parties of canons were all witnesses to the burgeoning cult of the Volto Santo, and it is probable that this was already identified with the laity and the commune. Legend (which still finds pious upholders at Lucca) would trace this cult back to the eighth century, but there is no certain evidence before the late eleventh. The first clear mention of it, as has often been remarked, comes from that unlikely teller of holy tidings William Rufus of England, who liked to swear by the 'Face' of Lucca.[41]

Rangerius – who, as bishop from about 1097 to 1112, had to try to restore post-Gregorian normality to the strife-torn church of Lucca – refers to the Vultus, as we shall see, obliquely, if at all. It is clear from his enormous verse life of his predecessor Anselm[42] that he regarded Martin as the proprietor of the cathedral and the diocese. The goods of the Lucchese church are the 'bona Martini' (l. 4644); those who despoil it 'Martinum violant' (l. 4899). In an important passage Rangerius sketches three ages of Christian society: gold, silver and bronze. He associates Frediano with Martin as a representative of the age of poverty, and (therefore) of gold: 'As was Martin, so too was Fredianus.... Each was poor and each a foreigner.' [*Qualis Martinus, qualis fuit et Phrigianus.... Pauper uterque fuit et peregrinus uterque.*] Their poverty simply illuminated their miraculous powers (ll. 4381-6). With the coming of the age of silver, which was an age of increasing wealth, the heroic virtues dimmed somewhat, but there were some compensations in the form of lavish expenditure on the building and adornment of churches. Consult writings that are now worm-eaten, says Rangerius, and 'you will read of the many treasures of our Martin' [*Martini nostri praedia multa legis*]. There was harmony between clergy and laity, like that of the mind united with the body, as both sought to sanctify their respective paths (ll. 4393-428).

Thus Rangerius contrives a rebuke to both the *milites* and the *populus* of the succeeding age, which was one of rampant luxury. He bears fascinating, if somewhat oblique, testimony to the association of demographic growth with social, religious and political change. There was more to the growing power of the urban laity and their increasing visibility in twelfth-century sources than sheer force of numbers, but that force must not be forgotten. Rangerius seems to have believed that the tumults produced by change occurred first in the secular world, and that the church was only gradually sucked into them: 'As the people was, so the priest began to be' [*At sic ut populus, sic incipit esse sacerdos*, l. 4443]. Population growth and immigration from the countryside compounded the problems: 'Thus from an increased number of people/ a multiplying crop of vices was bound to arise/ And a rude people originating from villages and crags/ Imported madness, as they pursued ease.' [*Sic de numero populorum multiplicato/ Exoritur scelerum multiplicanda seges/ At genus incultum villis et rupibus ortum/ Ingessit rabiem, dum fugit ad requiem*, ll. 4547–50.] The imitation of French ways was one symptom of the moral bedlam that was setting in (l. 4541). A people hitherto desirous chiefly of gain and peace and quiet [*populus quondam questus et pacis amator*, l. 4575] became caught up in class warfare and demagogic politics. Opposition to the campaign for the purification of the church was part of these upheavals.

This was the world which gave birth to the commune, at Lucca as elsewhere. It was also the world, and the time, which produced the first solid evidence for the cult of the Volto Santo at Lucca, which was well established by 1100. In 1107 Paschal II issued privileges to both the bishop and the canons of the church of San Martino guaranteeing their respective rights to a share in the offerings to the *sacrarium Vultus*. In a description of the altars in the cathedral as they were before the rearrangement which Rangerius undertook in 1109, both an 'old cross' and the Vultus are mentioned. In 1118 or 1120 Rangerius's successor Benedict consecrated the chapel of the Vultus in the cathedral.[43] It is perhaps odd, therefore, that Rangerius nowhere explicitly names the Vultus, either in his life of Anselm or in a sermon which seems likely also to be his, written to commemorate the dedication of Alexander II's rebuilt cathedral.[44] One might have thought that it would have served him well as an emblem of the devotion of the authentic Lucchese church to the Crucified Christ, and that he would have taken the opportunity afforded by the sermon to list it among the sacred treasures of the cathedral, but he does not. It must have existed when he wrote; what, therefore, did it mean to him?

There is an enigmatic passage in the life of Anselm which may hint at an answer. It heralds the transition from the age of silver to the age of bronze: 'But where there is no moderation in riches, and foreign religion has begun to make the cross frequented, as is usual, from the enjoyment of wealth and freedom, decency and uprightness and sacred order perish.' [*Ast ubi diviciis non est modus et peregrina/ Religio celebrem coepit habere crucem,/ Ut solet, ex opibus et libertate fruendis,/ Et pudor et probitas et sacer ordo perit.* ll. 4429–32.]

A number of words here challenge interpretation. What, for example, exactly is *peregrina religio*? And what exactly did Rangerius mean by the 'cross'? All that is clear is an association with unbridled wealth and the consequent 'perishing' of 'decency, uprightness and sacred order'. It is possible – but only possible – that Rangerius is referring to the riches that came within the grasp of the custodians of the Cross, and perhaps of the populace generally, when it became a popular attraction with pilgrims.[45] As to the impact of *peregrina religio* in general, we may recall Rangerius's disapproving words about the aping of French ways. There was no altering the facts of geography that made Lucca a staging post on the way to Rome. The author of the sermon for the dedication of the cathedral (perhaps Rangerius himself) had commented that the original dedication was attended by visitors not only from neighbouring cities but from as far away as France.[46] The Lucchese money-changers and other dealers had their stalls in the open space in front of the cathedral, and it was in fact 'in the time of bishop Rangerius' that they committed to writing their oath to 'commit no theft nor trick nor falsification within the court of St Martin nor in those houses in which men are given hospitality'.[47] Despite this precaution, the compilers of the *Codex Calixtinus* at Santiago de Compostela, within a generation of Rangerius's death, were naming Lucca among the centres, Italian and other, where the pilgrim might reasonably expect to be swindled.[48]

There seems to be no way of ascertaining whether the Vultus, around 1100, was identified as the possession of a party in the Lucchese church, or whether it was already in some sense 'popular'. The issue was fairly clear by 1181, when an agreement was recorded between the canons of San Martino and the consuls of the 'fraternity of the Holy Cross'. The latter clearly already had its own independent *operarii* ('clerks of works'), who were responsible for collecting offerings and seeing to the material requirements of the cult. On four major feast-days – those of St Regulus, the Exaltation of the Cross, the Dedication of the Cathedral and St Martin himself – and also on Holy Saturday and at the May Litanies, the *operarii* of St Martin and the *operarii* of the Fraternity were each to set out their table in the church, 'and what God there gives them, without fraud they shall share half and half'. However, on the feast of the Cross, the *operarii* of the Cross (later also referred to as the *operarii* of the Vultus) were to have two-thirds of the offerings, leaving a third to the 'old *operarius* of St Martin' [*antiquus operarius S. Martini*]. The consuls of the fraternity were also to have all the candles apart from the three offered by Corsagno, San Quirico in Venere and Medicina; dependent communities were obviously already offering candles at the Feast of the Exaltation. On other feast-days, the *operarius S. Vultus* could put out his table and have what God gave him, and on Sundays he could go round with a collecting bowl, but at Christmas and Pentecost he could do so only after the regular offering had been made, and he had no rights at funerals.[49]

The Feast of the Cross was becoming what it has remained down to the present day: the great civic festival of the Lucchese year. Some time between 1119 and 1124 Calixtus II conceded to Bishop Benedict the right to wear the *pallium* on the great festivals of the year, including the feasts of Martin and Frediano, and of the dedication of the cathedral, but there was no mention of the Exaltation of the Cross.[50] In 1120, announcing the results of an early arbitration between the canons of the cathedral and of San Frediano, he had prescribed that six of the latter, with the prior, should attend solemn mass at the cathedral on the feasts of Martin and Regulus, and that the *maior missa* was not to be celebrated at San Frediano on those days.[51] At no time, in the records of this dispute, is there any mention of a contested right to celebrate the Exaltation of the Cross. Although it was firmly located in the cathedral, that cult was, we may surmise, ever more clearly identified with the laity and the commune. It seems plausible, especially if we remember the fragmentary evidence that the cathedral canons had secular backing in their disputes with San Frediano, to suppose that the ruling elements in lay society had made common cause with the clergy of San Martino, or at least come to terms with them.[52]

Some twelfth-century *translationes* were narrated in such a way as to identify the lay rulers of the city as little more than mere spectators; of others it is impossible to know what special interests, if any, they served. An inscription on a sarcophagus still preserved in the shadows behind the high altar of what at the time was the church of San Giorgio (later San Paolino) at Lucca records the discovery in 1197 of the holy bodies of Paulinus, bishop and martyr, Severus martyr and Theobald martyr, 'in the time of the Emperor Henry, the Lord Cardinal Pandulf, Guido bishop of Lucca and Guido priest of this church' and certain other named persons.[53] This *inventio* may have been the genuinely fortuitous consequence of rebuilding work, which might well enforce the translation of relics, whether from an old to a new shrine within the same church or to a completely new church. Paulinus, thus brought to light, was destined for a second *inventio*, and for a future as a civic patron, but not for some while yet.

The normal motivation of *translationes* and *inventiones* was likely to be the enhancement of the prestige of the possessing or receiving church and clergy, and of their power to attract offerings. Petronius, the ancient bishop of Bologna whose relics, with many others, were brought to light in 1146 in the church of Santo Stefano which he himself had reputedly built, was (like Paulinus) ultimately destined for a great future as a civic patron, but here too this was not an immediate development.[54] The *inventio* of the virgin Justina, the apostle Mathias, and – most ambitious of all – St Luke, at the church of St Justina at Padua in 1176, was probably an event of similar type, prompted by similar ambitions. Both *inventiones* were described by monastic authors, who stress the unanimity of urban society in its rejoicing at the discovery or rediscovery of heavenly patrons.

According to the narrator of the Paduan *inventio*,[55] since a disastrous fire in 1172 the whole population of the city had been unusually thoughtful on the subject of its saints, and desirous of relocating those who were lost to view; like St Ambrose eight hundred years earlier, the clergy held up to remembrance a sacred past which the urban community was to join in celebrating. In both the Paduan and the Bolognese narratives, the *populus* is evoked chiefly as the audience and as the beneficiary of miracles; but the presence of the consuls as witnesses of the *inventiones* is recorded in both cases, and at Bologna they were actively involved in so far as they swore to uphold safe conduct for those who, in obedience to the bishop's directive, came annually from all over the diocese to do homage to Petronius on his feast-day. At Padua, St Luke did miracles for individuals from Monselice and from as far away as Verona; and all the peasant inhabitants of the village of Montagnana came in a body to do homage to him, singing and bearing gifts. The saint, firmly located in an urban setting, brought his devotees to town.

Alba Orselli comments on the generic way in which the Bolognese *populus* is described, while noting the more specific reference to the consuls, and suggests that the bishop's extension of the feast to the whole diocese concerned the clergy and 'the laity *qua* the flock of the diocese, rather than as members of the *civitas* or as in some sense bound to it'.[56] Perhaps this is too fine a distinction. The catchment area of an urban church was increasingly understood to be that of the city itself. The power of the metropolis over the countryside, even if ecclesiastical in its origins, now had to be exercised in co-operation with men who were more than just members of an anonymous mass of *fideles*. The monastic narrators of Padua and Bologna were well aware of this, even if they mentioned the consuls only briefly. Although the saints might still be the property of the clergy, the practical co-operation of the lay rulers of society was increasingly necessary to the successful management of the cult, as it was necessary to the bishop's maintenance of his diocesan jurisdiction.

Sometimes it is possible to suspect that a translation had the cultivation of the urban laity in view from the beginning. In 1144 Bishop Atto of Pistoia – himself a Spaniard, and knowing of the devotion of his people to St James – took steps to obtain a relic of the apostle from the fountainhead, Compostela itself – or so we are told by Contarinus, 'clerk' and 'chancellor' of the city of Pistoia.[57] This was to all appearances an adroit piece of public-relations work on the part of a Vallombrosan abbot turned bishop, a man without local connections, who had been compelled as recently as 1138 to excommunicate the consuls when they violated the property of the church. There is no clear evidence of a pre-existing cult of St James at Pistoia: Atto's motives may plausibly have been both to strengthen his own prestige and to attract pilgrims to Pistoia at a period when traffic along the Via Francigena was enriching the custodians of the Volto Santo at nearby Lucca.

Atto knew, we are told, that the church of Pistoia possessed a valuable contact at Compostela in the person of Rainerius, a deacon of Pistoia who went to France *causa discendi* and spent time in Paris and later in Winchester, before going (presumably as a pilgrim) to Compostela, where his talents were recognized by the formidable bishop Diego del Gelmírez. Though he did not know Rainerius personally, Atto wrote to him to solicit his good offices in obtaining relics of St James for the church of Pistoia. Allegedly word of Atto's reputation reached the ears of the archbishop of Compostela, who acceded to the tearful entreaties of Rainerius and the canons of the church of St James, separating a portion of the relics of the head of the apostle and consigning them in a suitable container to two Pistoiese citizens, Tebaldus and Medius, who, as pilgrims to Compostela, had delivered Atto's letter. They also took back to Pistoia letters from the archbishop, which Contarinus claims to have read, in which he joined with Rainerius in begging Atto to build a suitable chapel for the apostle in the cathedral of San Zeno (as Rainerius would, indeed, have known it).

The chapel was built in 1144–45 at the western end of the cathedral (it is now in the south aisle of the nave). Atto consecrated it on 24 July, the vigil of St James. Immediately the miracles began. As is usual in such collections, the tales Contarinus relates delineate a catchment area for the power of the relics which extends from the neighbourhood of the church itself to the communities of the Pistoiese territory and ultimately to Florence, 'which at that time was unfriendly to Pistoia', and even to the diocese of Bologna. A man of San Baronto (a community centred on a monastery in the mountains eight miles from Pistoia) received a cure for his nervous paralysis from the relics, and thereupon set off for Compostela itself. The cure of a Florentine boy, brought in a wagon by his mother, was witnessed by natives of Pistoia and by Florentines, Lucchese and others who had come 'from farflung parts'. James then demonstrated his power by working miracles in Florence itself; it was proper that the beneficiaries should come to Pistoia to give thanks, and Contarino claims to have talked with one of them. The significance is heavily underlined: 'When the Florentines knew the truth of this miracle, although they were at that time very hostile to the Pistoiese, many of them began to come to St James with excessive veneration, barefoot and clad in woollen garb, especially women in compunction of heart, as if inspired from heaven.'

Atto, as far as we can see from the surviving sources, had taken the initiative at Pistoia, and he was now assisted by a pope who was doubtless aware of his earlier local difficulties with the consuls. In November 1145 Eugenius III wrote to the bishops of Siena, Volterra, Florence, Lucca and Luni, drawing their attention to the miracles that were occurring by James's intercession at Pistoia and urging that they should in no way permit pilgrims to be obstructed from flocking there. In another letter written on the same day he granted an indulgence of seven days to all who devoutly visited the shrine.[58] Institutions rapidly grew up to service the new cult. In 1148 and again in 1153, Atto was making grants to a hospital of San Jacopo. In October 1148 the consuls were present, and reciprocated the bishop's generosity by agreeing to the payment of an annual cense of one pound of wax at the feast of San Zeno. In April 1153, the rectors of the hospital bound themselves to render one pound of oil annually on the vigil of San Zeno.[59] Within a generation of his coming, James had acquired his own *Opera* for the receipt of offerings,[60] which may well have been an autonomous body run by laymen from the beginning, as it evidently was when its vernacular statutes were published in 1313. More miracles were added to Contarinus's compilation in 1201 and later in the thirteenth century. The author of one of these addenda underlined the central message: 'Therefore, brethren, let the clergy and people of Pistoia rejoice together with the whole bishopric ... since Jesus Christ has deigned to grant us so great a patron, because the whole city is illuminated by his protection.'[61]

The story of James's coming to Pistoia and the range of his subsequent miracles well illustrate the values and expectations that were bound up in the cults which became official in the city-states that were taking shape in the twelfth century. James's physical presence guaranteed a patronage which extended in the first instance over the city and the *episcopatus*, and therefore over the communities which the commune of Pistoia would claim to rule; but his influence, on behalf of Pistoia, could extend throughout Tuscany and even, more vaguely, beyond, attracting the interest and, of course, the offerings of pilgrims. He established a charismatic presence on which the official devotions of the city as a political community rapidly came to be focused, clearly with the compliance of the bishop in whose church that presence was located; the Volto Santo (however long it had actually been in the cathedral) seems to have achieved something very similar at Lucca.

The probability is, furthermore, that by 1200 James, like the Vultus, was the focus of the compulsory rituals of homage which the commune exacted from its subjects. Certainly subject communities were involved in the celebrations of his feast-day; this is indicated by the reminder sent in 1221 to the inhabitants of Lamporecchio and Batoni that they must send their archers to the *festa* and guard the roads leading to Pistoia.[62] By the late twelfth century it was becoming common throughout city-state Italy for rural communities and lords who submitted to the authority of the commune to bind themselves to make offerings at the altar of the patron on his or her major feast-day. Statutory regulation of these proceedings survives only from the thirteenth century, but evidence for their occurrence in the twelfth century, though patchy, is fairly widespread. For example, from the 1130s onwards the inhabitants of Imola were repeatedly forced to agree to render *pallia* to both Bologna and Faenza on the feast of St Peter, who, by a convenient chance, was the patron saint of both cities.[63] They as frequently relapsed into disobedience, but Master Tolosanus of Faenza recorded with satisfaction under the year 1184 that 'after the Faventines had thus subdued all their enemies they were entitled to an annual tribute of *pallia* from a number of communities including Imola, and a payment of wax [*pensio cere*] from many castles'.[64] At a similar date the commune of Siena was beginning to impose ceremonial obligations at the Feast of the Assumption on lords and communities which submitted to its authority.[65] The punishment of the failure of the inhabitants of the Garfagnana to make their offerings at Lucca at the feast of the Cross in 1244 is one indication of established custom,[66] and by this time regulations of the practice are beginning to appear in communal statutes. By this time, also, some at least of the games and races which marked the patronal festival, such as the ancestor of the famous *Palio* of Siena, were taking place.[67]

In many cities by the end of the twelfth century, therefore, the bishop's church, if not the altar of the bishop's patron, was providing the venue for a ceremonial which – while it grew out of the homages rendered by episcopal tenants and subjects, and although the cathedral clergy benefited from the offerings – was increasingly controlled by the lay power. Bishops in Italy, as elsewhere in Europe in the late twelfth century, can scarcely have been insensible to the multiple pressures on their authority. In pursuit of their political aspirations, the laity, sometimes opportunistically and also inconsistently, allied itself with heresy and a more generalized anticlericalism. Growing papal power had repercussions on episcopal power, but, perhaps more immediately, there were the clashes of papal and imperial interests in the peninsula, which afforded opportunities, at least temporarily, for urban politicians hostile to all types of ecclesiastical jurisdiction to advance their cause.

If one contrasts the veneration accorded to ancient bishop-saints with the treatment city-state Italians often meted out to their living bishops, one might conclude that by and large they felt that the only good bishop was a dead bishop, and, by a perfectly logical extension of that principle, that the only saintly bishop was one who had been dead for a long time. Early in the century efforts were still being made to supply bishop-saints where none existed. Bernardo degli Uberti of Parma, who was consecrated by Paschal II almost immediately after his consecration of the new cathedral of Modena, was 'canonized' by his successor as bishop, and his legend emphasized his services to his city – for example, his defence of Parma against aggression from Piacenza and Cremona. No such effort was made on behalf of Buonsenior of Reggio, despite his impeccable credentials, as if the existence of the ancient bishop-patron Prospero made it unnecessary.[68] Later in the century, saintly bishops seem more clearly to have remained possessions of the church rather than of the city in a wider sense. To be reputed a saintly bishop by the church was not necessarily a passport to lay popularity. The exception who may prove the rule is Ubaldo of Gubbio, who died in 1160 after a long reign.[69] Even if they were not saints themselves, however, Italian bishops around the year 1200 were more than ever persuaded of the value of the saints in their dealings with their unreliable and even irreverent citizens.

The transaction which brought the arm of St Philip to Florence in March 1205[70] was, on one level, the result of contacts between Bishop Pietro (who died in 1203) and several clerics of Florentine origin who had risen to high office in the Latin kingdom of

Jerusalem, including the late patriarch Monaco and the prior of the church of the Holy Sepulchre, Raniero. It was Raniero who actually bore the relic to Florence, combining this errand with that of requesting Alberto Bishop of Vercelli to accept election as the new patriarch of Jerusalem. The relic was received by the bishop-elect of Florence, Giovanni da Velletri, erstwhile prior of San Frediano at Lucca and a man well known to the Pope, who commissioned a narrative of the translation. He was accompanied, we may note, by the *podestà*, and the relic was installed not in the cathedral, but in the Baptistery. Philip had come to add his protection and patronage of Florence to that of the Baptist. He had another function, too: as a prophetic exponent of Trinitarian doctrine, he would make 'the upholders of the orthodox faith rejoice and the damnable troop of the heretics tremble'.

It is possible to supply a context for all this in local politics and the relations of Florence with the Pope, who was doubtless well-informed about the whole transaction.[71] Sufficient of Innocent's letters to the Florentines and to Giovanni da Velletri around this time survive to justify the conjecture that there had occurred, perhaps in the course of the year 1204 and as a result of the efforts of the bishop-elect, a shift among the Florentines in favour of accommodation with the church. What happened at Florence was bound to interest the Pope, if only because it had originally been Florentine Cathar missionaries who brought their heresy to his own city of Orvieto. Heresy and other more generalized forms of disobedience accompanied the pope's struggle to establish a working governmental structure in the nascent 'papal state'. Nevertheless, despite the utility of saints and relics as weapons in the struggle against such dissent, Innocent found it either unnecessary or undesirable to canonize Peter Parenzo, the Roman *podestà* whom he had sent to Orvieto and who was murdered there by the heretics.[72]

At Assisi, the greater citizens objected to the surrender of their fortress to the Pope in 1198.[73] The popular party opposed the pro-imperial policy of their betters, but was worsted as a result of defeat by the Perugians in 1202. In 1204 the Assisans' attempt to elect an excommunicate as *podestà* earned them a paternal reproof from Innocent.[74] It was an agreement in 1210 between the 'greater' and the 'lesser' citizens which permitted the completion of the new cathedral of San Rufino, and in 1212 Bishop Guido (who had extended his protection to Francis a few years earlier) performed an *inventio* and translation of the old bishop-saint. The narrative describing these events makes no specific allusion to troubled political or religious circumstances.[75] It invokes the well-worn topos of the saint whose relics, precious though they be, have become lost to view with the passage of time. The custodian of the hospital attached to the church of San Rufino received a triple vision of the martyr, directing him to the forsaken place of his burial, submerged in water in the *confessio*. The water, indeed, created difficulties: it could scarcely be believed that such an important tomb would be located in so inauspicious a place. The crucial role played by the bishop, as one known to be 'correct in life and prudent in action', is emphasized. The *inventio* was attended by the consuls and other citizens of Assisi, and the *universus populus* witnessed the installation of the relics in a new container in the altar at the east end of the cathedral.

Rufinus's bones had survived in their entirety, down to the smallest, and they were to be kept together. The point is underlined by one of the miracle stories appended to the narrative of the translation.[76] People from outside Assisi who had attended the ceremony gathered up dust from the original tomb, 'so that in honour of the holy martyr they could take it away to their own places'. They were able to get no further than a mile or so from Assisi before they were stopped in their tracks, found themselves walking in circles, or were otherwise prevented from progressing. The dust was returned to the canons, who, having deliberated upon the matter, enclosed it with the rest of the relics. If Rufinus wrought wonders for the outsider, as indeed he did, he was to do it at Assisi, and therefore for the benefit of the church and people who possessed a monopoly of his remains. The other miracles that were effected by the rediscovered saint display the customary mixture: some stories indeed celebrate his efficacy for the pilgrim and the foreigner, but for the most part he showed a natural concern for the interests of natives of Assisi, such as the students on their way to Bologna who lost the money they were carrying with them to pay their scholastic expenses, or the young girl who was falsely accused by her father and brother of unchastity, but with the martyr's help withstood the ordeal of hot oil. There were also, of course, the many from Assisi and neighbouring towns such as Foligno who required relief from disease.

Rufinus was the established communal patron. When the castle of Postignano submitted to Assisi in 1217, the inhabitants agreed to render a three-pound candle on his feast-day.[77] As the co-existence of the old martyr and the charismatic lover of poverty in Assisi graphically indicates, however, a new sort of sanctity was now making its appearance in the cities. Before the mendicant tide swamped most other claimants to holiness, there appeared holy men and women, charitable activists, sometimes also enthusiastic pilgrims, whose major claim to the veneration of their fellows was their exemplification of the religious possibilities open to the laity. A representative specimen was Raimondo of Piacenza, surnamed the 'Palmer' (d.1202), who was diverted by a vision of Christ from the endless pursuit of pilgrimage to a life of charitable activism in his native city.[78] Another was Homobonus of Cremona, the exemplary lay Christian, charitable, a peace-maker, and assiduous in his performance of his religious duties, who was promoted by his bishop, Sicard, and received the unique honour of canonization by Innocent III in January 1199, within a year of his death.[79]

Cremona was oddly short of saints, and Sicard had been doing his best with what he had. In 1195 he had translated saints Himerius and Archelaus, neither of them natives of the place, to a new marble shrine, 'and a great and glorious festivity took place', as he himself related.[80] Homobonus was an opportune candidate for promotion as a civic patron. He had good credentials and powerful backing, but there is little evidence, in the early years of the thirteenth century, that the Cremonese were so impressed by the honour the city had been done by his canonization that they desisted from their customary outrages against the church. It would be rash to suppose that in revivifying Archelaus and Himerius, and in advancing Homobonus, Sicard had ends in view that could be defined as consciously and narrowly 'political'. It would be similarly rash to deduce too much from the fact that a little over a month before the canonization of Homobonus Innocent had written to the people of Cremona (a city with a notable record of support for the Hohenstaufen) urging them to give no aid or support to Markward of Anweiler.[81] Yet any action undertaken, in Cremona or elsewhere, to buttress the influence of the church, to impress upon the populace their need for its saving grace, and to attract their loyalty and their offerings, was bound to have implications for the nature of the partnership that might be forged between the clergy and the laity, and therefore for the way in which power would be exercised in urban society in the future.

The urban laity is far from invisible in the twelfth century. In bringing apostolic relics to their cities, in performing and publicizing new *inventiones* of old local saints, the bishops were well aware of their audience. Furthermore, the leading members of the urban laity were no longer merely an audience. If the words *populus* and *civis* retain something of their old all-purpose ambiguity, the appearance of the *consul* and the *podestà* clearly signal the institutionalization of secular power to the extent that even hagiographers unselfconsciously record their presence at *translationes* and *inventiones*. They witness, they escort, they consent; the winning of the initiative is soon to follow.

Notes

1. There are several editions of the *Relatio*; I have used the one by G. Bertoni in *RIS* VI.i. On its language and context, see Golinelli, 'Cultura e religiosità a Modena e Nonantola nell' alto e pieno Medioevo', in *Lanfranco e Wiligelmo: Il Duomo di Modena* (Modena 1985), pp. 121–8; R. Bussi, 'Le istituzioni cittadine e Modena tra X e XII secolo', ibid., pp. 117–20.

2. Cf. the *vicinia* of Ferrara, p. 64 and n.10 below.

3. There had, for example, been violent dissensions at Piacenza in 1090 between *milites* and *populi*, which ended in a divinely inspired and exceedingly emotional 'peace movement' (*Annales Placentini Guelfi, MGH SS* 18, pp. 411–12). On the less differentiated language used in the *Vita Longior* of Geminianus, which Golinelli suggests should be dated to the eleventh century, before the burgeoning of the reform movement, see above, pp. 46–7. It is a moot point whether we should deduce from the failure of the author of the *Relatio* to mention 'consuls' (first mentioned at Modena as late as 1135) that a commune did not yet exist.

4. Described by Miller, *Formation*, p. 15. The Latin of the inscription reads 'Dat Presul signum populo munimine dignum/ Vexillum Zeno largitur corde sereno.'

5. Printed in E. Baluze, *Miscellanea novo ordine digesta*, ed. G. Mansi, 4 (Lucca 1764), pp. 65–7. For the manuscripts, see F. Barcellona in *I Santi Patroni Senesi*, pp. 31–3. The date of the translation is recorded in the *Kalendarium Ecclesiae Metropolitanae Senensis*, in *Cronache senesi*, p. 5. For the long-running dispute between Arezzo and Siena over this and other churches, see above, pp. 37–9.

6. *Ordo Officiorum*, p. 273. One of the cathedral's two major bells was named after Ansanus (p. 393).

7. Cammarosano remarks on the 'solidarietà tra autorità urbane e episcopato' at Siena in the 1120s; a tax was imposed on the whole territory to sustain the battle over the *pievi* (*Caleffo Vecchio* 5, pp. 35–6).

8. E.g. above, p. 42.

9. *Acta S* Sept. 1, pp. 238–9. The historical fact of the translation is attested by documents which refer to Regulus's body as being still in the church of Gualdo in 778 but in the cathedral of Lucca in 781–82: *Memorie e documenti*, 4, n.10, p. 15; n.86, pp. 136–9; n.88, p. 141; n.90, p. 144. For Rangerius, see below, pp. 73–5.

10. For this and what follows I am largely reliant on Benati and Samaritani, *La Chiesa di Ferrara*. Unfortunately this book, though full of information, is exceedingly difficult to use, being far from clearly organized, inadequately indexed and bereft of footnotes. For the *vicinia*, see pp. 41–2, 48–9, 69, 160, etc.

11. Ibid., p. 83.

12. Ibid., pp. 43–4. In fact relics of St Leo were already allegedly present at Santo Stefano in the previous century (p. 59). See also ibid., pp. 7–8, and cf. Lanzoni, *Le Origini delle Diocese Antiche*, pp. 449–51.

13. The *Chronicon Estense* records both the translation of 1103 and the placing of the body 'in Arca, ubi est' in 1116 (Muratori, 15, col. 299).

14. Benati and Samaritani, pp. 60–62, 124. The translation of the crucifix of St Luke may have been connected with Ferrara's aspirations to complete freedom of river traffic and freedom from royal tolls on the Po.

15. Text in Ughelli (*Italia Sacra* 2, pp. 519–26), who printed it in the full knowledge that it was probably *suppositiosum*.

16. Ibid., p. 526: 'De civibus autem nostris Ferrariensibus nobilibus et sapientibus duodecim eligimus nobiles & sapientes viros consules, qui magna libertate civitatem regant & populum & sua jura cum proprietate detineant, & romano more suum jus, & honorem detineant, & cum magna fortitudine suam consuetudinem teneant.' Cf. Benati and Samaritani, pp. 11, 73.

17. Benati and Samaritani, p. 62. Romanus's day was observed as a holiday in later centuries: ibid., pp. 382, 389.

18. Another attempt to launch a 'new' patron seems to have been made, some time after the 1140s, with the circulation of the fantastic story that in 1106 the Emperor Henry V had translated the relics of a certain St

Maurelius from Edessa to Ferrara. Daniel Papebroch suggested (*Acta S Maii* 2, p. 158) that the story originated after the institution of canons regular at the former cathedral on the south bank of the Po. Cf. Benati and Samaritani, p. 404: 'Si trattava di un patrono creato a metà del sec. XII nella transpadana cittadina in opposizione alla cispadana e alla nuova cattedrale.' The (evidently earlier) *Vitaliana* makes no mention of Maurelius, who had allegedly been a bishop of Voghenza/Ferrara. Why his relics had to come from Edessa, and when Henry V went to the Holy Land, is not made clear; the narrative also (deliberately?) suppresses any mention of Landolfo as bishop at the time of the translation, naming a 'Johannes' instead. The fact that two recorded bishops of Voghenza bear the names Mauricinus and Georgius (Lanzoni, *Origini*, p. 451) may go some way to explain the garbled association of St George with Maurelius in the legend. For the cult of Maurelius at Ferrara in general, and for evidence of later veneration of him at San Giorgio Vecchio and in the diocese, see Benati and Samaritani, pp. 8–10, 403–4; and p. 231 below.

19. *MGH SS* 20, p. 254.

20. The dossier is in Pasqui, 1, pp. 519–73.

21. *PL* 215, cols 51–2. The bishop had been resident at San Pietro for two centuries: see above, p. 38.

22. Pasqui 2, n.443, pp. 68–70.

23. Ibid., n.564, pp. 260–62. The act was approved by Innocent IV on 31 October 1250 (n.565, p. 263), and on 20 November 1252 the cardinal of SS Cosmas and Damian advised the clergy of the Pieve to accept the terms (n.579, pp. 278–9).

24. Ibid., n.605, pp. 328–33. The commune had long since received annual rents on the feast of San Donatus, for example from inhabitants of the castle of Montecchio in 1234 (ibid., n.518, pp. 204–6). As early as 1153, Munaldo, *rector et gubernator Aretinae civitatis*, received the cession of the castle of Vitiano *vice reipublice predicte civitatis et [ecclesie] beate Marie*, for which an annual *pensio* of two candles of 12 pounds was payable every year on the feast of San Donato (ibid., 1, n.357, pp. 482–4).

25. See below, p. 118.

26. See below, p. 84.

27. See above, p. 42.

28. Already in his life of Romuald, Peter Damian indicates that there was dispute as to whether the translation had really taken place (*FSI* 94, pp. 16–17): a *conversus* of the monastery shows Romuald how the martyr, in sacerdotal vestments, emerges at night from his tomb in the church at Classe.

29. *Spicilegium Ravennatis Historiae*, esp. pp. 538–45. For the ninth-century translation, see above, p. 42. Cardinal Hildebrand's sentence was printed by Mittarelli, 4, p. 49.

30. The thirteenth-century statutes of the city decreed that two *cerei* of

four pounds each should be taken annually to Sant' Apollinare Nuovo on the vigil of the saint's feast, and two similar *cerei* to Classe on the day itself; it was additionally specified that the *cerei* for Classe must be borne by the *podestà* and his officials in person: Ravenna C13, pp. 171–3. Salimbene of Parma referred to the dispute over Apollinare's relics as one that was still rumbling, and may imply that he believed the relics to be in the city (*Cronica*, 2, pp. 761–2):

> Et de hoc est maxima altercatio apud Ravenna de corpore sancti Apollinaris, quia illi de Classe, que condam civitas fuit, dicunt se illud habere. Illi similiter de civitate Ravenne se illud habere fatentur, quia revera quidam archiepiscopus Ravenna transtulit illud corpus sancti Apollinaris de Classe in civitatem Ravenne timore Agarenorum, ut in Pontificalis Ravenne pluries legi, et reverenter collocavit in ecclesia sancti Martini iuxta Sancti Salvatoris ecclesiam, que condam Grecorum fuit ecclesia. Quod autem inde fuerit postea remotum seu asportatum, per scripturam aliquam minime repperitur.

31. *Culto dei santi a Reggio Emilia*, pp. 123–45.

32. Some eleventh-century privileges for the monks in fact continue to describe the relics as lying in the suburban church, but the issue does not seem to have been controversial before the middle of the twelfth century. A collection of Prospero's miracles, written before the middle of the eleventh century, admittedly probably by a clerk of San Prospero in Castello, narrates the successive translations of the saint's relics as matters of fact: A. Mercati, *Miracula B. Prosperi*, pp. 215–16. For some reason Mercati believed that the author was a monk of the suburban monastery, a view not easy to reconcile with the latter's apparent standpoint, and not shared by Golinelli (*Culto dei santi*, p. 97 n.1).

33. *Historia Translationum*, Acta S Junii 5, p. 57. At least from the eleventh century Prospero was commemorated twice in the year, on his *dies natalitius* in June and on the commemoration of the original eighth-century translation in November.

34. Mercati, p. 203: 'vehementer suspecta'.

35. His disputes with the clergy of both the cathedral and San Prospero in Castello had required the intervention of the archbishop of Ravenna, which was also seen as necessary 'pro pace inter Reginos Cives et Capitaneos componenda': Golinelli, *Culto*, p. 124.

36. Ibid., pp. 142, 150. Although Guido was still abbot in 1172, he was accused by his monks of having reduced the community to a parlous condition and was deposed by Alexander III in 1173.

37. Reggio C13, p. 35.

38. Something of the story can be reconstructed from a succession of papal letters: Paschal II (*PL* 163, cols 281–2, 391–3); Gelasius II (ibid., cols 497–500); Calixtus II (ibid., cols 1096, 1242–3); Honorius II (166, cols 1287–

9); Innocent II (179, cols 145–6, 220–21, 303). In 1137 Innocent II gave the church of San Pantaleone to San Frediano (cols 335–6), but he had great difficulty in making his will prevail (cols 344–6, 566), and a few years later he was rebuking the consuls of the city for permitting attacks on the canons in connection with the cession of San Pantaleone (col. 631). In 1144 Lucius II reported that the prior of San Michele in Foro had excused himself for an attack on the brethren of San Frediano which had evidently resulted from the subjection to them of the church of San Salvatore (ibid., cols 902–3). In 1147 (the year in which he personally consecrated the new church and the new shrine of San Frediano) Eugenius III complained to the consuls about an assault that had been made on the bishop himself, when in obedience to the Pope's mandate he had (clearly reluctantly) endeavoured to introduce the brethren of San Frediano into San Pantaleone (180, cols 1256–7; see also earlier letters, cols 1054, 1083–4, 1193–4, 1205). Anastasius II complained of continued obstruction (188, cols 1018–19, 1025–6).

39. In 1149, two years after consecrating San Frediano, Eugenius proclaimed an indulgence of forty days for all those who attended the annual commemoration of the dedication: *PL* 180, col. 1404.

40. These adjudications were entered into the cathedral register: *Regesto del Capitolo di Lucca* (3 vols + index, Lucca 1910–39), 2, n.1314, pp. 189–92 (1173); 3, n.1714, pp. 168–70 (1194).

41. There is a considerable bibliography on the Volto Santo. See the brief account and references in D.M. Webb, 'The Holy Face of Lucca'. It is certain (cf. above n.9, p. 87) that in about 780, the vigorous Bishop Giovanni I had brought relics of the African bishop-martyr Regulus from the church of Gualdo, in the maritime region of Lucca's territory, to the cathedral, which was subsequently sometimes referred to under the names of both Martin and Regulus. Regulus's feast was of some importance in the Lucchese calendar and, significantly, John was later to be credited with the acquisition of the Volto Santo. Cf. the discussion in H. Schwarzmaier, *Lucca und das Reich bis zum Ende des 11 Jahrhunderts* (Tübingen 1972), pp. 336–68.

42. *Vita Metrica*, *MGH SS* 30.ii, pp. 1152–1307.

43. Webb, 'The Holy Face', esp. pp. 230–31.

44. P. Guidi, 'Per la Storia della Cattedrale', pp. 182–4; Webb, 'The Holy Face', p. 231.

45. That Rangerius was less than enthusiastic about unrestricted popular access to relics may be inferred from a passage in another sermon which is probably to be attributed to him, commemorating his translation of the relics of Regulus, and also of Jason, Maurus and Hilaria, to new locations in the cathedral. Alexander II had thought it good to bestow these relics 'in more hidden places, so that access should be rarer and more difficult and the sight of them the more highly prized and salutary,

because contemplation that is [available] every day and at will first does away with wonder and at length induces boredom'. They had therefore been placed in the crypt, but the stratagem did not have the desired effect, thanks to the negligence of the custodians and the importunity of those who demanded access. There is a strong hint that the crypt simply became a hideaway for gossip or worse, and it was therefore decided that it was better to 'recall the holy body from the shadows to the light'. Guidi, pp. 184–6. The passage is quoted by Webb, 'The Holy Face', n.32, p. 233.

46. Guidi, p. 183.

47. Translation in R. Lopez and I. Raymond, *Medieval Trade in the Mediterranean World*, (New York 1955), pp. 418–19. The inscription is still to be seen under the portico of the cathedral.

48. Quoted by Gai, 'Testimonianze jacobee', p. 180: 'Proh subdola cupiditas, qui ex pueris suis didascalos efficere curam, aut Podium, aut villam sancti Egidii, aut Turoni, aut Placentiam, aut Lucam, aut Romam, aut Barum, aut Barletum illos mittunt. His enim villis scola maxime solet esse tocius fraudis.'

49. *Memorie e documenti* 3.iii, pp. 144–5; Webb, 'The Holy Face', p. 228.

50. *PL* 163, cols 1300–301.

51. *Regesto del Capitolo*, 1, n.779, pp. 333–4.

52. It has been observed that there was co-operation between the commune and the bishop on other levels in the early twelfth century, for example in the building of a *castrum* at Colle San Martino in 1109: D. Osheim, *An Italian Lordship: The Bishopric of Lucca in the Late Middle Ages* (Berkeley, CA 1977), p. 72. Both parties were making acquisitions in the Valdinievole.

53. P. Guidi, 'La Chiesa di S. Paolino in Lucca', *Atti della Reale Accademia Lucchese di Scienze, Lettere ed Arti* 35 (1919), n.3, pp. 25–6. There is a good photograph of the sarcophagus in the article on Paulinus by R. Volpini, *BS* 10, cols 151–6. For his second *inventio* in 1261, see below, pp. 153–4.

54. *Sermo de inventione sanctarum reliquiarum*, in F. Lanzoni, *San Petronio*, pp. 240–50.

55. *De corporum SS. Iustina et Lucae inventione*, *AB* 11 (1892) pp. 354–8.

56. 'Spirito Cittadino', in *L'immaginario religoso*, pp. 197–8. Orselli cites other evidence for believing that the cult of Petronius, until at least the middle of the thirteenth century, was the property of the monks of Santo Stefano and secondarily the diocesan clergy. For its later development, see below, pp. 174–80.

57. *Acta S* Julii 6, pp. 59–68. For Atto, see the article by A. Pratesi in *DBI* 4, pp. 566–7, and the references there given; for his own cult, there are materials in *Acta S* Maii 5, pp. 194–203. See also L. Gai, 'Testimonianze jacobee', who, among much else, rehearses the reasons for doubting the authenticity of both the relic and the story, citing her own *L'altare argenteo di san Jacopo*. Doubts are raised, for example, about the date of the

alleged transaction (Diego del Gelmírez died in 1140) and about the real existence of the Pistoiese clerk at Compostela, Rainerius (although the mention of the schools he had attended at Winchester seems a curious detail to fabricate). Of more interest here are the bishop's motives for claiming that he had brought a relic of the apostle to Pistoia, and the subsequent development of the cult.

58. Ibid., pp. 27–8.
59. Zaccaria, *Anecdotorum Collectio*, pp. 327–9.
60. Mentioned in an instrument of 1 May 1174: Fioravanti, *Memorie storiche*, p. 181. For the statutes of the *Opera*, see above, p. 80, and below p. 114.
61. *Acta S* Julii 6, p. 67B.
62. Chiapelli, 'Storie e costumanze', (1919), pp. 8–9.
63. Ghirardacci, 1, pp. 78, 88; Tolosanus, pp. 31–2, 50, 52, 88.
64. Ibid., p. 91.
65. See below, p. 256.
66. *Gesta Lucanorum*, *MGH SS*, n.s., 8, p. 310.
67. See below, Chapter 3. For early evidence for the *palio* see below, p. 258.
68. Golinelli, 'Istituzioni cittadine', pp. 93–8. *Vitae* of Bernard are edited by P. Schramm, *MGH SS* 30.ii, pp. 1314–27.
69. A.M. Papi, 'Figure Episcopali Post-Gregoriane: Sant' Ubaldo di Gubbio', in *Pastori di Popolo*, pp. 179–203.
70. *Translatio Bracchii Santi Philippi Hierosolymis Florentiam*, in *Acta S* Maii 1, pp. 15–18.
71. Papi, *Pastori di Popolo*, pp. 22–4, 99–103 nn.3–23; D.M. Webb, 'The Pope and the Cities', pp. 142–3.
72. *S. Pietro Parenzo: la leggenda scritta dal maestro Giovanni canonico di Orvieto*, ed. V. Natalini (Rome 1936) (= *Lateranum* n.s. 2.ii). For the context, see M. Maccarone, *Studi su Innocenzo III* (Padua 1972 = *Italia Sacra* 17) pp. 19–61; Webb, 'The Pope and the Cities', pp. 139–42.
73. *Die Register Innocenz' III*, 1, ed. O. Hageneder (Graz 1964), p. 127.
74. *PL* 214, cols 365–6.
75. *Acta S* Augusti 2, pp. 817–24.
76. Ibid., p. 822.
77. Cristofani, *Delle Storie di Assisi*, pp. 39, 97–8.
78. *Vita* in *Acta S* Julii 7, pp. 645–57.
79. *Die Register Innocenz' III*, 1, pp. 761–4. For Homobonus, see A. Vauchez, *La Sainteté en Occident*, pp. 412–14; for Sicard's lost *Vita*, see E. Brocchieri, 'Sicardo di Cremona e la sua opera letteraria', *Annali della Biblioteca Governativa e Libreria Civica di Cremona* 11 (1958), pp. 103–4.
80. *MGH SS* 31, pp. 174–5, 176.
81. J. Böhmer, *Acta Imperii Selecta* (Innsbruck 1870), n.906, p. 617. Cf. Webb, 'The Pope and the Cities', p. 145.

PART II
THE CULT IN ACTION

CHAPTER 3

SAINTS AND STATUTES

Urban law codes begin to survive in large numbers from the middle of the thirteenth century, and become fuller and more elaborate thereafter. They are both an indispensable and an insufficient source for the study of the civic cult of the saints. On the one hand, statute collections included provisions, on all subjects, which were honoured either irregularly or not at all; on the other, legislators did not always deem it necessary, particularly before the later thirteenth century, to write down well-known customary obligations. The periodic codifications that were drawn up naturally did not include all of the ceaseless stream of conciliar enactments that were issued year by year. Many of these, even when they were intended to be of permanent effect, rapidly became redundant, while others, once incorporated into a formal collection, remained there for years even when they were dead letters. Only a thorough sifting of conciliar deliberations and communal account-books could give the complete picture, for any one city, of what was either intended or actually done to venerate the saints.

By themselves, then, statute collections would be a poor, or at least an inadequate, guide to practice; they rarely give a full picture of the official cult, and they delineate an ideal which was not always realized. Whatever their informative value, however, they have a rhetorical and ideological character, as affirmations of the values to which the rulers of urban society professed to subscribe on behalf of their subjects. They can give us at least some idea of what city governments thought they should be seen to be doing in honour of their saints; and the language in which they expressed

95

that intent is itself not without its interest. Taken together, they afford at least a glimpse of practices which may not be described, fully or at all, elsewhere. Account-books, where they survive, add valuable detail, but discursive descriptions of the annual urban round of sacred ceremonial are few, and the observations of chroniclers, though increasingly numerous and helpful in the fourteenth century, are by their nature haphazard and unsystematic. Many statute collections, furthermore, have been made accessible in print, thanks to the antiquarian and legalistic enthusiasms of Italian scholars, especially since the Risorgimento, although it is understandably rare for the whole sequence of a city's statutes over a period of centuries to have been published.[1]

What follows is a brief survey of the sorts of information it is in fact possible to glean from them, given these limitations. More detailed reference to particular episodes in a given city's history will usually be made at an appropriate moment in the chapters that follow.

The Statutes and the Cult

Statute law at its first appearance was in large part codified custom, and incompletely codified custom at that. It has been said of the influential compilation produced at Bologna in 1288 that its immediate predecessor and principal source, which was drawn up in 1267, was 'disordinatissima ed incompleta', with much left to custom and to the legal experience of judges and notaries; the 1288 edition was clearly intended to be more systematic.[2] A similar development can be observed in the legislative history of many other cities.

Some cities, and some cities at certain periods of their history, produced updated collections of their statutes more frequently than others. There are four extant from Lucca in the fourteenth century, dating from 1308, 1331, 1342 and 1372, a fact which reflects repeated changes of regime. In 1331, when the statutes were re-edited in the name of John of Bohemia, Lucca was in disarray after the death of Castruccio Castracani in 1329, and this continued until the inception of Pisan rule in 1342. In 1369 Lucca was able to purchase its liberty from the Emperor Charles IV, and a new statute was called for. By the 1390s the restored republic was under threat from the ambitions of the Guinigi family and the expansionism of Giangaleazzo Visconti, which provoked multiple Tuscan reactions. Paolo Guinigi made himself *signore* in the summer of 1400. Another statute revision was carried out after his fall in 1430, although it was not in fact produced until 1446. This recension was printed in 1490, and yet another new edition appeared in 1536.

Where such a sequence exists, it affords an overall view of both continuity and innovation. The Sienese pattern was different. The city produced a vernacular version of its late-thirteenth-century statutes, with a few additions, in 1309–10, and a new collection in 1337–39, but subsequent additions were not codified until 1544, when the republic was in the last years of its independent existence. In the interval, miscellaneous collections of enactments were copied up from time to time.[3] The statutes redacted for Foligno in the first half of the fourteenth century remained in force until the mid-sixteenth century, to be replaced by new ones, which 'at least nominally' lasted until 1816.[4] Early printed editions not infrequently substantially reproduced the codes that had been in force for a century or more.

The manner in which the statutes of Padua were assembled in the later thirteenth century enables us to see the layers in which a collection might be built up. The title 'De feriis nundinis et festivitatibus celebrandis' brings together statutes described as *vetus*, that is, 'made before 1236' (before the tyranny of Ezzelino da Romano), with others which date variously from 1257, 1265, 1269, 1274 and 1275 and are transcribed under the name of the *podestà* in whose term of office they were enacted.[5] The *vetera* reveal that the concerns of the early legislators were first legal, in a narrow sense, and secondarily commercial. Saints' days, and the major feast-days of the year, including Sundays, concerned them because they marked the *ferie* (the vacations of the law courts) and also the more general public holidays on which buying and selling and the carting of goods, with stated exceptions, were prohibited and barbers were not permitted to ply their trade. Their other concern was with markets and their regulation. Already at this 'primitive' stage, however, the June feasts of the Franciscan Antony (that is, his feast-day proper and its octave) were to be closing days for all except food shops.⁶ They ranked, that is to say, with Good Friday, the feasts of the Virgin and of the twelve apostles, and Sundays.

In 1257 there was a new provision for the honourable and reverent celebration of Antony's feast, and thought was taken for clearing the piazza in front of the church of ruffians, gamblers and women of ill fame. There was further amplification in 1275. It was stated that the officials and members of the fraternities were to attend on the vigil of the feast with *duplerii*⁷ and candles 'according to custom'; but the greatest solemnity was reserved for the octave and its vigil. The *podestà* and his *familia* were bound to attend the saint's church on the vigil, and on the octave itself he attended again, with the bishop and all the clergy, the marquis of Este, if he was in the city, and all the knights and ladies and fraternities. Also in 1275 a race [*palio*] was instituted, for which the commune was to provide a prize of twelve *brachia* (very approximately, yards or metres) of scarlet.

A brief survey of the statutes produced by another north-eastern city, Treviso, will illustrate how the legislative regulation of the official cult developed between the thirteenth century and the sixteenth.⁸ Only one rubric in Treviso's earliest thirteenth-century statute collection has any reference to saints. This declares that the men of Rocca Ceneta are to be left undisturbed in the possession and control of the relics of San Tiziano, a significant reminder that dominant cities were commonly suspected of being greedy for relics possessed by their subjects, as indeed they often were.⁹ It was only in the aftermath of the tyranny of Ezzelino and Alberto da Romano that the statutes began to incorporate regulations for the observance of saints' days. The edition produced for Gherardo da Camino in 1283–84 decreed that annual offerings were to be made to St Peter, the patron of the cathedral, and that the bishop and the *podestà* were to honour the feasts of St Francis and St Bartholomew; it also explained why.¹⁰ Provision was made for an offering at the tomb of the Camaldolese monk Parisius in the convent of Santa Cristina; a record of Parisius's miracles was to be compiled, and ambassadors were despatched to the Pope to seek his canonization.¹¹ A resolution of 1302 – that an official offering should be made to the Virgin on the Feast of the Assumption because she had liberated the city from various dire perils – was appended to this statute.¹²

For the edition of the statutes produced in 1313, after the expulsion of the Caminesi, a certain amount of excision, expansion and rationalization took place. A single rubric united the prescription of offerings for Francis and Bartholomew, briefly mentioned the offering to Parisius, and decreed that the commune was to build a church under the name of San Salvator, which was to be solemnly visited on 15 December every year by the officials, councillors and guilds of Treviso. The following rubrics enjoined the offerings to St Peter and to the Virgin and then other benefactions to local churches; then came the fossilized clause about San Tiziano. At first sight there appears no longer to be any reference to sending ambassadors to the Pope to seek Parisius's canonization. On 13 June 1315, however, various *provisiones* were added to the statute, some of which dealt with the 'burial and honouring' of the humble ascetic Henry of Bolzano, whose death a few days previously had been followed by miracles and popular excitement. It was stated that the miracles performed by both Henry and Parisius were to be registered, with a view to the canonization of both; and in the flush of piety generated by Henry's sanctity, certain prisoners were to be released and a notary who had been deprived of office was to be pardoned his alleged offences.[13]

The fact that official offerings to saints might be governed by either statute or custom emerges from an interesting episode during the first period of Venetian rule over Treviso, between 1339 and 1381. In 1371 the canons of the cathedral petitioned the Doge for a renewal of the old custom of official offerings to St Peter, St Mark and the blessed Henry, 'as is contained in a certain old statute, which custom has been hitherto maintained by the *podestà* and rectors appointed by the Doge'. In reply, the *podestà*, Giovanni Gradenigo, acknowledged his duty to make the proper offerings, and detailed the amounts he gave in alms to the religious orders in return for their services in saying mass for the officials; these were either laid down in the statutes of Treviso or (in the case of the Servites) were the subject of a ducal privilege (*grazia*) which he deemed was consonant with the statutes because the Servites, too, participated in the mass rota. However, this punctilious public servant pronounced himself unsure of his obligations where there was neither statute nor *grazia*. There was, he knew, 'custom' [*consuetudo*], but he was uncertain of its binding force. Custom alone, evidently, had governed the offerings made since the beginning of the Venetian occupation to St Mark and also to St Vitus (whom the canons had not mentioned), and custom could work both for and against offerings. Gradenigo calculated that he paid out £415 annually in offerings from the treasury of Treviso; according to the statutes, he said, it should have been much more, but 'by custom it has been thus limited and observed'. He asked for a clarificatory ruling on the subject of offerings to St Mark and St Vitus. Offerings to St Peter and to Henry of Bolzano were obviously provided for by statute; neither the *podestà* nor the Doge, in his final ruling, felt any need to mention them. The Doge, Andrea Dandolo, recapitulated the state of the argument, acknowledged Gradenigo's request for enlightenment, and ruled that out of reverence for Mark and Vitus, 'about whom there is no statute' [*de quibus non est statutum*], their feasts were to be observed and the canons to receive their portion.[14]

Neither hitherto nor subsequently was there any mention in the statutes of a civic offering to St Liberalis. Liberalis had been adopted as a communal patron in the late twelfth century, and the statutes of the church of Treviso required the attendance of all the parish priests of the diocese, with their crosses and their *populi*, at mass at the cathedral on the morning of his feast-day; but although he was depicted on the communal standard with St Peter, his cult seems to have remained the responsibility of the clergy.[15] When the Venetians republished the statutes in 1574, Mark, as 'protector and defender of the duchy of the Venetians', figures in the invocation at the head of the statutes, taking precedence over Liberalis, 'defender and protector' of Treviso. The actual provisions for the official cult were left substantially in the form they had had since the late thirteenth century. Liberalis's feast-day was among the legal *ferie*, as was that of Vitus and Modestus. Three and half centuries on, the men of Rocca Ceneta were still safeguarded in their possession of the relics of San Tiziano.[16]

Another good example of development between the thirteenth century and the sixteenth is afforded by the statutes of Perugia, which display a considerable increase in system.[17] The statutes of 1279 (the earliest to survive, though not the first to be produced) were organized simply in *quaderni* (fascicules), not in 'books' or 'titles' distinguished by subject matter.[18] Regulations on holy matters occur inconsequentially. The *podestà* and *capitaneus* were to see that steps were taken to promote the canonization of San Bevignate, and, to avert pestilence and hail, the feast of St Stephen was declared a public holiday, on which no work should be done by man or woman. The festival of the main communal patron, Sant' Ercolano, is the subject of a composite clause, which begins by laying down the rate of subsidy available from the commune to any neighbourhood society or fraternity which wished to make a wax *cereus* (candle) or other offering for the *festa*. Whoever wished to make a *cereus* or to have one made was to offer sureties before the work began to the owner of the house in which it was to take place, insuring him and his neighbours against damage. Penalties were then laid down for the offence of throwing things at the offerings (that is, when they were hung up in the cathedral), with half of the fine going to the informer. Finally, the *capitaneus* was instructed to convene his council on the third day before the end of February to make arrangements for honouring the *festa*.[19] This was a common provision in early statute collections. The festivities as such were clearly established, but not as yet the subject of detailed written regulation; such regulation appeared, as often as not, to meet difficulties or obviate disorders. So it seems to have been at Perugia.

The Perugian example well illustrates one contemporary meaning of the word 'statuto'. It could designate either a collection of laws or a particular enactment; the latter might be read out at regular intervals in order to trigger action. In 1260 the council was petitioned to impose bigger penalties 'than is contained in the statute' for those who created disorders [*aliquam rixam seu mesclanciam*] on the vigil or feast-day of Ercolano.[20] The instruction to seek the canonization of San Bevignate was read out every year in May; it might then be resolved that the *podestà* and *capitano* should this year be dispensed from the obligation to take action. The confirmation of this *statuto* and the decision to copy it into the collection put together in 1279 was in fact made at a time of waning enthusiasm for Bevignate's cause.[21]

The statutes collected in 1279 were superseded by a more systematic and better-articulated edition promulgated on 15 September 1342, which came into force on 1 April 1343. This remained law until 1389, when certain 'organic reforms' were made which were then gathered into a new compilation published in four books at the end of March 1400, which received the approval of Pope Martin V in 1416. This was the source of 'the definitive edition' which went into print, in four separate volumes, between 1523 and 1528. By 1343 the need for a great deal more system and fullness was evident and an arrangement into books and chapters was adopted. In the twenty-fourth rubric of the first book, it was specifically stated that in order to avoid the recurrent necessity of convening the council to make the arrangements and authorize the expenditures necessary for *luminarie* (the term commonly used for the ritual attendance with lighted candles at a saint's festivity) the power to do so should be delegated to the *priori d'arte*. The festivals in question were named as those of Sant' Ercolano, San Costanzo, the Assumption, the Invention of St Stephen at the Dominican church, St Louis of Toulouse and Ascension Day. The processional order of the guilds was laid down, to avoid the quarrels over precedence which invariably occurred when they gathered to honour the vigil of the Assumption and the vigil of Ercolano; the same order was to apply to the processions to San Costanzo and San Domenico, and there were penalties for infringing it. The vigil of Sant' Ercolano and the day itself were both declared to be public holidays; as was usual, there was provision both for secret accusation against offenders, the accuser to get half the fine, and for inquiries to be made by the *podestà* and *capitano*.[22]

The third book of the statutes included lists of legal vacations, in no very precise chronological order, and public holidays. The latter continued to include the feast-day and octave of St Stephen, for the reasons stated in 1279. The rubrics dealing with crime include penalties for blasphemy, aggravated penalties for crimes committed at certain times including the weeks before and after Sant' Ercolano and the Assumption, for disorderly conduct at times when processions or *luminarie* were being held, and for 'playing on horseback' in the city or suburbs on either the vigil or feast-day of Sant' Ercolano. Finally, there is provision for the liberation of prisoners at certain festivals.[23]

The statutes printed in 1526 display a marked continuity with those of 1343 in some respects: for example, although a few alterations were made to the list of *ferie*, no one bothered to sort it into chronological order.[24] The most striking difference between the two collections, however, is the minute detail in which the offerings to be made by the officials and religious of the city, which were to be paid for by the commune, are enumerated. These festivities were numerous, but the arrangements for the *luminaria* of San Costanzo served as the model for others, which made some abbreviation possible.[25]

Invocations

Statutes can be regarded generically as a form of propaganda, in which a city's rulers enunciated the principles on which they claimed to conduct themselves. An invocation of God, the Virgin and the saints often (though not invariably) forms part of the *proemium*, and has the effect of establishing the relationship between the city, its rulers and the heavenly powers. The patron or patrons are commonly designated in formulaic terms which evoke the nature of this relationship. Often only the single, principal patron is mentioned; but it is not unusual for a list of names to be given which identifies at least the central group in the current 'pantheon'.

Very occasionally, the commune's veneration of its patron is described as having an explicitly spiritual purpose. The offerings made to San Feliciano at Foligno were intended 'for the salvation of the souls and bodies of the citizens of the stated city', while at Piacenza the feast of the Assumption of the Virgin, to whom the cathedral was dedicated, was to be celebrated 'for the salvation of the souls of the citizens of Piacenza and of all their dead'.[26] More typically, the saints are invoked simply and inclusively as 'patrons', 'defenders' and 'advocates', not only in the *proemia* of the statutes but elsewhere in the body of these texts (for example in the clauses regulating the *feste*) and in other comparable documents such as treaties and alliances. The same range of terms, drawing on the same fund of ideas, appears everywhere. At Cremona, Himerius and Homobonus were the 'special protectors and advocates of the city of Cremona',[27] while St Emidio was 'patron, protector and defender' of Ascoli Piceno.[28] The soldier-martyr Antoninus was described in the fourteenth-century statutes of Piacenza as *defensor*, but in the 1321 *Statuta Mercatorum* he is the *vocabulum* of the city, a formulation which recalls the use of the patron's name as a war-cry.[29]

Sometimes the saints were described outright as the 'governors' of their cities. It is hard to know what special significance, if any, should be attributed to this usage, but it is interesting that it is by no means universal.[30] In 1315 the Virgin, Peter and Paul and Liberalis were designated 'protectors and governors' of Treviso and its *districtus*;[31] at Osimo in the Marche, according to its 1342 statute, the confessors Leopardus, Vitalianus and Benevenutus were, with the Virgin and Peter and Paul, 'the most reverend protectors, chiefs [*capita*] defenders and governors of the city of Osimo and its *contado* [*comitatus*]'.[32] San Feliciano was *protector, defensor, gubernator ac advocatus* of the commune of Foligno.[33] More frequently, it was implied that the saint interceded with God for good governance, upholding and guaranteeing, perhaps supervising, the executive authority of his earthly representatives. Thus at Florence in the 1320s it is stated in one place that John the Baptist is 'the especial patron and defender' [*precipuus patronus et defensor*] of the commune, in another that it is he 'under whose protection the city of Florence is governed' [*cuius patrocinio gubernatur civitas Florentie*]. More elaborately, the Florentines hoped 'that God, by the prayers of the blessed John the Baptist, would defend and uphold and preserve in good and happy state and always increase from good to better the Commune of Florence'.[34]

The patron's constituency was variously described. In the 1306–07 statutes of the revived Modenese republic, St Geminianus appears as 'patron, protector and special defender of the city and people of Modena' [*patronus, protector et defensor precipuus civitatis et populi Mutine*] or 'defender and advocate of the commune and people of Modena' [*defensor et advocatus comunis et populi Mutine*]. The title *defensores populi Mutine* was also borne by the city's earthly governors.[35] Elsewhere, Geminianus is *defensor* or *patronus et defensor civitatis Mutine*, and of its dependent territory [*districtus*].[36] These phrases imply that Geminianus, as patron of the dominant city, wields a superior power over lesser communities which had come to form part of Modenese territory. Such communities would each have had their local patron. The statutes of the Tuscan rural communes sometimes mention solely the local patron, as when

Siena's subject Sovicille proclaimed in 1383 that St Laurence was its *singulare advocato protectore e difenditore*.[37] Alternatively, they may reveal layers of patronage. In 1397, Castiglione degli Ubertini, recently acquired by Florence as a consequence of the subjection of Arezzo, named SS Stephen, Fabian, Sebastian and St Michael the Archangel as its *patroni, protectores, defensores et gubernatores*, but the statutes were entitled 'to the honour, praise and reverence of the most glorious saint John the Baptist, patron and governor of the city of Florence and of its county, strongholds and district'. Here, at least, John was a 'governor', as if so to describe him strengthened and sanctioned the city's authority over its dependent territories.[38]

That the Florentines may have been particularly insistent on such expressions is rather suggested by the 1360 statutes of Montopoli, once a Lucchese dependency, which had submitted to Florentine rule in 1349. Not only the Virgin, Peter and Paul and the Baptist, but an up-to-the-minute roster of Florentine patrons, Zenobius, Barnabas, Reparata and Anne, were invoked.[39] The Florentines kept up to date when, later in the century, they produced statutes for the subject communities in the Mugello headed by Borgo San Lorenzo: St Victor's name was now added to the list of those 'under the name and protection of whom the city of Florence is ruled and governed'.[40] Viewed from this angle, the rural communes resembled the urban guilds, in that they too formed part of a still loosely conceived 'state', accepting the obligations of obedience to the centre (ceremonially symbolized by their offerings to the principal urban patron), but retaining their own corporate identity (ceremonially symbolized by their offerings to their own patron). The 1376 statute of the *Corte dei Mercanti* in Lucca begins by invoking God, the Virgin, the Volto Santo, St Peter prince of the apostles, the blessed confessor St Martin, the blessed martyr and first bishop of Lucca Paulinus, and only then 'the glorious martyr *messer* St Christopher, protector of the college and corporation' of merchants of the city of Lucca'.[41] The communal government, by identifying itself with the supreme patron, claimed a monopoly, unifying force within a 'state' which in actuality consisted of miscellaneous interests and organizations.

The bodily presence of saints often called for special expressions, even if they were not a city's most important patrons. At

Vicenza in 1264 the credit for ending the tyranny of Ezzelino da Romano was given to the Archangel Michael, and the bishop was promoting a new cult of the Crown of Thorns, but an incoming *podestà* was to remember in his oath the old local martyrs Felix and Fortunatus, 'in the consolation of whose most sacred bodies we rejoice, by whose protection we are guarded, for the salvation of the city of Vicenza and of its district and of the whole community'.[42] Contemporaneously at Verona, the bodily presence of St Zeno was recognized in virtually identical terms.[43] At Pisa, where the Virgin was patron of both cathedral and commune, the statutes expressed the hope that the twelfth-century merchant-turned-hermit Ranerius, 'whose body lies in the major church of the city of Pisa', would give the city his protection.[44] The fourteenth-century statutes of Osimo even incorporate a description of the *inventio* in 1296 of the ancient bishop-patron Leopardus, whose 'most holy body' had lain hidden since time out of mind. He was discovered to have a silver plaque on his breast carved with the image of a bishop and pastoral staff and inscribed with his name in gilt letters. Apart from ecclesiastical dignitaries and the whole chapter, the *podestà*, numerous nobles and other honourable persons, invited or not, were present.[45] The citizens of Todi were conscious of the honour due not only to their chief patron, Fortunatus, but to all the saints whose bodies 'rest and are guarded and celebrated' in the cathedral church.[46] It seems highly probable that wherever a saint was bodily present, the communal authorities recognized their duty to pay the appropriate homage.

Legal and Public Holidays

The minimal form of recognition of a saint's day to be found in the laws of the city-states is its inclusion in the list of legal holidays [*ferie* or *dies feriati*]. All statutes contain a list of *ferie*; sometimes the vacations of the criminal courts were less numerous than those of the civil courts, the need for criminal justice being, evidently, constant and pressing. Some of the legal vacations were simply seasonal (like, for example, the late summer harvest period); others hinged on the major and universal feasts of the Christian calendar (Christmas, Easter week, Ascension Day, Pentecost, and so forth).

The feast-days of a large handful of great saints – for example, all the Apostles – were almost universally included; so too were those of the most celebrated ancient martyrs, such as Laurence and Catherine of Alexandria. Some obviously popular saints such as Stephen do not always appear by name, because their days fell within a recognized holiday period, in his case the Christmas vacation. The lists of *ferie* produced in different cities therefore have an extensive common core; they also all have their peculiarities – notably, of course, the feast-days of local patrons and, very often, the name-saints of all the urban and suburban parishes. A list included in an influential compilation, such as the Bolognese statute of 1288, might serve as a model for legislators in other cities,[47] but Bolognese saints such as Petronius, Vitalis and Agricola and Proculus would not expect recognition elsewhere.

There is a similar mixture of the universal and the local in the more restricted lists of days which were to be regarded as full public holidays, when all were to abstain from work and all shops were to be shut. These varied considerably in length and comprehensiveness. At Faenza in 1415, the days affected included all Sundays and a short list of the major festivals of the year: Christmas, Epiphany, Easter, Pentecost, the Assumption and All Saints.[48] The Pistoiese *Statuto del Comune* in 1417 gave a somewhat longer list, including, for example, all feasts of the Virgin Mary and those of the Apostles and Evangelists.[49] The list prescribed in the 1476 statutes of Ferrara was much more extensive, including numerous saints' days which ranged from those of Agnes, Mary Magdalen, Laurence, Catherine and Lucy to the canonized saints of recent times, including Bernardino of Siena.[50] At Verona at the same period the statutes laid it down that no one was to presume to profane with manual labour any day dedicated to Christ himself [*maiestas altissimus*]; also excluded were days of obligation [*de precepto*] as indicated by the church, and those on which the bishop and clergy, in consultation with the *podestà*, should decide. The only days specifically named were the feasts of San Zeno and of the Veronese St Peter Martyr.[51] The Sienese statutes compiled in 1545 similarly avoided giving a lengthy list, referring to Sundays and others that were observed by precept or local custom.[52]

However long or short the list, the regulation of closing days could become exceedingly complicated, given the evident practical necessity for certain services to remain available, either seasonally or at all times. In 1415 the Faventines achieved a fairly economical statement of the permitted exceptions to the closing rule, but the Pistoiese, at much the same period, were less succinct. The 1417 Statute of the Commune included a lengthy rubric which, it was stated, superseded all previous *Statuta et Reformationes* on the subject.[53] Wine and bread could be sold, and beasts shod, on any day. Apothecaries and cobblers 'and others' were permitted to open the doors of their shops only until terce, but apothecaries on whose premises a doctor was resident could remain open at all times for the confection of medicines. At this point the legislators remembered that tradespeople had families and dependants who often lived over the shop, and wrote in a permission for them to get in and out all day. When a festivity fell on a Saturday, no restrictions at all applied. As a further afterthought, tailors were explicitly permitted to exhibit their wares (until terce) on feast-days. The awful consequences of not permitting butchers to sell fresh meat at all times between 1 May and 1 October were now remembered, and permission was duly given. The clause ends with the parting shot: 'And doors [*portelli*] are to be understood as those by which persons can enter the aforesaid shops and not others.'

This, however, was not all. The Statute of the *Popolo* proceeded to add another rubric governing the opening hours of spicers or perfumers and mercers.[54] They were not to open at all on some feast-days, but on others, which are enumerated, they could keep restricted hours. However, if someone died and required burial, or a case of serious illness arose which brooked no delay in obtaining the proper medicine, they could attend to the matter at any time. It had to be remembered, furthermore, that on three notable holy days – those of St James, St Bartholomew and the Holy Cross – there were big markets anyway in Pistoia, and then of course no restrictions applied; while during Lent grocers could open on any day for the sale of salt fish.

The Pistoiese provisions, which seem to give us a glimpse of legislators thinking, none too nimbly, on their feet, were unusually elaborate, but some of the exceptions they enumerate are common enough: for example, that apothecaries could prepare medicines at any time, or butchers sell unsalted meat during the heat of summer. The lawmakers of Ascoli issued a general permission to 'all merchants or goldsmiths' to keep their doors open thoughout holidays 'but not keeping anything on the counter' [*non tenendo alcuna cosa ne le banche*].[55] Luca Landucci recorded in 1481 how the Florentine apothecaries, of whom he was one, decided to cope with the problem of holiday opening by choosing four of their number, by lot, to stay open all day. In 1510 there was a prohibition on opening shops from 20 June till the festivities of St John were over, which Landucci thought hard on poor shopkeepers, as the exceptions were only for bankers and wool and silk merchants.[56]

The statutes of rural communes often indicate the holy days that are to be observed locally. Here, the setting is characterized by the occupations that are proscribed on holy days. At Montagutolo in the Sienese territory in 1280 it was forbidden (without special permission) 'to go to the mill with any load of grain' on St Dominic's day, 'nor to cart flour or wood'; 'straw and grass and water' seem to have been permissible. On a number of other days, including the feasts of the Apostles and Evangelists, 'no person may work or saddle any beast'.[57] The inhabitants of San Vito all' Incisa, however, could, according to their 1379 statutes, do such things on such days 'in case of necessity', and they could take their merchandise to Florence or Figline without penalty. At Ascoli Piceno the prohibition on labour 'does not extend to anyone who makes or carries hay'.[58] Such exemptions were in fact common, at least for the purpose of carting grain or hay to the mother city. At Ferrara in the fifteenth century, however, the prohibition was absolute on Mary days and the feasts of the Apostles,[59] while the legislators of Verona stipulated that the *festivitates* listed in the urban statute were to be observed by the inhabitants of the *distretto*, with penalties for work or carting, and no apparent exceptions were made.[60]

Additions to the list of public holidays, and to the longer list of legal *ferie*, were made for many reasons; movements of devotion and special interests which were certainly not always narrowly 'political' thus impinged on the sphere of the public cult. The Perugian decision to honour St Stephen with a full public holiday, as we have seen, rested on his identification as a protector against 'all the injurious water which is commonly called hail'.[61] Pisa's acquisition of the relics of Efisus and Potitus from Sardinia in 1316 resulted in their appearance in the list of 'closing days' laid down by the merchant court in 1321.[62] At Florence in 1325, the feasts of Louis of Toulouse and Thomas Aquinas, both very recently canonized with the backing of Florence's patron and ally Robert of Naples, were not only *feriati* but kept as full public holidays, along with that of St Barnabas, who had become a civic patron thanks to notable military victories obtained on his day (11 June) in 1269 and 1289.[63] In 1333 the Sienese government received a petition that the feast-day of Joachim and Anna be observed, in honour of the Virgin, as a public holiday; the feast was kept with special enthusiasm at the hospital of Santa Maria della Scala, and the petitioners alleged that many Sienese were already abstaining from business on that day.[64] The Perugian list of *ferie* in 1343 included the feast-days not only of the city's ancient local patrons but of the mysterious San Bevignate, whose canonization the commune had sought, and Pope Martin IV, who had died in the city in 1284.[65] The list of *feriati* included in the statute produced for Treviso in 1385, during a period of rule by the Carrara lords of Padua, intruded the Paduan saints Antony and Prosdocimus.[66] In 1401 the Florentine guild of the Calimala, patrons of the Baptistery, obtained that the feast of the Baptism of Christ be celebrated; in the guise of the 'eighth day after Epiphany' it was included in the 1415 list of *ferie*.[67]

The list of *ferie* in the printed Pistoiese statute of 1546 contained a number of novelties, when compared with earlier versions.[68] The appearance of Blaise and Sigismund in the list can be explained thanks to a marginal note in a fifteenth-century list, which draws attention to the conciliar deliberations of 20 October 1479. This was a plague year, and the Pistoiese had thought it timely, in view of Blaise's expertise with sore throats and Sigismund's efficacy in cases of fever, to add their days to the list of those that were *feriati* 'for all civil cases and [cases of] private debt' [*pro omni causa civili & debitis privatis*].[69] Less in need of explanation is the inclusion of St Joseph, given that his cult had been assiduously promoted over the previous century,[70] and of Vincent Ferrer, Bernardino da Siena and Nicola da Tolentino, who had all been formally canonized during the same period. All these names appeared in the list of *ferie* in the statutes of Ferrara, now under papal rule; so too did Homobonus of Cremona.[71] Joseph and Nicholas of Tolentino were newcomers also in the list given in the sixteenth-century statutes of Faenza; other new names were those of St Peter Celestine, the plague and pilgrim saint Roche or Rocco, and Savinus and Peter Damian, two of the four 'Holy Protectors' of Faenza whose group identity was crystallizing at just this period.[72] The ancient and the modern, the local and the universal, continued to rub shoulders in these lists, but the inclusion of saints newly held up by the church for universal veneration was becoming normal by the sixteenth century.

The Offering to the Patron

It has been stated that statutory regulation of the urban cult is sparse before the middle of the thirteenth century. The example of Siena well illustrates a typical progression from a situation in which the patronal festival was governed largely by custom, which seems still to have obtained when the great statute of 1262 was issued, to a much more detailed and systematic written regulation of the ceremonial by the closing years of the century.[73] The succinct provision of the statute of Reggio Emilia in 1242 for the festival of San Prospero is as full as anything we can expect to find before the middle of the century, and it provides an outline which in later times and other places would be amplified:

> In honour of God and the blessed confessor Prospero we wish it henceforth to be observed that all knights and citizens and other honourable persons of the bishopric of the city shall be bound to come to the feast of St Prospero in the summer, and that they shall be in the city on the feast of St John and of St Prospero; and the *podestà* shall be bound eight or fifteen days before the said feast to hold an assembly, and to have the said custom read in it, and to ensure that it is observed in all particulars and to have it publicly proclaimed throughout the city.[74]

It was in fact common to charge the *podestà* with the responsibility for proclaiming the feast a week or so in advance, and for holding a council in order to make the necessary arrangements. That, in fact, might be the extent of the statutory regulation. The processions which culminated in the offering to the patron frequently took place on the vigil of the feast; the afternoon of the feast-day itself was the customary time for the races, jousts or other jollifications that might by custom accompany it. It is relatively unusual for a detailed order of procession to appear in the text of the statutes themselves; the rules, if they were written down, were written down elsewhere. The authors of the Florentine statute of 1325 were able to assume that the order of precedence to be observed in the procession for the Baptist was specified in the guild ordinances [*in ordinamentis societatum*].[75] The Perugians, in 1342–43, thought it necessary to spell it out precisely because of disputes among the guilds and societies.[76]

The method by which the citizen body was to be organized for the purposes of the *offerta* may be specified. At Perugia, at Faenza[77] and elsewhere, the offering was made at the great solemnities of the year by the guilds, but the Florentines, as Villani records, made a deliberate change in 1306, decreeing that henceforth attendance at the offering to St John should be under the standards [*gonfaloni*] of the *popolano* neighbourhood societies.[78] The statute of 1325 speaks of an obligation on all males of the city and suburbs aged over fifteen.[79] At Lucca also, all males aged from fourteen to seventy had to attend and to follow the candle of the urban neighbourhood to which they belonged [*contrata* or *brachium*].[80] The statutes of Parma from the mid-thirteenth century insisted, in steadily increasing detail, on attendance with the *vicinia*. The phrasing of the early-fourteenth-century statutes suggests that the citizen's obligation to make offering was analogous to his obligation to pay taxes, which were also assessed on a neighbourhood basis.[81]

In a number of statutes, however, only the offerings to be made by the civic officials and the subject communities of the *contado* are specified; citizen obligations are not mentioned. The *Breve Populi* of Spoleto in 1296 mentioned only the offerings due from the *castra* (the 'castles' or fortified villages of the countryside).[82] Conversely, there may be no mention of *contado* obligations. As often as not, the duty of subject communities to attend and the quantity of the offerings required of them were laid down only in the terms of their submission to the 'mother' city, which, as we have seen, begin to survive from the closing decades of the twelfth century. They were only occasionally included in the *statuti* of the rural communes.[83]

Albeit briefly, the lawmakers of Reggio made plain in 1242 the obligation on the notables of the *episcopatus* to attend the patron's *festa*. The use of the word *episcopatus* is an explicit reminder of the origins of the commune's territorial jurisdiction, and of this ceremonial, in the bishop's power over city and diocese. At neighbouring Parma, also, the thirteenth-century statutes referred to *contado* obligations in ecclesiastical rather than political terms: candles were to be presented at the Feast of the Assumption on behalf of every 'parish and provostship of the bishopric of Parma and [every] baptismal church' [*plebatus et praepositura episcopatus Parmae et ecclesia baptismalis*].[84] The Lucchese statute of 1261 does not survive, but the rubrics respecting the feast of the Holy Cross have been preserved; already a number of *plebes* are named which were obliged to bear a twelve-pound candle to the feast 'for the honour of the most holy Sign and of the city' [*pro honore illius Santissimi Signi et pro honore civitatis*]. It is already specified that two months before the feast the governors of Lucca's subject communities, 'both in the diocese and outside it', should be summoned to receive their instructions aurally. Noteworthy also is the fact that in several places it is provided that the bishop should be asked to ensure that his subjects, including those 'beyond the Arno', fulfilled the stated obligations, and also that he should 'compel' every priest of the diocese to attend.[85] In 1308 the bishop of Luni was to ensure the attendance of the men of Carrara and Sarzana and 'other communities of his in the jurisdiction of Lucca'.[86]

The statute of 1308 included an exceptionally detailed list of subject communities and their obligations on the feast of the Exaltation of the Cross, the patronal festival of the Volto Santo, in September.[87] It is organized territorially, and ends with a list of communes which were also enumerated, with some difference of order, in the statute of 1331, under the subheading 'Terre olim pistoriensium'.[88] Their presence as tributaries to the Holy Cross in 1308 was a result of the joint rule established by the Lucchese and the Florentines over Pistoia in the opening years of the fourteenth century in the wake of that city's murderous factional divisions. The conquest of Lucca by the Pisan Uguccione della Faggiuola in June 1314 destroyed Lucchese hopes of hegemony over northern Tuscany – hopes which Castruccio Castracani spectacularly revived, only to be thwarted by premature death. In 1331, with the fresh disaster of that death not far behind them, the Lucchese were only too aware what a change in their fortunes had been wrought by Uguccione della Faggiuola. So they appended an explanatory note to the list of subject communities: 'although there are lands and castles listed above which today are not subject to the commune of Lucca by reason of the change in the city's condition which took place on 14 June 1314, they have been left there as a memorial of the territory of the past, but nothing is to be done about or against them, nor are the officials bound to do so'.[89]

When the statute was reissued under Pisan rule in 1342, the *terre olim Pistoriensis comitatus* were deleted, but the lament of 1331 was repeated.[90] It was repeated again in 1372, in an emended form of wording that reflected Lucca's renewed sense of its relationship to the Emperor since Charles IV, in 1368–69, liberated the city from the Pisans.[91] By the time that, in 1446, a new statute was produced for the republic restored on the fall of the native tyrant Paolo Guinigi in 1430, Florentine aggression had whittled the Lucchese territory down to even smaller dimensions. The new statute acknowledged the fact, referring to the *districtus sex milliarorum*, and omitted laments which must by now have seemed to belong to a remote antiquity.[92]

Lucca's near neighbour Pistoia entrusted the regulation of the festival of St James to the body which had the general oversight of the saint's cult: the *Statuti di San Jacopo* were declared to have the force of statutes of the people. The Pistoiese Statute of the *Podestà* of 1296 simply referred to the *podestà*'s obligation to set a guard on the cathedral during the period of the feast of St James, and to seek out and fine citizens who had failed to discharge their obligations.[93] The Sienese statutes, after 1287, stated the existence of both citizen and subject obligations as a fact, but never included a list of the latter; they were separately enumerated, from the 1220s on, in a succession of *Libri Censuum*.[94] In 1415 the Florentines, their dominion massively increased by the acquisition of Arezzo, Pistoia and Pisa *inter alia*, included in the statute a full list of their subjects' obligations.[95] The cities of one region of Italy could therefore display a wide variation in the manner and detail of the statutory regulation of their patronal festivals.

As to what form the required offerings took, there was further variation. The list of offerings due from the *contado* in the Lucchese statute of 1308 consists entirely of candles [*ceri*]; the more important subject communes had to provide a *cereum fioritum*, that is, an outsize candle with elaborate ornamentation, which might be as much as thirty-five pounds in weight. A label [*breve*] bearing the name of the community offering it had be fixed to each candle (or pound of wax, if the offering were made in that form). 'And the chief *operarius* of the Holy Cross shall instruct the notary to register each candle as it is removed from the holder on the day of the festivity or that day after, and the pound [weight] of every great candle, so that it may be known if communes have committed fraud and which communes have rendered or not.'[96]

These wax tributes were usually destined for the decoration and illumination of the mother church. The costly piece of cloth known as a *pallium* or *palio* (or sometimes *bravium*) seems to have been awarded as a prize in races (such as the famous Sienese *Palio*) before it was demanded as an offering at patronal festivals. The only *pallium* mentioned in the Lucchese statute is the one to be provided as the prize in the race run on St Regulus's Day.[97] At Pisa also the requirement was for candles, but in 1268 Count Federigo Lancia, who had forgotten to order his candle for the Feast of the Assumption, had for the time being to reoffer two silken *drappos* which he had offered the previous year: the facts were solemnly recorded before a notary.[98]

In the course of the thirteenth century some dominant cities began to exact the tribute of a *palio* from at least some of the dependent lords and communities in the countryside. Perugia required *palii* from some important subject communities in the later thirteenth century, although this is not apparent from the statutes;[99] the statutes of its Umbrian neighbour Spoleto, however, referred to the *cerea et bravia* brought to the city for the Feast of the Assumption.[100] The Sienese traditionally required candles, although some communes which made submission in the mid- to later fourteenth century were bound to present a *palio*. Many other communities which had a long history of subjection to Siena, such as Montalcino, continued to render *ceri*.[101] In 1400 it was stated in the Consiglio Generale that offerings which were meant to be in the form of wax must be so rendered; the cathedral authorities had on occasion accepted sums of money instead, to the detriment of the decoration of the church.[102] The offerings made at Foligno on the eve of the feast of San Feliciano, however, which were also explicitly intended for the *Opera* of the cathedral, were expressed at the rate of twelve pence per hearth.[103]

At Treviso early in the fourteenth century, by far the greater part of all offerings made by the citizens at great festivals was in the form of candles. The officials of the commune, however, were obliged to offer a *palio* or a silver chalice at the feast of St Peter, and, in gratitude to the Virgin for her manifold favours, a *palio* worth fifty pounds was borne before the *podestà* to her church on the Feast of the Assumption. This *palio* was an 'emblem of victory' [*signum victoriae*].[104] Like the *baldachino* under which the Sacrament was carried in the Corpus Christi procession, or the 'cloth of honour' before which the Virgin and Child commonly sit enthroned in painted altarpieces, it betokened both sacrality and power. As such it was exacted from those whose public homage most strikingly demonstrated the authority of the commune. A *palio* purchased at communal expense was offered to Sant' Emidio by the chief officials of Ascoli, along with those offered by the subject territories.[105] At Pistoia, the *podestà* and *capitano* were bound to offer a *palio* to St James at their own expense, while the *Opera di San Jacopo*, which received all offerings, provided from stock both the *palio* for the race and one for the prior of the *anziani* to offer, while they were authorized to hire *palii* to the rectors of the guilds, for all of which they were paid.[106] In the Statute of 1330, a new rubric extended the demand for a *palio* to the chief communes in the territory of Pistoia.[107]

Villani's well-known description of the *festa* of San Giovanni as it was celebrated during the brief rule of the duke of Athens at Florence in 1343 suggests that the appearance of *palii*, offered by Arezzo, Pistoia, Volterra and other larger towns and tributary nobles, was a novelty which 'together with the offering of the the *ceri* made a noble *festa*'.[108] In 1415 the vast majority of Florence's subjects still rendered simply a *cereum*; the larger communes which were obliged to give a *cereum fioritum*, and the communes and lords who rendered a *palio*, as also did the Florentine *podestà* and *capitano del popolo*, were listed separately. A separate rubric dealt with the *palii* owed by recently conquered Pisa, and also by Arezzo.[109]

The dominant city exacted recognition of its authority from the communities of the surrounding territory at the altar of the patron; it was obliged also to uphold the discipline of civic life within its dependent communes, and that meant, *inter alia*, upholding the respect due to local patron saints. The statutes of rural communes, accordingly, contain numerous provisions for the compulsory attendance of the inhabitants, bearing their candles, at their own patronal festival, and for the observance of holidays.[110] Similarly, the urban merchant community would ensure that its members honoured the prescribed festivals. The Lucchese Merchant Court was responsible for ensuring, by writing letters in or by the month of March every year, that Lucchese merchants dwelling in Provence, France, Genoa or Venice sent wax or money in good time 'to make candles to bear to the *luminaria* of the Holy Cross'.[111] At Pisa, the *Breve dell' Ordine di Mare* provided for an offering to be made on behalf of the consuls of Tunis.[112]

The thirteenth-century statutes of Parma display a range of typical concerns about the patronal festival, including the quality of the candles to be offered and even the uses to which they were likely to be put. The candles were to be of wax, without admixture of glue or soap, and without artificial colour. In the 1255 edition of the statutes, it was stipulated that four *Fratres Poenitentiae* (members of the Franciscan 'third order'), to be appointed a month beforehand, were to have a strict monopoly of making the candles for the Feast of the Assumption. They would meet the requirement that the wicks were to be of cotton or flax only, and would sell the candles in the piazza.[113] This arrangement was abandoned only a little later in the century, however; although quality controls were to be maintained, 'anyone who can make candles' was to impress a seal on them, a copy of which was to be deposited with the appropriate officials; and 'anyone' who could make 'candles et candelabra' [*canellas et duplerios*] for himself and his household was permitted to do so at home. The lawmakers of Faenza were prepared to accept that the candles could be made around a rod or cord, but laid it down that the weight of that rod or cord must be recorded and checked, in the presence of the guild consuls, against the weight of the finished article.[114] Apothecaries were sometimes warned that they must make the candles for the *contado* of the same quality as the candles that were offered by the citizens.[115]

While it was usual for the supreme patronal festival which required offerings from city and *contado* to be centred on one saint and one church, a single saint was sometimes venerated at more than one shrine, and honours were sometimes more or less evenly divided between two saints domiciled in different churches. Arezzo illustrates the first possibility, Piacenza and Forlì illustrate the second. At Arezzo the *podestà* and his *familia* had to divide their compulsory offerings to San Donato in half, one to be rendered at the church of Santa Maria della Pieve on the vigil and the other at the cathedral on the day itself. The offerings of 'each and every castle and vill of the *contado* and district of Arezzo' were to be similarly divided between the churches.[116] At Piacenza, the Feast of the Assumption was solemnly celebrated at the cathedral by the *podestà* and the whole city, but it was on the feast of the ancient soldier-martyr Antoninus that the offerings from dependent *castra* and *ville* were required; the proceeds were divided between the cathedral and the church of St Antoninus, which had been a cathedral in the early medieval period.[117]

At Forlì the twin patrons were a complementary couple of a type sometimes found elsewhere: the ancient Bishop Mercurialis and the soldier-martyr Valerianus. The former lay in the monastic church that bore his name, the latter in the cathedral church of the Holy Cross. It was on St Mercurialis's day that the city was supposed to receive *pallia* in tribute from its subjects. The commune was then bound to offer one of these *pallia* to Mercurialis and one to Valerianus on his day; if the *pallia* had not in fact been received, they were to be purchased at public expense. The *podestà* and *anziani*, together with the officials and councillors and also the guilds, were obliged to offer candles annually at both shrines.[118] The two saints performed other complementary functions: an incoming *podestà*, before he entered the palace, was to visit the cathedral and the shrine of St Valerianus to ask that God should deign to grant his aid to the Roman church, to the *podestà* himself and to the city; if the Holy See or the legate appointed a *capitano*, he was to do the same, but at the church of St Mercurialis.[119]

The patron's festival was in many cities marked by the release of selected prisoners at his or her altar, which was also often done at Christmas or Easter. The Aretines in fact insisted on restricting the practice to Good Friday, stating specifically that it was not to take place at the feast of St Donatus.[120] The fortunate prisoners would be provided at public expense with a small candle to offer at the altar. The principle, and its limitations (for example, what types of prisoner were or were not eligible for release), might be stated in the statutes, but the ritual would be the subject of a petition before the communal council as the festival in question approached, and the identity of the prisoners to be offered might be the subject of debate. It was commonly stipulated that no prisoner could be so presented twice in a lifetime, or that no one guilty of serious crime, or in debt to the commune, or in debt for more than a certain amount, qualified; sometimes it was made clear that 'poor' or 'wretched' prisoners were intended. At Perugia five prisoners were to be released on Good Friday, and two each at Christmas, at the feast of St Ercolano, and Corpus Christi, and (an unusual provision) two female prisoners, if such could be found, on each festivity of the Virgin Mary; if no women were available, one male prisoner could be released instead. Sodomy, cursing [*maledictio*], forgery, and blaspheming God or the Virgin, disqualified.[121] To institute this practice could be a way of marking a new solemnity – as at Siena when in 1450 the shape of the festivities for the newly canonized Bernardino was decided, and again in 1462 after the canonization of Catherine.[122]

Other Processions and Offerings

In many cities the statutes recorded the institution of honours, which might take the form of offerings, processions and races, in recognition of victories or deliverances experienced on a saint's feast-day. One historian of medieval Treviso systematically distinguishes those which commemorated particular events from those which honoured the established patrons of the local church. Several of the former were in fact never incorporated into formal statute collections: Epiphany (in celebration of the victory of Guecellone Tempesta over the partisans of the Marquis of Este in 1327); St Mark (the first Venetian takeover of Treviso, 1342); St Andrew (the end of Carrara tyranny, 1388); St Lucy (the initiation of the second Venetian regime, 1391).[123] Celebrations of this type might, however, come and go. St Lucy received honours at Parma in recognition of the fact that the Sanvitalesi faction had been expelled from the city on 13 December 1295;[124] but after the major beneficiary of this event, Giberto da Correggio, was himself driven from Parma in 1316, Lucy disappeared from the revised statutes.

The statutes of 1347 said that the feast of St Bovo was to be celebrated because it had been on his day, in 1341, that Parma was liberated from the detestable tyranny of Mastino della Scala; but when in time Bernabò Visconti acquired power over Parma, the festivities were suppressed in deference to the feelings of his consort Regina, Mastino's daughter.[125]

Solemn processions at which the attendance of the guilds and the officials of the commune was required multiplied for a variety of reasons. The fifteenth-century statutes of Vicenza stipulated an order of the guilds and corporations which was to be observed whenever solemn processions were held.[126] The celebration of the patron normally remained unique in that the offerings of the countryside were required then and on no other occasion. For example, when, in the mid-fourteenth century, a solemn procession was decreed at Pistoia for St Zeno, it involved the urban population and the officials, but not representatives of subject communities.[127] In the fifteenth century there were three *oblationes generales* at Ferrara: for St George, St Dominic and St Antony (of Vienne). Only for St George, the ancient patron and protector of the city, was the full attendance of the urban corporations and the offerings of the *contado* required; it was specifically stated that the rural communities, the doctors of the *studio* and the college of notaries were not obliged to attend on Dominic and Antony.[128]

Civic officials commonly had to meet more obligations than the mass of the populace. The thirteenth-century statutes of Ravenna required the attendance of all the men and women of the city at the celebrations of San Vitale and of saints Ursicinus and Barbatianus at the cathedral, and at the church of St Theodore *a Vultu* in the first week after Pentecost, in honour of the Holy Spirit. The *podestà* and his officials had the duty of attendance at certain other festivities, for example the feasts of St Andrew, St John the Evangelist and St Apollinare; they were obliged personally to bear candles to Classe.[129] According to the statutes produced under Venetian rule in 1471, however, 'the whole people of the city of Ravenna, male and female' was theoretically required to attend the morning mass on a long list of feast-days at the principal churches.[130]

Miracles as well as victories could generate public celebrations. In 1342, the authorities of Osimo in the Marche declared:

since God is marvellous and glorious in all his works, and redeemed with his precious blood the human race, expelled from the delights of paradise, it behoves the whole Christian people to pay wholehearted reverence to that same blood; wherefore we decree and ordain that on the day of the blessed virgin Lucy, on which the miracle of the blood of the painted crucifixion took place in the church of St Nicholas, a solemn feast shall be celebrated by the gonfalonier and the priors of the people and the council of the people of Osimo and the whole people of Osimo with tapers, candles and a *palio*, to be offered every year in the church of St Nicholas aforementioned.[131]

In some places the statutes make it apparent that the patronal festival was distinguished from other solemnities by the organizational principle adopted for the procession. At Florence and at Parma, as we have noted, citizens were bound to attend on the patron with their neighbourhood societies. Other festivities were left to the guilds. The Florentine *artes* were bound every year to offer a candle to St Philip at the Baptistery,[132] and at Parma the offering to St Lucy was to be made by the officials, *capita societatum* and the *societates, misteria, artes et alios civitatis Parmae* in the same way as for St Hilary.[133] It was the more striking that the short-lived celebration of St Bovo was to be organized by *vicinia*, as if it were second in importance only to the Assumption.[134]

From the later fourteenth century onwards, the statutes of many cities reveal the advance of the feast of Corpus Christi to become one of the year's greatest public solemnities, and attest the close association of the feast with the guild community by laying down the processional order to be observed by the guilds. Corpus Christi was almost universally listed among the *ferie* by the mid-fourteenth century; its development as a festival directed by the public authorities came later.[135] There were, in sum, an increasing number of occasions in the year when the magistrates paraded their authority and their allegiance to God, his saints and his church, in his name exacting displays of reverence and obedience from the populace.

Races and Games

Meanwhile, the opportunity was not missed to multiply races and other festivities which afforded further opportunities for display, but were also deemed to give pleasure and 'comfort' to the common people. The races which frequently marked not only the patron's feast-day but other occasions, both sacred and secular, are a common subject of statutory regulation, but once again the statutes vary in the amount they feel it necessary to say about them.

The Aretine statute of 1327, to take one example of many, stated the rules for the *pallium* which was to be run annually for San Donato, laying down the course which was to be followed by the contestants.[136] The late medieval statutes for Reggio Emilia provided for a rerun in case of a contested decision.[137] At Faenza, the 1410 statutes included lengthy regulations for races to be run for the Feast of the Assumption and on St Peter's Day for a *bravium*, with a pig [*porchetta*] weighing at least sixty pounds as second prize, a string of garlic as third, and a cock [*gallo*], with two ounces of spices, to be presented to the herald [*tubator*].[138] The triad *bravium, porchetta* and *gallo* was to be found in several other places, normally as first, second and third prize respectively, while a string of garlic might be derisively offered as the equivalent of a wooden spoon. During the period of their rule over Ravenna in the later fifteenth century, the Venetian authorities provided these prizes for races run in honour of both Sant' Apollinare and San Vitale.[139] At Como, where the race for St Abundius was, very fittingly, contested by boats on the lake, the second prize was twenty-two pairs of gloves (not unknown elsewhere), and the booby prize a string of garlic and some salted fish.[140] Even where the regulations are not spelled out, references to races associated with the patronal festival are common. At Lucca, however, it was neither the Volto Santo nor St Martin who was honoured by a race, but the martyr-bishop Regulus, whose relics had lain in the cathedral since the eighth century and who was sometimes regarded as a co-patron of the cathedral. The compilers of the 1308 statute thought it unnecessary to do more than specify that the race should be run and the expenses met 'according to the usual custom'.[141]

At Verona in the late thirteenth century there were two races, one on horseback and one on foot. The latter won literary fame when (in *Inferno* XV, 121–4) Dante likened Brunetto Latini, resuming his eternal running in hell, to the victorious contestant:

> e parve di coloro
> che corrono a Verona il drappo verde

> per la campagna; e parve di costoro
> quelli che vince, non colui che perde.

These races had traditionally been run on the first Sunday in Lent [*dominica totius populi*] in honour of the Virgin and St Zeno.[142] By the fifteenth century the number of races run at Verona had increased to four, including one for asses and a foot-race for women, but they had been shifted from the Sunday to 'Fat Thursday', out of a sense of religious decorum. Women's races took place elsewhere; the question whether reputable women could be expected to run a race in public was openly confronted at Verona. A prize of six *brachia* of fine green cloth was to be contested by *mulieres honestae*, even if there was only one of them; but if no honest woman was to be had, 'then prostitutes shall be accepted in addition' [*tunc in supplementum accipiatur de prostitutis*]. The race run by *equi masculi et integri* for twenty-five *brachia* of crimson velvet, of course, remained the most prestigious.[143] At Faenza also, in the early sixteenth century, the authorities were insistent that the races for the Assumption and for the feast of SS Peter and Paul were not to be contested by mares.[144]

At Parma in the fourteenth century there were both races and jousting on the day after the Assumption; similarly at Ascoli Piceno on the feast of Sant' Emidio there were races, and 'each and every gentleman and [everyone] capable of jousting and playing with the lance and with arms on horseback' [*tucti et singuli gentili huomini et acti ad jocare con l'aste et armigiare ad cavallo*] were to be in readiness to perform.[145] The desire to make the patronal festival in all respects the pivotal day in the city's social calendar was expressed in the effort to restrict the ceremony of knighting to that day. At Pistoia there were penalties for getting oneself knighted during the two months preceding the Feast of St James, while the authorities at Parma demanded that all knighthoods were to be conferred on the Feast of the Assumption, 'so that the said festivity shall be more honourably celebrated'.[146]

The new races introduced in the fourteenth and fifteenth centuries were sometimes of an entirely secular character, but they were also commonly instituted, certainly when the time of year permitted, as part of the commemorative celebrations of a saint who had granted the city a favour and to whom thanksgiving was accordingly due. The Florentines were pioneers in the field. In 1325 regulations were in force for the *bravia* of not only St John the Baptist and of St Reparata, the ancient patron of the cathedral, but of St Barnabas, the celestial victor at the Battle of Campaldino in 1289. These were the three races known to Giovanni Villani, who estimated the total cost of the three *palii* in 1333 to be a hundred florins.[147] It was a mark of enhanced honour (and expense) if a foot-race was upgraded to be run *equester*. By 1355 Reparata and Barnabas had received this compliment; and St Victor was similarly rewarded for the victory he brought the Florentines over the Pisans in 1364, as the statutes of 1415 indicate.[148]

Image and Sacrilege

Sometimes preserved in the statutes are resolutions that images of a city's patrons, commonly flanking the Virgin, be painted on its walls or over its gates, and there are other references here and there to works of art that were directly or indirectly funded out of the public purse. The Perugian statute of 1343 decreed that 'una enmagine' of Sant' Ercolano, 'well carved, honourable and fine' [*relevata biene, onorevole e bella*], should be made to be carried at the head of the procession of the guilds and artificers every year on his feast-day.[149] The obligatory offerings that were made to St Philip at the Florentine Baptistery were to be converted into *picturae* for the decoration of the church, a slightly more specific variant of the common stipulation that offerings be used solely for the benefit of the church where they were made.[150]

Resolutions in favour of artistic or architectural commissions in honour of the saints are, of course, more normally to be found in other sources. The presence of such pious declarations of intent in statute collections can sometimes be connected with the political context in which the collection as a whole was produced. On the restoration of a republic in Modena in 1306–07 it was declared that a statue of St Geminianus bearing a standard and flanked by two angels was to be carved in finest marble, inscribed *Iustitia, misericordia, veritas et pax* (Justice, mercy, truth and peace) and placed on the façade of the cathedral facing the piazza.[151] At both Vicenza and Verona in the late thirteenth century, St Christopher, among other saints, was to be depicted over the gates of the city, presumably to exercise his well-known protective role over travellers. In both cities, St Peter was among the other saints who were to be depicted by the side of the Virgin, at Verona 'with the keys in his hands'.[152] This possibly indicates a specific desire to demonstrate loyalty to the Roman church in the wake of the expulsion of Ezzelino da Romano. At a similar period, the Pisan statutes were requiring the repair of the images of the Virgin and other saints over the gates of the city, and indeed for their provision where they were supposed to exist, but did not.[153] At Osimo in 1308 it was laid down that the image of San Benevenuto, the late bishop of the city, should be painted on the gates with those of the Virgin and St Christopher, 'so that honour may be paid to them by passers-by'.[154] The statutes of Camerino in 1424 wished the Virgin, their chief patron Venantius, and not only Christopher but Antony of Vienne to be so depicted.[155]

The interests of the saints in general were (theoretically) protected by laws against blasphemy, which might be associated in the minds of legislators with the playing of games of chance, or, as at Ferrara, with outrages against images. The Ferrarese laws exacted the amputation of the right hand for the desecration of images of Christ or the Virgin, and protected lesser saints with the threat of a fine of twenty-five pounds. Failure or refusal to pay the monetary penalties could in theory result in draconian physical punishment.[156] According to the 1567 statute, any Jew who was convicted of any of these offences was to be burned alive, and in such cases extra-legal, inquisitorial procedures could be used. Secret accusation was encouraged, and a share in the fine promised to the informer. The statute added a further unpleasant touch, promising potential informers that, apart from this share in the proceeds, they could expect 'great reward from the divine majesty and the greatest honour among men'.[157]

For the most part, there was a single penalty for all blasphemy. Niccolò d'Este's code for Modena, however, prescribed a top rate of fines for blasphemy against God and the Virgin, a medium rate for Modena's patron Geminianus, and a bottom rate for all other saints.[158] In some codes, a distinction was made between *cursing* God or the Virgin and merely swearing by 'any bodily part', whether shameful or not, of God, the Virgin or any other saint.

In 1424 the lawmakers of Camerino adopted this distinction, and also doubled the penalties for all sorts of 'insult' and recourse to arms at Christmas and Easter and on the feast-days of the two patrons, Venantius and Ansovinus. Failure to denounce instances of blasphemy to the authorities was punishable by a fine.[159] At Spello, a chest [*cippus*] was to be provided at public expense and kept in the communal palace for the receipt of secret accusations of blasphemy.[160] At Todi, at least by the sixteenth century, the authorities went further: the *podestà* and the *capitano* were each to keep such a locked chest in their respective palaces, as were the priests of the urban churches.[161]

It will have been observed that although there is a predictable family resemblance between the codes produced in different cities, there is no guarantee that matters dealt with in one city's statutes will be dealt with, either in the same amount of detail or at all, in the statutes of its neighbours. This is most obviously the case, perhaps, in the regulation of the patronal festival itself: sometimes left to custom and the administration of the *podestà* in consultation with the councils; sometimes presumed to be dealt with in the ordinances of the guilds or deputed to a quasi-autonomous body such as the Opera di San Jacopo at Pistoia; sometimes spelled out in considerable detail in the statutes themselves. Sometimes also, as we have seen, the statutes concern themselves only with citizen obligations, those of the *contado* being specified elsewhere; occasionally the reverse is true. The fact that, once a year, such a ceremony would take place invariably emerges, but that is sometimes all that can be said.

The absence from the statutes of saints such as Liberalis at Treviso is a salutary reminder, also, that a round of celebrations of saints who were in various ways regarded as urban patrons because of their traditional connections with the local church – not to mention, of course, a host of other saints with no such connections – went on without the legally stipulated intervention of the officials. The lists of legal holidays furnish an index of the recognition accorded by the secular power to a spectrum of observances, universal and local, ancient and recent, which were only to a very small degree of its own making. It is the more obvious, therefore, that when a saint's feast is added to the *ferie* or becomes a full public holiday, as when a saint's name is added to the list of those receiving an official offering, or when a new race is instituted, something must have occurred to prompt such explicit recognition of the city's obligations. That something might be a political event; but it might be a papal canonization. The picture is, for the most part, one of a close integration of lay and ecclesiastical interests, but it is a moving rather than a still picture.

What can be said of the statutes can in fact be said of the life and practices of the cities themselves: that they did (and said) basically similar things in a hundred and one subtly different ways. In exploring the official cult of the saints in its development over time, we shall have frequent occasion to be reminded of that fact.

Notes

1. For convenience and brevity, statute collections are cited here by the name of the city and the date of recension or (for early printed editions) publication, and listed alphabetically in that form in the Bibliography, where full references are given. Citations are by page number unless there is no printed pagination.

2. Bologna 1288, 1, p. x. For the earlier recensions, see Bologna 1245–67.

3. For the statutes of Lucca, see S. Bongi, *Inventario*, 1, pp. 31–7; for the statute of 1308 in particular, A. Mancini, *Storia di Lucca* (Florence 1950), pp. 101–8. For Siena, *Guida-Inventario dell' Archivio di Stato di Siena* (2 vols, Rome 1951), 1, pp. 61–76.

4. Foligno C14, 1, pp. viii–x.

5. Padua C13, pp. 180–84.

6. The 'octave' was the eighth day after a feast. For the veneration of Antony at Padua, see below, p. 149.

7. These were 'double' candles, or candelabra, whose holders were often elaborately decorated. As an offering, they constituted a special mark of honour.

8. Treviso C13 includes laws dating from 1207–18 (vol. 1) and from 1231–33 and 1260–63 (vol. 2). In Treviso C14 the 1313–15 recension, produced in 'the last phase of the free commune', provides the basic text, supplemented by the statute issued by Gherardo da Cammino in 1283–84 and the 'carrarese' of 1385. The Venetian statutes are in Treviso 1574.

9. Treviso C13, 1, p. 39 (see also 2, p. 31). Ceneda, site of an early diocese, was one of the communes absorbed into the city of Vittorio Veneto in 1866. For Tiziano, see A. Maschetto, *BS* 12, cols 509–14.

10. Treviso C14, 1, pp. 111, 113–14. For the background, see below p. 151.

11. Ibid., pp. 112–13. For Parisius, see below p. 141.

12. Treviso C14, 2, pp. 109–10.

13. Ibid., 1, pp. 110–17, 204–6.

14. Avogari, *Memorie del Beato Enrico*, pp. 108–13.

15. Ibid., pp. 194–5. For Liberalis, see I. Daniele in *BS* 8, cols 5–9.

16. Treviso 1574, pp. 36–9. The *feriati* (for which in general see below pp. 106–7) are listed on p. 131v. The statute produced in 1385 for Francesco Carrara, which otherwise altered little, introduced a list of *ferie*: Treviso C14, 2, pp. 315–16.

17. There is a brief history in Perugia 1343, 1, p. xii; see also *Archivio di Stato del Comune di Perugia, Inventario* (Rome 1956), pp. 9–13.

18. Perugia, Archivio di Stato, *Statuti* 1. A continuous numeration of the rubrics has been supplied in more recent times. Rubrics 1–86 were privately printed, incomplete, by A. Fabretti at Turin (n.d.) under the title *Statutum Comunis Perusii anno MCCLXXIX digestum*.

19. *Statuti*, fol. 4 (r.25); fol. 14v (r.82); fols. 59v–60 (r.444).

20. *Regestum Reformationum Comunis Perusii ab anno MCCLVI ad annum MCCC*, 1, p. 131.

21. L. Kern, 'A propos du mouvement des flagellants', pp. 49–51. Cf. below, pp. 145–6.

22. Perugia 1343, 1, pp. 133–5.

23. Ibid., 2, pp. 62–6 (holidays); 72–3, 93–4, 244 (blasphemy, etc.); 349 (prisoners).

24. Perugia 1526, p. xxxviii (r.81).

25. Ibid., pp. ci *verso*–ciiii *verso* (rr.380–418).

26. Foligno C14, p. 289: 'ad salutem animarum et corporum civium civitatis eiusdem'; Piacenza C14, p. 229: 'pro salute animarum placentinorum civium et omnium defunctorum eorum'.

27. Cremona 1485, a.ii.

28. Ascoli 1377, p. 3.

29. Piacenza C14, pp. 215, 4.

30. For the possible significance of the designation of the Virgin as a governor of Siena, see below, pp. 259–62.

31. Treviso C14, 1, p. 661.

32. Osimo C14, 2, p. 861.

33. Foligno C14, 2, p. 289.

34. Florence 1325, 1, p. 5; 2, pp. 1, 310: 'ut Deus precibus beati Iohannis Baptiste defendat et manuteneat et conservet in bono et felici statu et semper de bono in melius augmentet Comune Florentie'.

35. E.g. Modena 1306–07, 1, p. 99.

36. Ibid., 1, p. 11; 2, p. 157.

37. *Fonti sui Comuni Rurali Toscani*, 1, p. 121.

38. Ibid., 3, p. 171: 'ad honorem,laudem, et reverentiam gloriosissimi Sancti Johannis Baptiste, patroni et gubernatoris civitatis Florentie eiusque comitatus, fortie et districtus'.

39. Ibid., 5, p. 397. Writing to the men of Montopoli in 1382 about emendations of the statutes, the Florentine priors declared that Peter, Paul and the Baptist, as well as Montopoli's own patron Stephen, were *capitanei, protectores et defensores communis et terre Montistopoli* (ibid., p. 356).

40. Ibid., 9, p. 1: 'sotto il nome e patrocinio de' quali la città di Firenze si regge e governa'. For the fourteenth-century enlargement of the Florentine 'pantheon', see below, pp. 164–8.

41. Lucca 1376, p. 9.

42. Vicenza 1264, p. 8: 'quorum sacratissimorum corporum consolatione gaudemus et patrocinio munimur ad salvamentum Civitatis Vicentie ejusque districtus et tocius comunancie'. Elsewhere (p. 1) the martyrs are referred to as the *sancta corpora Vicentie civitatis*.

43. Verona 1276, 1, p. 21: 'cuius sacratissimi corporis consolatione gaudemus et patrocinio munimur'.

44. Pisa C12–C14, p. 339.

45. Osimo C14, 1, p. 462.

46. Todi 1551, Dist. II r.16. These expressions do not, however, appear in the thirteenth century: cf. Todi 1275.

47. As suggested by Fasoli and Sella, Bologna 1288, 2, p. 41.

48. Faenza 1415, p. 276.

49. ASP *Statuti e Ordinamenti* 12, fols 22 r–v.

50. Ferrara 1476 [p. 141v].

51. Verona 1475, Lib. IV, r.7.

52. Siena 1545.

53. Ibid., fols 22v–23.

54. *Statuti* 14, fol. 54.

55. Ascoli 1377, p. 318.

56. *Florentine Diary*, pp. 32–3, 240.

57. Siena C13–C14, 1, p. 13.

58. *Fonti sui Comuni Rurali* 7, p. 84; Ascoli 1377, p. 319. For some Umbrian exemptions, see Foligno C14, 1, pp. 20–21; M. Roncetti, 'Statuti di Torgiano del 1426', *BSUSP* 59 (1962), p. 128. Exceptions were also often made at the time of the vintage.

59. Ferrara 1476, p. 142.

60. Verona 1476, Lib. IV, r.7.

61. Perugia, Archivio di Stato, *Statuti* 1, f. 14v: 'Ad evitandam omnem pestem & omnem aquam nocivam que grando generaliter appellatur.'

62. Pisa C12–C14, 3, p. 258 and n.

63. Florence 1325, 2, pp. 95–6. These statutes were in fact produced in a brief interval between the *signoria* of King Robert himself over Florence and the election of his son Charles in December 1325. For Barnabas at

Florence, see below, esp. pp. 152–3.

64. ASS CG 114, fol. 41, 20 August 1333.

65. Perugia 1343, 2, p. 62. For San Bevignate, see above, p. 101.

66. Treviso C14, 2, pp. 315–16.

67. ASF *Libri Fabarum* 47, fol. 77, December 32 1401 (Consiglio del Popolo): 'in favorem Consolum Artis Calismale quod celebretur dies in qua dominus noster Yhesus Christus fuit batizatus per manum S. Johannis Batistae'; Florence 1415, 1, p. 189.

68. Pistoia 1546, pp. 54v–55.

69. ASP *Provvisioni* 45, fol. 99v. The 'signpost' is in *Statuti e Ordinamenti* 15, fol. 57v.

70. For instances of recognition of Joseph in the later fifteenth century, at Ferrara and elsewhere, see below, pp. 229–30.

71. Ferrara 1567, pp. 59–60.

72. Faenza 1527, pp. xxii r–v. For the Holy Protectors, see below, pp. 171–3. The other two, Terentius and Emilianus, were automatically included because they possessed titular churches in the city.

73. For a fuller discussion, and criticism of the suggestion that such written regulations existed already in 1200, see below, n.30, p. 271.

74. Reggio C13, p. 35.

75. Florence 1325, 2, p. 304.

76. Perugia 1343, 1, p. 133.

77. Faenza 1415, p. 292.

78. Villani, IX.87. Cf. below, pp. 205–6.

79. Florence 1325, 2, p. 303.

80. Lucca 1308, pp. 44–5.

81. Parma 1316–25, p. 113:

> ...et ire quilibet cum vicinis suae viciniae sive illius viciniae in qua solvit coltas et facit alias faciones. Et quaelibet vicinia civitatis Parmae sive vicini ejusdem teneatntur et debeant, quando deferunt canellas ad ipsum festum, portare et portari faciere confalonem, qum portare et portari facere teneatur confalonierius ipsius viciniae; et sub ipso confalone et post ipsum confalonem vadant et ire teneantur omnes vicini.

82. Spoleto 1296, pp. 51, 53.

83. The 1360 statute for Montopoli specifies the obligation to offer *unum honorabile cereum floridum* annually at the feast of the Baptist: *Fonti sui Comuni Rurali*, 9, p. 405.

84. Parma 1255, p. 202.

85. *Memorie e documenti*, 5.i, pp. 11–14.

86. Lucca 1308, pp. 45–6.

87. Ibid., pp. 36–44.

88. ASL *Statuti* 4, pp. 86–7 (modern pagination).

89. Ibid., p. 89.
90. *Statuti* 5, p. 103 (modern pagination).
91. *Statuti* 6, fol. 75v:

Et licet alique terre & castra de quibus supra fit mentio modo non subsint de facto sub obediencia lucani comunis et non possit fieri exactio contra eas, tamen ad perpetuam rei memoriam cum de jure et ex antiquissima consuetudine & possessione & ex forma privilegiorum imperialium pertineant ad lucanum comune de eis facta est in hoc statutorum volumine mencio specialis.

92. Lucca 1490, III.31 (no pagination).
93. Pistoia 1313, p. 22 (r.xlvi); 1296, pp. 35, 122. For a description of the Pistoiese statutes see E. Altieri-Magliozzi, *L'Archivio di Pistoia*, pp. 23–36.
94. See below, p. 256.
95. Florence 1415, 3, pp. 301–13. In the 1325 statute there had been only a brief statement of principle and a precautionary stipulation that the communes of Poggibonzi, Catignano and Gambassi, and all those conceded by Pistoia to Florence, were bound to make an offering: Florence 1325, 2, p. 311.
96. Lucca 1308, p. 45. *Cerea fiorita* were commonly required from the more prosperous dependent communes: Villani (X.ccxv) describes the 'castellated' ceri exacted from certain communes on their submission to Florence.
97. Lucca 1308, p. 35.
98. Pisa C12–C14, 1, n.1, p. 264.
99. In 1216 Perugia required *unum pallium vel cereum valentem C solidos denariorum* from Montone: V. Ansidei and L. Giannantoni, 'I Codici delle Sommissioni al Comune di Perugia', *BSUSP*, 1 (1897), p. 151. In 1259 the money tribute previously owed by Cagli was converted into a *palio*, which had to be carried on a pole to the church of Sant' Ercolano: ibid., 3 (1897), p. 199. In 1269 Arezzo exacted a *pallium* of purple silk from Borgo San Sepolcro which similarly had to be borne on a *lancea sive asta* (Pasqui, *Documenti*, 2, p. 417).
100. Spoleto 1296, p. 51. Orvieto similarly made mixed demands of its subjects, as appears from the submissions included in the *Regesto degli Atti del Commune* compiled in 1339: *Ephemerides Urbevetani*, ed. L. Fumi (2 vols, *RIS* 15.2), 1, pp. 97–123.
101. For example, Chianciano (1346) and Radicofani (1352); Lucignano, which in 1359 was required to offer a *cero*, in 1390 promised a *palio*: Nardi, 'Il territorio', pp. 98–9, 100, 126.
102. Cecchini and Neri, *Il Palio*, pp. 41–2.
103. Foligno C14, 2, p. 289. The value of the wax to be offered could be expressed in terms of money or weight or both. Simple money payments were more often exacted as part of treaty settlements, as for example in

1364, when the Florentines demanded 10,000 florins annually for ten years from Pisa, payable on St John's day (Filippo Villani, 102).

104. Treviso C14, 1, p. 115.
105. Ascoli 1376, p. 322.
106. Pistoia 1313, pp. 7–8, 10.
107. ASP *Statuti e Ordinamenti* 4, r.25, fols 16v.
108. Villani, XIII.8
109. Florence 1415, 3.
110. See, e.g., *Fonti sui Comuni Rurali*, 2, pp. 179–80, 267 (S. Maria a Monte); 3, pp. 39–41 (Castelfranco di Sopra); 4, p. 126 (Montecarlo), etc.
111. Lucca 1376, p. 59.
112. Pisa C12–C14, 3, pp. 568–9.
113. Parma 1255, pp. 201–3. By the end of the century the responsibility for supplying the candles was imposed on one *providus vir* from each *porta* of the city: Parma 1266–1304, p. 157.
114. Faenza 1415, pp. 291–4.
115. For example, the authorities at Siena in the 1330s were anxious to maintain or increase the value of the offering from the *contado* and decreed (ASS CG 109, fol. 74v, 26 March 1330): 'Piacciavi di fare fermare ch' e pizzicaiuoli che fanno i cieri del contado facciano di quella ciera che fanno quelli de la citta.' This stipulation was written into the revised statutes of 1337–39: 'Statutum est quod pizzicaioli et alii facientes cereos de comunitatibus faciant de illa cera qua faciunt cereos civitatis...' (ASS *Statuti* 26, fol. 246v).
116. Arezzo 1327, p. 70. A similar arrangement was upheld under Florentine rule, and the Florentines even extended the practice: see below, p. 222.
117. Piacenza C14, p. 230.
118. Forlì 1359, pp. 92–4.
119. Ibid., pp. 42–3.
120. Arezzo 1327, p. 71.
121. Perugia 1343, 1, p. 212; Perugia 1526, r.187, fol. 64v.
122. See below, pp. 302, 308.
123. Marchesan, *Treviso Medievale*, 2, pp. 186–93.
124. Parma 1266–1304, p. 158.
125. Parma 1347, pp. 79–80. The *Chronica Abbreviata de factis civitatis Parmae* (*Chronica Parmensia*, p. 382) records both the institution of the festivities and their suppression. Between 1341 and 1344, in fact, the Correggio *signori* minted coins with Bovo's effigy: *CNI* 9, p. 406, pl. XXVII.7.
126. Vicenza 1490, p. 102. Manuscript notes added to the British Library's copy towards the middle of the sixteenth century expanded the list of processions; the feasts of Joseph, Bernardino, Jerome, Peter Martyr and Vincent Ferrer and the Feast of the Visitation were among the additions.

127. See below, pp. 159–60.

128. The rubric *De oblationibus generalibus que fieri debeant in anno* is on p. 173v according to the manuscript pagination supplied in the British Library copy of Ferrara 1476, which lacks title page or pagination.

129. Ravenna C13, pp. 167, 169–72. Cf. above, n.30, p. 88.

130. Ravenna C13, p. 77.

131. Osimo C14, 2, p. 956.

132. Florence 1325, 2, p. 303. In response to the discovery of a conspiracy in 1340, the Florentine authorities ordained an annual procession to San Giovanni to be performed by all the guilds on All Saints' Day (Villani, XII.119).

133. Parma 1266–1304, p. 158.

134. Parma 1347, pp. 79–80.

135. For further observations on the celebration of Corpus Christi, see below, Chapter 6; for Sienese regulation of the festival in the mid-fifteenth century, see below, pp. 303–5.

136. Arezzo 1327, pp. 69–70.

137. Reggio 1582, Lib. VII, c.20.

138. Faenza 1415, pp. 194–5.

139. Ravenna C13, pp. 79–80.

140. Como 1355, 1, p. 106.

141. Lucca 1308, p. 35. By the late fifteenth century, the race had been moved to the Feast of the Holy Cross on 14 September; see below, p. 214.

142. Verona 1276, 1, pp. 61–2.

143. Verona 1475, Lib. I, r.35. One annalist places the change in 1434: *Memorie Istoriche raccolte da Giacopo Rizzoni*, in *Cronica della Città di Verona descritta da Per Zagata* (3 vols, Verona 1745–49), 2, p. 223. See also *Cenni intorno all' origine e descrizione della festa che annualmente si celebra in Verona, l'ultime venerdì del carnevale* (Verona 1818).

144. Faenza 1527, Lib. VII, r.1.

145. Parma 1316–25, p. 114; Ascoli 1377, pp. 321–3.

146. Pistoia 1296, p. 122; Parma 1266, p. 155.

147. Florence 1325, 2, pp. 307, 436–7; Villani, XII.93.

148. ASF *Statuti di Firenze* 16, fols 237v, 249v; Florence 1415, 3, pp. 315–16. Matteo Villani records the upgrading of Reparata's race in 1353 (III, 85); and Filippo Villani the institution of Victor's in 1364 (99).

149. Perugia 1343, 1, p. 135.

150. Florence 1325, 2, pp. 303–4.

151. Modena 1306–07, 1, p. 99.

152. Vicenza 1264, pp. 3–7; Verona 1276, 1, pp. 651–2, repeated verbatim in 1475, Lib. IV, r.20.

153. Pisa C12–C14, 1, pp. 52, 264.

154. Osimo C14, 1, p. 155.

155. Camerino 1424, p. 17.

156. Ferrara 1476, p. 147 (manuscript pagination).
157. Ferrara 1567, Lib. III, r.1 (pp. 141 a–b).
158. Modena 1488, Lib. III, r.26.
159. Camerino 1424, pp. 207–8.
160. Spello, Archivio Municipale, *Statutum Civitatis Hyspelli*, 1360, fols 50 r–v (Lib. II, cap. 3).
161. Todi 1551, Dist. III, r.115.

CHAPTER 4

BUILDING THE PANTHEON

New Saints and Old

The identity of the chief patron, to whom the commune would require its citizens and subject communities to render ceremonial obedience, was established by 1200, and in the vast majority of instances would not subsequently be altered, whether the decision was in favour of the patron of the cathedral, another ancient saint domiciled elsewhere in the city, or a recent newcomer such as St James at Pistoia. This supreme patron did not necessarily stand on a lonely eminence; there might be a number of saints, old and new, in the cathedral church, or in other prominent urban churches, who had a claim to official recognition. Despite the unquestionable value of stability and (in every sense) venerability, changing times and new situations in most cities created a need to add to the number of their heavenly protectors. There was no universal pattern, however, and some cities paid official court to a much larger number of saints than others.

In the eyes of the rulers of the communes, ancient local saints stood for more than just the power of the bishop and his clergy, which the communes in a number of respects challenged. The saint's cult and relics symbolized, and guaranteed, the historic continuity of the urban community itself. They represented a source of authority and security on which governments which were, perhaps, all too conscious of their own impermanence and provisional character, needed to draw. To be seen to maintain the veneration due to them was to associate oneself with legitimacy and tradition.

One ancient type in many places retained its ancient potency. Not only did bishop-patrons where they were already established, as at Modena, Milan, Verona and Arezzo, continue to be invoked as the guardians of their cities (usually alongside the omnipresent Virgin), but new ones were set up, for example at Parma, Lucca and, most spectacularly of all, Bologna. Lucca in the fifteenth century officially venerated a veritable roster of ancient bishops. No fewer than five were invoked by way of preamble to the revised statute produced for the republic restored after the fall of Paolo Guinigi in 1430, and printed at the end of the fifteenth century.[1] Martin was present as patron of the cathedral, Regulus by virtue of the presence of his relics, and Paulinus, Frediano and Theodore as ancient bishops of the city, real or supposed. That ancient bishops were not necessarily intimately associated with modern bishops was illustrated by the rise of Petronius to become the chief patron of the city of Bologna. Never associated with the cathedral of Bologna, by the end of the fourteenth century he had outdistanced, if not actually supplanted, St Peter, patron of the cathedral and the original patron of the commune, and acquired his own church.[2]

The diversification of the urban pantheon was, in a sense, initiated by those communes which felt the need, in their early years, for a patron of their own. When the commune of Florence appropriated the Baptist, leaving Zenobius and Reparata to the cathedral clergy, or the Pistoiese adopted James rather than Zeno, or the Lucchese the Volto Santo rather than Martin, they were setting a distance, if only a short distance, between the commune and the saint or saints who stood for the bishop and the cathedral clergy. In several Tuscan cities, however, a new, or renewed, emphasis was being laid on the bishop's old saints by the middle of the fourteenth century, and statutory offerings were instituted to saints who had not previously been entitled to them. Sometimes, but not always, this reflected a recognition of the presence of the saint's relics in the cathedral, and therefore the city's special link with him and its special claim on his patronage. The cathedral patrons of Florence, Pistoia and Lucca all received a greater degree of recognition in the mid-fourteenth century, and so too at Siena did the ancient martyrs whose relics were possessed by the cathedral.[3] Now that the powers of secular government *vis-à-vis* the local church were for most purposes satisfactorily established, the lay rulers of society perhaps felt inclined to emphasize their association with the spiritual arm. The demonstration of the *pietas* of ruling elites, and of their alliance with the church, underlined their respectability and their claim to both moral and political authority. In cities which avoided 'despotism', the right to power was still perpetually contested, and self-defining elites needed all the ideological support they could get. The so-called 'despots', too, usually made it their business to play a leading role in the offering to the civic patron, and to advertise their sponsorship of the festivities.

This chapter will be principally concerned with the expansion of the pantheon and the appearance of new patrons. The diversification of the pantheon did not necessarily entail the promotion of hitherto unknown saints, but new saints were constantly appearing, and a variety of circumstances both fostered the need to multiply the number of a city's heavenly protectors and supplied the means of doing so. Among these circumstances were the incursions of the mendicant orders into urban society and the political emergencies of the thirteenth century.

In an Italian world shaped by the continuation and intensification of the conflicts that had developed in the later twelfth century between Pope and Emperor, between social groups within the cities, and between 'orthodoxy' and 'heresy', the friars rapidly established themselves as the New Model Army outside whose ranks, if the Franciscan Salimbene of Parma was to be believed, authentic modern sanctity could scarcely be found.[4] Their credentials were established at the highest level in this, the first century of formally established procedures for papal canonization. The canonized mendicant saints Francis, Dominic, Antony of Padua, Peter Martyr and, in due course, Louis of Toulouse and Thomas Aquinas rapidly entered the lists of those whose feast-days were kept as legal or public holidays and to whom civic governments made official offerings. While it was doubtless the case, as Salimbene implied, that jealousies existed between the secular clergy and the friars who seemed to be claiming a monopoly of sanctity, the mendicants were in actuality sometimes to be found co-operating with other clergy in the promotion of popular non-mendicant saints, which suggests both that they shared in local patriotism and that they saw such cults as an important instrument of pastoral provision.[5]

Whatever their provenance, new saints were almost invariably additional rather than central to an already-established public cult. In a few places, they were incorporated into the ranks of a city's chief patrons. The same Bishop Guido of Assisi who performed the *inventio* of Rufinus in 1212 also expressed anxiety lest the Pope should divert Francis's activities from his native place.[6] It is unlikely that the bishop could have foreseen how completely Francis would eclipse Rufinus in general fame, but although Francis (and Clare) took up a prominent position alongside him, Rufinus remained (and remains) the patron of the commune. At Padua, the Franciscan Antony, who came to be associated with resistance to the godless tyranny of Ezzelino da Romano, similarly assumed a dominant position, but he added his strength to that of the older patrons Justina and Prosdocimus.

In cities where the Virgin ruled the cathedral and, by common consent, the commune as well, her patronage was often reinforced by that of a saint or saints whose relics were present in the cathedral or elsewhere in the city. At Cremona, as we have seen, Bishop Sicard made what look very much like deliberate efforts, at the end of the twelfth century, to build up the strength of his church in terms of relics. Whether or not his efforts were successful in the difficult years just before and after 1200, the statutes later produced for the city under Visconti rule attest that the old imported Bishop Himerius and the recent layman Homobonus, both enshrined in the cathedral, were the 'special protectors and advocates of the city of Cremona', and that (while the Feast of the Assumption remained the chief civic festival) both these blessed confessors could expect the attendance of the *podestà* with his household on their feast-days.[7] The cathedral had meanwhile acquired the relics of another saint, the blessed Fazio (d. 1289), like Homobonus a layman and charitable activist, and the *podestà* and his *familia* were also to attend on him. For whatever motives, the Cremonese paid a lot of attention to charitable lay saints, among them the wine porter Alberto of Villa d'Ogna, who had been treated with withering scorn by Salimbene.[8] At Cremona as elsewhere, however, the statutes also enjoined the attendance of the officials at the major churches of the city on what might be termed representative feast-days, for example that of Thomas Aquinas at the Dominican church. This requirement expressed in ceremonial form the duty of almsgiving and protection of local churches which urban governments all acknowledged. Saints thus honoured belonged to the civic pantheon in the loosest and widest sense.

At Ferrara the attempt of the bishop and cathedral clergy to achieve the canonization of Armanno Pungilupo – who, to outward appearances, represented popular lay piety – was frustrated by an aggressive counter-campaign on the part of the Dominican-led Inquisition, which succeeded in 1301 in obtaining his posthumous condemnation as a Cathar heretic.[9] Shortly afterwards, an official procession and offering to St Dominic were instituted, the second of the three *oblationes generales* which were being celebrated at Ferrara by the fifteenth century.[10] Salimbene, predictably, thought that the Paduans should be content with the genuine saint, the Franciscan Antony, whom God had given them, and give up their nonsensical cultivation of the layman Antony the Pilgrim; but although the greater Antony was always accorded a higher rank, Antony the Pilgrim enjoyed official honours at Padua from 1269 on (two years after his death), and worked numerous miracles there until well into the fourteenth century.[11]

Not all new saints were candidates for civic recognition; some, obviously, achieved more public importance than others. That Zita of Lucca had become popular within a generation of her death is suggested by the fact that the statutes of 1308 called for a guard to be set on the church of San Frediano on the vigil of her feast, which was also a legal holiday.[12] We may also recall the testimony of those excellent judges, the demons in *Inferno* XXIII, who, gleefully ducking a corrupt Lucchese politician in boiling pitch, could assume that the reader would know where the '*anziani* of St Zita', whom they regarded as such promising material, came from. On general grounds of probability, one might have supposed that the local saint, bodily present in her relics, would have a special appeal to her fellow-citizens, even if it was limited by her affiliation with a particular church and a particular family, the Faitinelli, in whose household she had served all her working life. The Faitinelli, who experienced their ups and downs during the Lucchese political upheavals of the fourteenth century, endowed and adorned the saint's chapel in San Frediano, and sought burial in it.[13] Was it more to Zita's advantage to be associated with the Faitinelli, or to that of the Faitinelli to be associated with her? This patronage is a reminder of the networks of private interest which, often now invisible, underpinned particular cults: a cult might be almost entirely a private concern, almost entirely 'civic', or both.

The attributes of local physical presence and availability to worshippers certainly helped to make Zita's contemporary, Lucchesius, the chief patron of Poggibonsi in the century after his death in 1260. This reformed small tradesman, money-changer and social climber was invoked in the communal statute of 1300 after the Virgin (patron of the mother church of Poggibonsi) and St Laurence (patron of the Augustinians). With the passage of time he advanced to become the chief patron, and his festival became 'from both the civic and the liturgical points of view, the [chief] annual solemnity of the *paese*'. In a period during which Poggibonsi squabbled with its neighbours, notably San Gimignano, and suffered first destruction and then subjugation at the hands of Florence, Lucchesius offered appropriate little services to his fellow-citizens, apart from the normal run of healing miracles: prisoners at Florence awaiting condemnation, and a prisoner held at San Gimignano during a 'war' between the two towns, found themselves miraculously transported back to Poggibonsi. The language applied to Lucchesius in official enactments was of the familiar type: he was 'defender and protector of the said commune'; it was in his name [*vocabulo*] that the commune was 'governed and ruled'; he was to be celebrated so that 'in his mercy he may protect and defend our commune'.[14]

The day-to-day role of a Zita or a Lucchesius, we may surmise, was that of local people whose relics were perpetually and exclusively the possession of the local community. It would certainly be a grievous error to suppose that the appearance of a new cult, even if it inevitably possessed a social and perhaps also a political context, was the result solely of political contrivance. Civic authorities, in lending their support to new cults, were often probably responding, and felt themselves bound to respond, to spontaneous and unforeseen upsurges of religious feeling. Every city produced its own recipe for the enlargement of its cult; and for some to which the opportunity seemed to offer itself, this included a campaign for the canonization of local holy men or (less frequently) women. They were (for a long period between the mid-thirteenth century and the mid-fifteenth) uniformly unsuccessful, but this did not necessarily dampen local ardour for the *beati* in question.[15]

Treviso was unusual, in 1315, in having two saints to promote. In June of that year the death of the layman Henry of Bolzano, commonly known as San Rigo, was followed by intense excitement there. The rulers of the commune not only resolved to sue for the canonization of Henry but felt inspired to renew their earlier efforts on behalf of the centenarian Camaldolese monk Parisius, who had died in 1267 after (allegedly) eighty years as confessor to the nuns of Santa Cristina.[16] It is not clear whether either Parisius or Rigo was a politically significant figure in the narrow sense. The sources collected by Mittarelli suggest that Parisius gave counsel to the Franciscan Bishop Alberto, assuring him in 1262 that he could with confidence face charges laid against him at Rome by brethren of his order. After Parisius's death, Alberto conducted an inquiry into his sanctity and proclaimed an episcopal canonization. He then obtained a decree from the city council that the *podestà* would annually make offering with the people at Parisius's altar, and that the commune would make one hundred pounds available for the campaign for his canonization. Mittarelli believed that the bishop's promotion of Parisius was an act of thanksgiving for his own deliverance from his enemies. He was involved by family ties in a feud with the counts of Castelli, who murdered his brother, Brancaleone Ricci, perhaps in 1263. He then made common cause with Gherardo da Camino, and with his aid was restored to his place.[17] The decree prescribing the offering for Parisius and the commune's commitment to seek his canonization was incorporated into the statute Gherardo published after he assumed power over Treviso in 1283,[18] but even if the cult owed something to da Camino encouragement, Parisius was evidently not regarded as so intimately involved with one particular regime that his cause was dropped on its fall. Like Henry, he was an ornament to the city, an advertisement for its capacity to nurture holy men.

On 15 December 1312, Guecellone da Camino was expelled from Treviso. The citizens were summoned to revolt on that day by the sound of the bells of Santa Maria Maggiore, which led them to believe that it was with the Virgin's assistance that they had returned 'to a peaceful and tranquil *status communis*'. In 1314 a *palio* was voted to the church, so that God might hearken to the prayers of his mother and deign to preserve the city of Treviso, with all the inhabitants of the city and district, inside and out, in this happy condition [*in bono statu et pacifico et communi longissimis temporibus*].[19] On the day after Henry's death on 10 June 1315, the chief magistrates of the commune resolved that measures should be taken to honour him, so that God in his mercy, and through the prayers of the blessed Rigo and all the other saints, should preserve Treviso in a 'state' which, once again, was not merely 'good and peaceful' but *communis*. Two days later, the Council of Three Hundred passed a resolution which was to be incorporated into the volume of the statutes – that is, the new edition produced by the restored communal regime after the expulsion of Guecellone.[20] The resolution of 13 June, with the other documentation produced by Henry's burgeoning cult, provides a fascinating insight into what was involved in the communal sponsorship of a new saint.[21]

The heads of the Dominican, Franciscan and Augustinian orders were associated with the bishop and a commission of eight laymen in drawing up proposals for action. The burial was to be in a suitable place in the cathedral, to be decided upon by the bishop and others; in a fitting and beautiful chapel there was to be an extremely beautiful tomb, of alabaster or porphyry or other fine stone, with iron grilles around it 'for the conservation and good keeping of the body of the blessed Rigo' [*pro conservatione & bona custodia corporis B. Rigi*]. Within two months the *podestà* was to elect two suitable ambassadors to present the case for canonization to the Pope. A register of the miracles of both Parisius and Henry was to be kept, in two copies, one in the communal chancery and the other in the sacristy of the cathedral, so that in due season they might assist in the canonization process. Every year the *podestà*, with the other officials and the guilds, was to 'visit' the body of the blessed Rigo with *doppieri* and candles, as they did the blessed Parisius. When the time came for the translation of the relics to their new shrine, the *podestà* was to attend with all the officials. All expenses incurred 'on the body and conservation of the blessed Rigo' were to be met by the commune. All prisoners for debt who could achieve 'peace' with their enemies within fifteen days were to be released from the communal gaols and their condemnations cancelled from the records, out of reverence for the blessed Rigo. Specifically, the condemnation of Gerardo de Casale (a notary deprived of office by the commune) was to be annulled, 'as it is being said publicly that the said Gerardo did not commit so great an offence that he deserves to suffer further punishment'. Finally, all these resolutions were to be enrolled among the statutes and to have the force of statute, in the pious hope that God would promote the happy state of the city, bring concord among discordant citizens, and establish the enjoyment of perpetual peace.

Within a few days, thought had to be taken for the bread supply, because of the 'multitude of outsiders [*forensium*]' who were flocking to venerate the relics. The prisoners to be considered for release were identified and a vote was taken on every one, which revealed varying degrees of dissent; but a proposal to supply the necessaries of life to Henry's son Lorenzo was carried *nemine contra*. Various administrative complications were ironed out: compensation was voted for the collectors of the usual levy on bread, which had been suspended on 17 June to ensure an abundant supply. On 8 August the commune accepted the offer of a loan to enable it to pay the five hundred pounds it had voted for the building of the chapel and shrine. A competent overseer was appointed to the work early in October. Payments were made to the individuals who had been collecting offerings. Rigo's image was painted, with that of the Virgin and St Lucy, on the wall of the public palace. Another loan was accepted, in mid-December, to make possible a second payment of five hundred pounds.

In January 1316 the bishop made a proposal which ran counter to the intentions of the commune, and therefore provoked debate. He had come to the conclusion that the miraculous effusion of blood from the corpse, and the many miracles that had taken place at the site of the original burial, strongly indicated that it should remain where it was, and not be moved to a new location. Furthermore, the proposed site was too constricted for the numbers of people who would wish to frequent the shrine, and, apparently, so low that the 'big and beautiful' columns that were intended to support the *arca* would have to be cut in half, 'which would be a great shame'. There would be no room for the numerous wax images which were already there, and continued to be put there by the sick who received cures. Suggesting, therefore, that Henry remain where he was, he announced his intention of supplying one thousand pounds immediately to continue the restoration of the cathedral 'in the same way it has been begun', invoking the names of Peter, Liberalis, Henry, and the other saints whose bodies lay in that church; he would recoup the money from the offerings of the faithful. It was as if the bishop wished to remind the officials that the cathedral was the shrine not just of the new saint whose interests they had espoused but of others who, by reason of long antiquity and association with the church and the city, had a claim on his, and their, attention.

The matter was now considered by the Council of Three Hundred, who voted that the relics should be placed in the new shrine, proposing certain necessary alterations to the fabric to make room for it and for one or two flanking altars. In April the bishop renewed the consultations, carefully observing that he intended to do nothing new without the knowledge and consent of the *podestà* and commune. On 21 April arrangements were determined for the translation on the first Sunday in May. A major concern was to ensure the integrity of the relics.[22] The precious body was to be transported in the iron-bound wooden casket it now occupied and placed upon the stone shrine, while twelve large and splendid *doppieri* burnt around it; with the greatest possible speed it was to be surrounded by iron bars, tipped with iron spikes which would serve to support candles and also to preserve the shrine from damage. All the aforesaid was to be at the expense of the commune.

The story did not quite end there, although, as Henry's biographer later acknowledged, the excitement was at its greatest intensity in the first three months after the saint's death. In September 1316 two Ferrarese prisoners petitioned for their release in the name of the blessed Henry. The initiation of the campaign for canonization was delayed by the need to wait on a new papal election, then fatally hampered by lack of funds. In mid-century Henry was none the less safely established alongside Peter as the recipient of official offerings at the cathedral. Vauchez is clearly right to emphasize the striking extent of communal initative in the promotion of the new cult, which extended over matters which might have been thought to pertain to the church;[23] but almost equally interesting is the evidence of both interplay and tension between the bishop and the officials. There was clearly a large area of shared values and common concerns. The officials had to take note if God's will, declared in miracles, seemed to have sanctified a particular site for Henry's resting place, and clergy and people alike were interested in preserving his patronage in its entirety for Treviso by preventing dissipation of the relics.

Sometimes, where any evidence survives, it is possible to discern, or at least guess at, not merely the motives for seeking a canonization, which might seem fairly obvious, but the existence of crosscurrents of opinion among the rulers of urban society. The citizens of Perugia, in the wake of the flagellant excitement which had its origins there in 1260, espoused one of the odder of these saintly causes.[24] The only evidence for the existence of the hermit Bevignate seems to have been his appearance in visions to Raniero de Fasoli, the lay penitent who was the instigator of the devotion. These visions encouraged Raniero to persist in his demands that the bishop should promote a penitential movement. They culminated when Bevignate appeared in order to explain that a letter that the Virgin had left on Raniero's table contained a summons to penitence lest God, irritated beyond endurance by the sins of mankind, should destoy the world. From June 1260 onwards, the *Annales Decemvirales*, the records of Perugia's supreme council, contain references to the campaign for canonization, which had to be renewed whenever there was a change of pope, a not infrequent occurrence in the late thirteenth century. The secular authorities were assisted by the Templars who, until their suppression in 1312, had charge of the church that was built in Bevignate's name.

Occasionally signs of discouragement appear in the records, not least because of the expense in which every fresh attempt involved the commune. Every year in May, the original 'statute' which imposed the duty of seeking the canonization on the officials was formally read; in 1273 the notary Branduccio suggested that the matter should not be pursued, while Oddo Oddi was for referring it to the bishop. In 1276 it was decided to suspend the statute for the time being, but despite renewed disagreement it was resolved in February 1277 to write to Perugian ambassadors who were already at the curia on other business, instructing them to take the issue up. The notary Branduccio appears to have become a vigorous proponent of the canonization; in 1277 the enthusiasts obtained a resolution that if those deputed to plead the cause with the Pope should refuse or procrastinate, they were to be fined for every day's delay. A fresh repulse from the curia prompted another decision to dispense the officials from applying the statute; the issue was frozen until the Pope should come to Perugia or circumstances otherwise change for the better. The statute was none the less incorporated in the collection put together in 1279.[25] In 1285 the *podestà* and *capitano* were enjoined to conduct inquiries in the church to ascertain whether Bevignate's relics were really present (a good question, it might be thought). Hereafter, despite Branduccio's best efforts, there was a lack of enthusiasm for trying again. The 'statute' was still present in the statute collection of 1343.[26] More to the point was the continued recognition of Bevignate's feast-day among the *ferie*.[27] In 1453 the authorities declared his day a full public holiday, defiantly stating: 'although he is not enrolled in the catalogue of saints, it is not to be doubted that he is in celestial glory and among the number of the saints, both because of the sanctity of his life and the frequency of the many and manifest miracles which through his merits the divine goodness in his life and death has performed'.[28]

The much more fragmentary records of the attempt of the commune of Osimo to obtain the canonization of a very different candidate, Bishop Benevenuto Scottivoli, similarly suggest the problems of expense and the resultant divided counsels which attended such enterprises. A native of Ancona, Benevenuto was appointed administrator of the see of Osimo in 1263, when it was deprived of independent episcopal status as a punishment; Urban IV entrusted it to him when it was restored in 1264, and in 1269 also appointed him governor of the March of Ancona.[29] He died in 1282, and virtually all that is known of the canonization campaign which began two years later is derived from two letters written to Jacopo Gozzolini, a noble of Osimo who was *podestà* of Matelica and was appointed one of the ambassadors to pursue the cause with the Pope.[30] Benevenuto might have been thought a good Guelf candidate, and there is in fact some indication that his support came from nobles around the bishop. In March 1284 the Florentine *podestà* of Osimo, Lamberto Cavalcanti, wrote to Gozzolini informing him of his appointment as ambassador and instructing him to make all necessary preparations for his departure after Easter. Hard on the heels of the decision of the Council of the Commune, a group of noble friends also wrote to him from Osimo, supplying a little more detail about the circumstances. The decision had been taken at the petition of the bishop, who said that he had been rebuked by 'lord Jerome' and other magnates for not having urged the case earlier. There had not, apparently, been any difficulty in obtaining the council's approval; the choice of ambassadors had been delegated to the guild priors acting in co-operation with the bishop. The choice had fallen on Gozzolini, and three others, who are named as Sinibaldo, Leopardo and Gasino.

The problem was finance. The guild priors, who are described as 'apparently ill-intentioned' [*velut malevoli*], professed to understand that it had been decided in the Council that no tax would be raised to cover the expenses of the embassy; instead, they proposed to sell a house for a hundred pounds. To Gozzolini's friends this seemed an intolerable deception of the commune, and they proposed that they should in his name go before the Council and express his willingness to undertake the embassy at his own expense, on the understanding that no tax-collection would be made before the first of August. They were evidently anxious lest Gozzolini's reputation should suffer if his fellow-ambassadors should publicly declare their willingness to go at their own expense, with no word from him. To judge from a letter written in 1292 by Bernardo, Cardinal-Bishop of Praeneste, Gozzolini and Leopardo at least had carried out their charge, for he recalled that they had in his presence attested to Benevenuto's miracles. The cardinal referred to Benevenuto as both *sanctus* and *beatus*.[31] The campaign was no more successful than other communal initiatives of the period; but none the less, a cult resulted. According to the communal statutes, Benvenuto's feast was to be kept as a holiday like those of the Virgin and the ancient saints of the cathedral Leopardus, Vitalianus and Victor.[32] It is interesting to note that a solemn *inventio* of the old bishop-saint Leopardus was conducted in 1296, at the very time when the cathedral authorities were promoting the veneration of a recent bishop.[33]

The Aftermath of the Hohenstaufen

The future political shape of Italy was not immediately apparent on the death of Frederick II in 1250. The ultimate outcome waited upon the defeat and deaths, in 1266 and 1268 respectively, of his bastard son Manfred of Sicily and his grandson Conradin, the last Hohenstaufen claimant to the imperial title. The downfall of the regimes of the da Romano brothers in north-eastern Italy, of Oberto da Pallavicino further west, of Tuscan Ghibellinism, each had its own history and took place on different time-scales. Although the chronology and the details varied from place to place, the general trend is clear, if only in retrospect. Everywhere parties were coming to power which were prepared to espouse the cause of the church, to permit the operations of the Inquisition and to profess themselves ready to extirpate heresy and uphold clerical liberties. Everywhere the mendicant orders, who had come to be deeply embroiled in the anti-imperial struggle, cemented their place in urban society; and everywhere saints new and old shared the credit for the happy outcome of the struggle against Antichrist and his cohorts.

The commonplace assumption that the victorious must have God on their side had taken on a special colouring in years of alliance with a church which proclaimed itself to be fighting for ecclesiastical 'liberty'. It was against this background that the honours publicly paid to saintly patrons were in many cities augmented by offerings and other festivities commemorative of notable political and military events, which assured the populace that a victory, or the expulsion of a tyrant, had the stamp of celestial approval.

Saints' days were easily adaptable for commemorative purposes. Even the most secularly minded writers frequently dated events by them; perhaps only notaries thought habitually or readily in terms of a more abstract dating system, Roman or 'modern'. To credit saints with victories over the ungodly that had been achieved on their 'days' became a standard means of enlarging the civic pantheon, in a manner which was specifically identified with the ascendant powers in urban society. In many places, therefore, the pantheon came to exhibit a many-layered structure with, perhaps, one layer of universally venerated saints; a second of saints, both ancient and modern, whose cult was ancient or whose relics were preserved locally; and another consisting of newly instituted commemorative celebrations, which might well implicate saints who had had no previous cult or bodily presence in the city.

The cities of north-eastern Italy which had suffered the tyranny of the da Romano family in the mid-thirteenth century furnish examples of enlargements of the public cult in the late thirteenth and early fourteenth centuries which both incorporated commemorative festivities and gave recognition to the new orders, but also indicated the continuing enthusiasm of the townsfolk for saints native to the place. At Verona, the late-thirteenth-century statutes simply expressed the continuing eminence of the Virgin and Zeno, and indicated no specific additions to the public cult, but the city had a claim on the recently canonized Dominican St Peter Martyr. Milan might have his body, but Peter was a native of Verona [*oriundus verone*], and, as the statutes published in the fifteenth century indicate, his day became not only a legal but a general holiday.[34]

At Padua, however, circumstances made a mendicant saint into the major patron of the city. Stories were told of how the great Franciscan preacher Antony had withstood Ezzelino to his face; it was appropriate that he should be posthumously associated with the liberation of the city. It was on the octave of his feast, 20 June, that a crusading army, under the archbishop of Ravenna, successfully assaulted Padua in 1256. As Salimbene tells the story, a Franciscan lay brother in the army rode round the camp on a mare, carrying a makeshift standard and calling upon the soldiers, in the names of Christ, Peter and Antony, to cast away fear and trust in victory; another lay brother, even more helpfully, reverted to the trade he had followed in the world (in Ezzelino's employment, in fact) and constructed a siege-engine for the crusaders. It was because of the timing of this victory that the Paduans celebrated the octave of Antony's feast with more enthusiasm than the feast-day itself. By contrast, Salimbene adds, the Bolognese of the church party could not bear to hear Antony mentioned, as it was on his day in 1275 that they suffered a grave defeat at the hands of the exiled Lambertazzi party and their allies from Forlì and Faenza.[35] To blame a great saint thus for a defeat sustained on his day might be thought to be the logical corollary of the belief that saints could bring victory, but it is not often given explicit expression.

At Vicenza St Michael the Archangel was adopted as one of the patrons of the commune because it was on his feast-day, 29 September 1259, that Ezzelino da Romano's vicars had left the city, two days after their master's death. The Hermits of San Michele accordingly received a grant towards the building of their church, the Archangel was to be depicted over one of the five gates of the city, and a race to be run for a piece of 'scarlet' was instituted on his day.[36] The Dominican bishop, Bartolomeo da Braganza, was meanwhile able to forward his interests and those of his order by endowing the city with a distinguished relic. Bartolomeo had been translated to Vicenza by Alexander IV in 1256, but while Ezzelino still lived he was forced into exile. He received from Louis IX the gift of a *spina* from the Crown of Thorns, which he brought to Vicenza in 1260, after Ezzelino's death. The place where he built a Dominican church to enshrine it was reputedly a resort of Satan, presumably a haunt of heretics.[37] The communal statute of 1264 recorded a resolution that the bishop would henceforth bless the palms for Palm Sunday at the new church. A feast was instituted in honour of the Holy Crown, to take place on the first Sunday after Ascension Day and to be attended with candles, banners and musical instruments by the fraternities of the city. Among the reprobates excluded from the safe-conduct which encouraged all to come to Vicenza for the celebrations of the Holy Crown were the men of Prata and of Igna, 'who are of the blood of the perfidious da Romano'. The *podestà* was henceforth to take his oath in the name of the Thorn and of Vicenza's old martyrs Felix and Fortunatus, who – with the Virgin, Peter, Christopher and the Archangel Michael – were to be painted on the five gates of the city.[38]

At Treviso, celebrations of St Bartholomew and St Francis commemorated the fall of Ezzelino and Alberico da Romano. The statute compiled for Gherardo da Cammino in 1283–84 prescribed that the bishop and clergy should go on the vigils of Saints

Bartholomew and Francis and sing vespers at their respective churches; on the morning of the feast-day itself, the bishop was to celebrate mass, attended by the *podestà* with his household, who were to offer candles. It was emphasized that 'Such honour and joy is to be expressed as is appropriate to those who from death have come to life, from grief to rejoicing, from sickness to health, we who were liberated from wretchedness and snatched from the lions' den and from the savagery and grasp of Pharaoh by the sole mercy of our lord God.' A brief history is given, in colourful language, of the iniquitous tyranny of Ezzelino and Alberico. It had lasted over thirty years when Ezzelino fell in battle against the Cremonese beside the river Adda. Alberico promptly fled with his wife and all his children to the fortress of San Zeno, and the exiled citizens of Treviso returned to the city 'from divers parts of the world' on 4 October 1259, the vigil [*recte* the feast] of St Francis. The citizens later laid siege to Alberico for about four months, forcing him, on the vigil of St Bartholomew (15 August 1260), to take refuge in the citadel, only to be overcome and captured four days later. The statute now describes not only the execution of Alberico and his sons by the Trevisan, Paduan and Vicentine allies, but also how his wife and daughters were burned (whether or not as presumed heretics is not specified). Without a shade of misgiving or irony, the text emphasizes: 'we believe that all this came about miraculously through the power of God and his saints, we extol the mercy of Almighty God'.[39]

Further west, the credit for the embarrassing defeat that the citizens of Parma inflicted on Frederick II at Vittoria in 1249 undoubtedly went to the city's established patron, the Virgin.[40] By the early 1260s, however, the Virgin had a new assistant. St Hilary of Poitiers had impeccable anti-heretical credentials, which, in addition to his nationality, fitted the pious fraternity that bore his name, soon to be called the *Societas Cruxatorum*, to receive the patronage of Urban IV and Charles of Anjou.[41] The influence of the *Societas* was crumbling within a generation of its foundation, but Hilary himself endured. From later chronicle references it emerges that his feast at Parma was a public event of some consequence, marked by a procession involving all the guilds to the saint's church in the *borgo*. In 1310 it was celebrated 'in the usual way and by a great crowd' when the citizens received word from

Giberto da Correggio, who had attended Henry VII's coronation at Milan, that the Emperor was offering peace to Parma.[42] In the *Ordinarium* of the cathedral of Parma, revised in 1417, Hilary is in more than one place called *advocatus* of the city and people.[43] When, on the death of Filippo Maria Visconti in 1447, the Parmigiani proclaimed a republic and entered into an alliance with the Ambrosian Republic of Milan, Hilary was depicted in episcopal vestments at the head of the treaty, in company with Ambrose: above them, between the *stemme* of the two republics, was inscribed the word *Libertas*. Hilary functioned here as a political figurehead, specific to Parma as Ambrose was to Milan.[44]

In Tuscany, Florence, after the death of Frederick II, fought for pre-eminence as a self-consciously 'Guelf' city. On St Barnabas's day, 11 June, in 1269, the Florentines defeated the Sienese at Colle Val d'Elsa; still more importantly, they defeated the Aretines at Campaldino on the same day in 1289. Over ten years later, according to Compagni, the Florentine nobles recalled their part in this victory when they expressed their resentment of the 'popular' politicians who, in their view, had stripped them of 'the offices and honours of our city'.[45] Barnabas became a new, Guelf, patron as a new order emerged out of the ruins of the effort before and around the year 1300 to suppress noble factionalism and build a broadly based 'popular' regime. In 1311 Cardinal Arnaut de Pellegrue, nephew of Pope Clement V, who had had dealings with the Florentines as his uncle's legate in Italy in 1309-10, sent them a gift of relics of St Barnabas from the papal court at Avignon, knowing, as Villani said, of their great devotion to the saint.[46] After the not entirely easy relations of the first years of Clement V's pontificate, this graceful gesture seems to symbolize the *rapprochement* between the Florentines and the papal court, on the eve of Henry VII's imperial expedition to Italy. In 1325 the Statute of the *Podestà* included regulations for a foot-race to be run in honour of Barnabas, 'since he has been and is the protector and special defender of the people and commune of Florence and also of the *Parte Guelfa*'. The statute also preserves the resolution that a church dedicated to him should be built in Florence, 'as it is fitting that the commune and people of Florence and the *Parte Guelfa* should honour the blessed apostle Barnabas'.[47] In 1473, Benedetto Dei still listed the day on which Barnabas's *palio* was run as among the great festivals of the Florentine year.[48] It was the first of several commemorative celebrations that the Florentines instituted to mark days of triumph or deliverance.

It cannot and must not be assumed that every cult which originated in Italy in the tumultuous epoch of reaction against the Hohenstaufen and the first phase of the Angevin presidency of the Italian Guelfs was closely related to the political context. Sometimes, however, the circumstances are suggestive even where the political connection is not obvious. The seemingly fortuitous second *inventio* of St Paulinus at Lucca is a case in point.

In July 1261 the relics of several alleged martyrs were discovered in the church of Sant' Antonio, foremost among them Paulinus, who was described in an accompanying inscription as 'the first bishop of Lucca and disciple of the apostle Peter'.[49] Ten months previously Lucca had suffered temporary shipwreck, along with Florence and the rest of the Tuscan Guelfs, at the Battle of Montaperti. As the Lucchese annalist Tolomeo Fiadoni remarked: 'The state of Tuscany was totally transformed, because all of imperial Tuscany except Lucca and the Guelf exiles from Florence was converted to the Ghibelline party.'[50] Lucca was now a refugee camp for Tuscan Guelfs, and the Cardinal-Legate Guala was present in Lucca while Paulinus was discovered and celebrated. There were numerous Lucchese prisoners at Siena, one of whom, significantly, was the beneficiary of one of the rediscovered saint's early miracles.[51]

The *inventio* narrative explained that the Lucchese learned from the legend of the saint how the apostle Peter had sent Paulinus to Lucca, 'and how he preached and planted the faith, and faithfully baptized the Lucchese people; and how fondly he loved the city and fervently prayed that God would augment the Lucchese people and preserve them in unity without division and deliver them from heretical pravity and defend the city from the hands of its enemies in perpetuity'. This information supposedly derived from the account in the *Acta* of how Paulinus prayed before his martyrdom for the heavenly and earthly salvation of Lucca, and was assured by an angel: 'Through you, the Lucchese people will without doubt be increased, and with you as patron, the city will never be destroyed by the hands of its enemies.'[52]

The saint's prayers for Lucca, and the angel's assurances, had a great deal of point in the situation of the early 1260s, when it could not, perhaps, be foreseen how brief the triumph of Tuscan Ghibellinism would prove to be. The bishop ordered that the church where the relics had been found should henceforth be named San Paolino, and that the saint's day should be observed for ever. Could it be that he, and the other sponsors of the *inventio*, who perhaps included the papal legate, hoped to bolster the shaken confidence of the populace in Lucca's Guelfism by conjuring up a saint, and a legend, which emphasized an ancient linkage between the city and St Peter? The story conformed to an old model, which had already served for several civic patrons. Ptolemy of Lucca was well-informed enough to know that St Peter had sent Paulinus to Lucca at the same time as he sent Apollinaris to Ravenna and Syrus to Pavia; the Florentine Villani, however, who knew about Frediano, knew nothing about Paulinus.[53] He had not come altogether out of thin air. As we have already seen, he had experienced *inventio* in 1197, when he had been described as bishop and martyr, but not as a disciple of St Peter. This – or so at least it seems – was an addition made in or after 1261.[54] Was Paulinus intended by his rediscoverers in 1261 to be not merely Roman, but Guelf?

This time, at any rate, he endured. Both the Lucchese statute issued in the name of John of Bohemia in 1331 and the earliest surviving communal accounts show the civic authorities making a regular solemn offering to his church on his feast-day.[55] In 1341 the church was rebuilt on a larger scale, and in 1369, to mark the liberation of the city from Pisan rule, a recognition of the relics was performed in the presence of the Emperor Charles IV.[56] One of the *terzieri* into which the city was reorganized after the liberation of 1369 was named after Paulinus, and his legend, including his prayers for the perpetual defence of Lucca from adversity, had by the fifteenth century become the common property of vernacular verse chroniclers of Lucca's struggle against Florentine conquest between 1429 and 1433. Alessandro Streghi, who wrote a vast verse chronicle which went back to Lucca's mythical beginnings, included a paraphrase of the legend, including St Peter's sending of Paulinus to Lucca, the saint's prayers and the angel's reassurances. When Streghi imagined the saints in heaven rushing to intercede with God for the deliverance of Lucca from a conspiracy in 1430, Paulinus, 'primo pastor ... non fu lento/ A domandar la grazia' (the first shepherd ... was not slow/ To beg for grace').[57]

There were numerous supposed disciples of St Peter, such as Syrus of Pavia or Apollinaris of Ravenna, destined to their pastoral charge by the apostle himself.[58] As a late entrant Paulinus had to build up his position, but he did so with some success, although not to the extent that he ever supplanted the Volto Santo as the object of Lucca's emblematic cult. Like Hilary and Barnabas, he survived the transformation of the circumstances in which his cult had been created. Of all these saints, and others like them, it could be said that their *feste* became part of the social calendar, and they themselves became part of the history of their cities. The 'invention of tradition' itself has a long history.

Liberty and Hegemony

The extirpation of the Hohenstaufen did not, obviously, mean the end of political emergencies. Despite the disruptive effect of the imperial expeditions that were to come – those of Henry VII and Louis of Bavaria – a more powerful influence was exerted on the urban cult from about 1300 onwards by the power struggles within and between cities. Cities both large and small found themselves fighting for their liberty against their neighbours, whether those neighbours were princely dynasties or powerful 'republics'.

North-western Tuscany was not the least among the many cockpits of Italy in the early fourteenth century. The murderous turbulence of Pistoiese politics led in 1302 to the establishment of a Florentine–Lucchese condominium over the city. The careers of the Pisan Uguccione della Faggiuola and then of the Lucchese Castruccio Castracani threatened to alter the power balance in the region very much to Florence's detriment, but after Castruccio's death in 1327 Florence established a protectorate over Pistoia, and was among the players who not only nibbled at Lucchese territory but bid for control of Lucca itself, ultimately losing to Pisa. These events can be shown to have motivated innovations in the public cult of the communities involved, both large and small.

No visitor to Serravalle Pistoiese can fail to be aware of its strategic significance, perched on a spur between the valleys of the Ombrone and the Nievole, guarding the western approaches to Pistoia. It was not a fortunate position for its inhabitants, given the combined assaults on Pistoia of the Lucchese and the Florentines in the opening years of the century, and the continuing conflicts thereafter. Uguccione and Castruccio respectively began and completed its castle. According to a story reported by the Franciscan annalist Luke Wadding, a Lucchese assault on Serravalle, mounted after Pistoia surrendered on 11 April 1306, failed because (after four months of siege) St Louis of Toulouse appeared in great splendour on the walls on his feast-day, and the besiegers fell back in disarray. Thereafter the inhabitants vowed perpetual homage to St Louis on 19 August, which was suspended when Castruccio occupied the castle in 1322, but subsequently resumed. In 1427, by which time Serravalle had been taken under direct Florentine rule, expenditure on the *festa* was limited to 12 *libbre*. Louis was identified by his ancestry as Guelf, and few saints could have been more acceptable to the new overlords.[59]

On 7 February 1339 the Florentines acquired control of Pescia, hitherto a Lucchese possession in the Valdinievole between Pistoia and Lucca. Here there is some evidence of a tension between proponents and opponents of Florentine rule which found expression in the attempted manipulation of the cult.[60] St Dorothy, whose feast was celebrated on 6 February, was proclaimed the patron of the commune, in recognition of the end of Lucchese rule and of the exile of Pescia's Guelfs. Later additions to the civic calendar reflected the compulsory identification of Pescian interests with those of Florence: the defeat, on 17 February 1362, of a Pisan force sent to help the Lucchese to recapture Pescia was commemorated by the institution of a celebration of San Policronio; and in 1430, when Francesco Sforza's troops were repulsed from Pescia in the wake of the coup at Lucca which unseated Paolo Guinigi, the feast of saints Abdon and Sennen, which fell on 30 July, also became patronal. All these 'Florentine' cults were located in the church of Santo Stefano, which the new rulers had adopted as their 'chapel', and only much later intruded into the calendar of the mother church of Pescia, Santa Maria.[61] It was at Santo Stefano that, five days after the 'takeover', a parliament was held which elected four citizens to go to Florence to swear fealty.

Santa Maria was in fact temporarily desecrated by the Florentines in 1339 and used as a barracks for their troops. Perhaps its clergy and neighbourhood were identified with resistance to Florentine control. In August the priest of S. Maria, Sinibaldo, and one of his canons, Francesco di Uliviero Vanni, were petitioning the Florentines for the return of the keys of the church.[62] Francesco soon succeeded Sinibaldo as *pievano*, and in summer 1344 took part in a recognition of the relics of a local holy man, the twelfth-century charitable activist Alluccio. This was conducted by the bishop of Lucca, ostensibly at the instigation of Fra Pietro, rector of the hospital of Campugliano, in the parish of Santa Maria, where Alluccio was buried. This was a classic *inventio*, correctly conducted. The saint's relics are known to exist, though long neglected, and are sought and found; the seekers, however, do not dare to investigate their treasure without episcopal permission, which is duly sought and granted; after scrutiny of the saint's *Vita* and due deliberation with the senior clergy of the city of Lucca, the bishop authorizes the veneration of the relics, permitting the rector Pietro to translate them to another more honourable place if he should think fit, but not outside the diocese, and granting the standard indulgence of forty days for the saint's feast. The bishop's inquiries resulted in the proclamation that Alluccio was to be venerated as patron and intercessor of his native land.[63]

The episode makes interesting reading, not least because it makes no reference whatsoever to the Florentine presence at Pescia. The motives of Pietro and his associates in undertaking the *inventio* at this particular moment, and the bishop's interest in asserting his ecclesiastical authority over Pescia in the face of the Florentine intrusion, are left for us to guess at. Was it entirely coincidental that between late 1344 and early 1345 the priest Francesco and all his canons and chaplains were forcibly ejected from Pescia, and one Giovanni Cavalcanti, claiming apostolic authority, was placed in possession of the *pieve* by the bishop of Florence? In February 1345 the bishop of Lucca intervened, and by April it appears that Francesco had been reinstated.

Destined, partly by its own virulent factionalism, to be the prey of its Tuscan neighbours, Pistoia witnessed notable modifications to its public cult in the first half of the fourteenth century. The growing power of Florence over the city, however, in no way detracted from its established patronal cults. In 1316, as Pistoia entered under the protectorate of Robert King of Naples, a resolution was taken to renew the silver altar-frontal of St James. Among the saints depicted in small enamelled roundels on the frontal was Eulalia, who was reputed to have foiled an attempt by Uguccione della Faggiuola to take Pistoia on her feast-day in 1314. Later in the century Eulalia was represented on the altar of St James carrying a model of Pistoia and the chequered standard of the commune.[64] The cult of St Agatha at Pistoia seems to have originated at a similar period and in a similar context. In the later fourteenth century a sumptuous feast was held on Agatha's day, for which hunters in the *contado* were asked to provide. Four young girls, clad in white and crowned with olive leaves, bearing in their hands the arms of Pistoia, were by public decree meant to attend at the morning mass; they got a florin each for their trouble, and a dowry of thirty florins.[65] The feast-days of both Eulalia and Agatha were legal holidays according to the 1344 Statute of the *Popolo*, and they entered, in later centuries, into an iconographic partnership in Pistoiese art.[66]

Noteworthy innovations took place in the 1330s under the Florentine protectorate. It was established Pistoiese custom that the *podestà* and *capitano* who held office in the summer were each obliged to render a *palio* worth twelve Pisan *lire* to St James on his feast-day in July. So that their counterparts who officiated in the winter semester should not escape this duty, it was laid down in Chapter 25 of the Statute of the 1313 *Opera di San Jacopo* that 'those who are not in the said office in the month of July shall be bound to offer such a *palio* on the feast of St Martin or they shall be bound to offer this *palio* on another great and solemn day as the *operarii* of San Jacopo shall decide'.[67] In earlier medieval times Martin had been one of several saints sometimes named as patrons of the cathedral,[68] and a procession on his day was evidently still expected to take place in 1333. On 10 November the Consiglio Generale was asked, in the usual way, to consider what should be done to honour the festival. Ser Vanni Donati rose to propose that the procession should take place 'in the accustomed manner, with this proviso, that no one shall be compelled by the authority of this council to attend the procession'.[69] There is no apparent mention of the procession in subsequent records, and reference to St Martin seems in fact already to have vanished from the new version of the statute of the *Opera di San Jacopo* made in 1329.[70]

As Martin fell, however, Zeno rose. San Zeno had been formally acknowledged as the patron of the church and city of Pistoia, along with St James, from the earliest surviving statutes onwards.[71] It was only now, however, that explicit provision was made for the civic celebration of Zeno. On 2 December 1333, a few weeks after the last mention of Martin's procession, the council was reminded that 'the government was bound to take counsel about the procession of San Zeno, viz., in what manner men with their candles should attend this procession'.[72] When the same issue was raised in November 1336, explicit reference was made to Chapter 41 of the third book of the Statute of the Commune, which laid it down that the council should deliberate annually on the arrangements. In this debate, the officials of Zeno's own *Opera* rose to the occasion. Ser Parmigiano Pucci proposed:

> that the said procession should be honourably performed by the citizens of Pistoia on the day of the vigil of the feast of blessed Zeno at a suitable hour after vespers. And that it should be proclaimed by the *podestà* in the accustomed places in the city of Pistoia that all the men of the city should come at the stated hour to the procession, and from that hour all craftsmen's shops should be closed and remain closed until the feast-day had been celebrated so that no person exercised his trade from that hour and throughout the whole day of the feast and that two notaries be elected for each *porta* who should write down all the names of those who come to the procession with their candles in their hands.[73]

Ser Parmigiano was in effect proposing that the feast of San Zeno should henceforth become a test of civic discipline second only to the feast of St James. Three years previously Vanni Donati had urged that attendance at St Martin's procession should not be compulsory; that there was some opposition to Parmigiano Pucci's motion, for whatever reason, is indicated by the fact that although the routine proposal to make arrangements for the procession was passed by 110 votes to 6, his specific proposals were approved only by 85 votes to 26.[74] As far as Ser Parmigiano was concerned, however, the interests of the saint (and his *Opera*) had not yet been adequately secured. On 6 December 1337 he repeated his proposals of the previous year with some elaboration, and with the important proviso that what he requested should be done both this year and in future years. Furthermore, he asked that annually henceforth the *operarii* of San Zeno should be authorized to purchase at the expense of the commune a *pallium* worth twenty-five pounds, to be carried in the procession and offered by the *anziani* at Zeno's altar, before being 'converted' to the uses of the *Opera* in such manner as should please the *anziani, gonfaloniere* and the *operarii*. When the principle had been agreed, it was proposed that the chamberlain of the commune should be authorized 'without prejudice and without the need for any further decree' to pay the twenty-five pounds for the *palio* to Parmigiano and Giovanni Nolfi, *operarii* of San Zeno.[75]

The *operarii* of St James had not, meanwhile, been inactive on their own account. On 11 January 1333 they reminded the Council that the blessed Bishop Atto had been responsible for bringing the relics of St James to Pistoia, and for building the chapel of St James in the cathedral. They suggested that his body was insufficiently venerated, and proposed improvements to his tomb and altar, requesting a grant for the purpose. One councillor recommended the acceptance of the proposal and the granting of fifty or a hundred pounds; another suggested that agreement should be reached with the canons that all offerings made at the altar should be devoted to its repair and ornamentation.[76]

Should these developments in the Pistoiese public cult be related to the city's political circumstances under virtual Florentine rule? The association of the cult of St James with the pro-Florentine Guelf interest had already, as we have seen, been expressed in the work done on the saint's silver altar-frontal in 1316. It was certainly under the eye of Florentine officials that the discussions of the veneration of Zeno and Atto took place in the 1330s. Parmigiano Pucci, *operaio* of San Zeno, had been prepared to be identified as a supporter of the Florentine interest: on 26 December 1331 he spoke in the Consiglio Generale in favour of granting power to the Florentines.[77] Atto's Vallombrosan associations seem to have helped to secure him a Florentine public. Among the miracles excited by his translation into the cathedral of Pistoia in 1337 was the cure of a Florentine tailor, who was told by a Pistoiese woman:

'My friend, a certain saint has recently appeared in the city of Pistoia, Atto by name, who was once abbot of Vallombrosa, of very holy life, and then bishop of Pistoia: now that his precious body has been newly rediscovered, he is doing many and numberless miracles.' There were other Florentine beneficiaries in the course of the century, including a *podestà* of Pisa.[78]

To honour Atto was also, however, automatically to honour James. Reliefs on the tomb which Atto occupied from 1337 until in the seventeenth century he was translated to a chapel on the right of the high altar bear witness to his enduring claim to fame; they show him sending for, and receiving, the relics of St James.[79] Elsewhere in the cathedral there is ample evidence of the fourteenth-century alliance of James and Zeno. The tomb of Dante's friend and fellow-poet, the legist Cino da Pistoia (d. 1337), is crowned by statuettes of Zeno and James flanking the Virgin and Child; while the tomb of Bishop Baronto Ricciardi (d. 1348) shows the bishop himself presented to the Virgin and Child by San Zeno, while his nephew Bonifazio is presented by St James. Statuettes of both Atto and Zeno appear (with Eulalia) among those which flank the magnificent figure of James as pilgrim saint in the centre of the renovated and enlarged altarpiece in his chapel.[80] In 1348 a Pisan benefactor offered money to assist towards the provision of organs which should be placed in the middle of the church so that they might serve both the choir of San Zeno and the chapel of St James.[81]

Villani recorded that when Pistoia came to terms with Florence in May 1329, the Pistoiese Ghibellines ordered the eradication of all emblems of 'the eagle, the Bavarian and Castruccio' and placed on their banners 'the golden shells of San Jacopo'.[82] Would it be fanciful to speculate that Martin's disappearance from the revised Pistoiese statutes in 1329 had anything to do with his association with Lucca and 'that most pestilential tyrant Castruccio degli Antelminelli'?[83] Villani is our witness that on at least two occasions Castruccio made spectacular use of St Martin's feast-day – first in 1325 when he paraded the Florentine prisoners of war taken at Altopascio through the streets to mark the occasion; and second in 1327, when he entertained Louis of Bavaria for the *festa* and Louis proclaimed him Duke of Lucca and of the cities and bishoprics of Pistoia and Volterra.[84] After Castruccio's death in 1328,

Lucca declined into a prize over which German mercenaries and various Italian powers, Florence among them, haggled and squabbled. A notable feature of the public cult during the troubled years after 1328, a period when Castruccio tended to be remembered nostalgically at Lucca, was the increased emphasis placed on St Martin.

The 1308 Lucchese statute makes no mention of any communal celebration of St Martin's Day (11 November), although it does provide for the placing of a guard on the cathedral on the vigil of the feast to prevent criminal or indecent behaviour, a sign both of respect and of the expectation that large numbers of the faithful, especially devout women who might be molested by less devout men, were routinely expected to be present.[85] The robing, at public expense, of the statue of St Martin with the Beggar which stood high on the cathedral façade is first mentioned in the statute produced for John of Bohemia in 1331, as a custom 'hitherto observed'. Does this mean simply that it had not previously been thought necessary to put it in writing, or had it, and perhaps the festival as a whole, recently received added emphasis under Castruccio?[86]

Given the gaps in the sequence of account-books, it may be entirely fortuitous that the first extant record of expenditures on Martin's robing dates from 1334, but this was no ordinary year. Warfare made the customary celebration of the Volto Santo impossible and also, it would appear, prevented the running of the annual race for San Regolo on 1 September. The offerings normally made to St Augustine on 28 August and on the feast of the Nativity of the Virgin at the church of Santa Maria della Rosa on 7 September were paid for on time,[87] but these celebrations did not involve the convergence of large numbers of people from outside the city. On 5 November John of Bohemia's vicar issued a proclamation bidding all citizens and subject communities to bring their usual candles to the *luminaria* of the Holy Cross, which was going to take place on the vigil of St Martin. On 13 November the vicar's deputy announced that inquisition would be made to establish who in the city had not brought their offering, and similarly into defaulters from the communities of the *contado* and *distretto*.[88] The spicer Luporino had been paid on 10 November for the three hundred pounds of wax necessary for the candles that the *anziani*, their household servants and officials and the districts [*contrate*] of the city and suburbs were to bring to the *luminaria*. The accounts show that the customary ceremony of releasing prisoners had also taken place on St Martin's day.[89] On the 28th the *anziani* authorized payment of the expenses for the ceremony of robing the statue of St Martin and the Beggar, referring to 'a long-observed custom'. They also authorized payment for the three races (for men on horseback, men on foot, and women) that it had presumably been impossible to run on St Regulus's day (1 September); they too had been run on St Martin's day.[90] To permit the year to pass without the customary demonstration of obedience from citizens and subjects was clearly not to be tolerated, and St Martin's day was opportunely timed to serve as a fallback position.[91]

Whether or not the earlier silence of the statutes is significant, it was only in 1342 that Martin, *noster protector*, was awarded by statute the annual offering of forty pounds of wax that was already the commune's standard offering on major feast-days. This apparent innovation was accompanied by a new regulation prescribing penalties for unseemly behaviour in consecrated places, most specifically the cathedral.[92] The interests of Martin and the Holy Cross, unlike the interests of Zeno and James at Pistoia, were managed by one office of works. This is indicated by the fact that according to the 1331 statute the messenger of the *anziani* was to pay the *operaio* of the Holy Cross for the old vestments of St Martin. After 1369 the commune's method of paying for *luminarie* changed, and the *operarii* of the city's churches had to buy the wax themselves and claim reimbursement; the same official claimed the payments due to the Vultus and to Martin.

A glimpse of the Lucchese pantheon as it was popularly perceived in the fifteenth century is afforded by the doggerel poems which were written to celebrate Lucca's deliverance from the war of conquest which in 1429 the Florentines ill-advisedly launched against the city. One anonymous versifier declared, when a conspiracy to deliver Lucca into Florentine hands was unmasked in October 1430:

>Il nostro Santo Volto pretioso
>Non vuol che 'l crudo Popul Fiorentino
>Entri in Lucha palese, nè nascoso:
>Così non piace al buon San Paolino,

San Martino e San Regolo glorioso,
San Benedetto, ancora San Davino,
Et Santo Agnello, e ancor la beata Sita
Guardan Lucca, che non sia tradita.[93]

Alessandro Streghi more graphically imagines the saints in heaven kneeling before God to pray for Lucca's deliverance from conspiracy. The Virgin, Peter, Paul, the Baptist, Stephen, Laurence, Lucca's holy bishops, and every saint whose relics the city possessed, are mentioned in no particular order. Zita, too, runs to kneel and to pray 'for her Lucchese'.[94]

Florence: Saints and Power

Pistoia, Lucca, and a host of other places in both northern and southern Tuscany were put under pressure in the fourteenth century by the growing power of Florence, with consequences, direct and indirect, for their veneration of their saints, some of which we have observed. What of Florence itself?

On 20 October 1372 the Florentine Office of the Mint, the *Zecca*, commissioned from Jacopo di Cione the magnificent altarpiece of the Coronation of the Virgin which hangs today, in its original frame, in the gallery of the Accademia.[95] It depicts the old and the new in the Florentine 'pantheon' in its up-to-date form. The saints are grouped at the foot of the raised dais on which Christ crowns His Mother. Only John the Baptist and John the Evangelist stand; the rest kneel in front of them. To the left, Matthew is present as patron of the *Zecca*, with St Catherine. Behind them, St Anne can be seen holding a model of the city. This group is completed by Pope Victor, holding both the palm of martyrdom and the bays of victory. On the right are Zenobius, Barnabas and Reparata, with Antony Abbot behind them. A fleur-de-lys is visible on Zenobius's vestments; Reparata carries the communal standard, a red cross on white. The principal subject of the altarpiece expressed Florence's claim to a share in the universally available patronage of the Virgin; there were stories attached to the presence of several of the other saints.[96]

New admissions to the ranks of those who received official honours at Florence were strictly limited to those who had done the state some service. Barnabas was an early trailblazer. St Anne then helped to rid the city of the short-lived tyranny of the Duke of Athens in 1343. By expelling the tyrant on her feast-day, she avenged the insult done to her daughter, on the feast of whose Nativity he had taken power in the previous year.[97] Just over twenty years later, on 29 July 1364, Florence obtained a victory over Pisa which was both so complete and so unexpected, according to Filippo Villani, that the *Parte Guelfa* decreed the annual celebration of St Victor, whose day it was, as of a *patrono de' guelfi* (like St Barnabas, as Filippo explicitly observed). A chapel was founded in the cathedral (which was in process of rebuilding), and an annual offering by the *Parte*, a *palio*, and a public holiday were all instituted.[98] St Antony was also particularly associated with the Guelfs. In 1383 he was honoured by 'the most holy Guelf party' in recognition 'that the Guelfs had regained the regime and offices [*lo stato e gli onori*] in our city of Florence'.[99]

The authorities also, however, recognized their duty to do public homage to the ancient saints of the bishopric, Zenobius and the Syrian martyr Reparata. In the mid-fourteenth century the Florentines decided to realize the potential of Zenobius. In January 1331 a solemn *inventio* of his relics was performed, attended by the archbishop of Pisa and the bishops of Florence, Fiesole and Spoleto (who was a Florentine). Giovanni Villani records the event, and also describes the splendid reliquary in which the saint's head was now enshrined. The relic was to be annually displayed to the people, while the rest of the body was replaced with great devotion where it had been. The desire to make Zenobius visible and portable, so that he could enter more fully into the life of the city, is noteworthy. The bells of the cathedral rang almost continuously, day and night, for ten days, while the bishops granted indulgences to the populace who 'visited' the relic. If Villani is to be believed, it was all a great success.[100]

The chronicler's description suggests that this was an ecclesiastical rather than a communal initiative. It came in fact at a time when the authority of the bishop in urban society was in need of buttressing. Later fourteenth-century evidence, however, shows Zenobius invoked in the defence of secular establishment values. One dismayed observer of the Ciompi revolt in 1378 thought that Florence owed it to the prayers of the Baptist and Zenobius, together with other holy men and women of the land, that things had not been worse.[101] The 'Panciatichi' chronicler testifies to the processional use of his head on several occasions in the last two decades of the century.[102] In March 1382 Zenobius's head was carried in procession with many other relics, at a time of anxiety about subversive activity by exiles and two recently disbanded guilds. He helped to celebrate the news of the taking of Arezzo in November 1384, and the results of the scrutiny of June 1385 which established 'good Guelf citizens' in firm control of office.

The image of the Madonna of Impruneta was also carried in this procession, and a curious incident took place when the bishop refused to permit the image to precede the head of Zenobius. The disagreement threatened to create a riot, and the bishop and his entourage had to take refuge in the house of Bartolomeo Ridolfi. Eventually, by order of the priors, the procession continued, with the episcopal party going before and the image following some considerable way behind. Zenobius's identification with the bishopric, and therefore with the city, was presumably felt (at least by the bishop) to entitle him to precedence; or perhaps it was felt that a relic should precede an image, even if the image was of the Mother of God. Zenobius's influence, and that of St Philip in the form of his arm, was invoked to assure the stability of the city in May 1387, when the *signori* ordered a great procession after the political representation of the lesser guilds was cut back. In October 1390 both relics, and the Madonna of Impruneta, were exhibited with great pomp and splendour in the Piazza della Signoria. These solemnities had a multiple purpose: to induce God to stay the plague, and to bring peace between the Florentines, the Sienese and Giangaleazzo Visconti. As if it were not already apparent that Zenobius was acceptable to the Guelf establishment, on 25 May 1391 the *Parte Guelfa* went to make 'a most noble offering' to Zenobius. The chronicler explained that because he had belonged to the Gerolami family, which was regarded as Ghibelline, the *Parte* had never previously deigned to offer to him; but now all was forgiven and forgotten.

It has been suggested that over the long process of its building, the cathedral came more and more to express the dignity and the pretensions of an increasingly patrician ruling group.[103] The new cult of St Victor was located in the cathedral and not in the

Baptistery which, in time past, had received the relics of St Philip and St Barnabas. As an inhabitant of the cathedral, Zenobius benefited modestly from this trend. He received some fresh emphasis, for example, in 1432 when the *Arte della Lana* decided to translate him to a new position in the easternmost chapel, and to commission a new altar and shrine from Brunelleschi and Ghiberti.[104] A diarist noted how Pope Eugenius IV, on entering Florence in January 1439, went in great state to Santa Maria del Fiore and censed the head of Zenobius.[105] Zenobius also had associations with the Medicean church of San Lorenzo,[106] and his presence in the Florentine painting of the middle and late fifteenth century, from Domenico Veneziano to Botticelli, attests to some continued interest in him throughout the Medicean period, although at the end of the century his biographer, Clemente Mazza, was lamenting the public neglect of his cult.[107] If he never attained an eminence comparable to that of the Virgin or the Baptist or even some of his newer competitors, Zenobius and his relics at least belonged entirely to Florence. In this he resembled Geminianus at Modena and Donatus at Arezzo, and differed from Zeno at Pistoia or Martin at Lucca.

Reparata as well as Zenobius achieved greater fourteenth-century prominence. According to the statute of 1325, the Florentine *podestà* was obliged to see that the feasts of both Reparata and Zenobius were observed throughout the city, but it was only on the vigil of Santa Reparata that the officials were obliged to offer candles at the cathedral, which went to the benefit of the *Opera*.[108] In 1351, as Matteo Villani dolefully reported, the Florentine authorities tried to use the good offices of the newly crowned King Louis of Naples to obtain the arm of Santa Reparata from the abbey of Teano, but the abbess of Teano swindled them and palmed them off with a replica made in wood and gesso, which was discovered only in October 1356, when the masters who had been commissioned to adorn the relic with gold and silver and precious stones discovered its true composition.[109] The city fathers' determination to enhance the cult of Reparata led them, in 1353, to undertake a little historical research into the question of why the cathedral was dedicated to her, and why 'by ancient custom' a *palio* was run on her day. The story that they discovered (which was in fact already known to Giovanni Villani) was that it was on her day that Florence had been delivered in the early fifth century by the forces of the Emperor Honorius from the threat of the Goths, Suevi and Vandals under Radagasius. The imperial forces were few, and the prayers of Zenobius, then bishop, had been instrumental in the victory. It had to be admitted that the Florentines were not then 'in a state of great opulence' [*in troppa magnificenza*]; therefore they could institute only a *palio* of eight *braccia* of a cheap red cloth, which was run on foot from the cathedral to the gate of San Piero Gattolino. The now-established custom of the commemorative celebration clearly disposed contemporaries to project the practice far back in time. Now that the city was in a position to do a little better, the priors ordered twelve *braccia* of fine scarlet (which, according to the statute of 1355, might cost up to forty florins) and decreed that (like Barnabas's) the race should be run on horseback.[110]

The statute of 1415 bears witness to the institution of several more offerings in thanksgiving for victories in the generation since the Zecca altarpiece had been painted. St Julian was to be thanked for the defeat of the regime of the Ciompi in 1378 (although this is not explicitly stated in the text of the statute),[111] St Augustine for the victory obtained against the forces of Giangaleazzo Visconti in Mantuan territory in 1397,[112] and St Dionisus for the conquest of Pisa in 1406.[113] The public cult had something of the character of a series of commemorative tableaux of Florentine history. The saints favoured were not (as it happened) representatives of quasi-independent modern religious institutions, but figures from the remote sacred past. The first 'modern' or mendicant saint to be accorded the honour of the attendance of the priors, the captain of the *Parte Guelfa* and other notables at his festivity was, by a decision taken in August 1388, the Franciscan St Louis of Toulouse, whose Guelf Angevin identity was reinforced by the statement that he 'was of the royal house of France'.[114] In 1425 the officials of the *Parte* resolved in addition to make an offering to Louis at Or San Michele, where Donatello's great gilded bronze statue now stood.[115]

The Local Man

With the passage of time and the stilling of the echoes of the struggle against the Hohenstaufen, the defence of 'liberty' retained its spiritual overtones; the saints continued to be invoked, to act, and to receive thanksgiving, in its interest. This labour was often, as it were, divided between saints of different types: on the one hand the saint whose bodily presence, often of long standing, guaranteed his kindly interest in the local inhabitants; on the other the saint, previously perhaps unconnected with the city, on whose anniversary victory or deliverance had been experienced. In different ways, both met the need for saints who belonged to the city in a special, even exclusive, sense, and who had written chapters in a unique local history. The supremacy of the old-established civic patron, who might well be a local saint anyway, was rarely disturbed by these supplementary devotions. The biggest challenge to their standing that such patrons faced, in the fourteenth and fifteenth centuries, was usually from the all-conquering Virgin. Recent saints of local provenance also retained considerable appeal. Occasionally, however, the cult of a saint who was neither local nor recent, nor apparently associated with any specific victory, achieved civic prominence for reasons which may remain somewhat obscure to us.

The cult of the Spanish martyr Vincent at Vicenza, for example, emerged into prominence in the later fourteenth century. Although it was in the brief period of Visconti rule (1387–1404) that the church dedicated to him was built, no convincing reason for associating the saint with the Visconti has been advanced. The day of Vicenza's submission to Giangaleazzo (21 October 1387) was the feast of St Ursula, to whom a church was also dedicated. Vincent was not among the saints celebrated in the aftermath of the da Romano tyranny in the late thirteenth century, but it seems that his cult antedated the Visconti regime, if by only a few years, probably owing its impetus to a punning etymology which derived the city's name from the name of the martyr and perhaps reinforced by the further verbal association with the Latin *vincere*, 'to conquer'.[116] The fifteenth-century statutes offer no enlightenment, referring to Vincent simply as 'our fostering patron and protector [*almus patronus et protector noster*]'. Whatever his attractions, Vincent was obviously not the exclusive possession of Vicenza. The local martyrs Felix and Fortunatus were persistently referred to, like other saints whose relics were present in Vicenza, as 'holy bodies'. Their day, like St Michael's and the Feast of the Thorn, celebrated on the first Sunday after Ascension Day, were still numbered among the principal festivals in the fifteenth century. So was that of St Vitalis, which commemorated the Venetian takeover in 1404. The language of the statutes implies that Felix and Fortunatus were still presumed to exercise a special degree of patronage over the city, while the authorization of payments to subsidize the attendance of religious personages at the Feast of the Thorn, and the grant of safe-conduct in connection with it, suggests that this was the occasion on which the city authorities expected to play host to the greatest number of outside visitors.[117]

Where the supreme patron was a great saint to whom city or cathedral could not pretend to have an exclusive claim, there might be special incentives to introduce local talent into the pantheon. St Peter's peculiar property was his association with the papacy, which in certain circumstances could be a disadvantage rather than an advantage to him. Although he was a figure of princely power, he did not have the Virgin's ability so to multiply aspects, images and presences that her patronage could be felt and claimed in every city of Italy at once. Several 'cities of St Peter' afford particularly interesting examples of the process of the multiplication of heavenly patrons to meet local needs.

The cathedral of Treviso was among the many dedicated to Peter, who was declared in the statute of 1313 to be 'head of our city', and was therefore entitled to 'invocation' and 'honour'.[118] As we have already seen, both the diocesan clergy and the commune paid special regard to Liberalis, whose relics the cathedral possessed, and in the late thirteenth century and the early years of the fourteenth the city was rapidly acquiring both new saints and commemorative celebrations, as well as elevating the Virgin to a greater prominence than before. At Faenza, too (where the successor of St Peter was ultimate overlord), we can see evidence of both the need to claim a share of the Virgin's attention and the importance attached to protectors who could offer their bodily presence and exclusive patronage. Though they are worthy of attention, there is nothing in any sense abnormal about these developments. A more extraordinary development took place in Bologna, another city supposedly subject to the papacy, where Peter was all but displaced as supreme patron by another saint whose cult began, in relative obscurity, only in the twelfth century.

Peter was undoubtedly the chief and original patron of the commune of Faenza. As we have seen, already in the mid-twelfth century tribute was being exacted from subject communities on his feast-day. A capitular charter of 1136 described him as 'universal patron of the whole city and bishopric of Faenza'; the assembly met in the cloister of his church; and he was called upon in battle against Ravenna in 1145.[119] In 1226 and 1236, the Faventines were hailing Peter as their 'standard-bearer' [*vexillifer*]; when they found themselves in a tight corner in 1228, fighting shoulder to shoulder with some Florentines, they joined in calling upon their 'key-bearer' [*Clavigerum*] and the Florentines' Baptist.[120] In Lanzoni's view, Peter reigned alone at Faenza until the fifteenth century.[121]

It is apparent from the statutes produced in 1410 by Gian Galeazzo Manfredi with the permission of the Pope, however, that here as elsewhere the Virgin had established herself among the supreme intercessors in whom the commune officially placed its faith. The statutes begin by invoking, besides the Virgin and Peter and Paul, St Apollinaris (presumably as the patron of the metropolitan see of Ravenna) and the priest Terentius who, it seems, was the first of the later 'four holy protectors' to stake his claim.[122] The offering to be made by the officials and guilds at the Feast of the Assumption at the monastery of Santa Maria Forisportam is described at great length; a *bravium* of eight *brachia* of green cloth was to be contested. The feast of St Peter and St Paul was in fact to be celebrated on identical lines, with the difference that the *bravium* competed for on that occasion was to be of scarlet.[123] In so far as the wording of the statute betrays motivations, the purpose of the celebration of the Assumption was to secure the protection and intercession of the Virgin;[124] while Peter and Paul were 'the patrons and special defenders of this our city', and the desire to venerate them 'greatly' [*immense*] at their cathedral church was stated without further elaboration.[125] There was also to be an offering to the priest Terentius, 'whose body rests in the city of Faenza', which took place at his church. This was to be attended by the *podestà* or his vicar, and the *anziani*, together with the officials of all the guilds. Clearly, it was the saint's corporeal presence that commanded respect.[126]

The revised version of the statutes published by the papal government in 1527 adds another of the 'four holy protectors',

Emilianus, as well as John the Baptist and St Joseph, to the number of the saints 'by whose care and vigilance the city is preserved from all adversity'.[127] The regulations for offerings, including the feasts of the Assumption and of St Peter and Paul, were consolidated more economically than before into one rubric.[128] The church of St Terentius was one of three which received official oblations in the course of the year. By this time the concept of the 'four holy protectors' of Faenza was beginning to take shape. The four – Terentius, Emilianus, Savinus and Peter Damian – were saints who fulfilled the need for local connections and physical presence.

It was Lanzoni's view that the idea of classifying the four saints as a group under this title originated with the Imolese humanist Giovanni Antonio Flaminio, who compiled his lives of them between 1526 and 1534, prefacing the first, the life of Terentius, with a succinct explanation of the *raison d'être* of the patron saint.[129] In his life of Savinus, Flaminio described the saint as one of 'the four ... whom the people of Faenza by public vote established out of all the saints to be venerated by them as the special defenders of the city'.[130] An inscription in the cathedral in fact records a solemn vow taken in 1512 to keep the feast-days of these four saints with no less solemnity than Sundays, if God was pleased to avert the threat of the forces of Gaston de Foix, in the face of whose advance Raimondo Cardona, commander of the forces of the Holy League, had retreated within the walls of Faenza.[131] The feasts of Savinus and Peter Damian, however, are mentioned merely among the *ferie* in the statute of 1527,[132] and only Terentius receives an official offering, as he did already in 1414.

Of course, neither he nor his three colleagues had come from nowhere. The priests of urban churches dedicated to St Emilianus and St Terentius are mentioned in the mid-twelfth century; a *regio S. Terentii* is documented in 1157, a *regio sancti Emiliani* in 1182. In 1321 Bishop Ugolino ordered that these two saints should be celebrated in the city and its suburbs.[133] Terentius was a priest of uncertain date, Emilianus a peripatetic 'Scottish' bishop who died near Faenza on his way back from a pilgrimage to Rome. Savinus was an Umbrian bishop and martyr; he, or at least a saint or saints of the same name, was venerated and relics were claimed in several places in Italy, including Siena.[134] There was a *regio S. Sabini* outside the Porta Imolese in 1172. Although the cathedral of Faenza did not begin to celebrate Savinus's feast until some time after 1264, it was among the most solemn by 1367. In the fifteenth century his principal feast was celebrated on 7 December and his translation on 14 June. In 1448 an inventory recorded the possession of his arm; his chapel was newly built in 1471, and a marble *arca* commissioned for it from the Florentine sculptors Giuliano and Benedetto da Maiano.[135] Flaminio reported the belief, attested by Benedetto da Maiano's reliefs on the new tomb, that Astorgio II Manfredi had translated Savinus from the rural church of Fusignano, which Manfredi acquired, briefly, in 1438. Lanzoni suggested that the presence of a splendid Byzantine sarcophagus, fit for a martyr, in the church of San Savino at Fusignano gave rise to the belief that the saint himself was interred there.[136] It would not have been implausible for a *signore* to make a gift of such relics to the mother church of his capital city.

Peter Damian was, it seems, for nearly four hundred years exclusively the possession of the monks of his burial-place, Santa Maria Forisportam outside the walls of Faenza, where he was translated to a new shrine in April 1354. His feast-day, however, was declared a *feria* and rest-day in Galeazzo Manfredi's 1411 statutes for Brisighella and the Val di Lamone.[137] The enlargement of the walls of Faenza in the fifteenth century brought Santa Maria Forisportam within the city, which may well in itself have sharpened awareness of Damian's potential as another heavenly protector. The treatment of the other three 'holy protectors' suggests that by *c.* 1500 there was a keener sense of the need to harness the power of the saints who honoured Faenza as their resting place and to publicize their presence. Bodily presence within the city, however, was not everything. The statutes never awarded an official offering to the humble cobbler Nevolone (d. 1280), although he received burial in the cathedral.[138] The four holy protectors offered, in addition to their relics, varying combinations of higher status and greater antiquity. Savinus now lay in the cathedral, in a new and up-to-date shrine, and by about 1485 both Terentius and Emilianus also possessed new shrines.[139]

Like that of Faenza, the cathedral of Bologna belonged to St Peter, and so too, originally, did the commune. Peter received the *pallia* which, as we have seen, Imola was obliged to render to Faenza and Bologna at various times in the twelfth century.[140] Before 1200 St Petronius, though he was brought before the public eye by the *inventio* of 1141, remained the property of the monks of Santo Stefano.[141] His rise to the eminence expressed in the building of his huge church at the end of the fourteenth century reflects the need felt by the citizens to have a protector more precisely made to their measure and symbolic of their history than the prince of the apostles could be.

In the *Vita* written by a monk of Santo Stefano, perhaps around 1180, Petronius was already associated with the rebuilding of Bologna after its mythical destruction by the Emperor Theodosius II, but he was most important as the founder of Santo Stefano itself. The legend of Theodosius's destruction of Bologna was derived from a *mélange* of sources: Barbarossa's recent sack of Milan, and his threats to Bologna and destruction of her walls; the supposed destruction of Milan by Lambert in the tenth century, as told by Landulf Senior (itself a hotchpotch of traditions); Theodosius I's destruction of Thessalonica; and St Ambrose's reference, in a letter to Faustinus of Bologna, to the 'half-destroyed corpses of cities [*semirutarum urbium cadavera*]' to be seen in Emilia, which so contrasted with their antique glories.[142] St Ambrose bulked large in these miscellaneous recollections, and for a time he played a civic role at Bologna in his own right. It was well known that he had rebuked the first Theodosius for his treatment of Thessalonica, and forbidden him to set foot in Milan until he had done penance. He also had an authentic association with Bologna, in that he had been present at the *inventio* of the martyrs Agricola and Vitalis.[143]

If any saint, before 1200, was specifically associated with the history of Bologna, it was in fact Ambrose. The author of the *Vita* of Petronius imagined that Ambrose had extended his protection to Bologna and forbidden Theodosius to enter the city. The consuls deliberated in the church of St Ambrose, which was eventually to be destroyed to make way for the huge basilica of San Petronio. An offering was already made to Ambrose according to the statutes of 1250; it was not until 1253 that Petronius received one.[144] There is some evidence for knowledge of the content of the Petronius legend, though not necessarily for any particular interest in Petronius himself, in Bolognese academic circles: the glossators Azzo, Accursius and Odofredus used Theodosius's rebuilding of Bologna as proof of Bologna's standing as an *urbs regia*.[145] It was after the middle of the thirteenth century that the cult of Petronius began its advance. His fortunes were bound up with Guelf and popular politics, and sometimes explicitly with the Geremei faction;[146] but – in this, perhaps, somewhat resembling St Hilary at Parma – he proved able to surmount what might have been a limitation to become the distinctive symbol of Bolognese identity and autonomy in the face of a variety of challenges and adversaries.

His role in Bologna's history was promoted by three forgeries, perpetrated perhaps a little before the middle of the thirteenth century. The first of these was an alleged privilege of Theodosius II (d. 450) for the *studium* of Bologna. The second recorded Petronius's personal intervention with the Emperor to secure this and other wide-ranging privileges, which were proclaimed in the presence and with the consent of the then Pope (Celestine I, 422–32). Petronius (supposedly a Greek and a kinsman of the Emperor) was thus associated with the privileged status of the university (threatened in the early thirteenth century by secession and by Frederick II's attempted suppression in 1226) and with the territorial expansion of the city. Theodosius II was imagined to have authorized boundaries which included most of what Bologna was actually seeking to gain, in the mid-thirteenth century, at the expense of Imola, Modena and Ferrara. The minatory clauses at the end of the privilege echoed those of Frederick II's diploma for Bologna in 1220. The third forgery reproduced Ambrose's letter forbidding Theodosius I to enter Bologna, as imagined by the author of the *Vita*, with the improvement that not only kings but magnates were now forbidden to enter or 'deceive' Bologna. Although Gina Fasoli did not think they could have been intended seriously, these forgeries were copied into the *Registrum Novum* of the commune.[147]

There was more to come. A vernacular legend, dependent on the tale told in the *Registrum Novum*, was in circulation by the end of the century. Lanzoni supposed it to be a product of the heyday of the popular Guelf commune which effectively came to an end with the ascendancy of the Pepoli after 1327. A predictable feature of the development of the legend was the total confusion of the chronology and of the two Emperors Theodosius. Petronius, having obtained the privileges from Theodosius II at Constantinople, returns to Bologna, where his arrival is foreknown by St Ambrose (dead in 397, unfortunately for the plausibility of the story). Together with Ambrose and Ursicinus of Ravenna, Petronius proclaims the imperial privileges and rebuilds the city, planting four crosses in conspicuous locations. Ambrose solemnly writes down a prohibition against interference in Bologna by any king, prince, lord or tyrant. Petronius, meanwhile, having acquired a stupendous collection of relics, has the idea of building Santo Stefano in the likeness of the Holy Sepulchre; and the widow Eulalia, with his support, pays for the building of San Pietro. Petronius is also responsible for attracting scholars to the city.

By now Petronius had been linked to all that was most significant in Bologna's past and present. Although Ambrose retained a shadow of his former role, it was Petronius who demanded at Constantinople that the Emperor should enlarge Bologna's *contado*, and that 'the city should remain in liberty under the government of its citizens and never be subjected to any tyrant or temporal lord who might have power to destroy her. 'Thus', comments Lanzoni, 'Petronius became the rebuilder of Bologna and the founder of the commune, of the *distretto*, and of the *studio*.'[148] One might add, also, that through the widow Eulalia, he had an interest in the founding of the cathedral.

It was not until the later thirteenth century that Petronius, with Ambrose, began to be invoked in statutes and official documents. In the oldest extant communal acts, Peter appears alone as patron of the cathedral and commune. In the middle of the thirteenth century he was joined by Dominic and Francis, who may have begun to be regarded as civic 'protectors' after Innocent IV consecrated both their churches in October 1251. The presence of Dominic's relics in Bologna and the prominence of his brethren in the *studium* probably sharpened the competitive urges of Petronius's supporters. In a decree of 14 December 1284 the names of Petronius and Ambrose appear after those of God, the Virgin, Peter and Paul, Dominic and Francis; they are described as the 'holy defenders of this city', while Dominic and Francis are simply 'confessors'. In another decree, of 1299, they move ahead of their mendicant rivals.[149] In 1298 the government, confronting the expansionist ambitions of the Marquis of Este, put the militia companies in a state of readiness and ordered the making of a standard of vermilion silk with the figures of Petronius and Ambrose upon it.[150]

The years just before and after 1300 were clearly crucial in the development of Petronius's cult. In the statute of 1288, the officials were supposed to do reverence to Petronius and Floriano (another of the saints possessed by Santo Stefano) on St Stephen's day, a sign that the church, as much as the saint, was being honoured.[151] In September 1301, however, it was decreed that Petronius and Ambrose should henceforth be celebrated together, on the day either before or after the feast of St Francis (4 October). The wording of the decree suggests that the substance of the vernacular legend was by now in circulation: Petronius had endowed the city with many relics, repaired and rebuilt it, saved it from the snares of the devil, and crowned it with privileges for the *studium* and other immunities; his own bodily presence, in the monastery that he himself had built, was 'the pillar, so to speak, of our strength [*velut columna nostrae virtutis*]'.[152] Petronius's legend had been elaborated first in the shadow, as it were, of Ambrose's established reputation; now the positions were being reversed. Still Petronius had to yield precedence to Francis on 4 October, which was his 'own' day, but by the later fourteenth century he was being celebrated on 4 October and Francis's solemnities were shifted.[153]

At Pentecost in the year 1307, a poor sick man in the church of Santo Stefano saw that the way was open down to the well under the tomb of St Petronius. Drawn by thirst, he painfully made his way down to it and drank of the water with many devout prayers for the saint's intercession. He was instantly cured, and in the ensuing excitement another one hundred and fifty cures were recorded. The monks lost no time in presenting various petitions to the government. They asked that the piazza in front of the church should be provided with two or three awnings so that pilgrims might be protected from sun and rain, and that the commune should provide doles of bread and wine for the poor 'who cannot leave the place' . For as long as the miracles continued, no woman should be permitted to approach the church with 'lascivious ornaments', so as not to give offence to God or anyone else. Two brothers of the monastery should be elected to collect alms for the 'decent poor' and dispense them to the deserving with the aid of four good men from the parish. These same persons should be charged with the duty of collecting all offerings and gifts made to the monastery 'while these miracles last', and depositing them with the *podestà* month by month. Finally, the *podestà* should provide 'men, or hired troops' to prevent any tumult or disorders that might arise.[154]

The contention that the rise of Petronius illustrates the widespread preference for sacred personages who were native and exclusive to the locality[155] is, if anything, strengthened by the observation that other native saints were being publicized at precisely this time, perhaps in an effort to divide the spoils of civic recognition with him. According to Ghirardacci, the feast of the martyr Floriano (16 December), another possession of the monks of Santo Stefano, was declared in 1298 to be *feriato*; in 1303, in recognition of the miracles he had been doing, he obtained the honour of an official visit and offering on his feast-day.[156] In 1304 the monks of San Felice endeavoured to obtain this honour for their name-saint and other ancient bishops whose relics they possessed.[157] This same marked emphasis on the public recognition of native saints is also apparent in the latter part of the fourteenth century, the period of Petronius's final advance to the head of the Bolognese pantheon.

Petronius's new altar in Santo Stefano was consecrated in 1362.[158] In 1376 it was resolved that the communal and guild procession in honour of Petronius should take place quite separately from that of the clergy. Furthermore, the offering was to go not to the benefit of the community of Santo Stefano, but to pay for a head-reliquary for the saint. When this had been done, the offerings could revert to their earlier destination. The reliquary was executed in 1380 by Jacopo Roseto, with an inscription on the base recording its making 'in the time of the liberty of the popular and guild regime of the commune of Bologna' [*tempore libertatis regiminis popularis et artium communis Bononiae*]. Three years later the same artist executed another head-reliquary, for St Dominic, to which the commune seems to have contributed.[159] Henceforth, both saints could go in procession in time of public need, and so they frequently did in the fifteenth century.[160]

It has been observed that Dominic was the only saint among the co-patrons of Bologna who seemed able in these years to hold his own against Petronius.[161] Still, it seems, attempts were made to bring other saints into a position of civic prominence, and to win for them a share of official honours. In 1390, St Proculus, 'bishop and martyr of Terni, city of Umbria', was 'discovered' by the monks working in his church.[162] This Proculus had received an official offering under the terms of the statute of 1288,[163] but the present occasion was improved by the discovery, in the presence of the communal authorities, of another Proculus, supposedly 'a Bolognese martyr and knight', who may have seemed a plausible candidate for the role of civic patron. The new Proculus eventually took his place as a vigorous, scowling youth, carved by Michelangelo, on the *arca* of St Dominic.[164]

In the difficult closing decades of the fourteenth century, Petronius was more than ever needed to affirm Bologna's liberty in the face not merely of the papacy but of other ambitious powers close at hand. In 1377 the Pope had yielded to the city's insistent demand for autonomy by conferring the title of Vicar General on the legist Giovanni da Legnano. The decision to build a great new church in honour of Petronius, with its façade fronting the main square, can be seen as a means of announcing to all the world that Bologna's autonomy came from God; it can also be viewed, as Ghirardacci viewed it, in connection with the threat posed by Giangaleazzo Visconti to all the remaining independent powers of northern Italy.[165] Among the buildings which had to be demolished to make way for it was the old church of St Ambrose, who received partial compensation when Jacopo della Quercia depicted him, with Petronius, flanking the Virgin and Child on the great west portal of the new basilica. *Pietas* towards Ambrose could not be totally abandoned, but the growing menace of Milan may conceivably have contributed to his relative demotion within the Bolognese pantheon.

New regulations for the feast of Petronius were promulgated in 1393.[166] That he was now the city's patron in the fullest sense was indicated by the requirement of offerings from every vicariate of the *contado* and *distretto*, and from the civic authorities, dependent castles and nobles of Imola, as well as from every order of urban society. For a 'new' cult thus to appropriate these offerings was a quite exceptional development. The instructions to be carried out by the vicariates were notably explicit. The vicar, or his notary, was to approach the *anziani*, with his companions, and declare in a loud voice: 'These are your servants, the men of such and such a vicariate, who commend themselves to the blessed Petronius and to your lordships.' When they had done this, they were to pass on with their trumpeters before them, and were free to go. 'This order', the decree commented, 'is regarded as very useful, because by this action is demonstrated the fealty and obedience that the said communes and officials hold to the commune of Bologna.' In 1395 it was additionally decided that Petronius should be honoured by a race run on his feast-day for a *palio* worth fifty *bolognini d'oro*.[167]

It is noteworthy that Petronius's cult seems to have advanced in two surges, first in the later decades of the thirteenth century and again in the later decades of the fourteenth. In 1406 Cardinal Baldassare Cossa, on taking control of the city for the papacy after the Visconti interlude, coined *quattrini* with the saint's effigy, which were used until 1591.[168] Coins bearing Petronius's image, a mark of patronal status hitherto reserved for St Peter, had begun to appear in the late fourteenth century; in the fifteenth century the saints shared the honour, sometimes even appearing together. It might be hazarded that the papacy, given the intermittent difficulties of its relations with Bologna, saw sense in identifying both itself and St Peter with the saint who had come to symbolize Bolognese autonomy. Peter's attributes were established, and his image at Bologna did not differ from his image elsewhere; but almost from the beginning Petronius was distinguished by the model of the city that he bore in one hand, in token of his peculiarly protective role.[169]

Symbols of Power

The rulers of church and state, if not always in perfect harmony, co-operated in the display of the power which was necessary to the maintenance of the social order. The management of the cult of the saints who interceded for the well-being of the local community was an essential part of this co-operative enterprise. There is, as we have seen, ample evidence of the importance of the local holy man or woman, ancient or modern, in civic devotion. As the fourteenth century progressed, however, an increasing weight of public devotion was concentrated on objects that were universally available to Christians: the Virgin and the Eucharist. Urban governments responded accordingly.

The Virgin, above all by means of wonder-working images, possessed the power to imprint herself on the consciousness of the faithful in a particular visual shape. In 1292 an image of the Virgin painted on one of the pilasters of the loggia of Or San Michele in Florence began to work miracles. Villani reported that the Dominicans and Franciscans expressed scepticism about these miracles and, as a result, 'fell into great disrepute with the Florentines'. These events were at the origin of the company of Or San Michele; the laity sang *laudi* before the image, and it became an object of pilgrimage for all Tuscany at the feasts of the Virgin.[170] The decision, in 1294, to rebuild the cathedral of Florence in a more splendid form and to dedicate it to Santa Maria del Fiore was only one indication of her strengthened presence. The cult of the Virgin was authentically popular, but also satisfied the need of ruling elites for a devotion that was at once old and new, affective and authoritative. It cannot have escaped the notice of the Florentine authorities that neighbours and past or present enemies such as Pisa and Siena had long venerated the Virgin as their supreme patron.

A prolonged drought in 1354 provided the occasion for Matteo Villani's first mention of the image of the Madonna dell' Impruneta.[171] By early May the drought had lasted for more than three months, and it was perceived that prayers and continual processions had been of no avail. The citizens thereupon had recourse to 'the ancient image' [*l'antica figura*] of the Virgin at Impruneta. It was brought forth, and the commune organized an escort with many *doppieri*, mobilizing the clergy and all the orders, and including in the procession the arm of St Philip and the head of St Zenobius, with many other holy relics. The whole people went to the *porta* of San Piero Gattolino to meet the *tavola*, which was reverently accompanied by the Buondelmonti, as patrons of Impruneta, together with the men of the parish. It was then borne to San Giovanni and from there to San Miniato al Monte before being restored to its home. The results were immediate and gratifying, exceeding expectations. Later chroniclers make frequent reference to the processional employment of the Madonna of Impruneta at times of need and celebration.[172]

It was in explicit imitation of the Florentine recourse to the Madonna of Impruneta that the Madonna di San Luca, the Byzantine icon supposedly painted by St Luke that was kept in a hilltop church overlooking Bologna, began to be brought down to the city for use in processions. When this was first done, in 1433, in the face of appalling weather that seemed to portend famine, the instigator, Gratiolo Gratioli, urged that the Bolognese should imitate the example of the Florentines:

> who, when visited by tribulation, have recourse to God and his glorious mother, and issuing from the city in an ordered procession, went to the Madonna of Impruneta, where there is a holy image of the Mother of God by the hand of St Luke the Evangelist, and devotedly taking this image they bring it into the city and for three consecutive days accompany it processionally around the city with lights, psalms and hymns [thus obtaining] the remission of their faults and the happy outcome of their requests.

It seemed only sensible that as the Bolognese happened to possess a comparable image, they should do likewise. On 4 July Gratiolo went forth with the directors of the *Compagnia della Morte* and brought the Madonna down, still in foul weather, to be greeted at the gate by all the magistrates; and, wonder of wonders, no sooner did the image approach the gates of the city than a light wind began to blow and disperse the clouds. 'Devout processions', involving eight thousand people, took place on each of the next three days, and the government then decreed that the ritual should be repeated every year on the first Sunday in July in memory of the event.[173] It was at a similar period that the Sienese authorities too had their most venerated image of the Virgin cut down so that it could be carried in procession.[174]

During this same period a ceremony which was indubitably religious in character, although it carried a powerful political charge, was universally adopted in the Italian cities (as everywhere in Europe), and its management was appropriated by the civic authorities. By the middle of the fourteenth century the feast of

Corpus Christi was listed among the *ferie* in most cities. In the second half of the century we have increasingly frequent notice of processions which were at first the responsibility of houses of religious. The civic authorities would contribute to the festivity by sending offerings, and the magistrates might join in the procession. They then took the control of the procession into their own hands, and the cathedral church became the focus of the ceremonial, if it was not so already. The Corpus Christi procession added to the civic calendar a new celebration which in principle was universal rather than local in its frame of reference, and which demanded the attendance of the chief representatives of the commune as insistently as did the feast of the patron.[175]

It was in 1361 that processions involving all the clergy and religious and confraternities of the city began at Pisa; the *anziani* carried the *baldacchino*, and the Spine from the Crown of Thorns was carried behind the sacrament in the procession, which went from the cathedral to the Piazza degli Anziani, and returned to the cathedral.[176] In the closing years of the fourteenth century the Florentine authorities intervened to prevent disorders that had arisen out of the competition to dominate the celebrations of Corpus Christi, which were first associated with the Dominicans of Santa Maria Novella.[177] In the 1360s the Sienese government was contributing to the solemnities, which were then centred on the Carmelite convent; in the middle of the fifteenth century, by papal command, they were shifted to the cathedral, and updated regulations were produced for the procession, which, here as elsewhere, provided an opportunity to display the entire social hierarchy in an order centred on the *baldacchino*.[178] A Perugian chronicler records that in 1426 the papal governor ordered that all the guilds should assemble for a procession at Corpus Christi in the order they adopted for the feast of Sant' Ercolano. The procession was to go from San Domenico to the cathedral and back again.[179]

At Parma the festivity was originally in the hands of the guilds. In 1332 the four *misteria* (butchers, smiths, skinners and shoemakers) gathered in the *piazza del commune* and bore offerings to the hospital *in Capite Pontis*. This was to be done every year for the benefit of the hospital.[180] According to the 1417 *Ordinarium* of the cathedral of Parma, the Sacrament was to be borne from the cathedral 'to the hospital of the four mysteries *in Capite Pontis*, where this solemnity is specifically venerated in the city of Parma'. It was to be carried through different gates in alternate years, at the direction of the *anziani*, 'so that the whole city may rejoice in the virtue of the Sacrament', and the processional order within the city was to be so disposed by the citizens deputed for the purpose that 'the whole city may in eternity be gladdened by the salvific presence of that Body'. Not only were the civic authorities responsible for the ordering of the procession, but they had only recently increased their involvement by agreeing to supply the four candelabra that were carried about the sacrament. Four canons carried the *baldacchino* from the high altar to the main portal of the cathedral, and there handed it over to the officials who were to bear it in the procession. The author took the precaution of observing that if at any time in the future the commune should cease to provide the candelabra, the sacristan would have to supply them, as he had done in earlier times.[181]

Neither the Virgin nor the Eucharist was merely a symbol of power, but their effectiveness as such was enhanced by the universality of their scope and their appeal. It was an essential attribute of rulership that it should associate itself visibly, even ostentatiously, with devotions which mattered to men and women at all levels of society.

Notes

1. Lucca 1490, a.iiij *verso*:

   Cuius quidem compilationis sumpto a sancta & individua Trinitate principio & invocatis gloriosissima genitrice Cristi Maria & almifica croce & beatis apostolis Petro & Paulo nec non utroque Iohanne videlicet baptista & evangelista ac gloriosissimis Regulo archiepiscopo & Paulino martyribus & Frediano & Thoeodoro dicte lucensis episcopis & Martino confessoribus cristianissime civitatis Lucensis protectoribus & patronis nec non tota celesti curia triumphante incipit liber primus.

   Martin and Paulinus already figured in the invocation which prefaced the statute of 1372 (ASL *Serie degli Statuti* 6, fol. 2).
2. See below, pp. 174–80.
3. See below, Chapter 7, *passim*.
4. *Cronica*, 2, pp. 733–6. In this passage Salimbene mounts an attack

on the cults of the wine-porter Albert at Cremona and other popular uncanonized saints.

5. It is evident from the *Vita* of Zita of Lucca that the Franciscans and Dominicans co-operated with the regular canons of San Frediano in launching her cult in 1278 (*Acta S* Aprilis 3, 508A–B), and the orders were similarly involved in promoting Henry of Bolzano at Treviso (see below, p. 142) For mendicant predominance among canonized saints, see Vauchez, *La Sainteté*, pp. 309–10.

6. According to Thomas of Celano, *Vita Prima*, XIII.32; translation in M. Habig, *St Francis of Assisi: Omnibus of Sources* (London 1979) p.254. For the *inventio* of Rufinus, see above p. 84.

7. Cremona 1485, p. lxxxvi. For Sicard, see above, p. 85. Around 1320, statues of Himerius and Homobonus were placed flanking the figure of the Virgin over the main portal of the cathedral. For a time Himerius appeared on the city's coinage: *CNI* 4, pp. 193–4 and pl. XV, 17.

8. Cremona 1485, loc. cit. The offering to Albert was to be entirely for the benefit of the hospital at the church of St Matthias, any claim by the rector of the church notwithstanding. For Salimbene's strictures, cf. above, n. 4. For Fazio, see Vauchez, 'Sainteté laïque au XIIIe siècle: la vie du bienheureux Facio de Cremone (v. 1196–1272), *Melanges de l'Ecole Française de Rome, Moyen Age–Temps Modernes* 84.i (1972), pp. 13–53.

9. The dossier on Pungilupo (another object of Salimbene's scorn) was printed by Muratori, *Antiquitates Italicae Medii Aevi* (6 vols, Milan 1738–42), 5, pp. 93–150. Cf. Benati and Samaritani, pp. 286–7.

10. Benati and Samaritani, pp. 403–4, 381. The first of the *oblationes generales* honoured St George, who was and remained the patron of both cathedral and commune, and the third St Antony of Vienne, a saint with many claims to popularity as the archetypal holy hermit, a much-frequented object of pilgrimage and the protector of man and beast against epidemic disease. Benati and Samaritani, p. 381, interpret the offering to St Antony as signifying the 'ruralization' of Ferrara in the fifteenth century. Este enthusiasm for pilgrimage (Niccolò went to Vienne in 1433) suggests that other influences may have played a part.

11. *Cronica*, 1, p. 514; Padua C13, p. 181. The early biographies unfortunately do not survive; there is a fifteenth-century *Vita* by Sicco Polenton, *AB* 13 (1894), pp. 417–25.

12. Lucca 1308, pp. 12, 250.

13. C.A. Meek, *Lucca 1369–1400: Politics and Society in an Early Renaissance City-State* (Oxford 1978), n.37, p. 190. The Faitinelli were among those families named as 'potentes et casastici' in the Statute of 1308, and some at least went into exile in 1314. The only member of the family to hold office as *anziano* before 1369 did so in February/March 1342, in a brief interlude of Florentine rule before the Pisans established control. Bartolomeo Faitinelli was among Lucchese merchants who returned from

Venice on the restoration of republican rule at Lucca in 1369 (ibid., n.10, p. 34). However, members of the family had already built a chapel for Zita in San Frediano in 1321, and in 1373 Giovanni Faitinelli left money for its embellishment; in 1382 he commissioned a painting of her and instituted a daily celebration of mass in the chapel. Wills of 1383, 1388, 1389 and 1401 show members of the family choosing to be buried there, and it was to Antonio Faitinelli that Leo X in 1519 directed a bull authorizing the celebration of her feast (Vauchez, *Sainteté*, p. 281).

14. M. Bertagna, especially, for the cult before 1400, pp. 15–39, and for the *Vita*, pp. 449–57.

15. Vauchez, *Sainteté*, pp. 82–3, lists known requests to the popes, between 1198 and 1431, which were *not* followed by the opening of a process. All the communal initiatives (except Padua's for Antony) are among them. Padua was unsuccessful with Antony the Pilgrim. Cf. Vauchez, 'Patronage des saints', pp. 65–6.

16. The last attempt to obtain the canonization of Parisius and Henry was made under Venetian rule in 1347. With St Peter (as patron of the cathedral), the Virgin and Francis and Bartholomew, Henry and Parisius were established as the recipients of official offerings still in the statutes published by the Venetians: Treviso 1574, p. 37.

17. Mittarelli, *Annales* V, pp. 62, 86–7, 91–4, 241–2, 292, 295, 392–3. Mittarelli's earlier *Memorie della Vita di San Parisio* (Venice 1748), published anonymously as the work of 'un monaco camaldolese', devotes a little more space to the saint's relations with the bishop.

18. Treviso C14, pp. 112–13.

19. The phrase *status communis* does not lend itself to easy translation. It is probably best understood by analogy with *bonum commune*, 'the common good', and similarly has overlapping moral and political connotations.

20. Treviso C14, pp. 204–6.

21. Avogaro, *Memorie del Beato Enrico*, 2, pp. 1–74.

22. Cf. similar concerns about the relics of Geminianus at Modena and Rufinus at Assisi, above, pp. 61, 84.

23. Vauchez, *Sainteté*, pp. 277–9.

24. L. Kern, 'A propos du mouvement des flagellants', pp. 39–53.

25. Perugia, Archivio di Stato, *Statuti* 1, f. 4.

26. Perugia 1343, 2, p. 349.

27. Ibid., 63; and still in 1526, p. xxxvii.

28. Kern, p. 52.

29. See the article on Benevenuto by G. Odoardi, *BS* 2, 1252–53.

30. Compagnoni, *Memorie Istorico-Critiche*, 5, pp. 103–4.

31. Ibid., pp. 109–10.

32. Ibid., 2, pp. 474–5; Osimo C14, 1, p. 224; 2, p. 623.

33. See above, p. 106.

34. Verona 1475, Lib. I, r.35; II, r.1.

35. Salimbene, *Cronica*, 1, pp. 570, 571–3.
36. Vicenza 1264, pp. 6–7.
37. There is a summary of the life of Bishop Bartolomeo in *AS* Julii 2, pp. 277–87.
38. Vicenza 1264, pp. 201–2. The oath of the *communitas populi* included St Michael.
39. Treviso C14, pp. 110–13.
40. This is repeatedly emphasized in the *Cantus triumphales in Imperatorem Fridericum II*, in *Chronica Parmensia*, pp. 447–63, and also by Innocent IV, in a letter of 20 March 1250 reminding the city's rulers of the need to respect the privileges of the church, printed by Affò, 3, pp. 386–7.
41. E. Jordan, *Les Origines de la Domination Angevine en Italie* (Paris 1909), p. 364. On the *Societas Cruxatorum* as one of the orthodox vigilante groups which were organized to combat heresy and Ghibellinism, cf. N. Housley, 'Politics and Heresy in Italy: Anti-Heretical Crusades, Orders and Confraternities, 1200–1500', *JEH* 33 (1982), pp. 201–5. Hilary is mentioned several times, in connection with his Society, in enactments added in the 1260s to the statutes of 1255: Parma 1255, pp. 468–71.
42. *Chronicon Parmense*, pp. 119. There is a reference to the guild celebrations of the feast in 1389 in *Chronica Parmensia*, p. 398. The festivities instituted in honour of St Lucy in 1295 were to be modelled on those for Hilary: Parma 1266–1304, p. 158.
43. *Ordinarium Ecclesiae Parmensis*, pp. 37, 114. In the act of election of Bernardo da Carpi, bishop from 1412 to 1425, Hilary is invoked as 'patronus et advocatus hujus almae civitatis Parmae' (ibid., n.2, p. 3).
44. Pezzana, *Storia di Parma*, 2, pp. 555–6. The miniature is illustrated in *Le Grandi Famiglie d' Europa*, 8: *I Visconti* (Milan 1972), p. 109.
45. *Chronicle of Florence*, 1, 21, trans. D. Bornstein (Philadelphia 1986), p. 24. The occasion the magnates chose for this protest was, perhaps significantly, the guild procession to do honour to St John in June 1300.
46. Villani, VII.31, 131; IX.13.
47. Florence 1325, 2, pp. 436, 439.
48. *Cronica*, p. 93. Already in the Statuto del Podestà of 1355 the race was contested on horseback and the *palio* could cost up to 20 florins (ASF 16, fol. 249v).
49. On Paulinus, see the article by R. Volpini in *BS* 10 (1968), pp. 151–6. In *AB* 23 (1904), pp. 491–2, H. Delehaye reviewed the pamphlet warfare that erupted after the discovery in 1900 of the 1197 inscription, and Lanzoni summarized it in *Origini*, pp. 366–7. The narrative of the *inventio*, by Paganus, rector of the church of San Giorgio and San Antonio, is in *Acta S* Julii 3, pp. 260–61; the legend and miracles of Paulinus and his companions in ibid., pp. 258–72.
50. *Die Annalen*, ed. B. Schmeidler, *Scriptores Rerum Germanicarum*, n.s. 8, 2nd edn (Berlin 1955), p. 144.

51. *Acta S*, Julii 3, p. 272E–F. A Sienese chronicler refers to the Lucchese prisoners, who were liberated in 1265 (*Cronache senesi*, p. 219).

52. *Acta S* Julii 3, pp. 261, 270.

53. *Historia Ecclesiastica* (1, xiii), Muratori XI, col. 765; Villani, II.12.

54. Cf. above, p. 77. In November 1200, another *inventio* in the same church had supposedly brought to light the hermit Antonio. Antonio, according to another well-worn model story which was exemplified at neighbouring Pisa by the legend of San Torpete, had gathered up the relics of the martyred Paulinus and his companions and given them burial. The legend of Antonio as we have it looks as if it was in fact written to substantiate the *inventio* of 1261, in that it proclaims Paulinus to have been the first bishop of Lucca and a disciple of St Peter. The legend of San Torpete is in *Acta S* Maii 6, pp. 5–19; the legend of Antonio in ibid., Aprilis 3, pp. 476–8. The inscription that was allegedly discovered with Antonio's relics seems to have been somewhat thoughtlessly modelled on the 1197 inscription, in that it mentioned both Bishop Guido (who was indeed still bishop in 1200) and the Emperor Henry VI (who had died three years previously).

55. ASL *Statuti* 4, p. 189 (old foliation 96). The series *ASL: Camarlingo Generale, Mandatorie* records authorizations by the *anziani* of disbursements from the *camera*; the series *Entrata e Uscita* records actual payments, often dated two or three days later. I have principally referred to the *Mandatorie*, which survive, with gaps, from late 1333 (Camarlingo Generale 88); there are a few earlier volumes of *Entrata e Uscita*. A run of *Mandatorie* for the period 16 July 1330–10 March 1331 survives in *Anziani avanti la Libertà* 2, from f. 197. For the general characteristics of Lucchese records in the mid-fourteenth century, see C. Meek, *The Commune of Lucca under Pisan Rule, 1342–1369* (Cambridge, MA 1980), pp. 10–15.

56. *Acta S* Julii 3, pp. 262–3.

57. The seven final cantos of Streghi's verse chronicle were published by A. Pellegrini, 'Il Piccinino'. Streghi himself subtitled these cantos 'Il Piccinino' after the *condottiere* whom the duke of Milan sent to deliver Lucca from the assault the Florentines launched on it in 1429. The complete poem can be reconstructed from manuscripts in the Biblioteca Statale of Lucca. The legend of Paulinus is in Ms. 942, fols 22v–23v; his prayers on Lucca's behalf in 1430 are in 'Il Piccinino' 23 (1899), p. 400. For another vernacular versifier's rendering of the same scene, see V. Finzi, 'Di un inedito poema', pp. 256–7.

58. For the story of Apollinaris, see Lanzoni, *Origini*, pp. 464–75; for Syrus of Pavia, see Orselli, 'La città altomedievale e il suo santo patrono', in *L'immaginario religioso*. These earlier versions of the legend arose from attempts to assert or avoid metropolitan jurisdiction. Lanzoni calculated (ibid., p. 51) that pseudo-apostolic saints were in fact more numerous in France than elsewhere.

59. *Acta S* Augusti 5, p. 796; G. Serafini, *S. Lodovico d'Angio, Patrono di Serravalle Pistoiese* (Pistoia 1986). For Florentine devotion to Louis at this period, see below, p. 168.

60. I rely for what follows on A. Spicciani, 'Scopi politici degli interventi fiorentini nelle istituzioni ecclesiastiche', pp. 47–70. The situation was complicated by the fact that the diocese of Lucca, to which the Valdinievole belonged until the Florentine Pope Leo X detached it in the early sixteenth century, was under interdict as a a consequence of Lucca's adhesion to Lewis of Bavaria's schism.

61. In 1866 the municipality decided that it would no longer finance these cults, on the good *risorgimentale* grounds that they (especially the feast of Dorothy) constituted 'un ricordo doloroso della guerra civile', and in 1926 the cathedral clergy decided no longer to participate in them. The statutes issued under Florentine rule authorized the continued *luminaria* of the Assumption and the fair of St Leonard on 6 November. The early veneration of Mary and Leonard at Pescia is attested by the tombstone of the priest Rustico, who died in 1132.

62. Sinibaldo's continued obedience to the church of Lucca was indicated when in 1341 he attended as *plebanus plebis Pesciae* the consecration of the enlarged church of San Paolino in Lucca (*Acta S* Julii 3, p. 263).

63. *Acta S* Octobris 10, pp. 232–9.

64. L. Gai, *L'altare argenteo di San Jacopo del Duomo di Pistoia* (Pistoia 1984), p. 74, figs 91, 191. Eulalia is described by Gai as 'compatrona di Pistoia, ma sotto il segno dei Guelfi Neri e del partito filo-fiorentino'. An inscription on the foot of the altar-frontal records the name of Dardano degli Acciauoli, vicar for Robert of Naples (ibid., n.3, p. 187).

65. A. Chiappelli, 'Note del Culto di S. Agata', pp. 112–16; Fioravanti, *Memorie storiche*, p. 32. Chiappelli suggested that Agatha's cult may have originated privately with invocations of her against the frequent fires of the early fourteenth century, but acquired a public dimension when the Florentines and the Pistoiese came to terms on her day in February 1312. She had a chapel in the *palazzo pubblico* from 1313. In February 1341 a petition was presented to the Consiglio Generale asking that the *operarii* of St James should be made responsible for the ornamentation of the altar in honour of God, the Virgin and St Agatha which the present *anziani* were instituting 'in the new chapel in the new city palace'; the *operarii* were to provide the chapel with all necessities and appoint a priest from among the chaplains of San Jacopo to sing mass every day before the *anziani* (ASP *Statuti* 5, f. 96v). In January 1417 responsibility for the keeping of the feast was virtually delegated to the *operarii* of San Jacopo, who were asked to lend thirty pounds annually to the commune for the necessary expenditures (ASP *Provvisioni* 31, f. 165).

66. ASP *Statuti e Ordinamenti* 10, II.29, f. 60v. Eulalia was depicted with Agatha in an early-sixteenth-century fresco of the two saints in the church

of San Paolo. An attractive lectionary which was copied in 1486 by the canon Girolamo Zenoni and presented to the cathedral includes the offices of both saints: ASP *Documenti Varii* 2.

67. Pistoia 1313, pp. 10, 11–12. Chapter 27 then states that the *operarii* themselves shall give candles to the *familiares* of the *capitano* and *podestà* on the feast-days of St James, the Virgin and St Martin, and shall also have ten large candles made for the *anziani* and *gonfaloniere* and their notary 'for each procession of the said festivals'. The Latin version of the statute is in ASP *Statuti* 2, fols 58–65v.

68. Fioravanti, p. 131, recounts the story that in 406 news of a great victory won over the Goths by Stilicho reached Pistoia on St Martin's Day, giving rise to his adoption as patron. His name does not in fact seem to appear among those of the cathedral's patrons before the mid-tenth century: for examples, see *Libro Croce*, ed. Q. Santoli (Rome 1939), n.9 (944), n.7 (952), n.148 (1012), etc. Zeno always takes precedence, sometimes being named alone. At this date, of course, James does not figure at all.

69. ASP *Provvisioni* 4, f. 93.

70. In the text of the 1329 statute of the Opera (ASP *Statuti* 4, f. 17) there is a blank space under the heading of r.27 ('Quod potestas et capitaneus teneantur offerre unum palium'). R.28, which corresponds to r.27 of the 1313 version, omits any mention of St Martin: the *operarii* now have to provide candles only for the feasts of St James and the Virgin. The content of the missing rubric 27 is supplied by rubric 5 of the first book of the 1330 *Statuto del Popolo*, where it is stated that the offerings of the officials who are not holding office in July are to be made 'on some other day of great solemnity' to be appointed by the *operarii* (ibid., *Statuti* 3, f. 4). St Martin's Day remained, presumably, a theoretical possibility, but is not specified. Fioravanti, p. 134, stated that Martin was honoured at Pistoia by civic pomps which continued until 1334. One indication of a cult in the later thirteenth century is a provision that his day should be one of those kept as a public holiday in the city only, 'nisi esset in subsiduo vidue vel pupillorum, sine fraude' (Pistoia 1296, p. 169).

71. Pistoia C12, r.6, p. 46: the electors of the consuls take an oath to elect five suitable persons 'ad honorem Dei et sancti Jacopi et sancti Zenonis et populis Pistoriensis'. James and Zeno were regularly invoked together in the late thirteenth century as *patroni et defensores* and sometimes even as *sancta corpora* (e.g. Pistoia 1296, pp. xxxvi, lvi), and Zeno's feast was among those for which the *podestà* was instructed to ensure the bread supply (ibid., p. 157).

72. ASP *Provvisioni*, f. 99. Federigo Bertucci advised that the arrangements should be delegated without more ado to the *anziani* and *gonfaloniere*; it was still the annual custom to take a formal vote to delegate the arrangements for the feast of St James himself.

73. *Provvisioni* 5, f. 215. The reference was presumably to the statute of

1329, but the text of the *Statuto del Comune* of that year unfortunately does not survive. It seems reasonably safe to assume that the clause in question more or less resembled Book III, r.28 of the extant 1344 statute (*Statuti* 6, III. xxviii, f. 97v): 'Potestas teneat tenere consilium per octo dies ante festum Sancti Jacobi de ordinanda processione Sancti Jacobi, qualiter homines cum ceris in ipsa processione venire debeant. Et idem fiat de processione sancti Çenonis. Et de processione fienda quolibet anno die xxiiij maii propter memoriam & reverentiam Sancte Pacis.' The last reference was to a procession commemorating the peace made between Florence and Pistoia in 1329. It appears from e.g. *Provvisioni* 5 f. 244 (6 May 1337) that a *palio* was run on this day.

74. *Provvisioni* 5, fols 215r–v.

75. Ibid., fols 289 r–v. The following year, on 7 December, the annual expenditure of twenty-five pounds on the *palio* was authorized in the council, but it was evidently now deemed unnecessary to put the arrangements for the *festa* itself to the vote: ibid., f. 366. It must be noted that as San Zeno's *palio* went to his own *opera*, it was not a substitute for the offering on St Martin's day which had been destined for the *opera* of San Jacopo.

76. Ibid., 4, f. 30v. In April 1337 the *operarii* asked for authority to spend a hundred pounds of their revenues *ad opus dicte sepulture perficiende*: ibid., 5, f. 243v. In 1604 it was alleged, in documentation presented to Pope Clement VIII in favour of Atto's cult, that his body had been found to be miraculously incorrupt on its translation into the cathedral, 184 years after his death: ASP *Documenti Varii* 4, f. 11v.

77. ASP *Statuti* 28, fols 11r–v.

78. *Acta S* Maii 5, pp. 199–200. For Florentine miracles performed when the relic of St James came to Pistoia in 1144, see above p. 79.

79. Gai, *L'altare argenteo*, p. 36, fig. 10.

80. Ibid., p. 134, figs 187, 188.

81. ASP *Provvisioni* 9, fol. 160v (28 April 1348). A grant of 'ultra libr' centum' was proposed, in fact 150, the rest to be paid by the *Opera* of San Jacopo.

82. Villani, X.128: 'feciono ordine, che s' abbattesse ogni insegna d' aguglio e i Bavaro e di Castruccio e i parte ghibellina, e feciono per sopransegna a loro bandiere i nicchi dell' oro e san Iacopo'. It is difficult to tell with what degree of emphasis Villani records that on St James's Day in 1331 the lioness of the Florentine commune gave birth to two live cubs, and that on the very next day the Florentines took steps to exploit divisions at Pistoia so as to obtain the *signoria* of the city. Ibid., XI, 184, 185.

83. As he was described on 18 March 1330, in a deliberation copied into one of a number of miscellaneous volumes of provisions made by the Florentines: ASP *Statuti* 27, f. 15v.

84. Villani, IX.323; X.38. Castruccio's family connections, it may be

noted, were with the *contrata* and church of San Martino. Until the mid-thirteenth century the Castracani functioned as money-changers at a stall in front of the cathedral, and the Antelminelli, the magnate clan to whose *consorteria* the Castracani belonged, had towers and houses in the *contrata*: T. Blomquist, 'The Castracani Family of Thirteenth-Century Lucca', *Speculum* 46 (1971), pp. 459–76, esp. pp. 460–61. In addition, Martin could be reckoned a soldier-saint.

85. Lucca 1308, p. 12. A guard was also to be placed at the cathedral on the vigil of the Holy Cross, and at the church of San Frediano on the vigils of Frediano himself and Santa Zita; but, significantly, only in the case of the Holy Cross was this to be the direct responsibility of the *podestà*.

86. ASL *Statuti* 4, p. 115, 'De honore et reverentia beati Martini'. Coins issued by Castruccio after the battle of Altopascio omitted the effigy of the Vultus which was almost invariable on the Lucchese coinage, but did not substitute Martin: *CNI* 11, p. 79.

87. ASL *Entrata e Uscita* 10, f. 186–186v.

88. S. Bongi (ed.), *Bandi Lucchesi*, nn.41–2, pp. 22–3. The *festa* took place despite the interdict on Lucca in force since April 1328: a temporary suspension of this interdict had ended at All Saints 1334.

89. ASL *Entrata e Uscita* 10, f. 194, 195v.

90. ASL *Mandatorie* 89, f. 115–115v.

91. The same expedient was employed in 1383: payment was authorized on 16 November for the wax offered 'in Vigilia Festivitatis Sancti Martini proximi preteriti ad reverentiam Sancte Crucis & Sancti Martini predicti' (*Mandatorie* 106, f. 126v).

92. ASL *Statuti* 5, pp. 189, 136.

93. 'Our precious Volto Santo did not wish the cruel Florentine people to enter into Lucca, openly or in secret; nor did it please the good St Paulinus, St Martin and glorious St Regulus, St Benedict, St Davinus too, and the holy Angel, and also blessed Zita, look after Lucca so that it be not betrayed.' Finzi, 'Di un inedito poema', pp. 256–7.

94. Pellegrini, 'Il Piccinino', 23 (1899), pp. 400–401.

95. Kaftal, *Tuscan Painting*, cols 131–2.

96. For some manifestations of the cult of the Virgin at Florence, see below, pp. 181–2.

97. Villani, XII.17. A rubric 'De oblatione fienda die Sancte Anne' was inserted into the margin of the 1355 statute (ASF *Statuti* 16, fol. 75v). Later in the century a *palio* was instituted in her honour 'pro honore reipublicae & ad perpetuam memoriam libertatis civitatis Florentiae' (Florence 1415, p. 316).

98. F. Villani, 99. Cf. *Diario d'anonimo fiorentino*, p. 298: 'A dì 27 di luglio 1365 puosesi il paglio della Parte Guelfa a la torre della Parte, al Ponte Vecchio da Casa Rossi, per la vettoria del beato messer Santo Vettore papa, ch' avemo la vettoria contr' a' Pisani. E còrresi il suo benedetto dì

acciò che Iddio e 'l beato misser Santo Vettorio grazioso ci de' vettoria contr' a nostri nemici, là dovunque fossono, e così sia.' For Victor in Florentine iconography, see Frugoni, *A Distant City*, p. 152; Kaftal, *Tuscan Painting*, col. 130, fig. 137.

99. *Alle Bocche della Piazza*, p. 44. In January 1393 an execution was delayed 'acciò che non guastasse la festa di santo Antonio', and in January 1396 the captains of the Parte invited all the *maggiori cittadini* to attend an offering to Antony in the cathedral (ibid., pp. 146, 189).

100. Villani, X.168, p. 155. The reliquary bust is illustrated and discussed in Rossi, *Italian Jeweled Arts*, n.20, pp. 12–14, pl. xi. For the cult of Zenobius generally, see A.M. Papi, 'San Zanobi', in *Pastori di Popolo*, pp. 127–76.

101. *Tumulto dei Ciompi*, p. 119.

102. *Alle Bocche della Piazza*, pp. 33 (March 1382), 55 (November 1384), 59 (June 1385), 73 (May 1387), 99 (October 1390), 140 (1392). The relic was also used for less 'political' purposes – for example, in efforts to stop it raining, in 1392, 1393 and 1398 (pp. 141, 178, 212). The head of Zenobius accompanied that of San Donato of Arezzo in the procession to greet the new bishop of Florence in January 1386: see below, Chapter 6, p. 223. For the Madonna of Impruneta, see also below pp. 181–2.

103. Papi, *Pastori*, p. 140.

104. R. Krautheimer, *Lorenzo Ghiberti* (Princeton, NJ 1970), esp. pp. 141–2 (documents pp. 411–16). On the translation of the relics (May 1439), see Papi, pp. 149, 173–4 n.107).

105. Corazza, *Diario*, p. 79.

106. In a consolatory epistle written in 1463 on the death of Cosimo's son Giovanni, the humanist priest Francesco Castiglione described the church 'que etiam ob memoriam beati patris nostri Zenobii, in qua episcopalem tenebat sedem & beati Ambrosii pontificis non minimis sit laudibus exornata' (Biblioteca Laurenziana Plut. 54, 10, fols 96–96v). In a sermon written after the death of Cosimo in 1464 to promote the veneration of Pope Marcus, whose relics, it was claimed, had been discovered in San Lorenzo in 1444, Castiglione recounted the story that St Ambrose had bestowed the relics on Zenobius (ibid., Plut. 89 inf. 47, fols 116v–117), and included Zenobius among the saints in whose *patrocinium* the canons of the church were to trust (fol. 118).

107. Papi, pp. 150–51. A project, initiated by Lorenzo de' Medici, for the mosaic redecoration of the crypt which housed Zenobius's relics was interrupted by the fall of Piero in 1494 and, though a fresh competition was held for the commission in 1504, remained unfulfilled. A mosaic portrait of the saint, entered for this competition, survives in the Museo dell' Opera del Duomo.

108. Florence 1325, 2, pp. 378–9.

109. Villani, II.24; III, 15, 16.

110. Ibid., III.85. The 1325 statute had said only that the *bravium* should be of the colour and condition that the *camerarii* should decide; and it had still then been a foot race. Now Reparata's *bravium* was to cost twice as much as Barnabas's (Florence 1325, 2, p. 436; ASF *Statuti* 16, fol. 249v). A similar story was supposed to account for St Martin's early patronage of the cathedral of Pistoia and the holding, until the 1330s, of a procession in his honour; see above, n.68.

111. Florence 1415, 3, pp. 321–2. Cf. below, p. 207.

112. Florence 1415, 3, pp. 322–3.

113. Ibid., pp. 318–19; *Diario d' anonimo*, p. 354; Corazza, *Diario*, pp. 20–21.

114. ASF *Libri Fabarum* 43, fols 62, 63. The proposal elicited 150 votes in favour and 75 against in the *consiglio del popolo*. It was a period of effusive expressions of Florentine devotion to France; see, e.g., letters of the *signoria* to the French king in *Missive* 20, fols 30v–32v (20 October 1384); 21, fols 119v–120 (9 August 1389). In the latter they asked the king 'statum nostrum, quem incliti praegenitores vestre fundaverunt atque foverunt, sub vestre regie protectionis refugio conservare'. The *oblatio* to Louis is included in Florence 1415, 3, pp. 317–18.

115. Janson, *Donatello*, p. 46.

116. F. Lampertico, 'Il dominio dei Visconti a Vicenza ed il culto di San Vincenzo' in *Scritti Storici e Letterarii* (2 vols, Florence 1882–3), 2, pp. 163–85. In 1383 the Statute of the college of doctors invoked the saint, 'cuius a nomine Vincentia Civitas nuncupatur', ahead of Vicenza's established patrons (ibid., p. 169). R. Sabbadini, in a review of Lampertico, queried how any specific connection with the Visconti was to be established: *ASI* 13, pt 2 (1884), p. 281.

117. Vicenza 1490, pp. 100–102.

118. Treviso C14, 1, p. 113.

119. Tolosanus, *Chronicon Faventinum*, pp. 36 and n.41. Cf. above, p. 81.

120. Tolosanus, pp. 155, 172, 159–62.

121. 'Le "Vite" dei Quattro Santi Protettori della Città di Faenza', in *Chronica Breviora aliaque monumenta faventina*, pp. 295–6. In 1331 the *Statuto dell' Arte dei Calzolai* invoked him alone, after God, Christ and the Virgin, as *patronus civitatis et populi et comunis Faventie*; this despite their possession since 1280 of a saint of their own, the blessed Nevolone (see below, p. 173).

122. Faenza 1415, p. 31.

123. Ibid., pp. 291–5. In addition, the Annunciation was to be celebrated at the Servite church (pp. 295–6). The belief that Santa Maria Forisportam was the original cathedral of Faenza was expressed by Tolosanus, *Chronicon*, p. 6.

124. Ibid., p. 291: 'ut ab ipso D.N. eiusdem matris gloriosissime Filio precibus et intercessione hec civitas Faventie et ejus populus continue sint recomissi et semper a cunctis periculis deffensetur'.

125. Ibid., p. 295.

126. Ibid., pp. 296–7.

127. Faenza 1527, p. ii: 'quorum presidio & tutela ab adversis omnibus civitas ipsa servetur'.

128. Ibid., Lib. VII, r.1, p. lxiii. There was an *oblatio* at the cathedral on the feast of St Martin; this was essentially of the 'commemorative' type, in memory of the 'pacification' of the city achieved by Bertrand du Poujet on behalf of the papacy in 1328. For the building of a chapel in the cathedral in honour of St Martin and other honours, cf. Faenza 1415, pp. 116n., 285–6n.

129. 'Le "Vite" dei Quattro Santi', pp. 337–8. The passage is quoted above, Introduction, p. 3.

130. 'Le "Vite"', p. 347.

131. Ibid., p. 294.

132. Faenza 1527, Lib. III, r.xxi, pp. XXIIr–v. Terentius and Emilianus enjoyed this status automatically, because they possessed churches within the city.

133. 'Le "Vite"', p. 287.

134. There are articles on these saints by G. Lucchesi in *BS* 4, cols 1183–5 (Emilianus); 11, cols 701–16 (Savinus); 12, cols 372–4 (Terentius).

135. 'Le "Vite"', p. 289. Lanzoni interpreted this commission as signifying a claim to a whole body.

136. Ibid., pp. 322–4, 359–60.

137. Ibid., pp. 291–3.

138. *Petri Cantinelli Chronicon (1228–1306)*, ed. F. Torraca (*RIS* 28.ii), p. 42; F. Lanzoni, 'Una Vita del Beato Nevollone Faentino, terziario francescano, composta nel secolo XV', *AFH* 6 (1913); 'Cose Francescane Faentine', ibid., 14 (1921), pp. 435–41; A. Vauchez in *BS* 9, cols 839–40. His feast-day was honoured as a holiday by his own guild, which conducted its deliberations at his altar. Astorgio I Manfredi (1379–1405) may have entertained a particular reverence for him, to judge from the saint's appearance, kneeling in an attitude of prayer, on his coinage: *CNI* 9, 411–12.

139. A. Savioli, ed, *Faenza, La Basilica Cattedrale* (Florence 1988), pp. 90–105. Like Damian's, the relics of Terentius and Emilianus were not brought to the cathedral till after the Napoleonic dissolutions.

140. See above, p. 81.

141. A chronicler listed the relics possessed by the rebuilt cathedral consecrated by Lucius III on 8 July 1184: they included fragments of Peter's clothing, but nothing of Petronius (*Corpus Chronicorum Bononiensium*, 2, p. 48). For the cult of Petronius I have relied principally upon the following: F. Lanzoni, *San Petronio*; A. Orselli, 'Spirito Cittadino', in *L'immaginario religioso*; G. Fasoli, 'La composizione del falso diploma Teodosiano'; M. Fanti, *La Fabbrica di S. Petronio*.

142. Lanzoni, *San Petronio*, esp. pp. 58–67.

143. Orselli, 'Spirito cittadino', esp. pp. 209–14.

144. Bologna 1245–67, 1, pp. 440, 441–2.

145. Lanzoni, *San Petronio*, p. 125; Orselli, 'Spirito cittadino', pp. 215–26; M. Fanti, *La Fabbrica di San Petronio*, pp. 11–12.

146. In October 1315 the commune awarded an annual payment of twenty-five pounds to Santo Stefano 'ad hoc ut precibus dicti beatissimi Petronii protectoris et defensoris civitatis et partis guelfe et Jeremiensium civitatis Bononie, ipsa civitas et pars e bono in melius augmentetur...' (Fanti, *La Fabbrica*, p. 16).

147. Fasoli, 'La composizione', pp. 598–9.

148. Lanzoni, *San Petronio*, pp. 140, 151.

149. Lanzoni, pp. 153–4, lists these texts, with references. Orselli n.64, p. 215, comments that the text of 1284 could be interpreted as conferring a special distinction on Petronius and Ambrose.

150. Ghirardacci, 1, pp. 350–51.

151. Bologna 1288, 2, p. 190.

152. Lanzoni, *San Petronio*, p. 161.

153. Ghirardacci, 1, p. 429.

154. Ibid., p. 502; *Corpus Chronicorum*, 2, p. 282.

155. Lanzoni, *San Petronio*, p. 155.

156. Ghirardacci, 1, p. 364. Floriano begins to to be invoked as a patron in official documents *c.* 1380, at about the time when Ambrose disappears: Lanzoni, p. 161.

157. According to Ghirardacci, 1, p. 459, they were successful, and the custom was still observed in 1592; Fanti, *La Fabbrica*, pp. 13–14, however, says that the communal authorities declined to pay an official annual visit unless the monks met all the expenses. Not all the saints involved in such negotiations were natives: when, also in 1304, the nuns of St Augustine asked that their saint's day should be not merely *feriato* but *festato* so as to obtain his good offices with God, the proposal was carried *nemine contra* (ibid., p. 465).

158. Ibid., 2, p. 261. The altar also contained relics of Floriano and Thomas of Canterbury. In 1364 it was decreed that the old saints Vitalis and Agricola – also, of course, in the possession of the monks of Santo Stefano – should be honoured 'like other solemn feasts': ibid., p. 274.

159. Fanti, *La Fabbrica*, pp. 31–3. Miracles accompanied the opening of Dominic's tomb for the translation in February 1383 (Ghiradarcci, 2, p. 395; *Corpus Chronicorum*, 3, pp. 371–2).

160. See below, pp. 230–31.

161. Fanti, *La Fabbrica*, p. 33.

162. Ibid., p. 434; *Corpus Chronicorum*, 3, p. 378, where the discovery is dated December 1389. Fanti, pp. 14–15, suggests that this was an effort to promote a double cult incorporating the 'pastoral and political' aspects that were united in the figure of Petronius.

163. Bologna 1288, 2, p. 190. Proculus was sufficiently well known for Villani to mention his martyrdom by the Goths (III.1).

164. Ghirardacci, 2, pp. 396–7.

165. Ibid., pp. 438–9.

166. Ibid., pp. 467–8.

167. Ibid., p. 478.

168. Ibid., p. 572. The *bolognino d' oro* struck in July 1380 bore St Peter with the keys on one side and the legend 'Bononia docet' on the other. The coinage issued by Taddeo da Pepoli earlier in the century also showed St Peter (ibid., p. 138).

169. Cf. below, p. 235.

170. Villani, VII.155.

171. M. Villani, IV.7; R. Trexler, 'Florentine Religious Experience'.

172. For example: *Alle Boche della Piazza*, pp. 59, 99, 141, 178, 212; Corazza, *Diario*, pp. 20–21, 23–4, 27, 29–30, 35–6; Landucci, *Diary*, pp. 37, 57, 87, 232, 245, 255, 262, 268, 292, 297.

173. Ghirardacci, 3, pp. 34–6. See in general G. Lanzi and D. Ferrari, 'Le Processioni per la Madonna di San Luca in Bologna', *Il Santo* 24 (1984), pp. 207–27.

174. See below, p. 265.

175. See in general Rubin, *Corpus Christi*, especially pp. 243–71.

176. P. Tronci, *Memorie Istoriche della Città di Pisa* (Livorno 1682), p. 393.

177. Trexler lays stress on the potency of the cult of Corpus Christi as a symbol of majesty and its power to foster dissension: 'The Magi Enter Florence', pp. 154–7.

178. See below, pp. 304–5.

179. *Cronache della Città di Perugia*, p. 321. Perugia 1526, p. 102v, prescribed that the offerings made by the guilds and religious orders for Corpus Christi should, with minor exceptions, be those that were made for San Costanzo and the other major festivals of the year, and that the Dominicans were to receive from the commune one of the finest of the *bravia* that had been offered to Sant' Ercolano on 1 March.

180. *Chronicon Parmense*, pp. 219–20.

181. *Ordinarium*, pp. 167–75. The reference to the recent institution of the offering of the *duplerii* is on p. 72. The probable date was 1414 (Pezzana, 2, p. 159).

CHAPTER 5

RULERS, RITES AND RELICS

The cult in action, as an element – or rather, a complex of elements – in the public life of the Italian cities, defies simple description. What follows is merely a series of snapshots.

The Annual Round

Where an adequate series of account-books survives, it may be possible to follow the annual round of official offerings over an extended period of time. At Lucca, the lists of prescribed offerings in the three statute revisions of 1331, 1342 and 1372, viewed together with the communal accounts which survive in reasonable profusion from the 1330s onwards, suggest that the fourteenth-century routine was remarkably stable considering the city's many political vicissitudes. The practice of the Lucchese government was to consolidate its regular almsgiving into the form of payments, made in wax, on the feast-days of prescribed saints.[1] The Preachers, for example, received their offering on the feast of St Peter Martyr (later in the century, St Dominic) and the Minors on the feast-day of St Mary Magdalen.[2] Some churches (apart from the cathedral) received more than one offering. The church of San Frediano received offerings in November on the feast-day of Frediano himself, and also on the feast of St Catherine, who possessed a chapel in the church; in April there was an offering to St Zita.[3]

The liberation of Lucca from Pisan rule in 1369 and the re-establishment of a free republic were followed by a change in the way disbursements for *luminarie* were made, by a restriction of the number of *anziani* who were to attend each *luminaria*, and by some alterations of detail; but although the organization of the account-books changed, a fundamental continuity was (unsurprisingly) maintained.[4] The list of offerings laid down by statute in 1446 and in 1539 was substantially as it had been in 1372, which in turn displayed no dramatic differences from the lists of 1331 or 1342.[5] Certain novelties did, however, result from the liberation of 1369. A *palio*, unconnected with any named saint's day, was instituted on 6 April in celebration of the restoration of liberty, and an 'altar of liberty' was set up in the cathedral.[6]

Before the fifteenth century, it is not easy to obtain a more discursive view of the sacred year than is afforded by statutes and account-books, but the description of Pavia, written at Avignon by Opicino de Canistris in 1330, provides an approximation.[7] He was hoping to convince the Pope that Pavia deserved to be released from interdict, but he thought it well not to overstate his case. Civic religious life, at Pavia as elsewhere, was by no means un-problematical. Piety could not always be had to order, and the public authorities, while officially enjoining the decorum that expressed perfect obedience to God and his earthly representatives, also tolerated and even encouraged secular festivities which have seemed, to both contemporary moralists and modern historians, to have little to do with devotion.

Opicino acknowledged that although it was so well endowed with gifts and amenities, Pavia was torn apart by the discords of its citizens. The eagerness of almost all the inhabitants to perform their Easter duty and the Easter custom of releasing prisoners – 'not, however, evil-doers or robbers' [*malefici vel latrones*] – did not mean that all were perfect, or that there were no reprobates among them. Opicino's descriptions of the customs with which the citizens of Pavia marked the chief days of their religious calendar convey an ambiguous interpenetration of the spiritual, the superstitious and the carnal of which he himself was partly, but perhaps only partly, aware. It would be rash to think that such conditions were unique to Pavia.

Opicino attempts to distinguish between the processions and other devotions which involved the laity and those which were essentially clerical, but the distinction was clearly not watertight.

First among the processions involving the laity he lists the Christmas Day procession to San Salvatore Maggiore, which was accompanied by all sorts of musical instruments and involved the presentation of a *pallium* of silk or cloth of gold. The feast of St Augustine at San Pietro in Ciel d'Oro was similarly honoured, the commune presenting one *pallium* and the guilds others: 'They do this in several other churches as well, bearing a *pallium* and making offerings, not only out of custom but out of some special devotion or a victory granted on a particular day.' Opicino lays great stress on the the citizens' reverence for Augustine, whom they regarded as their 'special patron', whose bodily presence was at all costs to be safeguarded against removal by kings or princes; he was therefore, allegedly, kept 'in the deepest and most secret of places' so cunningly that he could not by any means be removed.

The ancient Bishop Syrus was the official patron of the commune, and his feast-day was marked by the usual tributes. A *pallium* and a lighted candle painted with his image and emblems was borne to the cathedral, followed by the *podestà* and all the chief people and nobility; another similar candle, traditionally presented by the inhabitants of Occimiano, followed. Then there were the candles of the guilds, decorated with the insignia of the city and the instruments of the guild in question; behind each came the consuls of the guild and its patron, if it had one, each carrying a small candle; then came the guildsmen, themselves bearing candles. The apparent solemnity of the order so far described was not, however, maintained. A castle made of pots was carried on a board before the guild of innkeepers, and this was broken up by youths in the entrance to the church. The birdcatchers carried a tree with small live birds suspended by their beaks from its branches, and this met a similar fate. Many other games were played during the procession of the *cerei*.

The races in honour of the patron took place on the feast of his translation. The horse-race, for a *pallium* of silk or cloth of gold, was undertaken by the squires [*scutiferi*] of the nobles on behalf of their masters; a roast pig and a live white cock were the other prizes. The *pallium* was at the disposal of the winner, though it might be offered to the saint. After lunch, men and women of low repute [*ribaldi et mulieres publice*] ran foot-races for prizes of salt meat and ribbons; less idealistic or more realistic than the Veronese at a later date, the Pavese did not expect women of repute to be involved in such goings-on.[8]

The enthusiasm of the people of Pavia for their Easter duty and for the Eucharist, which Opicino liked to emphasize, took some rather irregular forms. Those who could not, or for some good reason would not, take communion at Easter, even nursing infants, were not permitted to break their fast until they had been 'communicated' with an unblessed host. A child too small to swallow a host was given some drops of wine that had been blessed. At the feast of St Blaise, too, everyone had blessed wine to drink from the altar chalice.[9] Other festivals were marked by 'folk' customs. On the feast of the plague-saint Sebastian, 'little birds' [*avicule*] of cooked bread dough were blessed at the church of St Peter *ad Vincula*, and given to men and beasts alike to avert pestilence. The goldsmiths, who belonged to that parish, made little iron arrows, which were also blessed and carried by men in memory of St Sebastian and to obtain protection against arrow wounds. On the feast of St Agatha at the church of the Clares, boys wrote on scraps of paper the words that an angel, according to legend, had inscribed on the saint's tomb, and put them in fields and vineyards to guard against hail. At Pentecost, it was the custom in the cathedral and certain other churches to throw firewood, with pots, fruit and roses, down from the ceiling vault. As young boys ran about the church trying to catch the pots, a burning flax-stem was dropped down on their heads. 'These and things like them are childish [*puerilia*]', Opicino observes primly; 'let us now turn to works of devotion.'[10]

Decorum and Authority

Where, however, were the dividing lines to be drawn between piety, *puerilia*, and folk customs which even to contemporaries seemed superstitious or paganizing? A little later in the century a hostile observer, Pietro Azario of Novara, described the celebrations of the feast of San Marino which all Pavia – city and suburbs, men, women and dogs – came to see.[11] A young man concealed himself beneath a specially planted tree whose trunk and branches had been hollowed out, and, operating a system of ropes which went up through the cavities, caused a number of 'veils' of different shapes and sizes to move about. Other young men arrived in a variety of female costumes, carrying sticks and bread-baskets, and competed with one another to beat down the veils. If a small one fell it was simply put into a basket, but there were fights over the big ones, and hair and cloaks were torn. The decadence and impiety of the Pavese made a whore [*prostibulum*] of the city, where neither God nor the saints were revered. The customary observance of vigils simply provided an occasion for people of both sexes to assemble 'in search of indecency and pleasure [*causa stupri et deliciarum*]'.

Azario's strictures seemed to Opicino's editors confirmation of a hint dropped in the *Liber de laudibus* itself. Augustine's feast at San Pietro in Ciel d'Oro was an attraction for all Lombardy, and vigil was kept all night, with good guard provided by the authorities, 'lest any evil should occur'.[12] This, taken with Azario's critical observations, might suggest that the Pavese were unusually prone to defile sacred occasions with wanton behaviour. In fact they were certainly not alone in so doing, or in being thought likely to do so. Part of the point of Opicino's observation was that on this particular occasion flocks of visitors from elsewhere came to Pavia, which would almost automatically create problems of public order for the authorities. Similar arrangements for the policing of vigils were made by law elsewhere, for example in the Lucchese statute of 1308.[13] The statutes produced at Parma between 1316 and 1325 stated openly that many of the women of the city and diocese who came to keep vigil on the eve of the Feast of the Assumption were 'dragged violently out of the church by ill-intentioned clerks and laymen' and abused.[14] The Perugian statutes of 1342–43 noted that in consequence of the indulgence lately conceded by Pope Benedict XII for the feast of St Stephen at the Dominican church, many injuries, insults and offensive acts ['*molte engiurie e contumelie, detractione, violentie e offese*'] were inflicted on women from town and country alike, and even on 'foreign' women who wished to attend the celebrations of the indulgence, both in the church itself and outside it.[15]

The same statute collection put in writing the processional order to be adopted by the guilds, precisely in order to avert squabbles, observing sadly that processions and *luminarie* were frequently the occasion for disorders of all sorts.[16] Penalties were sometimes prescribed for throwing candles at other people, or at the altar.[17] A clause added to the revised Lucchese statute of 1342, and subsequently repeated, proscribed a number of enormities that might be committed in the cathedral or other consecrated places: gaming, offering merchandise for sale (except at the markets which accompanied the festivities of the Holy Cross and St Martin) and throwing stones or other missiles at the *ceri* which, having been solemnly offered, were hung up in the church.[18] Saints, churches and the festivals of the sacred year were evidently not treated with perfect decorum or devotion.

The press of people who assembled for *feste* constituted a possible source of disorder, particularly if they were in merry mood. In 1398 more than four thousand people gathered at the Carmelite church in Parma to keep the vigil of the Assumption, and drank a good deal; 12,000 people watched the *palio*.[19] In 1328 there was a conspiracy to deliver Orvieto to Louis of Bavaria on the day of the Assumption, because all the people would be at the cathedral.[20] There was a riot at Siena on 15 August 1343, in the aftermath of the expulsion of the Duke of Athens from Florence; it was fairly easily quelled, but left its mark on the communal accounts, including a bill for a broken trumpet. Siena's political troubles in the second half of the century, which witnessed a frequent succession of regimes, were also reflected in expenses for security at the *festa*.[21]

It was far from unknown for there to be quarrels about the arrangements or payments for a festival. As rulers of Arezzo, the Florentines noted in 1448 that 'there have often been dissensions among the citizens about the honouring' of the feast of San Donato, and elaborate arrangements were prescribed for the appointment of a committee which should have full powers to purchase the *bravium*, which was to be 'of the most beautiful crimson silk' and to cost at least fifty-five florins out of a grant of sixty; the remainder, and up to another five florins, was to be expended on offerings, on the customary lunch and other expenses connected with the *festa*. The priors were to be bound not in any way to interfere with the appointed committee in the execution of their duty, but to give them every assistance.[22]

The age of secularization, of games and races, was also the age of the proliferation of wonder-working images of the Mother of God and of the growing civic prominence of the feast of Corpus Christi.[23] As one positive expression of the power to influence, or even to control, what was publicly done in honour of Christ, the Virgin and the saints, the appropriation of responsibility for Corpus Christi was entirely consistent with the position that urban governments had increasingly assumed in relation to the cult from the twelfth century onwards. If, however, the civic authorities thought it salutary to insist on the correct observance of feast-days, they were equally alert to the ways in which feast-days might disturb the operations of law and order. In some cities, the criminal courts took fewer holidays than the civil courts. The release of prisoners on the feast-days of the Virgin at Siena, the Baptist at Florence, and other patrons elsewhere was a widely acknowledged pious duty, but the identity of the prisoners to be released was often the subject of intense debate.[24] Taddeo Pepoli, who dominated Bologna between 1337 and 1347, decreed that because of the sheer number of prescribed feast-days, debtors who had been proclaimed for six months or more could be arrested, even in their own homes, on all feast-days except the feasts of Christ himself and the Virgin, and those of the Archangel Michael and the Apostles.[25]

Measures were sometimes taken to ration the personal attendance of the supreme magistrates at festivities. The possible motives were various: to economize on expenditure; to ensure the availability of a quorum to attend to urgent business; or to enhance the status of the solemnities that *were* attended by the city's rulers. In the Sienese statutes promulgated in 1337–39 it was laid down that the Nine Governors and Defenders of the Republic would leave the public palace only to attend the Feast of the Assumption. Arguably, the status of the city's supreme festival and the identification of the Nine with the Virgin were both thus emphasized.[26] In 1308 the Lucchese statute specified only that the magistrates should attend the celebrations of the Holy Cross, but the statute enacted for Lucca under Pisan rule in 1342 began to enumerate the *luminarie* to which the *podestà* and the principal officials and magistrates were bound to go with an offering of as many candles as there were persons attending, to a stated maximum of so many pounds of wax. It was a respectable list. A further modification was made in 1372, when it was stipulated that only three of the *anziani* should attend *luminarie*, with seven remaining in the palace; it was up to them to decide both the quantity of the offering, although forty pounds of wax remained the going rate, and which of the communal officials should attend.[27]

In a number of cities in the course of the fourteenth century, organizations such as the guilds, which had hitherto claimed a position of quasi-autonomy and influence in the fluid structure of urban politics, found themselves placed under restrictions.[28] This trend had implications for the public cult of the saints. The direction of the cult and the enlargement of the pantheon could never be socially or politically neutral processes, however genuine the spiritual motivations behind them; those who enjoyed these powers visibly occupied a distinctive place in urban society, in their own eyes and those of their fellow-citizens. It is difficult, therefore, to distinguish the process whereby the 'state' claimed monopoly powers over the regulation of the public cult from the process by which the social elite affirmed their status. They invoked an ideal of unanimity in the veneration of the saints, just as in earlier centuries clerical writers had described, or imagined, an ideal unity of clergy and people in holy enterprises;[29] but it was a unity, or semblance of unity, that sometimes had to be maintained by force. Festivals meant, after all, the assembly of large numbers of people; they raised issues of public order. Only in exceptional circumstances have the streets belonged to the people, and it has not usually been a spectacle welcome to their betters.

Villani thought that the Florentine Baptistery, which was and would remain the focal point of the civic cult, was in the time of Frederick II identified with the Guelfs and as the burial place of the *buona gente*.[30] The saint's festival, in times of political tension, certainly became a battleground between elements in the urban population. In June 1300 the magnates, disgruntled at their treatment by the *popolo*, chose the occasion of the guild procession to St John to mount an attack on their opponents.[31] In 1306 the regime took steps to diminish the identification of the *popolo* with the guild community. The *popolo* was reorganized into eighteen *gonfaloni* (standard-bearing companies), and it was decreed that all *popolani* were henceforth to attend the offering to St John with these *gonfaloni*, whereas previously they had gone under the *gonfalone* of one of the twenty-one guilds. As the new banners bore both the arms of the *popolo* itself and the arms of Charles I of Anjou and Naples, the effect would be to make the procession to the patron a visual display of Guelf unanimity.[32]

In 1333 two rival *brigate* of Florentine craftsmen, the one dressed all in white and the other in yellow, organized games and entertainments throughout the month preceding the feast of St John. According to the chronicler Stefani, 'the artisans, with increased arrogance, every day created new feasts and games and other diversions'. One, involving 520 men dressed in white and the running of a white *palio*, was held in the *corso de' Tintori* (the dyers' street) in honour of Sant' Onofrio. Stefani, writing between 1378 and 1385 and an observer of the Ciompi revolt, noted that 'they still preserve this style of celebrating this festival on that day, though not on so large a scale'. He evidently thought it significant that the great flood which followed did more damage to that area of the city than to any other.[33]

The Duke of Athens (who permitted the dyers to form themselves into a guild) curried favour with the lower orders in 1343 by permitting the institution of six festive brigades of the *popolo minuto*; the chief of the largest called himself 'the emperor'. Such junketings, even when they were secular in character, were suspect enough, but the Duke also reverted to the old style of celebrating St John, and the *festa* was organized on a guild basis, 'in the ancient way, without *gonfaloni*'. Stefani followed Villani in his acknowledgement that the *festa* was a fine spectacle, but added that 'the citizens, remembering the offering with *gonfaloni*, and seeing the mean people and wool-carders being made much of and advanced, were deeply offended, because it was beyond all human and divine reason'.[34] The institution of celebrations of St Anne to commemorate the Duke's expulsion, like other innovations in the public cult later in the century, can be interpreted as an expression of Guelf upper-crust assertiveness, self-consciously confronting the lesser guildsmen and the lower orders.[35]

At the height of the summer of 1378, the lesser workers in the cloth industry, who were not permitted to organize themselves in guilds and had no access to political representation, flared into a short-lived revolt, the so-called revolt of the Ciompi, which intermeshed with dissensions among the city's leading politicians. The disturbances began shortly before the feast of St John, and the celebrations could not and did not take place. A month later, the offering to St Victor (which was clearly a Guelf establishment occasion) was poorly attended because of the state of emergency and the fears of good Guelfs.[36] Order was restored in the autumn and the priors decreed, on 1 October, that the *festa*, with the running of the *palio*, should take place on 18 October (St Luke's Day). Two weeks later, alarmed by news of fresh conspiracies, they countermanded these orders. A special ritual took place on the 18th. Thirty-one knights who had been created at the height of the revolt in July took the opportunity to be, so to speak, rebaptized as knights of the commune and people. On payment of a stipulated contribution towards expenses, they were presented with a lance, shield and pennant bearing the arms of the *popolo*, and together they presented a *palio* at the altar of St John. Although the representatives of Florence's subject territories and communities made their offering, neither the usual citizen procession with the *gonfaloni* nor the running of the *palio* took place; the priors wished to keep opportunities for assembly to a minimum.[37]

By an enactment of 1380, recapitulated in the 1415 statute, officials of the guilds or of the merchant corporation were strictly forbidden to institute any offering on a saint's day; the power to do so was reserved to the priors and the other principal officials of the commune.[38] The latter had already demonstrated their prerogative in February 1379 by instituting a celebration of St Julian the Hospitaller, whose feast was celebrated at Florence on 31 August, in specific commemoration of the defeat of the Ciompi.[39] When the Guelf grandees offered to St Victor, St Zenobius or St Antony, it was at the cathedral, which was being rebuilt in honour of the Mother of God. Theirs was the city's holiest public space; the celebrations of Sant' Onofrio remained a neighbourhood festival in honour of a neighbourhood saint.

Custom enshrined social prerogatives, and any departure from the norm was keenly observed. In 1332 eyebrows were raised when the butchers of Parma, who had always been accustomed to process to the feast of St Hilary together with the cobblers, smiths and skinners, went not with the other guilds, but accompanied by 'many of the greatest and noblest people in the city'.[40] The butchers had a history of influence in civic affairs, and they, together with the *dominae*, the wives and mothers of the best people, presented the two great candles that were made at the expense of the commune of Parma for the high altar of the cathedral, and lit on solemn feast-days.[41] The processions and ceremonies that were integral to the celebrations of the saints inevitably afforded opportunities for the display of status, and even intimidation. Already in the mid-thirteenth century Salimbene thought it was for reasons of both display and 'security' that Giberto da Gente (who, as he reported, had come to power with the assistance of the butchers) attended the solemnities of the Assumption at Parma accompanied by an armed bodyguard of fifty men.[42] On St John's Day at Florence in 1394 the authorities deployed 700 soldiers 'in an exhibition of military power'.[43]

The church could not be treated as a 'private' or subordinate organization, as the guilds could be. It had the power to make demands which had at the very least to be negotiated and accommodated, but it also had to accommodate the demands governments made on the cult for their own purposes. The command to attend at the shrine of the patron, enforceable on all orders of society, was issued in the name of the government. To institute a celebration which included this requirement, as the Pistoiese did when they consented to the solemnities for San Zeno in 1337, was a serious matter.[44] This particular example well illustrates how the enhanced reverence paid to episcopal saints by communal authorities in and after the fourteenth century fitted into a larger pattern. The tributes that secular governments, which had demonstrably acquired a high degree of control over the local church and its personnel, now required to be paid to the bishop's saints became another means of identifying themselves in the public eye with the sanctified and particular past of the urban community. Late-medieval rulers were increasingly designated *Magnifici*; their dignity was, in part, that of courtiers at the court of heaven, who paraded their status in public ceremonial. This was true of princes and republican magistrates alike. The defence of the communal order against tyranny might call forth impassioned appeals to the saints, but even if an individual ruler had his own cult preferences, he paid his respects to his city's established saints. The commune and people which the saint protected continued to exist under seigneurial management, as the official titles of many a *signore* attested, and the paternalistic functions of guardianship and protection claimed spiritual and saintly sanction.

There were several ways of publicly associating regimes with the virtues of the saints. In the ceremony of the robing of the statue of St Martin, which took place annually on his feast-day at Lucca, the charity of the saint and the charity of the government were with increasing clarity represented in one image. In 1331 it was declared that every year, on the vigil of St Martin, last year's garments were to be given to the messenger of the *anziani* in exchange for a candle of one pound weight which he was to present to the *operarius* of the Holy Cross; he was then to wear them publicly while riding on horseback about the town on St Martin's Day, 'so that he can be seen by all'.[45] In 1372, what had been described in 1331 and 1342 as a custom 'hitherto observed' is now laid down as a statutory duty 'for the honour and reverence of the blessed Martin, patron and protector of the city of Lucca'. The recipient of last year's vestments is no longer necessarily to be a named servant of the *anziani*; the *anziani* are given official permission to give them to whom they will, with the old proviso that they be borne by him on horseback around the town 'so that he may be publicly seen'.[46] From time to time the whim of a scribe permits us to see what sort of effect the government paid to achieve. In 1361, for example, an exceptionally full account of the expenditures on the robing ceremony enumerates payments to a draper for red and white cloth for Martin's robe and cap, to a furrier for fur trimmings, for two cords for the harness and the cap, to a goldsmith and a mercer for the horse's eye-pieces, and for the gilding of them and of the bridle and the silvering of the saint's sword, and to a tailor for thread and braid and for the sewing of the garment. Finally, payment was authorized to the *magistri* who had erected the wooden scaffolding necessary 'for the cleaning and garbing of the aforesaid image'.[47] In the fifteenth and sixteenth centuries it was stipulated that the vestments be given 'to some poor person' who, again, had to exhibit them on horseback, 'in memory of the miracles of the said beneficent confessor [*almifici confessoris*]'.[48]

Rulers, whether one man or many, did not always fulfil the obligations laid upon them. This might be out of negligence, or it might be the result of difficult circumstances. Guecellone da Camino, as ruler of Treviso, was apparently neglectful of communal obligations to the saints: on 15 April 1314 Costanzo, priest of the church of San Bartolomeo, complained that the statutory obligation to make an offering of £50 worth of wax to his church, in commemoration of the end of the da Romano tyranny, was not being fulfilled, representing this as a failure to perform a vow. The council voted 250 to 15, with three abstaining, in favour of making the offering. With the restoration of a free commune the following year, more care was taken of such matters.[49] At Parma in 1448 measures were taken to celebrate the forthcoming Feast of the Assumption with enhanced magnificence. Gratitude was especially due to the Virgin for her help in restoring Parma's republican liberty (after the death in 1447 of Filippo Maria Visconti); but it was admitted that the celebrations of the previous year had not been all they should have been. The prescribed offering of 35 *lire* had not been made, and was to be made up; the sacristy of the cathedral had suffered losses of sacred objects, and efforts were to be made to get them back.[50]

Even in adverse circumstances, every effort was usually made to fulfil the minimum demands of the occasion. The temptation to save money on offerings might be offset by the hope of a profitable return on the investment; similarly, as physicians found when they argued against the holding of processions during epidemics, it might seem urgently necessary to conduct propitiatory rituals, and to fulfil customary obligations, if the city was facing some sort of disaster. If it seemed essential not to conduct the prescribed solemnities at the proper time, postponement rather than outright abrogation was the rule. We saw above how at Lucca in 1334 the impossibility of celebrating either St Regulus or the Volto Santo at the appropriate time brought the feast of St Martin, two months later, into an unusual prominence.[51] The procession for St James at Pistoia took place in 1348, as did all the festivities of the Assumption at Siena in both 1348 and 1349, and in 1355 in the wake of the fall of the Nine.[52] In 1363, a raid by Pisan troops on St James's Day prevented the Pistoiese from running their *palio*, but Filippo Villani recounts that they swore that the *palio* would not be run at all unless it were under the very gates of Pisa, and so it came about. In the same year, a Sienese chronicler noted that the Pisans did not make their August *offerta* to the Virgin because of the plague, but postponed it to Candlemas of the following year. The Sienese themselves, however, resolved that the *palio* was to be run precisely in order to stay the plague, an indication that at this date the race as well as the offering could still be deemed to have religious value.[53] At Florence during the Ciompi revolt in 1378 the festivities for the Baptist, as we have seen, were postponed, and then celebrated only in part. A century later the Pazzi conspiracy caused less disruption: the celebrations, including the *palio*, were held on 5 July 1478.[54] In 1476, the Sienese yielded to the fear of plague and cancelled the *palio*; the money that would have been spent on it went instead to the making of a silver statue of St Sebastian.[55]

There may by the fifteenth century have been a sharper consciousness of a distinction between games and races and the more strictly sacred components of civic festivals. The statutes of Verona announced that it was fitting [*conveniens*] to move the races that had been run at Verona on the Sunday before Easter [*dominica totius populi*] to a time ('Fat Thursday') that was both outside Lent and away from the day that was sacred to the Lord. The lawmakers were, they said, 'changing the tradition of our ancestors for the better, for the sake of our religion, so that, with the word of the lord, the time which is God's should be rendered to God, and that which is the world's, to the world'. The Sunday was henceforth to be marked by a solemn procession in honour of God, the Virgin and St Sebastian, in the hope that 'by the intercession and merits of the glorious Virgin and martyr this city especially may be preserved untouched by plague'.[56]

The feeling that the *palio* was an essentially secular component of the celebrations that clustered about a saint's day sometimes found expression in postponements for reasons both of worldly convenience and of devotional propriety. These were not an uncommon occurrence at Ferrara, for example, in the late fifteenth century. In 1471 the *palio* of cloth of gold, normally run on St George's Day, was run instead on 26 May, apparently because Borso d'Este had earlier been absent at Rome with all his lords. When he was absent campaigning for the Florentines in 1478, however, his wife Eleanora of Aragon attended the vigil and their eldest son Alfonso, borne in arms with the candle carried before him, represented his father. In 1480 the offering itself was postponed until 30 April because the Po was in spate, and in 1481 the *festa* coincided with Easter and the *palio* was therefore postponed 'so as not to obstruct the devout performance of communion'. Ercole took the opportunity on this occasion to put off the whole celebration until Federigo Gonzaga of Mantua arrived to join in the fun; Giovanni Bentivoglio and Ascanio Sforza also came to attend the offering on the 28th of the month, and they then stayed to watch the races. In 1497 the *palio* was not run, as a mark of respect for the death of the Duchess of Milan.[57] Races and other entertainments might in fact sometimes be dropped or postponed, but the solemn *oblatio* to the patron, which affirmed the right relationship both of subjects to their government and of the city as a whole to the heavenly powers, went ahead if at all possible. In 1496 at Florence, the *festa* of St John, according to Luca Landucci, was not celebrated *except* for the procession and offerings.[58]

Chroniclers and diarists, who devoted more and more space to festivals, lend some support to the contention that after the later fourteenth century they had an increasingly secular character, but the issue is complicated by the already familiar difficulty of making neat distinctions between mental compartments. To Gregorio Dati in the first decade of the fifteenth century the annual round of festivities, especially the celebration of the Baptist, demonstrated the perfect fusion of Florentine piety with Florentine power. This *festa*, like 'santo Zenobio', the Assumption, Pentecost, Holy Trinity and Corpus Christi, was an occasion 'for doing all those things which show joy and hearts full of gladness'.[59] Seventy years later, Benedetto Dei, describing Florence's annual festivals as he had known them, made no explicit distinction between the more and the less secular: the Baptist, Corpus Christi, the merrymaking at Carnival, the *palii* in thanksgiving for victories. He defied anybody, Italian, Sicilian, Levantine or other, to show the like. All these *rappresentazioni e solennità* took place 'to the honour and reverence of almighty God and for the contemplation and pleasure of the most powerful Florentine people'.[60] An observer of the celebrations of Corpus Christi at Bologna in 1492 expressed the interpenetration of cultural values in a rather different, somewhat paradoxical, manner: 'Many things from both the Old and the

New Testaments were represented in the procession. The spectacles were so fine that many said that Roman antiquity had come back to life.'[61]

In all these festivals there was the same duality: a demonstration of power and opulence that was meant both to impress and to entertain. Large numbers of people – heralds, servants, porters, musicians, provisions merchants, craftsmen of all kinds – were involved and remunerated. Twice in the first half of September every year Lucca expected to play host to hordes of people from the *contado* and further afield, for the fair and races of San Regolo and for the celebrations of the Volto Santo. The race for Regulus and the commune's provision of prizes for it are already described as customary in the 1308 statute.[62] The commune was put to any number of incidental expenditures apart from the *bravia* and their decoration, but again, we are better informed in some years than in others about what was spent and how on these occasions. In 1346, during the period of Pisan rule over Lucca, fruits and nuts were thrown into the piazza from the palace on the occasion of the proclamation of the races, and wine was provided for the entertainment of the trumpeters and piper of the Pisan Commune, 'who came to us on the day of the race and accompanied the *bravia* around the city together with the trumpeters of the commune of Lucca'; they were also given a florin as a tip, 'for the honour of the commune of Lucca'.[63] The decoration of the trumpets, and the hiring of the wagons on which the *bravia* were displayed, all cost money. It was customary for the trumpeters and other servants of the commune to receive new clothes every year just before the feast of San Regolo, and a similar custom was observed in several other cities.

Urban governments proclaimed safe-conducts (sometimes specified in the statutes) for a period of so many days preceding and following major festivals in the expectation, or at least the hope, that large numbers of people, apart from those who were compelled to do so by law, would attend the festivities and the fairs that often accompanied them. The inducements were sometimes less than holy; according to the 1308 Lucchese statute, the fair of San Regolo was the one occasion of the year on which dice-playing was legally permitted.[64] Villani recorded that in 1335 Mastino della Scala raided the Florentine *contado* with impunity because Florence's 'captain and cavalry' were for the most part at Pistoia for the feast of San Jacopo. They may well have been on police duties, but in 1342 so many people were absent from Prato visiting the *festa* at Pistoia that a *coup* was attempted.[65]

The races and other sports held in connection with the *feste* were unquestionably a great attraction, and by the fifteenth century great princes and substantial citizens lower down the social scale were taking a serious interest in horseflesh. A Florentine diarist recorded that the *palio* of St Victor in 1406 was won by the son of the *polminaio* ('lung-seller') of the *Mercato*.[66] The *palii* assigned as prizes for these races might be specially purchased by the government, or they might be taken from among those offered by subject communities at the patronal festival. In 1434, a month after Montefalco had sent 'a fine *palio*' to Perugia for the feast of Sant' Ercolano, it was offered to the winner of a joust that was held in the piazza 'to give entertainment to the people'.[67] The statutes laid it down that one of the *palii* offered for Sant' Ercolano, 'if a suitable one were to be found', was to furnish the prize for a race run the following day; otherwise one was to be provided, as was already the custom for the race held on All Saints' Day, and trimmed with fox fur at the commune's expense.[68]

These races excited widespread interest. A Sienese chronicler noted that in 1429 Filippo Maria Visconti's Barbary horses won the *palio* of St John at Florence. The Duke, who within a very short time would once again be at war with the Florentines, returned the *palio* to Florence with the request that he might be permitted to endow a chapel in San Giovanni; the gift was accepted and permission given for the chapel.[69] In 1431, the lord of Faenza won the *palio* of St John's Day itself, and the Marquis of Mantua the one that was run the following day, 'santo Lo'.[70] In 1472 Jacomo di Ranaldo Pecci won both the *palio* of St John at Florence and the *palio* of the Virgin at Siena; in the following year he did even better, winning the *palio* of St John and three other prizes at Florence, then winning at Pisa and Siena and, on 14 September, 'the principal *paglio* of Lucca', rounding off his year with two more victories at Florence.[71] Luca Landucci told how his brother Gostanzo brought two horses back from the Levant in 1478; one he sold to the Duke of Urbino, and with the other, 'Draghetto', he won twenty *palii* in all between October 1481 and

June 1485, beginning with the *palio* of Santa Reparata, winning the races of St Anne and St Victor on several occasions, and twice winning at Siena, only to be cheated of first prize on one occasion and on the other to yield it, with politic grace, to Lorenzo de' Medici.[72] In 1492 a Sienese owner won the *palio* of St John with a Turkish horse he had bought in Constantinople, and sold both horse and *palio* to the Duke of Mantua for 800 ducats.[73]

It might be possible to chart a decline in the explicit expression of religious sentiment in connection with festivals and a growing absorption in sport, pageantry and splendour as the fifteenth century progressed, but, as the Savonarolan episode suggests, there was constant excitability and ambivalence in the face of secular values. It was more and more frequently reported in the fifteenth century that the authorities had decreed a festivity to give 'solace' or entertainment to the people, but these came in both spiritual and carnal versions. Contemporary observers had an omnivorous enthusiasm for *feste*, but however enraptured they were by displays of material splendour, they also knew when they were witnessing a spectacle that was 'beautiful and devout', and registered their appreciation of these qualities. Powerful superstitious emotions were still bound up with the commemoration of the saints, and worldly complacency could easily be dented, at least temporarily, by signs of divine disfavour. In 1488 Luca Landucci recorded the forebodings aroused by the gale that blew up on St John's Day and tore the *palii* suspended around the piazza to ribbons; this, he believed, happened because a Bolognese cutpurse was executed on the holy day itself.[74]

The social diaries of the north Italian princes in the fifteenth century, however, must have made it very clear that *feste* furnished prime opportunities to exchange courtesy calls, conclude marriage alliances and transact other diplomatic business. The wedding of Maria, daughter of Alfonso of Aragon, to Leonello d'Este in 1444 was conveniently timed to coincide with the celebrations of Ferrara's patron St George, and a representation of the dragon-slaying was mounted in the piazza, with a wood 'with many oak-trees' erected as backdrop.[75] Leonello was credited with a keen interest in sacred music; he ordered the sumptuous celebration of Corpus Christi and of the Assumption, and was responsible for a particularly splendid spectacle in honour of the canonization of

Bernardino of Siena. After him, Borso 'augmented the feast of St George with his offerings'.[76]

The Bolognese year abounded in spectacles of various kinds. Ghirardacci identified the holding of ever more elaborate *feste*, such as the excessively dangerous joust of San Petronio in 1471, as one of the means by which Giovanni Bentivoglio sought to make his mark on both Italian and European opinion as a prince to be reckoned with. He was an enthusiastic instigator, and even inventor, of games. In 1480 he held a sort of football match in the piazza 'to give pleasure and enjoyment to the people of Bologna'.[77] In 1501, however, faced with riots and the threat of political extinction, Giovanni knew what he had to do. He ordained a solemn procession in which the head of San Petronio, the emblem of Bologna's identity and autonomy, was carried. Mass was sung in the basilica of San Petronio, and Giovanni then returned home, the relic remaining in the basilica until the evening, when it was restored to its historic resting-place in Santo Stefano.[78]

Liberty and Imperialism

For much of the fourteenth and fifteenth centuries the men who ruled Florence, Siena and, more spasmodically, Lucca faced, in varying forms, the challenge of upholding the appearance of republican continuity and tradition while accommodating the realities of their own struggles for power and reputation; so too, in their way, did the Venetians. Elsewhere subjection either to a native *signore*, who would most probably uphold tradition, in his own interest and in his own way, or to a 'foreign' lord (possibly the Pope) or republic (Florence or Venice) was the norm. Cities like Bologna and Perugia, ostensibly part of the Papal State but not yet fully under papal rule, occupied a rather ambivalent position.

The role of an established patron first during a struggle to uphold 'liberty', and then under despotic rule, can be nicely illustrated from the history of St Geminianus at Modena. In an earlier chapter we saw the importance attached to the reverent preservation and treatment of the saint's relics on behalf of the whole people of Modena. In the thirteenth century, the saint's arm acquired considerable regional fame and was put to a variety of uses in times of crisis. In 1260 it was exhibited to Bolognese penitents who visited the city during the Flagellant excitement, and two years later, when the Bolognese were conducting solemn processions in an effort to break a severe drought, they were again shown the relic.[79] It was also used for political purposes. In 1287 a chronicler of Parma recorded how a coalition of neighbouring cities tried to impose internal peace on Modena, fearing that in its disordered state it might become prey to the Marquis of Este, whose territorial ambitions in the whole region were a matter of general concern. To add the persuasions of the saint, the archpriest of Modena came with all the clergy to the public palace, bearing the *brachium* reverently in procession with lighted candles, crosses and incense.[80]

These efforts notwithstanding, Modena fell victim to the Este. whose first period of rule over the city was nevertheless interrupted on 26 January 1306 by a popular uprising which expelled Azzo VIII. Between then and the end of January 1307 a series of enactments was recorded which closely interwove the practical and the ceremonial, and made frequent reference to Geminianus. They suggest both the intimate involvement of the clergy in the process of re-creating Modena's freedom and the determination of the commune and people to make it clear that they possessed a substantial, perhaps even a majority, shareholding in the saint. Two hundred years previously the citizen body had made plain their proprietary interest in Geminianus's relics; this was re-affirmed now.[81]

Geminianus was invoked, immediately after God Himself and His Mother, as 'defender of the city and district of Modena' and as 'patron, protector and special defender of the city and people of Modena'. With the other heavenly powers, he was besought ever to show aid and favour to Modena, 'and to grant a health-giving state of peaceful liberty and the grace that it may perpetually be well governed by its rulers'.[82] The new order was to be one of peace and concord, underwritten by the saints, especially Geminianus, but threatened by the subversive activities of the ousted Marquis of Este. A company of one thousand foot-soldiers, to be known as the *societas Sancti Geminiani*, was to bear the insignia of the saint on its shields and banners.[83] On 26 March it was laid down that an image of Geminianus, holding a banner in his hand, with two angels beside him, of whom one was to bear a banner and the other a cross, was to be carved 'in the finest stone', inscribed *Iustitia, misericordia, veritas et pax* and placed upon the facade of the cathedral overlooking the piazza. Every year, the anniversary of the city's liberation 'from the servile yoke of Pharaoh' was to be kept as a public holiday, with all shops shut. The bishop and cathedral clergy were to prepare an altar with all necessary ornaments above the main portal of the cathedral, facing the piazza, and there celebrate mass with all the clergy of the city and suburbs. As part of the solemnities, the arm of the saint was to be exhibited to all those present.[84]

Geminianus did not bear the burden of the people's defence quite alone. On 20 May 1306 payment was authorized to 'masters and painters' who had been commissioned by the *capitano del popolo* to provide images of the Virgin and Child and others (Geminianus is not in fact mentioned by name) on the *palazzo pubblico*. It was hoped that the saints depicted would deign 'to protect and increase the tranquil condition and liberty of the people of Modena'. To encourage them, a lamp was to burn every night before the images.[85] It was also clear that Geminianus remained the bishop's patron: on 15 June 1306 it was requested, 'in defence of the rights of the holy confessor Geminianus', that a cancelled statute concerning the digging of the lord bishop's canal be revived.[86]

As the months passed, it came to seem necessary to bring Geminianus's arm into the more routine operations of government. The members of the popular councils took an oath on the *brachium* in the cathedral; according to the unanimous resolution of the *defensores* of the commune, taken on 13 November, they were to be formally reminded of this oath at every meeting. The duty of reminder was incumbent on the tellers of the votes, who were also to remind the meeting 'of the present good and peaceful state of the city and people of Modena, and what would happen to them if the opposite came to pass'.[87] It is all too apparent that the upholders of the new regime were nervously determined to ensure that the people must not be allowed to forget the foul deeds 'of that perfidious and most evil tyrant, who for such a long time made that people bear his yoke on their necks'.

On 13 January 1307 new regulations were published for the

celebration of Geminianus's feast-day proper, 31 January. As so often, a market accompanied the festival, beginning three days previously and going on for three days afterwards, despite the unseasonable timing; provision was made for the breaking of the ice if necessary. The usual safe-conduct was proclaimed to all merchants, excluding criminals, exiles and all subjects of the 'evil tyrant, the Marquis of Este'. As one would expect, all householders in the city and suburbs were obliged to bear their candles to the vigil.[88] Ten days later the guild officials petitioned, referring again to the 'savage tyrant Azzo', that the offerings made by guild members at Geminianus's altar on 26 January should be collected, publicly registered and devoted to the building of a chapel in honour of God, the Virgin and St Geminianus. This chapel was to be at the west end of the cathedral, towards the piazza. The officials of the guilds and the 'defenders of the people' were to be its patrons for the time being, with the right of nomination and presentation of the priest or rector. It was stated with extreme emphasis that neither the bishop nor any other prelate was to be permitted to claim any rights of patronage over the chapel as a result of having confirmed the nominated priest. The chapel's accounts were to be audited every year on 1 March, and deliberations held as to what should be done for its 'honour and stability'. The bishop and chapter were to be requested to confirm these arrangements and to be present with all the religious and clergy of the city and suburbs to celebrate mass every year on 26 January having previously gone in procession around the cathedral. Furthermore, the bishop was to be petitioned by the guild officials to grant an indulgence of forty days for all those attending the solemnity.[89]

The dispositions made at Modena in 1306–07 were, perhaps, unusually detailed and unusually specific in their reference to the political context that had given rise to them; but, as we have seen, the underlying ideas were commonplace. The Estensi, reassuming control of Modena in 1336, felt able to continue the special festivities that had been instituted in 1306 to celebrate their expulsion, on the pretext that they commemorated the saint's triumph over Attila the Hun. They showed proper respect for Geminianus; indeed, their statutes were unusual in imposing a higher fine for blaspheming him than other saints.[90]

As this example indicates, when a city lost its independence, decisions had to be made about the treatment of the civic cult by the new management, but these often seem not to have been particularly problematical. The annual round of sacred events which had taken shape in most cities by the fourteenth century was unlikely to be radically altered despite changes of regime. Public rituals were believed to have both an objective value, in so far as they propitiated God, and a subjective value, in that they expressed obedience to the commands of earthly authority. Neither God and the saints, nor the populace, would be pleased by the abrogation of established forms of veneration; the needs of new regimes could therefore best be met by adding to them rather than taking away. This could be done in two ways: first, by requiring attendance, with an offering, at the patronal festival in the 'mother' city; second, by instituting compulsory observances in the 'subject' city itself.

In the first period of Visconti rule over Bologna, Archbishop Giovanni took care to keep up the established round of celebrations, but added, in October 1351, a compulsory celebration of St Columbanus's Day in commemoration of the beginning of his regime. All shops were to close, and all officials, masters and corporations were to accompany the *podestà* to the church of San Colombano.[91] In his brief period of rule over Bologna, Giangaleazzo Visconti endowed the fabric of San Petronio with 'a most sumptuous *palio* of brilliant red cloth' [*un richissimo Pallio di drappo cremesino*] and ordered that in future a similar one be contested every year at the saint's feast. After his death, his son and widow confirmed a privilege he had left in draft, which *inter alia* confirmed the statutes, customs and privileges of the fabric of San Petronio, and also laid it down that every year on the feast of SS Peter and Paul the ducal lieutenant should offer a *palio* to the value of 25 *bolognini* at the cathedral, as had hitherto been the custom. This was a case of a happy coincidence; for it was on the feast-day of St Peter, the city's and the cathedral's old patron, that, according to the Duke, he had acquired the dominion of Bologna in the summer of 1402.[92]

A similar picture emerges elsewhere in the Milanese empire, both earlier and later. By a special mandate of Galeazzo Visconti the *pallium* contested in honour of Sant' Antonino at Piacenza in

1372, as in the previous three years, was worth 120 gold florins; formerly, it had cost only 15. By a happy chance the prize was won that year by Galeazzo's brother Bernabò.[93] In 1389 Giangaleazzo Visconti communicated to the *podestà* of Parma his wish that the feasts of St Mary of the Snows on 5 August and St Gall on 16 October should be annually celebrated at Parma.[94] Agreeing terms with Parma in 1421, Filippo Maria Visconti directed that the expenses of the offerings at the Assumption and for St Ambrose, 'and of other saints', should be met out of the city's ordinary revenues, 'as has hitherto been the case'. Three years later Filippo Maria attempted to get a subvention from the *anziani* of Parma for the celebrations of the Nativity of the Virgin in Milan Cathedral, claiming precedent under Giangaleazzo, but the *anziani* resisted, apparently with success. That the ducal *camera* had by the end of Filippo's reign taken over responsibility for the expenses of the Assumption 'and for the offerings and festivities of many other saints' at Parma, emerges from the fact that when Francesco Sforza negotiated the acceptance of his rule in 1450 he affirmed that these arrangements would continue.[95]

The pageantry that accompanied the *joyeuse entrées* of Borso d' Este into Modena and Reggio in 1452 was nicely designed to illustrate the desired relationship between the prince, his subject cities and their saints. On his entry into Modena he was met by a triumphal car in the midst of which 'they had placed St Geminianus, surrounded on all sides by a multitude of angels, and distributing corn and money'. At Reggio, St Prosper was represented, also on a triumphal car, 'in the air between two angels' with a canopy over his head supported by three more angels. Beneath his feet was a rapidly turning wheel, on which eight angels with musical instruments were placed, making the most delightful music. One of the angels at Prosper's side pronounced a eulogy in the vernacular tongue, with deliberately clear pronunciation; the reader is left in no doubt that the common people were intended to hearken and understand. The angel, having finished his speech, turned to Prosper, who was holding a reproduction set of the keys of the city in his left hand and in his right a royal sceptre, smoothly asking him for these emblems of authority so that he might hand them over to the Duke. At this, the holy bishop elegantly praised Borso's many virtues and expressed his pleasure that his city should be ruled by such a man, before handing over the keys and the sceptre.[96]

Dominant cities, as well as *signori*, would of course make demands of the cities they came to rule. The Florentines were notably keen to do so, both by exacting tribute to be brought to St John and by instituting solemnities in subject communities. That officials might be overzealous in exacting such tribute seems to emerge from an addition made in 1355 to the statute of the *podestà*; penalties were prescribed for attempting to exact candles for the feast of St John from communes in the *contado* or *distretto* when it could be shown that the parish on which they depended had in fact fulfilled its obligations.[97] In their first statute for Arezzo in 1337, the Florentines required that St John the Baptist should be celebrated on the established Aretine pattern: at the cathedral one year and at Santa Maria della Pieve the next.[98] This requirement was predictably omitted from the statutes produced in September 1345, after the Aretines temporarily regained their liberty on the fall of the Duke of Athens. It was replaced by an offering to Arezzo's native martyrs, Laurentinus and Pergentinus, enjoined so that God might deign to preserve and increase the peace to which the city had 'respired' on the feast-day (3 June) of the martyrs, who (it is significantly emphasized) belonged to the city by both birth and martyrdom.[99] John the Baptist, naturally, returned when Florentine rule became permanent after 1384; according to an enactment of 1454, the offering to him was now made at the *pieve*.[100] The balance was a delicate one, but no more than the Venetians or the Milanese did the Florentines have much to gain by ostentatiously subverting the established observances of their new subjects, and they might indeed hope to win propaganda points by showing a paternalistic care for native traditions.

In 1385–86 an opportunity was rather fortuitously offered to them to demonstrate their *pietas* towards Arezzo's greatest saint. Even as Arezzo struggled, in the mid-fourteenth century, to assert its independence of Florentine control, the location of the relics of St Donatus was disputed between the cathedral and the *pieve*. In October 1353, seven years after the manufacture of the splendid head-reliquary which can still be seen in the *pieve*, a commission of prelates, acting at the request of the Bishop of Arezzo and also of the priors and *gonfaloniere di giustizia*, ruled that the cathedral possessed the body and the *pieve* the head; the clergy of the *pieve* were ordered to put away the body they had been exhibiting. The wording of the ruling has its significance. The body was to be venerated in the cathedral; the head was 'to be venerated by and shown to the people' [*venerandum et ostendendum populo*].[101] The *pieve*, that is, had been awarded possession of the mobile relic which, like the arm of Geminianus or the head of Zenobius, was suitable for popular exhibition or for processional use.

Thirty years later, the reliquary was looted from Arezzo by French troops in the military upheavals which preceded the final Florentine takeover of the city. It came into the hands of the Ordelaffi lord of Forlì, and in 1385 he returned it to the Florentines as rulers of Arezzo. The Florentines deliberated what to do with the holy object; the advice offered in the *consulte* was that it should be returned to its owners. The priors did this, but not before it had been solemnly carried in the procession which welcomed the new bishop of Florence when he entered the city in January 1386.[102] When the relic was at last returned, the priors accompanied it with a flowery letter which laid stress on their paternal care for Arezzo and the role the Florentines had played in plucking the city 'from the Inferno'; now, under the tutelage of Florence and Donatus, the Aretines could look forward to peace and prosperity.[103]

The arguments in favour of restoring the relic are not elaborated in the record. Was it a relevant consideration that the rest of the saint's body had remained in Arezzo throughout? For whatever reasons, the Florentines – who had not, after all, removed the relic themselves – either felt morally obliged to return it or reasoned that they had more to gain by doing so. In the fifteenth century the Florentines not only – as we saw above – arbitrated in disputes about the conduct of the *festa* of Donatus at Arezzo, but upheld the requirement of the attendance of all the officials at the annual exhibition of the head-reliquary at the Pieve.[104] The wording of the Florentine statutes for Arezzo preserves the distinction between the Baptist as 'the protector and advocate of the magnificent and excellent Florentine people' and Donatus as 'the special benefactor and advocate of the cite of Arezzo'.[105] The Baptist, might by virtue of being Florence's patron, also be the patron of its territory, but he could not be blandly asserted to be the patron of Arezzo as such. Florentine rule caused no interruption in the appearance of Donatus on the Aretine coinage, either between 1337 and 1342 or after 1384.[106]

There is an apparent contrast here with the fate of the relics of San Rossore, brought to Florence from conquered Pisa in 1422 by the monks of Ognissanti, who proceeded to commission from Donatello the reliquary bust which, in changed circumstances, went back to Pisa in 1591. The late-sixteenth-century historian Scipione Ammirato perceptively evoked the context of the 1422 'translation': it was, he said, as if Pisa, 'deprived of its liberty and its ancient honours, were also abandoned by its saints, and on the contrary the city of Florence were filling itself with pomp, with glory, with riches, and with blessing'.[107] There was, however, no way in which the Florentines could strip Pisa of its supreme patron, the Virgin herself, and no apparent evidence that they sought to obtain the relics of Ranerius or Torpete.

The forcible removal of relics in token of the subjection of one city to another was by no means unknown. In the later thirteenth century the men of the small Umbrian town of Bettona were engaged in resisting the aggression of Assisi, and sought to secure for themselves the relics of San Crispolto, a legendary evangelist of Umbria, by translating them from their original resting place to an oratory within their own circle of walls. The bishop and commune of Assisi protested, and at one time the arbitration of the Perugians was sought, but the men of Bettona evidently remained in possession.[108] In the fourteenth century the threat to Crispolto came from the Perugians themselves. For much of the century they were notably aggressive in demanding tokens of submission from their Umbrian inferiors, and they sometimes sought relics as spoil. In 1320, having assaulted the Assisan castle of Bastia, they carried off the relics of San Corrado to Perugia, while in 1327 they were prepared to resort to arms to force the Spoletans not merely to render a *palio* at the feast of Sant' Ercolano, but to accompany it with a form of words which explicitly acknowledged their state of vassalage.[109] Bettona submitted to Perugia in May 1351, and in August 1352 the Perugians appropriated the relics of San Crispolto, installing them in the cathedral church of San Lorenzo. In 1371, however, the papal general Gil Albornoz decreed that they should be returned to Bettona.[110]

This decision is unlikely to have been taken out of a mere sentimental regard for the rights of original possession. It was also Alborñoz who authorized the removal of the body of St Rophilus to Forlì from Forlimpopoli in 1362.[111] In the one case the papal authorities evidently felt the need to trim back the power the Perugians had exercised for decades in Umbria ostensibly in the name of the Pope and Guelfdom; in the other, Alborñoz had, from 1359, made Forlì his base for the pacification of the Romagna, and had resolved on the destruction of Forlimpopoli as a trouble spot. The translation of Rophilus was the slightly delayed consequence of that destruction, and of the emigration of the Benedictine community which had had custody of his relics to the church of San Jacopo in Strada in Forlì in 1360. In 1362 the bishop and authorities of Forlì requested the relics from Alborñoz, and the ceremony of their translation to a completely new shrine was marked by the proclamation of an indulgence, in what must be reckoned a calculated effort to relaunch the saint and his cult in new surroundings.

If a city's ability to appropriate relics from weak or weakened neighbouring cities might be constrained by considerations of policy or the intervention of a higher authority, its power over its dependent countryside was less subject to qualification. It was conveniently presumed that a saint must desire the superior style of veneration that would be his in urban surroundings. Giovanni Antonio Flaminio took it for granted that the supposed translation of St Savinus from the village of Fusignano to Faenza in 1448 was, from the saint's point of view, a promotion: 'For God did not suffer his holy martyr to be longer defrauded of the honour that was befitting. So he stirred up the minds of the faithful to remove him from so humble a place, so that he could be more fully and conveniently celebrated.'[112] Such rationalizations obviously expressed the viewpoint of the rulers of the cities. In 1378 there were supposedly discovered, in the church of Sant' Ercolano in the castle of Antognolla near Perugia, the head and one arm of the saint. As Pellini expressed it in the sixteenth century, the rulers of Perugia judged 'that it was not fitting that the relics of so glorious a martyr should be in any other place than the city', and it was resolved that the translation should be celebrated every year on 18 October.[113]

Just over a century later, however, in February 1487, an exposition of the (previously known) relics of Ercolano in the cathedral revealed that the body was 'intero e sano'.[114] This seems to have prompted the announcement that the head and arm that had been discovered in 1378 were not the relics of the more familiar Ercolano – who, as bishop of Perugia in the sixth century, had withstood Totila – but those of a first-century namesake, who was now declared to have been the first bishop of the city. It was another variant of a familiar tale: Apollinaris of Ravenna, Syrus of Pavia and more recently Paulinus of Lucca were other Italian bishop-saints for whom such apostolic connections had been fabricated. What better way of accounting for the superfluous head and arm than to credit them to a first-century Ercolano and thereby, at a stroke, acquire for Perugia a first bishop with correct apostolic credentials?[115] In the closing years of the century, supporters of Colomba of Reate waited upon the Perugian magistrates to defend her reputation and argue her case for better accommodation, and found them discussing the placing of the image of 'the most holy martyr and first bishop and advocate of our city, St Herculanus' on the great seal of the people. Colomba's backers cunningly observed that for seven years the Perugians had had a living advocate in their midst, who was now living in squalor.[116] In the end the proto-Erculanus did not carry conviction. At the end of the sixteenth century Pellini commented that the festivities decreed for 18 October had fallen into disuse, and speculated that this was because 'they had no information about the first Ercolano in those times, and we have not had any since'.[117]

Relics of Power

By whatever means it was achieved, by the mid-fourteenth century the amassing of relics on behalf of a city was likely to be carried out under the direction of the government. The story of the ill-fated Florentine attempt to obtain the arm of Santa Reparata has already been told; they fared better with their efforts to obtain some memento of John the Baptist, and from 1393 his relics joined their other treasures in solemn processions.[118] In 1360 the Sienese acquired a rich store of relics by purchase, via Venice, from the sale of the furnishing of Constantine's imperial chapel at Constantinople; they cost £1625.[119] They became the focus of an annual ceremony, attended by the *signori*, when they were solemnly exhibited annually at the Hospital of Santa Maria della Scala on the Feast of the Annunciation. Payments for the offering made by the *signori* on this occasion begin to appear in the account-books in the closing decades of the century; a chronicler recorded in 1413 that the new silver trumpets made for the *signori* were first used 'when they went to see the relics'.[120]

Gifts were always acceptable, undisguised appropriation might be possible, and the purchase of relics might seem a mode of acquisition appropriate to the commercialized world of the later Middle Ages, but the grand old tradition of the 'holy theft' (*furtum sacrum*) was not yet dead. The Perugian authorities lost no time in staking their claim to the Virgin's wedding ring, stolen by a disgruntled German friar from the Franciscan convent of Santa Mustiola at Chiusi in 1473, and asserted their determination to hold on to it in the face of the objections of the Sienese, who, as overlords of Chiusi, appealed to the Pope. On 9 August 1473 the Perugians resolved that anyone who counselled the surrender of the ring was to be adjudged an enemy and rebel to the commune. There was intense diplomatic activity for some months, and the Perugians turned a deaf ear to a broad hint, conveyed to them in December by a commission of cardinals, that the ring might best be handed over to the Pope himself. Two cardinals who, according to Perugian sources, had received payment from the Sienese to urge the Perugians to return it significantly died. Prisoners were taken, quite literally: in April 1477 a Perugian who had been held at Siena because of the affair escaped and made his way home. The ancient argument that had justified relic thefts in the earlier medieval centuries was called in aid of the Perugian case: it was clearly the Virgin's own will that had brought her ring to Perugia. It may have been more immediately material that Sixtus IV had been a friar of San Francesco at Perugia for some years, and had lectured on theology and philosophy at the *studio*. On 14 February 1474 he informed the priors that he would take no action to enforce the return of the ring.[121]

The incident had the effect of reawakening official interest in Mustiola herself at Chiusi and at Siena. If the ring itself was lost,

Mustiola herself could be found, and in May 1474 she was 're-invented' and celebrated.[122] According to communal records, the ring had been deposited in 989 in the convent that bore her name. In 1350 it was appropriated by the cathedral church of San Secundiano, which gave rise to litigation over the right to exhibit it three times a year. In 1420, by agreement between the bishop and the communal authorities, it was deposited with the Conventual Franciscans. The narrator of the *inventio* of Mustiola would have had his readers believe that this was done for greater security, because the church of Santa Mustiola was outside the walls. According to this account, the precious object was regarded as communal property, and the priors held the keys by which it was secured. The ring had thus played a familiar role in contests between authorities and communities within Chiusi, but it had now moved on to a larger stage.

Santa Mustiola now appeared to a certain maiden of Chiusi in a vision, and told her to inform the priors that if they were to have any chance of recovering the ring, they must first translate her relics from her ancient tomb. On subsequent nights she instructed two honourable matrons that the bishop should be given a similar message. The leaders of the community none the less dragged their feet, professing uncertainty about where the relics were to be found, and the saint had to multiply her apparitions until the town was in uproar. The *inventio* now proceeded to a successful outcome. The canons of Santa Mustiola had been deprived of the ring over a century before, but now that Chiusi had lost it altogether they could regain a focal position in the public religious life of the community by establishing first the presence in their church of the relics of the 'ancient advocate of the Chiusini' [*antica clusinorum advocata*], and second their right to keep them.

Deliberations on this latter subject were held on 11 June, in the bishop's audience room, in the presence of Sienese ambassadors who had been appointed six days previously to visit Santa Mustiola's newly discovered relics and report on the circumstances of the *inventio*. It was decided to leave the relics where they were, but it is clear that the issue was not closed. The contest was between the convent and the cathedral, and the Sienese seem to have been involved as arbiters rather than claimants. The Sienese government sent an offering to Mustiola on 3 July, and later in the month they elected six citizens to deliberate further on the custody of the relics. In September the authorities at Chiusi proclaimed the *festa* a public holiday.

The Perugians had scored a lucky hit in their ongoing squabbles with Chiusi, which concerned tracts of the Val di Chiana and Castiglione del Lago, and therefore also with the Sienese who had ruled Chiusi since 1416; furthermore, they had acquired an asset with which they might hope to counter the attractions of Assisi and the Indulgence of the Portiuncula.[123] They made elaborate arrangements for the custody of the ring. At first it was resolved that it should be kept in the public palace, beneath the altar in the chapel of the *signori*, in an iron casket which was to be securely locked and surrounded by an iron grating about the altar. The casket was to have seven different locks, and the keys were distributed between the bishop (or his vicar); the archpriest and chapter of San Lorenzo; the priors; the *Consoli della Mercanzia* and the *Auditori del Cambio* on behalf of all the guilds of the city; the *Collegio de' Dottori*; and the *Collegio de' Notari*. The grating was to have its own keys, and these were to be held by the superiors of the four chief orders of friars. It was envisaged that the relic would be solemnly exhibited three times a year – on 3 August, All Saints and Easter Day – when it would be borne with great dignity from the palace to the cathedral. In 1488 – 'per più dignità della religione', as Pellini put it – it was decided to translate the precious object to the cathedral.[124] The previous arrangements had not been without their hazards: in 1487 the visiting Archbishop of Cosenza was shown the ring before departing from the city, but not without a little difficulty caused by the refusal of Alberto de' Baglioni, who had quarrelled with the priors, to yield up the keys he was holding.[125]

The circumstances of the transfer have an interest of their own. A number of trends in fifteenth-century piety combined to promote devotion to St Joseph. The Ferrarese diarist Zambotti noted that on 19 March 1481 Joseph was 'canonized' by Sixtus IV, clearly seeing this as in fact an honour for the Virgin.[126] The cult of the Betrothal of the Virgin, fostered by the Franciscans (of whom Pope Sixtus was one), helped to focus attention on her spouse. The Franciscan Bernardino da Feltre – who preached a great deal in Perugia between 1485 and 1487, a period of plague and civil disorder – urged in 1486 that a chapel in honour of St Joseph and a confraternity in his name be founded in the cathedral. He himself subscribed as a founder member of the fraternity, which acclaimed Joseph as a 'glorious patriarch' and as the 'nurturer and governer [*nutrizio e governatore*] of our lord Jesus Christ'.[127] Another Perugian chronicler noted that on 19 March 1488 the feast of St Joseph, 'which was not observed before', was marked by a solemn procession in which the officials of the commune participated, and that at the urging of another Franciscan preacher the feast was observed in the city and *contado*, although 'before, no mention at all was made of it'.[128] On 31 July the ring was solemnly installed in the newly built chapel of St Joseph, and ten years later Perugino painted for it an altarpiece of the Betrothal of the Virgin.[129] It would seem that the possession of the ring helped to create the climate in which the newly promoted devotion to Joseph could take root at Perugia.

Urban governments evidently thought it important that a city should possess relics commensurate with its status. Bologna boasted sufficient attractions to ensure that the numerous travellers who, because of the city's position, passed through it *en route* elsewhere did not do so without a second look, and well illustrated the proposition that a city's stock of relics constituted not only an attraction to everyday pilgrims but a means of impressing distinguished visitors, who were bound to profess a wish to see what their hosts had to offer. Apart from the Madonna di San Luca, the relics of St Dominic had drawing power. In 1472 'the queen of Russia, daughter of the despot of the Morea' visited the shrine, and in 1484 Alfonso Duke of Calabria, as captain of the league against Venice, 'wished to visit the most holy body of the glorious Dominic and to see the Bible of Esdras and other notable things in that church'.[130] When in the fifteenth century the Madonna di San Luca was carried in procession, for purposes of propitiation or rejoicing, it was often accompanied by other treasures from Bologna's store of relics. The causes were various: news of victory over the Turks in 1456; a general state of alarm and despondency, caused by plague and news of earthquakes, in 1457; the proclamation of an Italian peace in 1468; more bad weather in 1474; earthquake in 1505. In 1456 the head of San Petronio, the heads of St Dominic and San Floriano and the hand of St Cecilia were among the items borne in procession; all these were employed in 1505, with the addition of the heads of St Isidore and St Proculus, the Virgin's fillet, a spine of the Crown of Thorns, and – a new acquisition in the preceding century – the head of St Anne, which Cardinal Niccolò Albergati had received as a gift from Henry VI of England at the Congress of Arras in 1435.[131]

The Public Image

There were new saints, including canonized saints, and new cults; there were, as ever, the old saints who lay to hand for *inventio*, 'recognition' and translation, and civic rulers were as prompt to associate themselves with these rituals of refurbishment as they were with new cults. Niccolò d'Este, for example, was present in 1410 when the relics of San Romano were ceremonially 'exposed' at Ferrara, carried in procession and returned to the church where they had lain since the twelfth century. Nine years later it was the turn of St Maurelius and the thirteenth-century *beatus* Alberto di San Giorgio, whose relics were in the suburban church of San Giorgio, which had once been the cathedral.[132] Later in the century the dukes of Ferrara issued coins which bore the image of St Maurelius, while continuing to uphold St George as the emblematic saint of the city. One issue of Borso d'Este depicted the Duke on the obverse receiving a standard from St George, with Maurelius on the reverse; Ercole had himself portrayed kneeling before a figure of Maurelius clad in episcopal vestments.[133]

The suggestion that republican governments tended to favour images of the saints on their coinage while princes and *signori* employed heraldic emblems[134] is obviously true to the extent that republics would not favour the use of private and personal heraldry; but in fact effigies of the saints appeared on a large number of princely issues. A necessarily cursory survey suggests no single rule. Saintly effigies tended not to appear on princely or seigneurial gold issues and high denominations, which were frequently used as vehicles for personal and dynastic emblems, but they commonly did on coins of middling value. At the other extreme, *denari* or *piccoli* usually lacked any form of elaborate decoration. A pattern once established in the coinage of a particular city might be maintained over quite long periods by successive regimes, which perhaps suggests the influence of technical and practical considerations as well as the appeal of conservatism. Where a change of regime is marked by a striking change in coin design, we may perhaps presume a deliberate propaganda intent.

That the saints were in many places identified with republican autonomy is, of course, beyond question. St John the Baptist was the invariable emblem of the Florentine coinage until the sixteenth century. In the exceptional circumstances of 1529 the republic produced a *scudo d'oro* with the significant inscription *Senatus Populusque Romanus* on the obverse and *Jesus Rex Noster et Deus Noster* on the reverse.[135] Whether in the face of the Medici or the Pope, embattled republicanism in the sixteenth century needed the ultimate assistance. Alessandro de' Medici produced a coin with the images of Cosmas and Damian,[136] and Duke Cosimo some coins with no saintly effigy at all, but the Baptist remained the Florentine 'trademark'.

Two other Tuscan republics which survived into the sixteenth century present quite different profiles. The inscription *Sena Vetus Civitas Virginis* appeared on a *doppio grosso* of the value of two *soldi*, struck at Siena according to an ordinance of 17 August 1279;[137] this remained standard on similar issues, while small denominations just bore the words *Sena Vetus*. Despite everything that Siena owed to the Virgin, she was not actually depicted on the coinage until after the repulse of the Florentines from the Porta Camollia in 1525.[138] Lucca, by contrast, began to depict the Volto Santo on its coins early in the thirteenth century, after Otto of Brunswick confirmed Lucca's already ancient minting rights.[139] The city's chequered political history saw many changes of regime, but the coins being produced under the republic that was reestablished with the fall of Paolo Guinigi in 1430 and thereafter preserved some elements of a remarkable continuity with those struck early in the thirteenth century. Not only did the Vultus remain Lucca's most distinctive emblem, but the inscription *Otto Imperator* still persisted, on some small issues, in the the sixteenth century. The improved standing of St Martin at Lucca in the fourteenth century was reflected in his appearance on a *fiorino d'oro*, and he was subsequently to be found sharing the fifteenth-century *ducato largo* and the sixteenth-century *zecchino* with the

Vultus.[140] After Urban VI's visit to the city in 1387, permission was obtained to depict St Peter on the florin. In the late-fourteenth-century context this signified a celebration of the restoration of Lucchese liberty, which Pope Urban V had assisted in 1369.[141] Not until the late sixteenth century did Paulinus make an appearance on the coinage.[142]

In a number of cities, the images of long-standing patrons often in fact first appeared on the coins issued by seigneurial rather than communal regimes. Either to introduce or simply to preserve the effigy of the patron on the coinage was to affirm the continuity of a city's traditions under seigneurial rule, and the legitimacy of that rule. At Padua, for example, Jacopo II Carrara (1345–50) had St Prosdocimus depicted on the two-*soldi* piece: no earlier Paduan coin had borne a saint's effigy. Francesco I 'il Vecchio' (1355–88) featured the hermit St Daniel on his *carrarese* of four *soldi*; Prosdocimus appeared on his golden ducat and on the *carrarese* also. Francesco II (1390–1405) 'il Novello' had not only Prosdocimus, but Antony and Justina, depicted on various issues.[143] Taddeo di Pepoli (1337–47) was the first ruler of Bologna to have the patron St Peter depicted on the coinage;[144] he appeared again under the restored autonomous republic between 1376 and 1401.[145] By the end of this period, as already noted, Petronius had begun to make his appearance, and although the popes, as rulers of Bologna in the early fifteenth century, evinced a predictable desire to have St Peter on their coinage, Petronius maintained a persistent presence on the *quattrino*. Eugenius IV had Peter on the ducat and Petronius on the *grossone*;[146] during his brief *signoria* over the city between 1438 and 1443 Filippo Maria Visconti preserved a similar pattern, while the Bentivoglio, as *conservatori*, promoted Petronius to the *doppio bolognino d'oro* or ducat.[147] Various coins issued in periods of 'liberty' gave the preference to Petronius, while the *bolognini d'oro* issued in the name of the later-fifteenth-century popes depicted Peter.[148] Throughout the century, it was Petronius, in episcopal vestments, who held a model of the city, as a number of episcopal patrons did on the coinage elsewhere in Italy. Geminianus at Modena was another, but, perhaps surprisingly, he appeared for the first time only under the rule of Ercole d'Este (1471–1505), perhaps reinforcing points made above about Este care for soliciting his support.[149]

At Como, Abbundius was introduced on the coins issued in the name of Louis of Bavaria. He figured regularly on the issues of Francesco I Rusca (1327–35) and frequently, though not invariably, on the coins issued by Azzo Visconti between 1335 and 1339, and thereafter under the renewed Rusca *signoria*, until the end of the century. Naturally, he stood for the short-lived *Respublica Abbondiana* until it, and Como's minting rights, succumbed to Francesco Sforza.[150] Hilary's image had appeared on the communal coinage of Parma since the later thirteenth century, and it was retained not only under the short-lived restored republic of 1447–50 but also on the coinage issued for Parma under the rule of Francesco Sforza.[151] Syrus also made his first appearance on the coinage of Pavia in the later thirteenth century. Here the tendency to omit the saint's effigy from seigneurial gold coinages can be observed.[152] The saint, however, continued to appear on other issues, and like Hilary and Abbundius he was the emblem of the republic briefly proclaimed on the death of Filippo Maria Visconti. A bust of him featured still on some of Sforza's issues for Pavia.

At Verona, Zeno's numismatic debut was achieved under the Scaligeri after 1259, but only, at first, in the form of an inscription. He flourished under seigneurial rule, graduating to a nimbed bust on the *soldo* issued by Bartolomeo and Antonio della Scala between 1375 and 1381, and to a full-length image on the *grosso* issued by Antonio alone (1381–87). Under Giangaleazzo Visconti he was shown enthroned in an attitude of benediction or as a half-length.[153] Himerius at Cremona, however, met a quite different fate: having appeared on a number of *grossi* during the communal period which came to an end in 1330, he vanished from the issues of the Visconti and Fondulo *signorie*.[154]

At Milan itself Ambrose maintained his presence in one form or another from the days of the *prima repubblica* in the mid-thirteenth century onwards. On some early *ambrosini d'oro* or florins, Gervasius and Protasius accompanied him on the reverse, and they continued to appear on certain issues until the regime of Azzo Visconti (1329–39); Archbishop Giovanni then reinstated them on his *grosso*.[155] Under the later Visconti and the Sforza, Ambrose established a virtually unshakable position on coins of middling value, and on many of the larger issues his presence is acknowledged in the appearance of a small bust or *testina*, which seems to have been regarded as the Milanese trademark, in much the same way as the monarch's head on a British postage stamp. It was under the joint rule of Galeazzo II and Bernabò, between 1354 and 1378, that his image was elaborated to show him with the whip with which he chastised heretics;[156] later, Galeazzo Maria Sforza's *grosso* showed him on horseback, pursuing Arians.[157]

The city model was a familiar attribute of the bishop-saint, on coins as in other media, but other patrons displayed it also. At Camerino the cult of the youthful soldier-saint Venantius received a boost in the later thirteenth century when his relics, looted from the city by troops of Manfred, were returned by Charles of Anjou at the instance of Clement IV.[158] At this date the counts of Varano were establishing a domination of Camerino which lasted until 1434, and their coinage favoured Venantius. The old bishop-saint Ansovinus had appeared on the coinage from the early thirteenth century, and under the popular government of 1434–44 both saints were depicted, but it was always Venantius who was holding the city model. The lengthening shadow of St Peter was falling over Camerino by this time, and Venantius clearly signified civic autonomy. Giulio Cesare Varano (1444–1502) distinctly favoured him, and in 1482 Crivelli depicted him holding both the communal standard and a model of the city in an altarpiece painted for the cathedral.[159] In 1480 Sixtus IV forbade Giulio Cesare to mint any coins or to permit anything other than papal money to circulate, and under papal rule St Peter superseded Venantius.[160]

Native patrons met a similar fate in some other cities which fell under the authority of the popes. The coins of Ancona had honoured St Ciriacus from the early thirteenth century, first in the form of an inscription and then, from *c.* 1300, with an image; he was supplanted by Peter under papal rule in the fifteenth century.[161] At Ascoli, on the other hand, St Emidius, who appeared throughout the period of the autonomous republic, continued to do so, although by the mid-fifteenth century it was in the form of an inscription only. Here, in fact, the mint seems to have been inoperative for much of the period between the end of Eugenius IV's pontificate and its final suppression by Leo X. In 1471 the citizens pestered Sixtus IV for permission to coin *piccioli* for a year to the amount of one thousand ducats; these duly bore Emidius's inscription.[162]

St Peter, as we have seen, had ambiguous associations at Bologna: on the one hand, he was the patron of the cathedral and the original patron of the commune; on the other, his image, here as elsewhere in the papal dominion, had obvious associations with a papal power which increasingly eroded civic autonomy. At Faenza, where he occupied a similar position, the coinage of Astorgio II and Astorgio III Manfredi of Faenza, between 1448 and 1501, featured him frequently, if not invariably.[163] At Mantua, too, the communal coinage between 1256 and 1328 paid homage to him as patron of the cathedral, but here there were distinct local peculiarities. An inscription on the coins issued before 1256 under episcopal rule commemorated Mantua's most famous son, Virgil, and this practice persisted under the Gonzaga. It was not until the reign of Gian Francesco (1432–44) that the dynasty's coinage began to associate it with Mantua's most precious relic. A representation of the reliquary of the Holy Blood first appeared on a silver *grosso* of 1436 and subsequently on the first Mantuan gold ducat, in 1460: it 'became a much favoured type on Gonzaga coins'.[164]

To represent the saints on the coinage was, of course, only one way of using visual imagery to associate them with the earthly powers. The works of art of all kinds, from reliquaries to frescoes and altarpieces, commissioned by urban governments to celebrate the saints were beyond number, and we must reckon with them the furnishings that were provided for the newly diffused feast of Corpus Christi. The most superficial survey of the saints in the production of Florentine or Sienese artists reveals a coexistence of the old and the new expressive of the variegated pantheon that had been created in the previous centuries. The Sienese were fond of painting comprehensive versions of their pantheon.[165] At Florence, the historic layers of the pantheon all found representation. Jacopo di Cione's Zecca altarpiece of 1372 has already been mentioned.[166] In the fifteenth century, the Baptist might be depicted alongside the ancient Bishop Zenobius,[167] or alongside a patron such as Barnabas, who had been acquired by the city in an intermediate period.[168] The new, and specifically the Medicean, appeared in the frequent depictions of Cosmas and Damian, who did not owe their prominence solely to their popularity, as physician-saints, in the plague-ridden late Middle Ages. In an encomium on

Cosimo de' Medici addressed in 1464 to Alessandro Gonzaga, the humanist priest Francesco Castiglione related how Cosimo had paid for the annual celebration of Cosmas and Damian in 'almost all' the churches of the city; Castiglione wished this to be seen as evidence of piety.[169] The popularity of the Magi with artists, similarly, owed much not merely to the obvious opportunities the subject afforded for glamorous display but also to the partiality of members of the Florentine ruling elite, not least the Medici and their clientele, for dressing up as the Three Kings.[170]

In the late-fifteenth-century Marche, Carlo Crivelli was kept busily employed by earthly patrons who wished to keep their heavenly patrons firmly before the public eye. His Camerino altarpiece has already been mentioned. In 1472, Bishop Prospero Caffarelli commissioned from him a polyptych for the Duomo of Ascoli Piceno in which Sant' Emidio, in elaborate episcopal vestments, stands impressively to the left of the enthroned Virgin and Child.[171] Crivelli also included Emidio in an unusual composition of the Annunciation, now in London's National Gallery, in which the saint, shown kneeling at Gabriel's elbow and holding a large model of his city, seems almost to be distracting the Archangel from his momentous errand. The painting is inscribed *Libertas Ecclesiastica*, and commemorates the announcement made to the people of Ascoli by the *anziani* at the Feast of the Annunciation in 1482 that Sixtus IV had conceded administrative autonomy to the city. The feast thereafter became the occasion for an annual procession. Crivelli's 'sole "historical" painting' is therefore a monument to a calculated act of paternalistic concession to local sentiment, and a 'celebration of a solemnity more civic than religious'.[172]

The city model as an attribute of 'the bishop or saintly protector' was immensely popular in fifteenth-century iconography.[173] It represents a significant development of the motif, which appears in mosaic and other media throughout the early medieval centuries, of the bishop or other eminent personage who, in the role of patron, presents a model of his church to the Virgin and Child. In the thirteenth century, Salimbene described how the women of Parma offered a silver model of the city to the Virgin to reinforce their prayers for deliverance from Frederick II.[174] In the later fourteenth century, Eulalia was depicted on the San

Jacopo altarpiece holding a model of Pistoia, and Jacopo di Cione showed St Anne thus in the Zecca altarpiece of 1372.[175] In southern Tuscany around 1400, the Sienese artist Taddeo di Bartolo was a specialist in the mode: examples from his hand are his San Gimignano for the *collegiata* of the town of that name, and, at Siena itself, the figure of Ambrogio Sansedoni in the entrance of the chapel in the *palazzo pubblico*. The city model subsequently became Ambrogio's common attribute, and Zenobius of Florence and Petronius of Bologna were only two of many other patrons who were similarly depicted.[176] Patrons lay and ecclesiastical, representing or working within regimes of all stripes, clearly favoured a picturesque mode of representation which so graphically evoked the unique identity of the urban community and its special relationship with the heavenly powers.

Notes

1. The 1342 list is in *Statuti* 5, pp. 104–6.

2. A flagellant confraternity in the Magdalen's name existed at the Franciscan church at least from the 1330s: Bongi, *Inventario*, 1, p. 11.

3. *Statuti* 5, pp. 104ff. The offering to Frediano was already legally required in 1331 (*Statuti* 4, p. 189), but the offering to Catherine seems to have been initiated by command of Marsilio de' Rossi, vicar for John of Bohemia in 1333, when special payments were authorized for wax for the *luminaria* of St Catherine at her altar in the Preachers' church and also at San Frediano: CG *Mandatorie* 88, fol. 72. Other new entrants to the 1342 list were St Lucy, at the church of San Michele in Foro, and San Donato; an official offering to St Martin is also first prescribed in this statute. The earliest surviving payment for Zita is to be found in CG 95, fol. 24v, dated 24 April 1346.

4. Grants made in alms for the half-year were now grouped together, and such expenditures as those on *palii* or on the robing of St Martin were listed under *Extraordinarii*.

5. These lists are to be found, respectively, in ASL *Statuti* 6, fols 76–76v; Lucca 1490, III.32; Lucca 1539, III.32. In 1391 a payment was made for an offering to the ancient Bishop Theodore at the church of San Donato, which replaced the one made, since 1342, to San Donato himself: CG 108, fol. 110v. In the fifteenth century Theodore was one of the bishop-saints invoked at the head of the statutes in the next century: see above, p. 136 and n.1.

6. The *palio* is enjoined in ASL *Statuti* 6, Lib. III c. 93, fol. 70. On 13 April 1382 an offering was made at the altar of liberty, and the *anziani*

were authorizing payments to a painter for an altarpiece and for a tabernacle to enclose the altarpiece: *Mandatorie* 106, fols 105, 133v, 141v, 143v.

7. *Anonymic Ticinensis liber de laudibus*, esp. pp. 32–40. Detailed accounts of patronal festivities based on archive sources are A. Chiappelli, 'Storie e costumanze'; and Cecchini and Neri, *Il Palio di Siena*. For Siena, see below, Chapters 6–8 *passim*.

8. For Verona, cf. above p. 123.

9. *Anonymi Ticinensis*, p. 30.

10. Ibid., p. 40.

11. *Liber gestorum in Lombardia*, ed. F. Cognasso, *RIS* 16.iv, p. 118.

12. *Anonymi Ticinensis*, p. 39 and n.1.

13. Lucca 1308, p. 12.

14. Parma 1255, p. 115.

15. Perugia 1343, 2, pp. 120–21, 'De lo engiuriante le fenmene a le perdonanze.' The forms taken by this indecorous behaviour included 'toccando cioè desonestamente, basciando, tregnendo, abracecando, pizecano, glie pangne de capo levando'.

16. Ibid., 1, p. 133: 'glie romore e glie gride, le meschie e l'ofese'.

17. E.g. Parma 1255, p. 202.

18. ASL *Statuti* 5, III.cxxxviii, p. 136; cf. *Statuti* 6 (1372), III.cxcviii, f. 76v.

19. Pezzana, 1, p. 265.

20. *Cronache senesi*, p. 479.

21. Cecchini, pp. 30, 33–7. A chronicler noted the broken trumpets and the closing of the Biccherna in 1343 (*Cronache senesi*, p. 543).

22. ASF *Statuti di communi soggetti* 24, fols 46v–47.

23. See above, pp. 182–4.

24. On the statutory regulation of this practice, see above, pp. 118–19.

25. Rodolico, *Dal comune alla Signoria*, doc. 59, pp. 262–3.

26. See below, p. 285.

27. ASL *Statuti* 5, II.xxi, pp. 104–5; ibid., 6, III.cxcvi, f. 76.

28. Taddeo da Pepoli, for example, reduced the independence of the guilds at Bologna: Rodolico, pp. 84–92.

29. Cf., e.g., the stories of the translations of Geminianus and Ansanus above, pp. 61, 63.

30. Villani, VII.33. For the suggestion that the cathedral acquired greater civic prominence from the later fourteenth century, see above, p. 166. Other churches (such as San Lorenzo and the Annunziata) were particularly identified with the Medici.

31. Dino Compagni, *Cronica* (II, 21), ed. I del Lungo, *RIS* 9.ii, pp. 63–4.

32. Villani, IX.87; Stefani, pp. 98–9.

33. Stefani, p. 173; cf. Villani, XI.217. In March 1382 named persons including several dyers and wool-carders were exiled because they had

held meetings at Sant' Onofrio with the intent of reinstating the two disbanded guilds: *Alle Bocche*, p. 39. Sant' Onofrio's day was *feriato* according to the statute of 1415 (1, p. 189), and Benedetto Dei recorded 'gran festa di Santo Nofri a la piaza degli Alberti e Tintori' in 1472 (*La Cronica*, p. 94).

34. Stefani, pp. 202–3: 'Onde li cittadini, che si ricordarono della offerta co' gonfaloni, e veggendo magnificare la gente minuta e scardassieri ed inalzargli, sdegnarono forte di ciò, perchè era fuori d' ogni umana e divina ragione'; cf. Villani, XIII.8.

35. Trexler, *Public Life*, p. 220–24.

36. *Il Tumulto dei Ciompi*, p. 115.

37. There are several accounts of these events: e.g. *Tumulto*, pp. 85–6, 148; *Diario d' Anonimo*, pp. 386–7.

38. Florence 1415, pp. 316–17.

39. *Tumulto*, p. 91. The feast of St Julian, patron of innkeepers, was celebrated in Florence on 31 August.

40. *Chronicon Parmense*, pp. 218–19.

41. *Ordinarium*, pp. 183, 185.

42. Ibid., p. 222; *Cronica*, 2, pp. 649, 654.

43. Trexler, *Public Life*, p. 222.

44. See above, pp. 159–60.

45. ASL *Statuti* 4, p. 115.

46. Ibid. 6, f. 76v.

47. ASL *Mandatorie* 98, no foliation, 12 November 1361. A similar account, for November 1369, which includes a payment 'pro purificatura et mundatura sculture Sancti Martini' is printed in *Riformagioni della Repubblica di Lucca (1369–1400)*, 1, ed. A. Romiti (Rome 1980), p. 171. A very similar custom is documented later in the century at Pistoia with the robing of St James on his feast-day (25 July): Chiappelli, 'Storie e costumanze' (1919), p. 71. It may have been this unseasonable courtesy to St James that gave rise in later times to a delightful folk tale in which the apostle was cast as a Tuscan peasant down on his luck. During the winter he was able to charm a dealer into letting him have two fine oxen on promise of payment when the harvest was in. In every subsequent year, when James, working in the fields in the heat of July, saw his creditor coming, he donned his winter cloak and professed not to realize that it was summer and that payment was due (B. Bruni, 'La leggenda di Sant' Jacopo', *BSP* 1, ser. 59, 1957, pp. 80–90).

48. Identical texts appear as Lib. III c. xxxiii in the editions of both 1490 and 1539.

49. Marchesan, *Treviso Medievale*, 2, p. 188. For the institution of this offering, cf. above, pp. 150–51.

50. Pezzana, 2, pp. 659–60. A tailor and another man gave 320 lire to buy two *palii*, one for the race and the other to be presented to the cathedral; but the money that would have been spent on the *palio* for the winner

of the women's race was assigned to relieve the distress of Piacentine refugees in Parma.

51. See above, pp. 162–3.
52. Chiappelli, 'Storie e costumanze' (1919), p. 1; Cecchini, *Il Palio*, pp. 30, 33.
53. F. Villani, LXIII; *Cronache senesi*, p. 604. The conciliar resolution to run the *palio* is quoted by Heywood, *Palio and Ponte*, pp. 66–7.
54. Landucci, *Florentine Diary*, p. 20. Cf. above, p. 207.
55. *Cronache senesi*, p. 873.
56. Verona 1475, r. 35.
57. *Diario Ferrarese 1409–1502*, pp. 67, 200; B. Zambotti, *Diario Ferrarese*, pp. 64, 74, 89–90. The *palio* was run for St George only from 1456, having previously taken place on the Feast of the Assumption (Benati and Samaritani, p. 410).
58. *A Florentine Diary*, p. 108. This may mean simply that the *palio* was not run, since the customary licences were granted to various sorts of entertainers.
59. Dati, *Istoria*, p. 90.
60. *Cronica*, pp. 92–3.
61. Hieronymus de Borsellis, *Cronica Gestorum & Factorum Memorabilium Civitatis Bononie*, ed. A. Sorbelli, *RIS* 23.ii, p. 112.
62. Lucca 1308, p. 35. Villani refers to the race for Regulus under the year 1289 (VIII.137).
63. ASL *Mandatorie* 95, f. 53.
64. Lucca 1308, p. 201
65. Villani, XI 51; XII.2.
66. Corazza, *Diario*, p. 19.
67. *Cronache della Città di Perugia*, p. 380.
68. Perugia 1526, r. 93, p. XLIv.
69. *Cronache senesi*, p. 811.
70. Corazza, *Diario*, p. 35. The editor is wrong to think 'Lo' an abbreviation of 'Lorenzo'; it was a usual Florentine locution for 'Eligio'.
71. *Cronache senesi*, pp. 871, 873. The reference to the principal *palio* of Lucca shows that by 1472 this had been shifted from St Regulus's Day to the Feast of the Cross. The statutes printed in 1490 (but drawn up in 1446) still have it on 'dies kalendarum Septembris videlicet in festo sancti Reguli' (III.xxxvi, f. k.iiii); in the edition of 1536 the *podestà* is to arrange the holding of the race 'quolibet anno in festo Exaltationis Almificae Crucis, die quartadecima Septembris' (Lucca 1539, pp. clxiii r–v).
72. *Florentine Diary*, pp. 33, 42.
73. Allegretti, col. 826.
74. *Florentine Diary*, p. 46.
75. *Diario Ferrarese*, p. 27.
76. Johannes Ferrariensis, pp. 32–3, 37.

77. Ghirardacci, 3, pp. 206, 222.
78. Ibid., p. 307.
79. Ghirardacci, 1, pp. 201–2.
80. *Chronicon Parmense*, p. 52.
81. Modena 1306–07. The introduction includes a brief survey of Modena's earlier legislative history, and of Estense rule (1289–1306). For the early-twelfth-century translation narrative, see above, pp. 61–2.
82. Ibid., 1, pp. 3, 8.
83. Ibid., p. 42.
84. Ibid., pp. 99–100.
85. Modena 1306–07, 1, p. 158.
86. Ibid., p. 180.
87. Ibid., 2, pp. 50–51.
88. Ibid., pp. 143–5.
89. Ibid., pp. 157–8.
90. See above, p. 125. For Borso d'Este's entry into Modena in 1452, see below, p. 221. The chapel built in honour of Geminianus was demolished in 1476 (Modena C14, p. lxiv).
91. Sorbelli, *La Signoria di Giovanni Visconti*, pp. 220–22, 449 (doc. 79).
92. Ghirardacci, 2, pp. 536–7, 539. None the less, the troops sent to Bologna by the Duchess in March 1403 were billeted in San Petronio, so that mass could not be said there (*Corpus Chronicorum Bononiensium*, 3, p. 491).
93. Giovanni de Mussis, *Chronicon Placentinum* (Muratori 16), col. 512. Antonino's tomb had been opened the previous year in the hope of breaking a prolonged drought (col. 511).
94. *Ordinarium*, n.5, p. 180.
95. Pezzana, 2, pp. 26, 240, 703 and App. 52.
96. Johannes Ferrariensis, pp. 41–2.
97. ASF *Statuti* 16, fol. 208v.
98. ASF *Statuti delle comunità soggette* 22, fol. 54v. For the special celebrations instituted at Pescia when it came under Florentine domination, see above, p. 156.
99. Ibid., 22 bis, fol. 4: 'Item quod in die festivitatis gloriosorum martirum Laurentini & Pregentini Civitas Aretine de qua traxerunt originem in qua fuerint corona martirum consecuti de guerrarum fluctibus respiravit ad pacem quam deus eorum reverentissimis meritis conservare & aumentare dignetur.'
100. Ibid., 24, fol. 92v. According to a statute dated 22 November 1416, a chest was to be kept at the Pieve containing the names of those who contravened the *ordinamenti & statuti* of the Florentine government (ibid., 23, fol. 27v).
101. J. Burali, *Vite de' Vescovi Aretini* (Arezzo 1638), p. 83. The reliquary bust is illustrated by Rossi, *Italian Jeweled Arts*, pl. xiii.

102. *Diario d'anonimo*, p. 463. The Panciatichi diarist (*Alle Bocche della Piazza*, p. 61) says: 'in questo dì vene in Firenze la testa di sancto Donato d' Areço, che era stata i[m]bolata dalla conpagnia de l'arme', which is either a misunderstanding or an ambiguous reference to the relic's first public appearance. On 15 January 1386 the lord of Forlì was thanked for returning the relic; on 9 March two speakers simply advised that the *caput Sancti Donati* should be returned to Arezzo (ASF *Consulte e Pratiche* 25, fols 27v, 28, 41v). The reference is wrongly given as *Consulte e Pratiche* 27 in *Diario d'anonimo*, n.1, p. 463.

103. M. Falciai, *Storia di Arezzo* (Arezzo 1928), pp. 185–6n.

104. ASF *Statuti delle comunità soggette* 24, f. 91v:

> Et quod domini priores una cum capitaneo & potestate Civitatis Aretini & eorum offitialibus & provisore & camerario gabellarum & notario gabelle & capitaneis partis & offitiailibus custodie & cancellario communis & camerario comunis aretii debeant quolibet anno in vigilia sancti Donati predicti de sero quando ostenditur caput beati Donati ire ad ecclesiasm plebis sancte marie ad faciendam oblationem cum cereis in manibus ad venerandas dictas sancta reliquias beati Donati predicti.

Still in the seventeenth century the officials went to the *pieve* on the vigil to offer at Vespers; on the feast-day itself they adored the body at the Duomo.

105. Ibid., fol. 2: 'protector & advocatus magnifici & excelsi populi Florentini'; 'singularis benefactor & advocatus civitatis aretii'.

106. *CNI* 11, pp. 2–12. The Aretine mint eventually ceased to function in 1520.

107. S. Ammirato, *Istorie Fiorentine* 6 (Florence 1826), p. 429; Trexler, *Public Life*, n.11, p. 5; Janson, *The Sculpture of Donatello*, pp. 56–9.

108. Cristofani, *Delle Storie di Assisi*, p. 112.

109. *Cronache e storie*, pp. 88, 92–3. The foundation at Assisi of a confraternity in the name of the ancient patron San Rufino, which is first heard of in 1329, has been interpreted as another reaction to Perugian imperialism in the 1320s: U. Nicolini, 'La Fraternità dei disciplinati di S. Rufino', in *Le Fraternite Medievali di Assisi* (Assisi 1989), p. 107.

110. *Cronache e storie*, p. 166 and n.; Pellini, 1, p. 927.

111. M. Maccarone, 'La traslazione di San Ruffillo nel 1362 e la sua arca in Forlì', *RSCI* 5 (1951), pp. 358–71.

112. 'Le "Vite" dei Quattro Santi protettori', p. 359. For much earlier instances of similar sentiments, see above pp. 42, 64.

113. Pellini, 1, pp. 1233–4.

114. 'Cronica Perugina inedita', p. 274.

115. On the legend of 'Twelve Syrians', see F. Lanzoni, *Origini*, pp. 298–303. An Ercolano figured among the companions of San Brizio, who,

while evangelizing Umbria, had been flung into prison and (in an early version) martyred. A variant had Brizio released from prison by an angel in company with St Peter, who ordained him bishop. He in turn ordained his companions to various Umbrian sees, including Crispolto to Bettona. Ercolano became bishop of Perugia, where he subsequently suffered martyrdom at the hands of Totila. This version, Lanzoni reasoned, must postdate the *Dialogues* of Gregory the Great, in which the story of Ercolano and Totila's destruction of Perugia is told. The author of the later *passio* of San Crispolto believed that these events took place in the first century AD; Crispolto and his fellows could be claimed as disciples, through Brizio, of St Peter. This dating, and Herculanus's supposed Petrine connections, must have made it obvious even to the uncritical that he could not have been the saint martyred by Totila.

116. *Acta S* Maii 4, p. 823. Colomba had in fact been accused of conjuring demons in the public square in favour of the cause of one of the civic factions.

117. Pellini, 1, p. 1234.

118. *Cronica volgare*, pp. 172–3; *Alle Bocche della Piazza*, p. 170.

119. *Cronache senesi*, p. 590 (cf. p. 159, where the price appears as £1525).

120. Ibid., p. 773.

121. 'Cronica Perugina Inedita', pp. 83–8, 105, 169–71; Pellini, 2, pp. 722–30; E. Ricci, 'La leggenda di Santa Mustiola'. Ricci rightly pours scorn on the ethics of the Perugian case, but seems unaware of the *furtum sacrum* tradition, on which see P. Geary, *Furta Sacra* (Princeton, NJ 1978).

122. The basic story is told by Ricci, who prints (pp. 147–55) a narrative of the *inventio* dated 25 May. F. Liverati, *Le catacombe e Antichità Cristiane di Chiusi* (Siena 1872), pp. 323–30, prints or summarizes many of the relevant documents. Agostino Dati (for whom, see below Chapter 8 *passim*) was among the Sienese citizens involved in summer 1474. Santa Mustiola had a cult at Siena itself, which the government frequently honoured in the fourteenth century with an offering of a 3-pound *cero*: see, for example, ASS Biccherna 148, f. 97 (July 1323), 187, f. 133v (1337).

123. A. Fantozzi, 'Documenta perusina ad indulgentiam Portiunculae spectantia', *AFH* 9 (1916), pp. 237–93.

124. Pellini, 2, p. 730.

125. 'Cronica Perugina inedita', p. 270.

126. *Diario Ferrarese*, p. 87: 'E cusì questo anno se hè comenzato havere in reverentia, ad honore de la Vergine Maria....' The Duke of Ferrara ordered that all craftsmen shut their shops as a mark of respect. The event was clearly not a 'canonization' in the usual sense. For Joseph's appearance in the *Breviarum Romanum* at just this period, see C.A., 'Le développement historique du culte de S Joseph', *Revue Bénédictine* 14 (1897), pp. 148–9; an office with nine lessons appears in 1482, a 'proper' office in 1490.

127. *Cronaca del Matarazzo, ASI* 16.ii (1851), n.5, pp. 7–8

128. 'Cronica Perugina inedita', p. 294.

129. L. Manzoni, 'I Quadri dello Sposalizio della B. Vergine dipinto da Pietro Perugino e da Raffaello di Urbino', *BSUSP* 4 (1898), pp. 511–34.

130. Ghirardacci, 3, pp. 214, 231. In 1480 Alfonso had been a guest of the Sienese at the now traditional viewing of the relics at the Feast of the Annunciation: *Cronache senesi*, p. 882.

131. Ghirardacci, 3, pp. 41, 162, 164, 199, 214, 334–5. For the head of St Anne, see J.C. Dickinson, *The Congress of Arras* (Oxford 1955), n.4, p. 196.

132. *Diario Ferrarese 1409–1502*, pp. 5–6, 15–16. The diarist does not specify that Niccolò was present on the latter occasion. For Romano and Maurelius in the twelfth century, see above, pp. 65–6, 87 n.18.

133. *CNI* 10, pp. 431–42. For Italian coinage, see P. Grierson, *Bibliographie numismatique* (Brussels 1966), pp. 104–10. I have used *CNI* here as a convenient compendium, aware of Grierson's comments on its shortcomings and need of revision.

134. P. Grierson, *Coins of Medieval Europe* (London 1991), p. 148.

135. *CNI* 12, p. 234 (pl. XIX, 7). In April–June 1540 the Perugians, at odds with the papacy in the so-called *Guerre del Sale*, produced an imitation of this coin: *CNI* 14, pp. 210–11; A. Bellucci, 'Monete Inedite coniate nella Zecca di Perugia durante la Guerra del Sale nel MDXL', *BSUSP* 4 (1898), pp. 535–42. The image of Sant' Ercolano was retained on the obverse, while the reverse showed a *croce fiorita* with one of a variety of legends expressing Christ's lordship, e.g. 'Augusta P. Civitas Christi'.

136. *CNI* 12, p. 244 (pl. XIX, 22, 23).

137. Ibid., 11, p. 355 (pl. XXII, 37).

138. Ibid., p. 393 (pl. XXIV, 32, 33).

139. Ibid., pp. 73–4, (pl. IV, 39–45) etc. The mint of Lucca was functioning in 650 and did not close until 1847 (ibid., p. 51). See also D. Massagli, *Introduzione alla Storia della Zecca*, (Lucca 1870) (*Memorie e documenti per servire alla storia di Lucca*, 11.2); T. Blomquist, 'The Second Issuance of a Tuscan Gold Coin: The Gold Groat of Lucca, 1256', *Journal of Medieval History* 13 (1987), pp. 317–25.

140. *CNI* 11, pp. 76–8 (pl. V, 7, 8), pp. 89–90 (pl. VII, 1–3), p. 95 (pl. VII, 21–32; VIII, 1–3).

141. Ibid., p. 83 (pl. V, 20).

142. Ibid., p. 148 (pl. IX, 23).

143. *CNI* 6, pp. 188–206 and pl. XIX.

144. Ibid., 10, pp. 6–7 (pl. I, 8); Rodolico, *Dal Comune alla Signoria*, pl. I.

145. *CNI* 10, pp. 10–13 (pl. I, 13, 14).

146. Ibid., pp. 31–4 (pl. II, 18, 20, 21) On one Eugenius IV *grossone*, however, Peter and Paul are seen together (pl. II, 19). According to Ghirardacci, 2, p. 572, Baldassare Cossa as legate in 1406 coined *quattrini* with the image of Petronius which were used until 1591, when the *gonfalone*

of the church and the keys appeared.

147. For Filippo Maria's Bolognese coinage, see *CNI* 10, pp. 34–7 (pl. II, 24–6); for the Bentivoglio, pp. 37–46 (pl. II, 26). Peter also appeared (pl. II, 27–8), but Petronius dominated the lesser denominations (pl. II, 29–33).

148. Ibid., pp. 46–52, pls II–III.

149. Ibid., 9, pp. 190–93 (pl. XIV).

150. Ibid., 4, pp. 181–7 and pl. XIV.

151. *CNI* 9, pp. 400–401, 408–10 (pls XXVI, 36; XXVII, 9, 10, 11). A thirteenth-century issue is illustrated in Grierson, *Coins of Medieval Europe*, n.247, p. 109.

152. *CNI* 9, pp. 496–8 (pl. XL, 28, 29); cf. C. Brambilla, *Monete di Pavia* (Pavia 1883), pl. VIII, where fig. 13 illustrates a gold issue of Galeazzo II (1359–78) which omits Syrus. Other issues of Galeazzo II, and also of Giangaleazzo and Filippo Maria, which do depict Syrus are shown in *CNI* 4, pp. 498–504, pl. XLI, 1, 2; and pl. XLII.

153. *CNI* 6, pp. 271–7, pls XXIV and XXV, 1, 3.

154. Ibid., pp. 193–8, pl. XV, 17.

155. Ibid., 5, pp. 56–60 (pls III and IV, 8, 9).

156. Ibid., p. 75, (pl. IV, 17).

157. Ibid., pp. 162–82 (pl. VIII, 15).

158. Lilii, *Camerino*, pt I, pp. 28–34, who transcribes a poem narrating the sack and restoration of the relics.

159. A. Bovero, *L'opera completa*, p. 94, pl. XXXIV–V, XXXVI. Another specialist in the representation of Venantius was Gerolamo di Giovanni: the catalogue of his works given by P. Zampetti, *Paintings from the Marches: Gentile to Raphael*, trans. R.G. Carpanini (London 1971), pp. 92–3, lists four frescoes depicting the saint (cf. pls 85–6).

160. *CNI* 13, pp. 206–51, pls XIII–XIV. Venantius in fact continued to make appearances on the coinage well into the sixteenth century.

161. Ibid., pp. 1–17.

162. Ibid., pp. 179–98.

163. Ibid., 10, pp. 414–17.

164. Ibid., 4, pp. 220–65; note by D. Chambers in *Splendours of the Gonzaga* (Catalogue of an Exhibition at the Victoria & Albert Museum, 4 November 1981–31 January 1982), n.41, p. 129.

165. Most notably the reliquary cupboard doors (the 'Arliquiera') painted by Vecchietta in 1450 for the hsopital of Santa Maria della Scala: H. Van Os, *Vecchietta and the Sacristy of the Siena Hospital Church*, pp. 18–22.

166. See above, p. 164.

167. For example, in Domenico Veneziano's St Lucy altarpiece in the Uffizi, or in the panel now in the National Gallery London, painted by Benozzo Gozzoli in 1461 for the Compagnia di Santa Maria della Purificazione e di San Zanobi at San Marco.

168. As in Botticelli's San Barnabà altarpiece in the Uffizi, painted for the church that had been built to commemorate the victory of Campaldino: R. Lightbown, *Botticelli, Life and Works* (London 1989), pp. 187–90.

169. Florence, Biblioteca Laurenziana Ms Plut. 53, 11, fol. 13: 'Solemnia sanctorum martyrum Cosme et Damiani quibus peculiari quodam amore ac reverentia afficiebatur, quam amplo, quam magnifico sumptu singulis annis per omnia fere civitatis templa celebrari curabat.' See also R. Trexler and M.E. Lewis, 'Two Captains and Three Kings: New Light on the Medici Chapel', *Studies in Medieval and Renaissance History* 4 (old series 14 1981), n.90, pp. 121–2.

170. R. Hatfield, 'The Compagnia de' Magi', *Journal of the Warburg and Courtauld Institutes* 33 (1970), pp. 107–61; R. Trexler, 'The Magi Enter Florence'. A procession representing the coming of the Magi, their call upon King Herod and their worship of the child is first recorded in Florence in 1390: *Alle Bocche della Piazza*, p. 89. The Magi were certainly not popular just at Florence. At Parma in January 1414 the celebrations of the election of a new rector of the *studio* seem to have been merged with the festivities of St Hilary, and they culminated in a *rappresentazione* of the Magi, who converged on the *piazza* from three directions and proceeded thence to the cathedral: Pezzana, 2, pp. 156–7.

171. Bovero, *L'opera completa*, pp. 90–92, pl. XXVa.

172. Ibid., p. 96, pls XLIII–VI.

173. See in general Frugoni, *A Distant City*, pp. 76–81; H. Millon and V. Lampugnani, eds, *The Renaissance from Brunelleschi to Michelangelo: The Representation of Architecture* (London 1994), pp. 674–8.

174. Salimbene, 1, p. 283.

175. See above, pp. 164–5.

176. Frugoni, pp. 77–9; Kaftal, *Tuscan Painting*, cols 29–34 (Sansedoni), 1035–44 (Zenobius); *North East Italy*, cols 859–68 (Petronius).

PART III

SIENA CITY OF THE VIRGIN

The title 'City of the Virgin' that is so often applied to Siena might disguise from the unwary the fact that numerous Italian cities claimed the Virgin as their patron. Where she was patron of the cathedral, for example, she was often (though not invariably) also the patron of the commune. The Feast of the Assumption – at Parma, Pisa, Spoleto or Orvieto, as at Siena – was the great civic festivity of the year. Even where she was neither patron of the cathedral nor the original patron of the commune she frequently shared, as she did at Faenza and Treviso, in the chief honours awarded by the rulers of the city. At Florence (where the cathedral, rebuilt between the end of the thirteenth century and the middle of the fifteenth, was rededicated in her name) and at Bologna, this awareness of the need to call upon her universally available mercy was focused on miraculous images.

What, then, gave the Sienese a unique claim on her? The story is of a commemorative tradition which is unusual in that the event from which it stems, the battle of Montaperti in 1260, came to be principally associated not with one of the saints on whose feast-day it occurred, but with the Virgin. It was a tradition, also, which can be shown to have developed over time.

Like supreme patrons elsewhere, the Virgin did not protect Siena quite single-handed. The city was rich in saints both ancient and modern, and the Sienese showed themselves as alive as any other people to the desirability of multiple heavenly patronage. Happily, the sources allow us to see at least something of how the activities of the mendicant orders, the attachment to local men whose relics were the exclusive possession of the city, the appeal of history and of the ancient traditions of the local church, all contributed to shaping the civic pantheon.

The Black Death struck Siena hard; Tuscany was increasingly dominated by Florence, and political stability within the city, especially after the fall of the regime of the 'Nine' in 1355, was elusive. For Siena, reckoning with the shifting interstate alliances of the fifteenth century added external strains to the internal strains caused by faction. This uneasy situation may have intensified the concern of the city's rulers with the public decorum embodied in the cult, which found expression here as elsewhere in the processions for Corpus Christi. Good fortune and close relations with the papacy, in the middle of the century, also gave Siena two canonized saints to add to the number of its 'advocates'. Above all, the city continued to call upon its supreme patron, as a source of help in extremity and as the guarantor of Siena's liberty and identity. It was in these circumstances that the story of the battle of Montaperti achieved its final form. On the eve of the fall of the republic to Florentine aggression in 1555, the verbal and visual image of Siena as 'The City of the Virgin' was clearly established.

The Sienese example is unique only in the sense that every Italian city has its own sacred history. In outline, at least, the Sienese story is better known than most. To look at it more closely should enable us not only to appreciate its special features, but to see how it exemplified and reflected the trends that shaped the civic pantheon elsewhere.

CHAPTER 6

THE VIRGIN OF MONTAPERTI

On 4 September 1260 an army consisting of the Sienese militia companies, some German horse lent by Manfred of Sicily and some Ghibelline exiles from other Tuscan cities, notably the Florentine noble Farinata degli Uberti, met and defeated the combined Guelfs of Tuscany, headed by the Florentines, at Montaperti on the river Arbia, a short distance from Siena. The verdict of the battle was to be reversed and the Sienese were to be forcibly brought back into the Guelf camp when they met defeat by the Florentines at Colle di Val d'Elsa in June 1269, but Montaperti remained an undying memory of a glorious moment of victory over the old enemy.

The event is baldly described in Sienese annals, both Latin and Italian, which were copied in the fifteenth century. One Italian version gives a vivid sense of what was at stake in 1260.[1] The Guelf forces were on their way to fortify Montalcino, one of the small places in southern Tuscany which had been bones of contention between Florence and Siena for years. The first act of the Sienese after the battle was to raze Montalcino's defences. This account makes no mention of any ceremony of submission to the Virgin or supernatural influence on the outcome of the battle, but the annalist was in no doubt that it was through Manfred's benevolence, in the shape of his German cavalry, that Siena had had the victory.

A very different story, however, was already in circulation. An anonymous chronicle, which went down originally to 1361 and was completed in 1392, already contains the outline and some of the ornamentation;[2] the so-called Montauri chronicle, which was copied towards the end of the fifteenth century from a somewhat earlier original, contains a full version which has been much used by modern historians and will be used here as the basis for an examination of the tradition.[3]

According to this account, Florentine ambassadors at Siena made exorbitant demands, including the slighting of the city's defences. The Sienese were uncertain how to respond, but the Ghibelline leader Provenzano Salvani urged resistance, and suggested hiring the troops of Manfred of Sicily, which happened to be on hand. The money was found thanks to an ostentatious gesture from the immensely rich Salimbene Salimbeni, who brought 100,000 gold florins from his palace in a cart draped, *per più magnificenzia*, with cloth of gold and olive branches, remarking that if necessary there was more where that came from. The Germans had the position explained to them through interpreters, and were delighted with their handsome new contract, as they did not think much of the Florentines. Every Sienese shopkeeper, stall-holder and craftsman hastened to open up and put his wares at their disposal. Meanwhile, the city's rulers appointed Bonaguida Lucari to provide the populace with moral leadership. He organized an immense penitential procession, which culminated when he and the bishop joined in laying the keys of the city on the altar of the Virgin. A notary was on hand to record the city's deed of gift of itself to the Queen of Heaven. The chronicler describes the order in which the militia companies left the city, and then the battle itself.

That this narrative would have appealed to a popular and patriotic readership in fifteenth-century Siena there can be no doubt. The later fourteenth century had again seen Florentine and Sienese interests clash in southern Tuscany, to the detriment of Siena. With the acquisition of Arezzo in 1384 and Pisa in 1406, the Florentines definitively established their Tuscan hegemony. In 1399 the Sienese, like the Pisans, reacted to their fear and resentment of the Florentines by openly accepting the *signoria* of the Duke of Milan, Giangaleazzo Visconti, who was advancing, seemingly irresistibly, to the mastery of Italy. After 1403 they returned to a posture of alliance with the Florentines which was often put under strain – not least in 1429, when the Florentines launched what turned out to be an ill-considered assault on Lucca. Under the leadership of the firebrand Antonio Petrucci, and in alliance with Filippo Maria Visconti, the Sienese entered openly into the war against Florence in 1431, persuaded (though not without misgivings) that Lucca's cause was their own. This tension between fear of Florence's designs and recognition of the necessity of friendship with their overmighty neighbour continued to mark Sienese policy.[4] It must therefore have given fifteenth-century Sienese readers great pleasure to learn that at Montaperti every Sienese seemed an 'Orlando' to his opponents – or, as the Ventura version has it, 'un Ettore novello'.[5]

It is no easy matter, however, to decide how 'historical' the story is, despite the fact that these accounts have often, even if only implicitly, served as the foundation for historians' assertions about the events of 1260.[6] Understandably, it has been asked how much of the authentic thirteenth century there is in texts which have so obviously received a great deal of embellishment. D'Ancona believed that the Ambrosiana text was 'in great part old and almost contemporary ... The base is evidently old, with some changes and above all with amplifications and glosses; but beneath the restoration the primitive image can be recognised without difficulty.'[7] Giuseppe Rondoni, discussing Sienese popular traditions, did not directly address the problem of the date of the accounts, but stressed the elements of 'popular exaggeration' and 'fantastic ornament' in them.[8] Alessandro Lisini, editing the Montauri chronicle in 1939, thought the narrative of the battle was written about the end of the fourteenth century, and 'gleaned from popular traditions a century after the battle, and certainly mixed up with fabulous and exaggerated details, out of municipal pride, very much alive then'.[9]

It was the art historian E.B. Garrison who mounted the most sustained attack on the value of these narratives.[10] After an exhaustive analysis he succeeded in establishing what for him were the fundamental points at issue. First, none of the texts as we have them was copied before the fifteenth century. Second, texts which had been used to establish a dating of 1260 for the so-called Madonna del Voto which is still in the cathedral were of no use for that purpose: they demonstrably reflected the topography of the cathedral at a time when the disposition of altars and even the identity of images as they were before 1300 had clearly been forgotten.

Garrison derived wider conclusions, which may be more questionable, from his analysis. Speaking of the accounts generally, he observes: 'Whether they transmit a nucleus of reliable information or not, they are very obviously in this respect "fictionalised"; they must be looked upon in the same way as some modern historical novels, which though reporting gross events accurately enough nevertheless embroider them in a similar way.' The burden of proof, in Garrison's view, was on those who contended that a genuine historical tradition was preserved in these admittedly elaborated narratives. To think otherwise

> is to fly in the face of the sober principles of modern historiography. On the contrary, in view of all the evidence, it must be assumed that most of the tales told in the historical writings with which we are dealing here were made up out of whole cloth during the fifteenth century ferment of humanist fantastification.[11]

The principles of modern historiography may perhaps remain sober without being quite as abstemious as Garrison would have had them. Leaving aside the fact that there is nothing particularly 'humanistic' about the obvious embroidering the story has undergone, the analogy with the modern historical novel, superficially attractive, is probably inappropriate. The historical novel is often the product of intensive and detailed research, which the Montaperti narrative is very unlikely to have been. It is for precisely this reason that as soon as it is shown that there is independent evidence for any of the elements in the story, it becomes difficult to dismiss it as 'made up out of whole cloth', and we have to accept that 'a nucleus of reliable information' has undergone a process of transmission and elaboration which does not exactly correspond to the treatment of fact in either the 'normal' chronicle or the historical novel. There is no way of proving that the ceremonies the Sienese later professed to believe had taken place on the eve of Montaperti took place in the form described in the legend; but the tradition of the Virgin's rulership over the city, and its possible connection with the battle, may be more amenable to investigation. Is there any evidence for a *change* in the Sienese conception of the Virgin's patronage which can convincingly be connected with Montaperti and its aftermath?

If the Sienese appealed to the Virgin in 1260, it was because she was not only the mother of all mercies, but already the special patron of the church and city of Siena. In the twelfth century the communal seal had borne the image of the Castelvecchio, but after 1252 it depicted the enthroned Virgin and Child, with the inscription *Salvet Virgo Senam Veterem, quam signat amoenam*.[12] In the 1250s and 1260s members of a new brotherhood of Florentine origin devoted to the Virgin, the *Servi di Santa Maria*, or 'Servites', were in the process of establishing a house at Siena. The 'Ghibelline' Sienese government showered the Servites and other orders with privileges and assistance in their building programmes, a fact which has prompted the suggestion that it was especially anxious to demonstrate its orthodoxy and dampen any threats of pro-papal agitation.[13]

Among the early patrons of the Servites at Siena were the great Tolomei family, who offered them land in 1259. The vicissitudes of the Tolomei in this period are instructive if we are to consider the very real divisions which threatened Sienese political society as it confronted the Florentine threat in 1260.[14] Descendants of the minor feudal aristocracy of the countryside, and now bankers with a papal and international clientele to think of, they participated in the Sienese government throughout the period of the rise of the *popolo*. The General Council of the Commune met in the church of San Cristoforo, which faced (and faces) their *palazzo* across what is now Piazza Tolomei. It was here that the deliberations took place which resulted in the decision to resist the Florentines and supplicate the Virgin in September 1260. Already in 1240, however, Tolomei property had suffered damage from the *popolo* in fighting between the factions known as the Twenty-Seven and the Twenty-Four. The Tolomei fought at Montaperti, but like other families of similar standing they felt compelled to withdraw from the city late in 1262. Their return was delayed even after Manfred fell at Benevento in 1266, because of popular fears that the readmission of such families would mean magnate control of the city. In July 1269 the Sienese Ghibellines were defeated at Colle Val d'Elsa, where Provenzano Salvani was killed. When the Tolomei and their like returned to Siena the following year, a fresh reversal drove the leading Ghibelline families out, and the houses of the Salvani were destroyed; Palazzo Tolomei was rebuilt with stones taken from them.[15] As in other Tuscan cities, constitutional restraints were placed a few years later on the participation of such noble families in the political life of the city. The need to construct a constitutional balance which combined a safe 'Guelf' orthodoxy with a sufficiently 'popular' character was strongly felt for the rest of the century.

Whatever else had to be thrown hastily overboard after the deaths of Manfred and Conradin and the defeat at Colle Val d'Elsa, it was not conceivable that a Guelf regime would jettison the leadership of the Virgin, even if the Ghibellines had appealed to her and even if she was associated with Montaperti. She was the established civic patron, and the arrangements for her veneration, as we shall shortly see more fully, display an essential continuity through the years before and after 1260 which parallel the provisions of the patronal cult in other cities. Furthermore, her role in the charitable civic piety of the confraternities, burgeoning in Tuscany at precisely this period, showed that she laboured at all times to establish social peace and order, which might not otherwise be come by easily, if at all.

The Feast of the Assumption on 15 August was the central landmark of the Sienese year, the occasion on which the inhabitants of both city and *contado* had to demonstrate their obedience to the authority of the commune by doing reverence to its patron. From the middle of the twelfth century, individuals and communities who submitted to Sienese rule (including, in 1212, troublesome Montalcino) bound themselves to make their offerings at the Feast of the Assumption.[16] From the 1220s onwards, these obligations were listed in a *Liber Censuum* which was re-edited in 1334 and again in 1400.[17] At least from the late 1240s, heralds went about reminding subject communities, federate *signori* and citizens of their obligations; there is record also of steadily increasing official expenditure on the festivities.[18]

There are no detailed regulations for the Feast of the Assumption in the statute of 1262, although it is referred to in several places as an established part of the city's life. For example, covered roadways were declared to be a nuisance both when troops were on the move and 'on the feast of blessed Mary'; therefore there was to be a thoroughfare through the city open to the sky.[19] From two chapters in the distinction devoted to crime and punishment, it is apparent that the festivities generated some disorder. 'Lest any cause for scandal should arise', all citizens were to come to the cathedral together with the other inhabitants of their *contrada* of residence, and not otherwise; they were to come by day and not by night; and they were to bear candles, but not candlesticks: 'And whoever shall bear a candlestick, or shall cause one to be borne, shall be punished by a fine of one hundred *soldi*.' All citizens between the ages of eighteen and sixty, both permanent residents [*habitatores assidui*] and and 'foreign' citizens [*cives forenses*], were to attend. A particularly watchful eye was to be kept on any dereliction of duty by *cives forenses*.[20] The obligation to attend at the *festa* is in effect mentioned only when it is deemed to have become necessary to regularize it and prevent disorders or inconvenience.

The statute does, however, specify certain marks of respect to the patron that were to be the regular responsibility of the government. Apart from its obligations to the *Opera* of the cathedral and to the hospital of Santa Maria della Scala, the commune was bound to pay for two great candles to burn day and night before Mary's altar in the cathedral, and also for a lamp to burn day and night before the *carroccio* (the ceremonial war-chariot of the commune) 'ad honorem Dei et beate Marie Virginis'.[21] In specific memory of Montaperti, it was decreed that the Twenty-Four and the other officials of the commune should, when the bishop so requested, designate a site for a chapel to be built in honour of God, the Virgin and those saints on the day of whose solemnity the Lord gave the Sienese victory over their enemies. Here the Sienese were following what we have seen to be common practice in other cities at a similar period.[22]

In the statute compiled after 1274 by the Guelf government which ruled in nominal obedience to Charles of Anjou, we find that the commune is still undertaking to pay for candles before the altar of the Virgin, although the victorious *carroccio* of Montaperti is not mentioned. A new regulation, 'for the more solemn and honourable celebration of the feast of the blessed Mary' [*ut festum beate Marie solempnius et honorabilius celebretur*], stipulates the attendance of Siena's subject communities at the *festa*. All were to render on the vigil of the Assumption offerings of candles determined on a tariff related to the amount of tribute they paid annually to the commune, which, as we have seen, was laid down in the *Liber Censuum*. All candles offered in the cathedral 'on the feast of St Boniface and all those offered as cense payments [*pro censu*] on the vigil of Blessed Mary or at any other time' were to go to the *Opera*, and so did the money tribute (as well as the candles) owed by Montalcino.[23] St Boniface was one of the saints on whose day the Lord had deigned to give the Sienese victory over their enemies, as the 1262 statute put it, while the memory of Montaperti is kept alive also in the mention of Montalcino, whose flirtations with Florence had been one of the major causes of enmity between the two cities.[24] Lastly, the statute repeats the clauses of the 1262 statute penalizing scandalous behaviour on the way to the cathedral for the celebrations of the Assumption, with the addition of penalties for snatching another man's candle.[25]

There is a considerable advance here in the explicit regulation of the festival, but the relevant provisions are still scattered throughout the statute. They were amplified and consolidated to form one long chapter of the statute compiled under the magistracy of the 'Nine', which assumed power in the summer of 1287, and in this form they were translated entire into the vernacular version of the statute that was made in 1309–10.[26] A few new provisions were appended to this statute. In October 1309 the *consiglio della Campana* resolved that no shops were to be permitted to open on 15 August, and that no buying or selling of livestock was to be permitted in the city or the suburbs. Exceptions were made for the buying and selling of *cera lavorata* (the wax for the offerings to the Virgin) and for the necessities of the sick and the dead; while – appropriately, in view of the Virgin's role as a peacemaker – it was to be permitted to draw up wills and contracts of peace, although the making of other types of contract was forbidden.[27] In June 1310 it was decreed that a *palio* of 50 lire should be provided annually on 14 August, 'for which a race shall be solemnly [or, formally] run' [*al quale palio si corra solennemente*]. This was to begin in the coming August: 'And the aforesaid things are to be put into the constitution of the commune of Siena, so that they may be observed in perpetuity in honour of the glorious Virgin.' This may be the legislative birth certificate of the celebrated *palio*, but its history, like that of the other honours paid to the Virgin, is older: in 1232 a jockey was fined for failing to observe the rules of the race.[28] The next full recension of the statutes, in 1337–39, amended and built upon the foundation that had been laid, adding the significant proviso that the Nine, the supreme officers of the commune, were not to leave the public palace for any festival except the Feast of the Assumption, the unique civic solemnity of the year.[29]

In its increasing elaboration and systematization from the later thirteenth century on, the legislative regulation of the patronal festival at Siena follows a pattern not dissimilar from that to be seen in other cities. Down to 1262 and beyond, at Siena as elsewhere, it was custom that regulated the celebration of the Assumption.[30] Have we any grounds for supposing that the Virgin's official role at Siena was in fact altered or enhanced in or after September 1260?

The text of Montalcino's submission to Siena, drawn up four days after the battle, on 8 September, is highly suggestive.[31] The Montalcinesi were assembled in the *campo* at Siena before the victorious *carroccio*, which is described as having been made

> in honour and reverence of almighty God and the blessed Mary ever Virgin, who is defender and governor of this city, and of the blessed George, and to the honour and exaltation of the most invincible lord King Manfred, and to the honour and exaltation and augmentation of the aforesaid city and people... [*ad honorem et reverentiam omnipotentis Dei et beate Marie semper Virginis, que est defensatrix et gubernatrix civitatis ejusdem, et beati Georgii, et ad honorem et exaltationem invictissimi domini regis Manfredi, et ad honorem et exaltationem et augmentum civitatis et populi prefati...*]

The eye is immediately caught by the intrusion of St George, and to this we shall return. Of immediate interest is the fact that Mary is denoted not only *defensatrix* but *gubernatrix* of Siena. These words are not applied to Mary in earlier texts recording submissions to the Sienese commune; nor, in fact, were they used when another troublesome town, Montepulciano, made its submission on 5 July 1261.[32] It is tempting to speculate that their appearance in the context of Montalcino's submission expresses a status that had been officially accorded to the Virgin in a formal act of homage five days previously.

An intriguing equivalent appears in the clause of the 1274 statute which allots the offerings made on the feast of St Boniface, and those made by Montalcino, to the *Opera* of the Virgin, 'receiver and governor' of the city [*dicte beate Marie virginis receptricis et gubernatricis civitatis senensis*].[33] *Gubernatrix* reappears, we note, in association with a reference to Montaperti and the submission of Montalcino, while the purpose of the grant of the offerings has specific reference to the governance of the city: it is hoped that the Virgin will intercede with God 'so that he will govern the city and [its] men, always improving [them] from good to better' [*ut civitatem et homines gubernet semper de bono in melius augmentando*]'. The Nine who ruled Siena after 1287 were also *Gubernatores et Defensores* of the commune and people.[34]

The Virgin simultaneously governs and protects. The later chroniclers imagined that in September 1260 the Sienese called upon the Madonna of Mercy. According to the *Anonimo*, when the city had solemnly given itself to the Virgin, 'by this means and by prayer to the Mother of Mercy, she defended us from so great a danger'.[35] The Montauri chronicler describes the people as calling out 'misericordia, misericordia, Madre nostra reina del cielo'.[36] These accounts, we have noted, were written long after the event, but it is worth remembering that the period of Montaperti was also a great growth period of pious confraternities which invoked the Virgin in these terms.

What Meersseman judged to be the earliest known confraternity of *laudesi*, devotees coming together to sing the hymns known as *laude*, was in fact founded at Siena in 1267.[37] In 1262 the bishop of neighbouring Arezzo had confirmed the statutes of a Dominican Marian confraternity which proclaimed: that 'we citizens of Arezzo have voluntarily come together to seek the divine mercy by works of mercy, to relieve the manifold necessities of the decent poor especially, and of widows and orphans, also to assist as suitable opportunity arises religious places, impoverished monasteries, hospitals and prisoners'. The further aims of the confraternity were 'to procure charity and love and concord one with another, for the establishment of peace and the promotion of the good of all', with the assistance of God, of his most merciful Mother, and of the precious martyr-bishop Donatus. The fraternity was to be named after Holy Mary of Mercy, both because it was dedicated to performing acts of mercy, and because it was commended to the Queen of Mercy, 'by means of whose regime and leadership' [*per cuius regimen et ducatum*], it was hoped and believed, it would be sustained and promoted. In several places the Virgin is described as 'advocate', and in the final chapter the hope is expressed that through her patronage '[who is] leader and head of our fraternity' [*que dux est et caput fraternitatis nostre*] its members would merit admission 'to the heavenly congregation of celestial citizens' [*ad supernam congregationem celestium civium*].[38] The civic role of the Virgin's devotees and their faith that she would conserve the *bonum statum* of the city were thus explicitly stated.

Under one aspect the confraternity was an attempt to construct a community which, like the religious order to which it was affiliated and the city of which it was a part, eschewed monarchical forms of rulership in favour of officers elected for fixed terms. It was, in theory at least, intended to embrace disparate groups – laymen and clergy, men and women, townsmen and countrymen, Aretines and others – in an ideal fellowship. The Virgin as *caput et dux* was to be the keystone, the transcendent symbol of leadership and unity. The parallels with the situation and aspirations of the commune itself are suggestive. The Montauri chronicle dramatizes the divisions among the Sienese on the eve of Montaperti: there were those who thought that some concession at least had better be made to the Florentine demands. Buonaguida Lucari, 'a layman, of good spiritual life, of a great family of Siena, a gentleman', is the exemplar of up-to-date lay piety, ideally qualified to lead a divided citizenry in a mass pious exercise. Provenzano Salvani had reminded his fellow-councillors that the Sienese were 'commended' [*raccomandati*] to Manfred. Buonaguida, in his address to the people, repeats the word and builds it into a significant antithesis: 'You know, *signori Sanesi*, that we are commended to King Manfred; now it seems to me that we should give ourselves and all we have, all the city and *contado* of Siena, to the queen and empress of eternal life.' The contrast is between a conditional, perhaps temporary, relationship and an act of permanent and complete self-surrender. The humanist Agostino Dati, writing in 1456–57, was to express a related antithesis: on the one hand, the earthly lord Siena claimed never to have had; on the other, the transcendental absolute prince she had never lacked.[39]

Buonaguida's words as we have them, like Dati's, were written down in the fifteenth century, but they express something of the thirteenth-century situation. Siena was in desperate need of a leader to preserve her all-too-fragile unity, and to overstress her subjection to Manfred (especially in retrospect) or any earthly prince was unacceptable. The Virgin could step into the role. As a degree of political stability was achieved in the later years of the century and thereafter, Mary held a watching brief over the activities of her earthly representatives, the Nine human 'governors and defenders' of the commune. She is thus portrayed in the fresco commissioned by that regime from Simone Martini for the great council chamber of the *palazzo pubblico*; the inscription on her throne conveys her continuing interest in good government.[40] Government was vested in the hands of men who were, naturally, obedient to the will of the Queen of Heaven. When that relative stability was shaken and Siena's standing in the world seriously diminished under the impact of plague, economic change and Florentine competition, the tradition associated with the battle of Montaperti could be reactivated, if only to assuage wounded pride.

The Virgin – uniting, as we have seen, the attributes of leadership and mercy – sanctioned the routine operations of official piety. In March 1330, on the pious pretext of serving the interests of the Virgin Mary, 'to whom we are commended', the Nine recommended that the rates at which the communities of the *contado* paid their annual wax tribute should be reviewed, alleging that in the forty years since the current assessment was made, some of these communities were 'much increased in value' [*molte melliorate*]. To safeguard the value of these offerings, the apothecaries who made the *ceri* for the *contado* must make them of the same wax they used for the *ceri* of the city.[41] There was further discussion of the issue in the following December, when penalties were prescribed for failure to make the correct offering.[42] In August 1334, the usual resolution was taken to release certain prisoners at the Feast of the Assumption, 'since the faith, hope and sincere devotion of the Sienese is and reposes especially in the most holy mother of God, Mary ever Virgin and ever glorious, as in her who is truly head, leader and defender of the city, *contado* and jurisdiction of Siena, and she is the most special and singular queen of mercy and pity'.[43]

The fifteenth-century chroniclers had both such official expressions and the long intervening tradition of the piety of the confraternities to draw on as they visualized what happened in

1260. It is thus, surely, that we can account both for much of the language they use and for the appearance – in the Montauri chronicle, three appearances – of the image of the Virgin's protective robe. It appears already, once, in the version of events found in the late-fourteenth-century *Anonimo*. The Florentines were amazed at the size of the assembling Sienese forces, which indeed seemed more numerous than they were. In addition: 'That night, about midnight, they had seen a radiance over Siena so that it seemed like day, and it covered all Siena like an awning [*a modo d'un padiglione*].'[44]

By the time the Montauri account was written the image had been amplified, and it makes no fewer than three appearances in the narrative.[45] The *Anonimo* had remarked that the city adopted a pure white standard to lead the way to battle; the Montauri chronicler describes the standard of the *terzo di Camollia* as 'all shining white silk; which standard was made larger than the others, because it signified the mantle of the glorious Virgin Mary, all pure, white and clean'. When the hostile camps were drawn up facing each other, the watchers from the city saw 'a shadow like a mantle' entirely covering the Sienese camp. Some said, 'It's the smoke from the great fires in the camp'; others said, 'Not so, for if it were smoke it would move; it must be something else.' Out of devotion it was taken to be the Virgin's mantle guarding and defending the forces of Siena. Those in the Sienese camp, meanwhile, looking towards the city, saw a mantle-shaped shadow (instead of the 'radiance' of the *Anonimo*) over it, and interpreted this also as the Virgin's robe.

The image of the *Madonna della Misericordia* has been much studied.[46] Perdrizet discusses the use of the mantle as a symbol of protection, for example in certain marriage and other legal rites. The idea of the Virgin's protective cloak and the literary sources for it were older than the 1260s, but it is doubtful whether the visual image which later became familiar was as yet available widely, if at all. In the 1220s Caesarius of Heisterbach told of a Cistercian who was granted a vision of Paradise and was distressed to see none of his brethren present, until the Virgin lifted her cloak and displayed an enormous multitude of them clustered beneath.[47] A rather different thirteenth-century text is worth noting because it, too, associates the protective mantle with victory on the battlefield secured under the Virgin's patronage. In 1250 Pope Innocent IV reminded the citizens of Parma how the Virgin had assisted them in inflicting an embarassing defeat on Frederick II, 'spreading out the constant canopy of her protection over you'.[48]

In the course of the thirteenth century the image was adopted or appropriated by other religious orders; Duccio's *Madonna of the Franciscans* is the earliest Sienese artistic treatment of the motif of the Virgin's protective robe.[49] It was frequently associated with pious confraternities, although these, as we have seen, stressed the majesty and rulership of the Queen of Heaven as well as her mercy. It was for a confraternity in the Florentine Dominican church of Santa Maria Novella that the Sienese Duccio in 1285 painted the huge enthroned Madonna which is now in the Uffizi.[50] The two great Sienese civic images of the early fourteenth century – Duccio's *Maestà*, painted for the cathedral between 1308 and 1311, and Simone's fresco in the *palazzo pubblico*, probably executed in 1315 – are again images of majesty and rulership in the setting of a court of saints and angels. Duccio's altarpiece was borne ceremonially from the painter's workshop to the cathedral in 1311 amid pious demonstrations such as might have done honour to the reception of a relic, and renewed supplications for the Virgin's protection against all adversities, traitors and enemies.[51] Simone's Virgin is particularly striking in her resemblance to an earthly queen; this was the Virgin who, as Agostino Dati was to remark, had literally never been absent from the counsels of the republic.[52] Two of the earliest Italian representations of the Coronation of the Virgin are Sienese: the stained-glass *oculus* designed for the cathedral in 1287 and a panel attributed to Guido da Siena. Sienese artists and patrons, just before and after 1300, were certainly receptive to images of the Virgin which emphasized her regality.[53]

The image of the Virgin spreading the mantle of her protection over the city entered into Sienese civic art only in the later fifteenth century, when the literary tradition of the battle was fully formed. A unique feature of Sienese civic art is the series of 'Biccherne', the painted covers that were commissioned, often from notable artists, for the account-books of the commune. In 1451 the image of the Virgin hovering protectively over Siena appeared on a

Biccherna cover for the first time.[54] Earlier in the century she had been depicted on one of the inlaid wooden choir-stalls made for the chapel of the *palazzo pubblico*. Here she is seen above the city, though not spreading her cloak over it, holding a scroll with the words 'Receive my city and govern it justly' [*Accipe civitatem meam et iuste guberna*]. Sano di Pietro painted her in rather similar pose consigning the care of the city to Pope Calixtus III in the 1450s.[55]

By this time, as we have seen, the full story of Montaperti was being copied and recopied, and the Virgin of Montaperti was being called upon in present emergencies. In 1446, the chronicler Fecini reported that the *Opera* commissioned 'a mantle for the Virgin Mary', while in the following year he recorded a 'fine procession with the *Madonna della Grazie*, that is [the image] to which the keys of the city were given for the defeat of Montaperti'.[56] The authorities had given permission for the venerated ancient image, mistakenly believed to be the one before which the citizens made their submission in September 1260, to be cut down so that it could be carried in procession.[57] Within a few years, Agostino Dati would sum up the whole tradition in a historical work that was prompted by political crisis, and a generation later the Sienese for the first time re-enacted the imagined ceremonial of the eve of Montaperti in the hope of healing their internal divisions.[58] The association of the image of the Madonna della Misericordia with Montaperti was made explicit in the woodcut frontispiece of a book by Lancelotto Politi, later a polemicist against Luther, in 1502.[59] In 1525, in celebration of the repulse of Florentine and papal forces from the Porta Camollia, the government commissioned a full-blown Madonna della Misericordia for the church of San Martino.[60] Then, and only then, did an image of the Virgin, spreading the mantle of her protection over the city, appear on the Sienese coinage.[61]

The development of the image of the Virgin who both ruled and protected is one thread linking the events of 1260 and the visualization of them in the fifteenth century. A rather different, but equally intriguing, way of approach to the historical authenticity of the Montauri account is to examine St George's role at Montaperti. What, indeed, was St George doing at Montaperti, and why is he invoked in the document recording the submission of Montalcino four days later?

It is stated in the statute of 1262 that George, the 'knight of knights' [*miles militum*] has been elected the principal standard-bearer of the commune and its foremost defender; he is to be invoked in all its affairs; through his prayers and merits God has granted the Sienese victory against the Florentines and all their allies. It might indeed be said that the credit for the victory as such is given to him. The statute goes on to provide for official contributions to the celebration of his feast-day, and for assistance to the rebuilding of the church of San Giorgio, 'since the church of the most holy George of Siena has been newly begun to the honour of his blessed name and work is continuously going on on it, at the expense of the Germans...'. A church dedicated to him was to be built on the site of the victory, and the saint is eulogized in progressively more excited terms.[62]

The Montauri chronicler knows all about St George's role at Montaperti. When the troops went forth from the city, the Sienese captain Count Aldobrandino consulted with Count Giordano, captain of the Germans, and announced: 'It is nearly day; let us give order that everyone have breakfast and take comfort in the name of God and of the glorious Virgin Mary and of the glorious messer St George, noble knight.' The Germans rode out in the name of God and St George; George was their battle-cry.[63] The chronicler goes on to relate how the Germans used their booty to build the church, and tells further how the Sienese used to hold a *festa* there on St George's Day:

> In front of the church, with a wood, and a man armed like St George on horseback who fought with a dragon which came out of the wood, which dragon was made of painted terracotta, and was carried by a man, and a maiden stood on one side in prayer – and they ordered that this festival be celebrated in perpetuity in memory of the battle of Montaperti.[64]

This was done 'for a long time', and when the piazza in front of the church could no longer hold all the people who wanted to come, it was transferred to the *campo*, at the foot of the *palazzo*; but 'a long time afterwards', the Sienese being on good terms with the Florentines, the festival was removed from St George's Day and held at the Dominican church in Camporeggio in honour of the blessed Ambrogio Sansedoni.

The chronicler's time-scale is vague; but the vernacular statute of 1309–10 includes a regulation, dated May 1306, that there shall be a *festa* on the feast-day of the blessed Ambrogio, and that a *palio* of 25 *libre di denari* shall be provided, 'for which a race shall be solemnly run, as is the custom in the city of Siena'.[65] Did this regulation represent the culmination of the process of substitution recorded by the chronicler? George was still commemorated in the 1274 statute, despite the reversal of Ghibelline fortunes,[66] but he subsequently disappeared. Clearly he did not vanish from the popular memory, and Montaperti obviously could not simply be expunged from the Sienese patriotic record, least of all as there remained recurrent causes of dispute with the Florentines which were sharpened in and after the later fourteenth century. From the official point of view, however, there were obvious reasons to prefer to emphasize how the Virgin, the universally acknowledged defender of the unfortunate and the desperate, had extended her protection to Siena in 1260. Already in 1316 the Sienese, under threat from Pisan and German forces, were advised by 'an old man of the house of Piccolomini' that they should promote unity and recall all exiles, as a sign to their enemies of their readiness to defend themselves, 'as already in the past we have been defended against others and above all the siege of the Florentines with the aid of the Virgin Mary, who has always defended us from every assault and every evil'.[67]

There are indications, then, that the Virgin's status as the *ruler* of Siena was more clearly formulated as a result of Montaperti, even if commemorative celebrations of the victory still involved other saints. The tradition seems to have taken on its definitive form by the early fifteenth century, and while it is beyond dispute that there are fantastic, or at least fictional, elements in it, there seems little justification for dismissing it as 'made up out of whole cloth'. The Montauri chronicler, it can be shown, got the days of the week right;[68] he knew about St George[69] and about Ambrogio Sansedoni. The story as told by the chroniclers can be accepted both as an intriguing reflection of a real historical tradition and as a document of the religious and patriotic taste of its time. It described a special relationship between the Virgin and the people of Siena which gave them an unassailable title to a sort of greatness. Perhaps the Virgin could lend dignity to regimes whose weight in the world grew less and less. Certainly, as Garrison perceived when he postulated a 'surge' of interest in Siena's past in the mid-fifteenth century, the story of Montaperti would lose none of its popular appeal in the retelling.[70]

Notes

1. Muratori 15, col. 33; cf. the Latin version edited by J.F. Böhmer, *MGH SS* 19, p. 230.

2. *Cronaca senese di autore anonimo del secolo XIV*, in *Cronache senesi*, pp. 57–61.

3. *Cronaca senese conosciuta sotto il nome di Paolo di Tommaso Montauri*, in *Cronache senesi*, pp. 194–217. Before the Montauri chronicle came to light in 1899, historians drew on other, similar, versions of the story. Langton Douglas, for example used a manuscript in the Biblioteca Ambrosiana, copied in 1445: *A History of Siena* (London 1902), n.1, p. 85. Douglas cited in support of his reliance on this text the judgement of A. d' Ancona and O. Bacci, *Manuale della Letteratura italiana*, 1 (Florence 1892), p. 149. A more widely known account was copied in 1442 by a minor painter and vendor of artists' materials called Niccolò di Ventura. This is printed, with some alterations, in G. Porri (ed.), *Due Narrazioni sulla Sconfitta di Montaperto tratte da antichi manoscritti*, published, separately paginated, with *Il Primo Libro delle Istorie Sanesi di Marcantonio Bellarmati* (Siena 1844). See now also, especially for the fifteenth-century sources and setting for the cult, B. Kempers, 'Art and Ritual in Siena Cathedral', who reproduces some of the miniatures from the Ventura manuscript.

4. T. Terzani, 'Siena dalla morte di Gian Galeazzo Visconti alla morte di Ladislao d' Angio Durazzo', *BSSP* 3rd ser. 19 (1960), pp. 3–83; A. Pellegrini, 'Siena in un poema inedito del secolo XV', ibid., 2nd ser. 5 (1898), pp. 411–23; idem, 'Tre Anni di Guerra tra le Repubbliche di Firenze e di Lucca 1430–1433', *Studi e Documenti di Storia e Diritto* 19 (1898), pp. 171–89. The tone of Sienese chroniclers in this period suggests that whatever official Sienese policy was, fear and resentment of the Florentines were commonplace: for examples, see Muratori 19, col. 422; ibid., 20, cols 13–14; *Cronache senesi*, pp. 764–5.

5. Porri, *Due Narrazioni*, p. 71.

6. Bowsky, for example, writes of the Montaperti war: 'The conflict marked the city's dedication to its new sovereign protectress, the Virgin Mary' (*A Medieval Italian Commune*, p. 160) and, again: 'The city was first dedicated to the Virgin on the eve of the battle of Montaperti' (ibid., pp. 274–5). Waley, however, speaks of the dedication of the city *after* the Battle of Montaperti (*Siena and the Sienese*, p. 139). Peyer (*Stadt und Stadtpatron*,

n.13, p. 79) blandly describes the Montauri chronicle as 'the best source' for these events, quoting from it, for example, the 'fact' that at Montaperti the Sienese made mock of the ineffectual protection afforded to the Florentines by their saints Zenobius and Reparata (p. 50, citing *Cronache*, p. 212.) (Cf. Trexler, *Public Life in Renaissance Florence*, n.10, p. 4, who follows Peyer here.)

   7. Cf. n.4 above.
   8. Rondoni, *Tradizioni popolari*, p. 50.
   9. *Cronache senesi*, p. 194.
   10. Garrison 'Sienese Historical Writings'. See also 'Towards a New History'.
   11. Garrison, 'Sienese Historical Writings', p. 25.
   12. The inscription may be translated 'May the Virgin save ancient Siena, which she makes lovely'. A. Middeldorf-Kosegarten, 'Zur Bedeutung der Sieneser Domkuppel', *Münchener Jahrbuch der bildenden Kunst* 21 (1970), p. 78, illustrates both seals. The 1252 seal was depicted in the lower border of Simone Martini's *Maestà* in the Palazzo Pubblico (Martindale, *Simone Martini*, pp. 206, 208–9 n.5, pl. 8).
   13. F.A. dal Pino, *I Frati Servi di S. Maria, dalle origini all' approvazione 1233 ca.–1304* (2 vols, Louvain 1972), 1, pp. 844–5. The statute compiled by this government in autumn 1262 contained provisions against heretics which included some stringent new regulations inserted in response to the petition of the bishop and the mendicant orders: Siena 1262(a), pp. 119–22); 1262(b) (1895), p. 318.
   14. The history of the family is summarized in G. Prunai, G. Pampaloni and N. Bemporad, *Il Palazzo Tolomei a Siena* (Florence 1971); see pp. 9–27 for the period down to the re-entry of the *grandi famiglie* in 1270.
   15. Ibid., pp. 80–81; *Cronache senesi*, p. 224.
   16. Cecchini and Neri, *Il Palio*, pp. 11, 14–15, print and illustrate the document of 1147 in which the *signori* of Montepescali offer an annual cense. Later submissions are to be found in *Caleffo Vecchio*, 1, pp. 29–31 (the counts of Frosini), pp. 34–5 (the church and men of Paurano), pp. 87–90 (the men of Asciano), etc. Montalcino's submission, 12–19 June 1212, is in pp. 149–53.
   17. O. Redon, *Uomini e Comunità del Contado Senese nel Duecento* (Siena 1982), pp. 224–5, publishes the data from the 1223 *Liber Censuum*. Not all early cense payments were due on 15 August, but this became the rule by the early thirteenth century. The texts of 1334 and 1400 are published by Nardi, 'Il territorio per la festa dell' Assunta'.
   18. Cecchini, pp. 19–20. The Biccherna record of expenditures on the feast of August 1281 is printed in ibid., pp. 141–2.
   19. Siena 1262(a), p. 276.
   20. Siena 1262(b) (1894), pp. 149–50. These were persons, usually rural

nobles, who had accepted Sienese citizenship although they did not normally reside in the city.

21. Siena 1262a, p. 26.
22. Ibid., p. 29. For commemorative celebrations of victories, see above, esp. pp. 119–20, 124, 165.
23. ASS *Statuti di Siena* 3, fols 1 r–v.
24. Three saints called Boniface were confused in Sienese tradition. The St Boniface whose feast falls on 4 September was Pope between 418 and 422. According to Odericus (*Ordo*, p. 362) the Sienese in fact celebrated on that day the bishop of Ferentino commemorated by Gregory the Great, whose feast is properly celebrated on 14 May: 'De Sancto Bonifacio episcopo & Confessore novem Lectiones de proprietate ipsius in primo libro Dialogorum Beati Gregorii.' Under 13 May, Odericus records (p. 324): 'Festum Sanctae Mariae ad Martyres celebratur ... quia tali die primo Bonifacius Papa templum Romae, quod Pantheon vocabatur, abjectis idolis, ad honorem Beatae Mariae Virginis & omnium Martyrum dedicavit.' This was Pope Boniface IV (619–25, feast-day 25 May), who obtained from the Emperor Phocas permission to convert the Pantheon to Christian worship as a church dedicated to the Virgin. The cupola of the rebuilt cathedral may have been associated with the cult of the Virgin, and with Pope Boniface and the Pantheon (Middeldorf-Kosegarten, 'Zur Bedeutung', esp. p. 85, where it is observed that Odericus's reference 'at least indicates that Sienese spirituality in the early thirteenth century was informed about the significance of the Pantheon as a Marian church'). The fourteenth-century chronicler Agnolo di Tura referred to the altar of St Boniface, above which the image of the Madonna to which (he believed) the Sienese people had vowed obedience in 1260 was removed when Duccio's *Maestà* was installed on the high altar in 1311 (*Cronache senesi*, pp. 90, 314). For plans in the 1450s to refurbish the chapel of St Boniface, see below, p. 306. Garrison ('Towards a New History', p. 11) comments that by 1467 the designation of an altar and chapel of St Boniface had been dropped. The belief that Boniface was Sienese and the original patron of the cathedral none the less entered Sienese folklore; see, e.g., Tommasi, *Dell' Istoria di Siena*, 2, p. 14. In the eighteenth century Girolamo Gigli (*Diario Sanese*, 1, p. 156) notes under the date 14 May (i.e. the feast of Boniface of Ferentino): 'S. Bonifazio, a cui fu dedicata una volta la nostra cattedrale in memoria di Bonifazio VI [*sic*] Papa Sanese, secondo che scrisse il Tizio: ma non se ne hanno documenti sicuri.' For the resubmission of Montalcino to Siena after Montaperti, see below p. 259.
25. *Statuti* 3, fol. 119v.
26. *Statuti* 5, fols 17–19v; Siena 1309–10, pp. 64–8.
27. Ibid., pp. 360–62.
28. Ibid., p. 366; Cecchini and Neri, p. 20 and pl. 4, where the

condemnation of the jockey is reproduced.

29. See below, p. 285. Agnolo di Tura records that in 1310–11 the *signori* took up residence in the new *palazzo* 'e non escano fuore se non per le feste principali' (*Cronache senesi*, p. 312).

30. The Sienese statutes have been credited – wrongly, I believe – with an unusual precocity in this respect. Cecchini (*Il Palio*, pp. 12, 131–2) illustrates a notarial copy, presumably made for the cathedral, of the consolidated regulations drawn up for the Nine in or after 1287. The notary attested that 'dictum capitulum constituti inter alia contenuta in statuto Comunis Senensis existenti in Biccherna Comunis Senesis vidi legi et inveni'. Cecchini believed that this text, and therefore the written Sienese regulation of the Feast of the Assumption, dated, at least in part, from 1200. His contention arose from the dating of a clause which lays it down that a sacristy shall be built in the cathedral for the receipt of the offerings: 'Et factum est hoc capitulum anno Domini MCC, indictione XIIII., de mense septembris.' Cecchini perceived that the mention of the Nine later in the text must date the copy after 1287, but asserted (p. 16): 'this ordinance which has come down to us in a copy shows that, while the first part reproduces the original statute of 1200, the second part has a modified text of a later date, after the Nine had come into power in 1287.' This, as he might also have remarked, would also have to account for the mention of the tribute payable by Montalcino, which cannot date from 1200, as Montalcino did not submit to Siena until 1212 (see above, p. 256 and n.16). It was noted above that the clause about the offerings due on the feast of St Boniface and the offerings from Montalcino appears in the statutes for the first time in 1274 (*Statuti* 3, fol. iv). Cecchini observed (n.9, p. 129) that the text was 'repeated' in the 'statute of 1295'; it is in fact identical with the relevant rubric of the statute of 1287–89 (see above p. 258) and of the Italian version (Siena 1309–10, 1, pp. 64–8). The fact that the clause about the sacristy appears neither in the 1262 statute nor in that of 1274 is one obstacle to believing that it dates from 1200. It would be odd if an ordinance promulgated in 1200 had dropped out of view for perhaps half a century, only to be resurrected in this manner in or after 1287. It may be noted, also, that when specific dates are assigned to ordinances in the 1287 statute and the 1309–10 vernacular recension, they are normally recent enactments, i.e. later than 1274. The vernacular text, for example, includes ordinances dated 1277 (1, p. 108), 1281 (p. 251), 1288 (p. 78), 1289 (p. 266), etc. A survival or revival from 1200 would be in every way exceptional, not to say anomalous, and scrutiny of the date assigned to the clause about the sacristy in fact reveals that either the year or the indiction must be wrong. No part of the year 1200 was of the fourteenth indiction. The Sienese began the indiction on the Feast of the Nativity of the Virgin on 8 September, and, according to their reckoning, 1–7 September 1200 would have been the *third* indiction; 8–30 September, the

fourth. A spot-check of indictions given elsewhere in the 1287 and 1309–10 statutes suggests that they are uniformly correct. In the absence of other considerations, it would be possible to defend the date of 1200 by supposing that a scribe, somewhere in the process of transmission, wrote 'xiiii' for 'iiii'. However, this simple explanation is undermined by (a) the absence of the *capitulum* from the 1262 and 1274 statutes; and (b) the observable practice, in 1287 and 1309–10, of dating only new enactments. The latter consideration makes it plausible to suppose that the ordinance about the sacristy was promulgated between *either* 8 and 30 September 1285 *or* 1 and 7 September 1286, which would have been the fourteenth indiction. It is virtually certain that the scribal error, unnoticed and perpetuated by the redactors of the vernacular version and by the notary who copied the text for the cathedral, was in the year. It cannot be emphasized too strongly that this argument has nothing to do with whether or not ceremonies in honour of the Virgin involving offerings from the citizens and subjects of the commune took place in 1200; undoubtedly they did. It is highly unlikely, however, that the regulations governing the festivities existed in anything like the written form that they had in and after 1287.

31. *Caleffo Vecchio*, 2, n.628, pp. 846–52.

32. Ibid., n.629; for some other instances of saints as 'governors', see above, pp. 104–5.

33. ASS *Statuti* 3, fol. iv. *Receptrix* is an interesting and unusual substitute for *defensatrix*. The glossaries suggest that it was not a common word: Cicero uses it in the Second Verrine, 4, 8, to describe Messana as 'praedarum ac furtorum receptrix' and this is the usual meaning of the masculine form *receptor* (a receiver of stolen goods or protector of guilty persons), although other meanings are recorded such as arbiter or mediator, or tax collector. St Ambrose uses the feminine *receptrix* of the Ark and of the soul 'as "receiver" of the Word. Such meanings have obvious Marian possibilities, while the connotation 'protectress of the guilty' fits the Virgin's known generosity to the unworthy who put their trust in her.

34. As were their immediate predecessors, the Fifteen (1280–87): *Cronache senesi*, n.2, p. 225. The Virgin was designated on other occasions *capud et dux* of the city of Siena (in a grant of exemptions to tenants of the bishopric in 1274, *Caleffo Vecchio*, 3, 1098) and *capo e difenditrice* (in the petition to the Nine for her better honouring, 1309: Siena 1309–10, 1, p. 361). The nature of the Virgin's authority was clarified in the preamble to the statute of 1337/9 (*Statuti* 26, fol. 1): it is she 'sub cuius protectionem Senarum Civitas gubernetur'.

35. *Cronache senesi*, p. 58: 'per questo modo e orazione fatta alla Madre di Misericordia, ci difese da tanto pericolo'.

36. Ibid., p. 202.

37. G. Meersseman, 'Le Congregazioni della Vergine', in *Ordo*

Fraternitatis 2 (= *Italia Sacra* XXIV) (Rome 1977), pp. 1030–32. This study is an amended version of the author's 'Etudes sur les Anciennes Confréries Dominicaines, III: Les Congrégations de la Vierge', *Archivum Fratrum Predicatorum* 22 (1952), incorporating *inter alia* his 'Note sull' Origine delle Compagnie dei Laudesi (Siena 1267)', *RSCI* 17 (1963).

38. Idem, 'Le Congregazioni', pp. 1015–27. There is an English translation of these statutes in *Early Dominicans: Selected Writings*, ed. S. Tugwell O.P. (London 1982), pp. 436–51.

39. *Cronache senesi*, p. 201. Cf. below, p. 299.

40. Descriptions in E. Borsook, *The Mural Painters of Tuscany from Cimabue to Andrea del Sarto*, 2nd edn (Oxford 1980), pp. 19–23; A. Martindale, *Simone Martini*, pp. 204–9.

41. ASS CG 109, fols 74–5. Cf. above, n.115, p. 132.

42. CG 110, fols 98v–100v: 'Imperciò che a onore di si grande festa niuna persona si conviene ch'abia scusa di non recare la sua imposta'. Reference was made to the new rates since 1330 in the revised statute of 1337–39 (Cecchini, p. 149). A register of these dues was drawn up in 1334 and preserved in the cathedral archive, and subsequent *Libri Censuum* were based on this (cf. above, n.19).

43. ASS CG 115, fol. 114: 'Cum fides, spes & sincera devotio senensium specialiter sit & quiescat in sanctissima matre Dei Maria semper virgine perpetua gloriosa tamquam in ea que vere est capud dux & defensatrix civitatis comitatus & iurisdictionis Senensis & ipsa specialissime et singularis sit regina misericordie & pietatis...'.

44. *Cronache senesi*, p. 58. The *Anonimo* does not explain the image, but he remarks that the Virgin was afterwards similarly portrayed on the portal of the cathedral *Opera*, 'con quella padiglione da chapo'. The reference to the portal of the *Opera* is presumably to the lost painting by Simone Martini described first by Ghiberti and subsequently by Vasari: Martindale, p. 202.

45. *Cronache senesi*, pp. 203, 207.

46. P. Perdrizet, *La Vierge de Miséricorde* (Paris 1908); C. Belting-Ihm, '*Sub Matris Tutela*': *Untersuchungen zur Vorgeschichte der Schutzmantelmadonna = Abhandlungen der Heidelberger Akademie der Wissenschaften, philosophisch-historisch Klasse* 3 (1976); G. Schiller, *Ikonographie der christlichen Kunst*, 4, 2, *Maria* (Gütersloh 1980), pp. 195–6.

47. *Dialogus Miraculorum*, ed. J. Strange, 2 vols (Cologne 1851), 2, pp. 79–80.

48. Affò, *Storia di Parma*, 3, pp. 386–7: 'continuum protectionis suae super vos umbraculum protendentis'.

49. Schiller, n.34, pp. 195–6, mentions the visions on the eve of Montaperti, but regards the panel as connected not with these but with the 'monastic' tradition. The present argument would support that view, if it is accepted that the description of the visions is in fact a late derivative of

that very tradition. There seems to be agreement that the first recorded appearance of the fully developed image was on the banner of a Roman *Confraternitas Comendatorum Virgini*, which received its statutes from St Bonaventure in 1264 or 1267: Perdrizet, p. 64. The earliest surviving exemplars come from the early fourteenth century – for example, Lippo Memmi's panel for a confraternity in Orvieto Cathedral.

50. White, *Duccio*, pp. 32–45, 185–7.

51. *Cronache senesi*, p. 90; translation in White, *Duccio*, pp. 96–7.

52. See below, p. 299. It has been suggested that 'Duccio's idea of representing the Madonna as liege-queen surrounded by her courtiers was certainly a new one in Italian painting', with the influence behind it not only of courtly French art, but of the imagery of the *laudes*: E.T. de Wald, 'Observations on Duccio's *Maestà*', in *Late Classical and Medieval Studies in Honor of Albert Mathias Friend Jr*, ed. K. Weitzmann (Princeton, NJ 1955), pp. 362–86.

53. G. Cor-Aschenbach, 'The Earliest Italian Representation of the Coronation of the Virgin', *Burlington Magazine* 99 (1957), pp. 328–30. White attributes the *oculus* not to Cimabue but to Duccio: *Art and Architecture in Italy: 1250–1400* (Harmondsworth 1966), p. 157; *Duccio*, pp. 137–40. For Sienese representations of the Virgin generally, see H.W. Van Os, *Marias Demut und Verhherrlichung in der sienesischen Malerei 1300–1450* (The Hague 1969).

54. The Biccherna covers have been frequently discussed and published; here I cite *Le Biccherne*, ed. Borgia. For the 1451 cover, see n.58, pp. 156–7. Later images of the hovering Virgin survive from 1460 (coronation of Pius II, n.63, pp. 166–7) and 1467 (a time of earthquakes, n.65, pp. 170–71).

55. Now in the Pinacoteca Nazionale, Siena: K. Christiansen, *Painting in Renaissance Siena*, p. 40; E. Gaillard, *Un peintre siennois au XVe siècle: Sano di Pietro 1406–1481* (Chambéry 1923), pp. 63–6. For the political circumstances, see below, pp. 299, 303, 305–6.

56. '[L]a Madonna delle Grazie, cioè quella a cui fu dato le chiavi della città per la sconfitta di Montaperto'. This procession was conducted in hopes of a league with the Venetians; another, in 1449, was to avert the plague: *Cronache senesi*, pp. 858, 859, 860.

57. Garrison, 'Towards a New History', p. 10. It is interesting that at the same period the Bolognese were beginning to make processional use of the Madonna di San Luca, in explicit imitation of the Florentine use of the Madonna dell' Impruneta: see above, p. 182.

58. See below, p. 310.

59. *La Sconficta di Monte Aperto. Impresso nella alma citta di Siena per Symione di Nicholo cartolaio Nel anno Mccc.ii. A dì xxviii di Aprile.*

60. Burckhardt, *Siena the City of the Virgin*, p. 94.

61. G. Gigli, *La città diletta di Maria* (Rome 1716), pp. 43–4 and pl. 73;

D. Promis, *Monete della Repubblica di Siena* (Turin 1878), pp. 57–8. Promis expresses doubts about any immediate connection between Montaperti and the appearance of the phrase 'civitas Virginis' on the coinage (30).

62. Siena 1262, pp. 54–6.

63. *Cronache senesi*, pp. 209–10. As if to confirm the context in which he had thus impinged on Sienese affairs, George was invoked alongside God and the Virgin when Count Guido Novello, as vicar for Manfred, promised Siena assistance in her war against Orvieto in an instrument of 16 October 1264 (*Caleffo Vecchio*, 3, p. 1020).

64. Ibid., pp. 221–2.

65. Siena 1309–10, 1, p. 85. For Ambrogio Sansedoni, see further below, esp. pp. 278–9. For the *Giuochi Georgiani* and the commemoration of Ambrogio at a later date, see Heywood, *Palio and Ponte*, pp. 75–81, including a translation of an account printed in 1509.

66. ASS *Statuti di Siena* 3, fols 7v–8. The text is identical to the version in Siena 1262, pp. 123–4.

67. *Cronache senesi*, p. 359.

68. Garrison, 'Sienese Historical Writings', p. 41.

69. This chronicle also preserves a curious footnote to the story of St George at Siena. It gives the most detailed account of the efforts of the Sienese military captain and politician Antonio Petrucci, in and after 1429, to involve his rather reluctant fellow-citizens in the active defence of Lucca against the besieging Florentines. In 1429 he was appointed *podestà* of Lucca by its lord Paolo Guinigi, but the appointment was rescinded under Florentine pressure. Petrucci took this ill, and prepared to force his way into the city. The chronicler imagines him addressing his companions: 'Ora è 'l tempo, fratelli miei, al nome di Dio e di San Giorgio saremo vitoriosi' (*Cronache senesi*, p. 814). Of course St George was a favourite saint of the military man; but might not the redactor of the chronicle have had the German war-cry at Montaperti, which he had reported elsewhere, in mind?

70. 'Towards a New History', p. 10.

CHAPTER 7

VIRGIN WITH SAINTS

If the Virgin was a queen, she must have courtiers about her. It was legitimate for the Sienese to hope that spokesmen for the interests of Siena would be prominent among them. Four saints whose relics lay in the cathedral of Siena began to assume this civic role around 1300. They were first so represented, kneeling at the feet of the enthroned Virgin and Child, in the *Maestà* of Duccio, painted between 1308 and 1311.[1] The concept was an elaboration of the enthroned Virgins, surrounded only by courtier-angels, which Duccio himself, Cimabue and Giotto all painted for confraternities, and which made possible the gratification of the particular interests and attachments of patrons.

The chief of the Sienese four, Ansanus, sometimes called the Baptizer, is depicted as youthful and beardless. As we saw above, he had reputedly come to the cathedral in 1107, removed by the Sienese from the church on the Arbia which marked the place of his martyrdom and burial and had been one of those in dispute for centuries between the bishops of Arezzo and Siena.[2] Crescentius, still more youthful-looking, was a fourth-century Roman boy-martyr whose relics Pope Stephen II may have given to Bishop Ansfridus in the mid-eighth century.[3] Savinus, a martyr-bishop originally buried at Spoleto, was widely venerated, and his relics were claimed in many places in Italy.[4] Victor was a soldier-martyr of somewhat debatable provenance, shown as swarthy and bearded in token of the belief that he was African.[5]

These four saints were to become a familiar sight in Sienese iconography. Their 'bodies' [*corpora*] were claimed by the cathedral in 1215.[6] Three of them appeared flanking the Virgin in the stained-glass *oculus* for the cathedral in 1287, but Victor was absent, his place supplied by St Bartholomew, who, as Odericus tells us, possessed an altar in the cathedral.[7] In 1215 Victor had no altar of his own; his head was venerated in the altar of San Savinus, which, like that of Ansanus, had already been one of the cathedral's principal altars before 1190.[8] By the end of the thirteenth century, however, he was commonly invoked by the bishops along with his future companions.[9]

It was the presence of these saints in the cathedral, the centre of the public cult of the Virgin, that entitled them to their place around her throne. Their appearance in Duccio's *Maestà* signalled their emergence into the broader civic domain. Only a few years later they established their presence in the *palazzo pubblico*, presenting their petitions on behalf of the city to the Queen-Virgin in Simone's fresco. Their adoption of a civic role resulted in minor modifications to their iconography, particularly Ansanus's. The artist who, in 1336, executed the miniature of the Assumption of the Virgin which gives the register known as the *Caleffo dell' Assunta* its name included at the corners of the frame of the main miniature small busts of Crescentius, Victor and Savinus. In the initial 'I' below he showed Ansanus holding the black-and-white communal standard, the *balzana*, which would become his frequent attribute thereafter.[10] Simone Martini had already depicted him with the *balzana* in the altarpiece (now in the Uffizi at Florence) which he painted in 1333 for his altar in the cathedral, the first of a series of commissions in honour of the group of saints.[11]

By this time also, Ansanus, alone of the four, had become legally entitled to an annual offering from the officials of the commune, an honour which he upheld in the teeth of competition from saints of a newer vintage. A fresco painted in the choir of the cathedral by Ventura Salimbeni early in the seventeenth century expresses the long-term outcome of decisions about the civic cult taken by the city fathers in the course of the 1320s. It shows Ansanus baptizing a model of the city of Siena held by the Dominican *beatus* Ambrogio Sansedoni.[12] This somewhat curious iconographic device was a means of bringing together saints of totally different date and provenance who had claims on both the attention and the gratitude of the Sienese.

In October 1326 the Consiglio Generale heard a petition that the government should do honour to Ansanus on his feast-day (1 December). The rulers of the city were reminded that Ansanus had miraculously converted their ancestors to the Christian faith, when they were followers of the perfidy of the devil; he had subsequently liberated the Sienese from 'divers perils'. 'Out of reverence for so great a saint,' the Nine were asked to decree, 'as your predecessors have ordered for several other saints', that 'his holy feast be devoutly celebrated in your city of Siena, all citizens ceasing from all servile work'. The *podestà* or the vicar and the other officials of the commune were to be bound to attend 'with fitting lights' [*cum luminariis decentibus*] and the offerings were to be converted by the clerk of works into ornaments for the saint's most glorious body.[13]

The reference to the 'several other saints' whose cults had been sanctioned by predecessors of the present Nine is unspecific, but it is not, perhaps, too risky a guess that the saints of the mendicant orders were meant, for at Siena they were uncommonly popular and abundant. Perhaps the petitioners in favour of Ansanus, most probably men associated with the cathedral and its *Opera*, which would profit from the proposed offerings,[14] thought it a good idea to remind their fellow-citizens of the ancient traditions of the diocese, especially at a moment when, on the one hand, the rebuilding of the cathedral was under consideration and, on the other, the impact of the orders of friars on urban life was arguably reaching its height. Old 'episcopal' saints, as we saw above, were achieving a greater degree of civic recognition elsewhere in Tuscany at just this period; it is sufficient to recall the *inventio* of Zenobius at Florence, or Ser Parmigiano Pucci's lobbying on behalf of San Zeno at Pistoia only a few years later.[15]

Ambrogio Sansedoni, who died in 1278, was a friar of local and noble birth who had won fame in both Italy and Germany as a preacher, and in Siena itself as a counsellor to the government, an organizer of pious confraternities, and the friend (before and after his death) of young girls in search of a good marriage. He was credited with interceding successfully with Pope Gregory X to obtain Siena's release from interdict in 1273. On his death the bishop and the government were quick to approve his cult, and vote assistance to the building and adornment of his chapel and altar. Early in the fifteenth century Taddeo di Bartolo showed him carrying a model of the city in the entrance to the chapel in the *palazzo pubblico*, where, it may be noted, his figure corresponds to that of Judas Maccabaeus on the opposite jamb: both men were found righteous in the sight of God, and obtained pardon and favour for their people.[16]

If the other mendicant houses in Siena around 1300 had produced no one of quite equal stature, they had still proved remarkably fertile in *beati*. The Franciscans could boast as one of their tertiaries the holy comb-seller Pier Pettinaio, to whose prayers the arrogant Pia Tolomei attributed her relatively advantageous situation in Dante's Purgatory. The exemplar of upright business practice and strenuous lay piety, he too had received government grants to help launch his cult on his death in 1289.[17] The Augustinian local hero, Agostino Novello (so surnamed to distinguish him from the older and greater Augustine), was not a native of Siena but a southerner who had been a lawyer and servant of Manfred, which perhaps endeared him to some Sienese. He fought (on the losing side) at Benevento in 1266, then retired to the Augustinian hermitage of Lecceto near Siena. In an altarpiece painted at some time in the 1320s for the Augustinian church, Simone Martini later depicted him performing homely miracles, above all for children.[18] The Servites could boast of the blessed Joachim (d. 1305), who is still venerated as a special benefactor of children and epileptics, and whose life was written some time between 1325 and 1335.[19]

Joachim's biographer evokes an atmosphere of emulation among the admirers of these saints. In May 1310, at the Indulgence of San Galgano at the Cistercian monastery some distance from Siena, a number of people gathered around a fire, as it was chilly, and began talking about the life and miracles of Ambrogio Sansedoni and Pier Pettinaio, and 'of other good people, whom they had themselves known and had lived in their time'. This prompted someone to wonder aloud why God had not granted Joachim any miracles; and immediately a Servite lay brother who was present inwardly vowed a wax image of himself to Joachim if he should be cured of a swelling which a doctor was due to cut out the following day. His cure inaugurated the series of Joachim's miracles.[20] The emphasis on the contemporaneity and familiarity of these holy men to a Sienese public is noteworthy; it was a factor in obtaining public recognition for them.

By the time Ansanus received his official offering, all these new and deserving saints had in fact, at one time or another, been accorded honours by the Sienese government. In 1306 the government resolved that a *palio* should be provided at public expense, to be run, 'according to Sienese custom', in honour of Ambrogio Sansedoni.[21] On 29 March 1321, the Consiglio Generale agreed that thirty pounds should be spent to honour the blessed Joachim, which also honoured God and the Blessed Virgin, and in June 1324 the government asked for retrospective approval of several disbursements, of which one had been 'to honour the feast of the blessed saint Agostino Novello'.[22] These were, it seems, occasional and not regular expenditures, but official offerings for the feasts of Pier Pettinaio and Ambrogio Sansedoni had become more or less routine.

In December 1323 the *podestà*, the *capitano del popolo* and other officials bore candles amounting to one hundred pounds in weight to the feast of Pier Pettinaio, the scribe of the Biccherna noting that the expenditure had been authorized by the Consiglio Generale.[23] The following March the Nine themselves, together with the officials of the commune, bore a total of one hundred and thirty-two pounds of wax in offerings to the feast of Ambrogio Sansedoni, authorizing the expenditure without apparent reference to the council.[24] Both the size of the offering and the personal attendance of the supreme magistrates indicated the status of the festival; Ambrogio, it seems, was honoured at a slightly higher rate in terms of both the quantity of the offering he received and the august rank of his congregation, but neither actual practice nor the amount of detail in which the scribes of the Biccherna thought it necessary to record it was consistent from year to year.[25]

When Ansanus's supporters petitioned for similar honours in October 1326, therefore, they could rightly claim that the government had indeed been spending money on a number of other saints in recent years. Two years later, however, all such offerings were threatened by what appears to have been an economy drive. Vauchez drew attention to this incident and to the mendicant response, but the story can be taken beyond the point at which he left it.[26]

On 10 November 1328 the Nine brought forward a package of measures, explicitly motivated by the need to cut expenditures and increase revenue. The first, which concerned the granting of pardons (for a price) to certain banished and condemned persons [*exbanniti & condempnati*], was proposed and considered separately. Three proposals were then read and debated together. The first of these was a measure compelling certain natives of Massa who were resident in Siena or its suburbs to take out Sienese citizenship, while the third proposed the setting up of a committee to consider new regulations for the commune's almsgiving and pious benefactions; it was in fact set up, and reported a month later on 14 December.[27] The proposal which most concerns us here was the second: 'that the lords nine should not be able to go in person to any festivity or send or offer any *doppieri, ceri*, offering or money, etcetera' [*quod domini novem non possint personaliter ire ad aliquam festivitatem vel mictere vel offerre aliquos dopplerios ceros empsenum vel pecuniam etcetera*].

All these proposals excited some opposition. Issues involving *exbanniti & condemnati* were always contentious, and the government's proposal was passed on the first vote only by 192 votes to 92.[28] The triple proposal was then put to the vote, and opposition was slightly more muted, yielding figures of 207 to 72. The final vote on the first proposal was 191 to 80, conforming to the frequent pattern that once the issue had in effect been decided by the first vote, a few councillors would either cast their votes in favour or abstain on the second ballot. The final vote on the second, triple proposal, however, went against this trend: 158 councillors backed it, but 113 dissented.[29] Vauchez may well have been right to surmise that it was the proposal to ban the magistrates' attendance at the *festivitates* that excited this unusual degree of opposition, but it is impossible to be sure. As he rightly indicated, however, the orders were not slow to respond, and it is reasonable to suppose that they knew they would have backing among the people who mattered in Sienese politics.

On 16 February 1329 the prior of the Dominicans petitioned for the abrogation of the statute of 10 November.[30] In so doing he glossed it slightly. According to him, it had laid down that the Nine could not attend any festival except as specified by the statutes [*nisi per formam statuti*]. He pointed out that the statutes in fact had nothing to say about their attendance at *any* festival. He was right in the latter contention, but the words 'nisi per formam statuti' do not in fact appear in the original form of the proposal put forward on 10 November. Perhaps it was assumed by all concerned that the festivities for the Assumption were so deeply embedded in custom that they could not possibly be affected; it would indeed have been bizarre if the proposal had been so interpreted as to exclude the Nine from paying homage to the Virgin at the Feast of the Assumption. The *palio* that was run in honour of Ambrogio Sansedoni was enshrined in statute, but, as Vauchez correctly points out, the offering made by the officials on his feast-day, as on the feast-day of Pier Pettinaio, had, at least in theory, to be petitioned for and granted annually. The effect of the act of 10 November would have been to determine that whoever else might attend and bear offerings, the Nine themselves in future *could not* do so.

It was to head off this threat that the Mendicants now moved. The Dominicans pointed out that there was not a city in Tuscany which did not have its own saint who was solemnly venerated; this was true, but not entirely to the point unless the Virgin's position was going to be threatened as a result of the loose drafting of the new statute. In emotional language, the petition begged that:

> the aforesaid officials may and should, and indeed the Council should, as has been hitherto the custom, go to the festival of St Ambrogio, your most noble fellow-citizen; whom you knew, whom you have heard, whom you have loved with pure affection and reverence, whom your hands have touched, by whom the words of eternal life have been most generously exhibited and expounded to this city.

The Franciscan petition was presented on the same day. It had been the custom since the death of the blessed Pier Pettinaio for the officials to attend the divine office at the church of the Minors on his day. The Franciscans, too, could lay stress on their saint's Sienese nationality, and the indubitable benefits that accrued to the city from its possession of him. Perhaps mindful of the fact that they were not the only ones in the hunt, the Minors urged the value of multiple patronage: 'the city is preserved so much the more safely in so far as it has more great advocates with the supreme defender, that is God Himself [*tanto magis civitas servetur incolumis quot plures apud defensorem summum id est ipsum Deum magnos habuerit advocatos*]'. The Franciscans were emboldened to demand that the Nine, the *podestà*, *capitano* and other officials should in future be bound to attend the *festa*.³¹

Both the Dominicans and the Franciscans obtained their wishes fairly easily, by votes of 223 to 79 and 221 to 81 respectively. The petition put forward by the Hermits a few days later on behalf of Agostino Novello had a rougher passage. As Vauchez remarks, the council minutes record that one speaker, Jacopo di Piero, the *maior sindicus*, actually rose to demand the rejection of the petition. We can only speculate as to the reason: was it that the saint was not Sienese-born, although he was a lover of Siena? Did his following have unacceptable political associations? Or was it simply a last-ditch attempt to salvage what had been official policy? Anyway, the Augustinians requested only that the Nine and the other officials should be *permitted* to attend the *festa*, with such escort as seemed fit to them. They obtained their wish by the comparatively close vote of 154 to 77.³² This was on 20 February; it was not until 19 April that the Servites and the Carmelites presented petitions in favour of the blessed Joachim and St Nicholas of Bari respectively. Clearly the latter had realized that they could not be left out just because they had no local *beatus* to offer. St Nicholas was one of the most universally venerated saints in Western Christendom, and either this or influential backing for the Carmelites may be reflected in the lack of opposition to the institution of official honours to him: the vote was 183 to 33, for Joachim 156 to 58.³³

The effect of the petitions that were heard and approved by the Consiglio Generale in the early months of 1329 was to put official offerings to the saints in question on a regular footing, and to exempt them from the requirement of annual petition. The government measure of 10 November had been well-timed to save a little money, for the feast-days of both Ansanus (who was presumably equally affected by the measure) and Pier Pettinaio fell in December, and the communal accounts for the latter half of 1328 indeed show no record of any official offering to either saint. Now there would in fact be an extra expense to meet in December: the offering to Nicholas on the 6th. In December 1329 offerings were indeed made to Ansanus, to Nicholas and to Pier Pettinaio,³⁴ and the communal accounts for the first half of 1330 record offerings to Ambrogio and Agostino Novello, though not apparently to Joachim.³⁵ The sums that were being spent on these offerings may seem respectable, but if we compare the amount laid out on wax for offerings (including those for the Assumption) in, say, the second semester of 1329, with what was spent on regular almsgiving to the orders and other churches and pious institutions over the same period, it becomes apparent that there were only modest savings to be made by denying Ambrogio Sansedoni or Pier Pettinaio their candles, while all expenditures on offerings or alms pale into insignificance beside the amounts that had to be disbursed to *condottieri*.[36]

For a year or two Ansanus, although he received his offering, did not achieve quite the marks of ceremonial respect that were accorded to the mendicant saints. In both December 1329 and December 1330 a large number of one-pound candles and a small number of two-pound candles were borne to his feast, while Nicholas of Bari and Pier Pettinaio were honoured by the offering of four *doppieri* in their ornamental holders.[37] In 1332 the Biccherna record does not specify what form the offerings took, although it is clear that considerably less was spent on Ansanus than on Pier and Nicholas, to whom, furthermore, the Nine and the major officials bore their offering 'in accordance with the form of the statute'.[38] In 1334 Ansanus and his rivals were alike being presented with six *doppieri* of ten pounds' weight apiece. However, the bishop's saint on this occasion also received no fewer than sixty two-pound *ceri*, while Pier and Nicholas each received only one two-pound *cero* and five of one pound.[39] The spotlight had perhaps fallen on Ansanus with the installation of Simone Martini's new altarpiece, which is dated 1333, in his chapel; a similar differential marked off his offering in 1335, and it was even greater in 1336.[40] Although gaps in the Biccherna records make it impossible to reconstruct the entire series, it is clear that, as one would expect, Ambrogio Sansedoni, Agostino Novello and Joachim all graduated at the same period to the award of six *doppieri*. More was spent on Ambrogio, who received a larger number of supplementary *ceri*.[41] A tendency to esteem Ansanus on the bishop's side, and Ambrogio on the mendicants', above their fellows, was evidently already established. Generally, practice was being standardized at a level which would be laid down in the revised statute of 1337–39.

We can agree with Vauchez that the whole episode demonstrates the influence the mendicant orders wielded in Sienese society, but the story was not over in 1329. Ten years on, in fact, the government implemented a part at least of its original policy. Describing the restrictions placed on the movements of the Nine while in office, Bowsky observed that, according to the statute of 1337–39, they were not permitted to leave the *palazzo pubblico* for any *festa* but those of the Assumption, Ansanus and Ambrogio Sansedoni.[42] This in itself would have signified that the orders collectively had lost some ground; but Bowsky was mistaken. In the new statute, that part of the 1328 proposals which had barred the Nine from leaving the palace to attend *feste* was reaffirmed. Someone, however, had spotted the anomaly implicit in the earlier proposals. The Nine were now strictly forbidden, on pain of a fine of £50, to go 'to any feast unless to the feast of the glorious Virgin in the month of August' [*ad aliquod festum nisi ad festum Beate Virginis Gloriose de mense Augusti*]. The saints and their backers did not, however, lose financially, and in that respect the proposals of 1328 were not merely abandoned, but reversed. Detailed provision was made for the discharge by other, lesser, officials of what had once been the Nine's ceremonial obligations:

> the other festivals to which the Nine have been accustomed to go shall be honoured in this manner by the commune of Siena, viz., that the rectors and all the foreign officials and all the orders of the city of Siena, except the Lords Nine, shall go in the accustomed manner with others, every year, to the feast of the blessed Ansanus and to the feast of the blessed Ambrogio, accompanied by the councillors of the Consiglio della Campana and those other Sienese citizens whom they wish to associate with them. To those other festivities which the Lords Nine have been accustomed to attend, only the Chamberlain of the Biccherna with a religious companion and the four provisores shall go, each carrying his candle. Notwithstanding which, to each of the said festivities, including those of saints Ansanus and Ambrogius, shall be borne six wax *doppieri* of ten pounds' weight each, with holders painted with the arms of the commune and people of Siena, at the expense of the commune, to be left in the church in which the *festivitas* takes place for the illumination of the body of our lord Jesus Christ, and the authorities in charge of the said churches must leave them to be consumed for that purpose, and if they do not do so, that church shall be deprived of the said *doppieri* automatically and in perpetuity.[43]

A further brief chapter then laid it down that expenses 'for the offering and for bearing lights to the honouring of St Ansanus' [*pro oblatione & luminaribus deferendis ad reverentiam sancti Ansani*] were not to exceed the sum of £25. The offering to Ansanus is mentioned once elsewhere in the statute. The rubric laying down the regulations for the Feast of the Assumption repeated the clause, dating from 1274, which guaranteed to the *Opera* of the cathedral 'all the *ceri* offered at the feast of blessed Boniface and by way of cense to the commune of Siena at any time and also the *feudum* of 30 pounds annually payable to the commune of Siena by the commune of Montalcino', with the addition, after the name of Boniface, of 'blessed Ansanus'. His offering too, as its promoters in 1326 had intended, was to be the property of the *Opera*.[44]

The payment to 'messengers and porters' who bore the offerings to the various *feste* in December 1336 may hint that already the Nine were not attending in person. In 1333 it was stated that 'the officials of the commune' carried the *doppieri* to the feast of Agostino Novello, while those for Joachim were 'sent' and those for Ambrogio were 'offered'. Such phrasing is ambiguous, but the latest specific record of an offering made by the Nine in person seems to refer to the feasts of Pier Pettinaio and Nicholas in December 1332.[45] In 1337–38 the Biccherna records attest that the practice desired by the redactors of the statute was in fact being followed, except that more was spent on Ansanus than they seem to have wished. All three of the saints honoured in December 1337 once again received the six ten-pound *doppieri* which expressed the respects of the supreme magistrates, but seventy one-pound candles were made for Ansanus's feast, together with five two-pounders; Nicholas and Pier merely received two two-pounders and nothing else. Ansanus altogether cost £56 2s. the other two saints £29 17s. each.[46]

How should we interpret the shifts of the 1320s and 1330s? An episcopal saint had been proposed for civic honours, perhaps in reaction to the profuse award of offerings to the saints of the orders in recent years. The whole system, if it can be so called, was then challenged, apparently on the grounds of cost. Briefly, thanks to the rearguard action mounted by the Mendicants, a small group of privileged saints found themselves better off than before, in that they were guaranteed offerings that their supporters had previously, at least in theory, had to petition to obtain. Within a few years the government had restated its policy, but not, it would seem, with economy primarily in mind. The saints could rely on their offerings, but not on the supreme compliment of the attendance of the chief magistrates of the commune.

This need not affect the contention that economy had been the motive in 1328. Vauchez pointed out that the late 1320s were troubled times for Tuscany, with the incursions of Louis of Bavaria, a prolonged drought and an increase in the number of poor in Siena.[47] Precisely between 1326 and 1328 Siena was nominally subject to Charles of Calabria. In such circumstances economies on holy purposes might well seem two-edged. It was all very well to save money, but perhaps, in accordance with a sort of celestial Keynesianism, rulers needed to spend to obtain divine favour. In this troubled period: 'not only is there no decline in the magnificence of the feast of the Assumption, but it is perhaps more magnificent than ever.'[48] Whatever the motives of the government in 1328, the ruling that was finally enshrined in the statute of 1337–39 had the effect on the one hand of doing something to satisfy *pietas* towards the city's principal saints, and on the other of emphasizing the uniqueness of the Virgin's status as the city's patron above all others and the exclusive bond between her and her earthly representatives as governors of Siena, the Nine. It may also be noted that for some years there was no further multiplication of regular statutory offerings, although other offerings were sometimes, for special reasons, made to religious communities on the feast-day of their patron saint.[49] Admirers of the Virgin's parents, in 1333, or of Andrea Gallerani in 1347, asked only that the relevant feasts should be 'kept and celebrated' in the city.[50]

This treatment of the six favoured saints seems to have continued for some years after the fall of the Nine in 1355. The centrepiece of the offering remained the six *doppieri* in their decorated holders. In the second half of the century, however, the account-books show that the Sienese government was responding to a diversity of new pious demands, some of which, at least, may be connected with the Black Death. In consequence of a miracle of the Virgin during the pestilence, the commune began in 1352 to build the *cappella del Campo* at the foot of the *palazzo pubblico*.[51] It became customary to celebrate the Feast of the Annunciation at the *cappella del Campo*, and the occasion was also annually marked by a viewing of the relics which the government purchased in

1359 for the hospital of Santa Maria della Scala.[52] Also in the 1350s, the commune began to pay for *doppieri* to be sent to the church of Santo Spirito at Pentecost.[53]

The growing involvement of the commune in the celebration of Corpus Christi was another feature of the Sienese public cult of the later fourteenth century which differentiated it from the order with which the Nine had been familiar. The celebration of Corpus Christi was at this period centred on the Carmelite church, but the records show the government stepping up its participation. In 1357 four *doppieri* in decorated holders were sent to the 'Mantellini' (the Carmelites) for the feast; in 1363 the commune paid as well for twelve *doppieri* for the 'illumination' of the city for the feast [*ch'andaro a luminando per la città per la detta festa*].[54] In June 1365 the Carmelites petitioned the government of the Twelve for a grant to enable them to obtain a tabernacle for the Sacrament which would rival the *Corporale* of Orvieto. A chronicler recorded the making of such a tabernacle at a cost of £200.[55] From 1370 the feast at the Carmelite church was sponsored by the *Arte della Lana*, which had a chapel there.[56]

By about 1380 a new pattern was beginning to emerge, and the six old patrons began to lose a little ground. The accounts for the early summer of 1382 are illustrative. In June, apart from offerings for St Petronella, St Barnabas and for St Onofrio and Santa Maria delle Grazie at their respective churches,[57] six *doppieri* were purchased for the offering of Santa Maria della Grazie at the cathedral. For Corpus Christi, twelve *doppieri* in holders and eighteen *doppieri a mano* were paid for, of which four *doppieri*, as before, became the property of the Carmelites.[58] Meanwhile, although Ambrogio Sansedoni was still receiving the tribute of six *doppieri*, plus fifty other *ceri*, Joachim now received only four *doppieri* and fourteen other candles, and it seems beyond doubt that the same applied to Agostino Novello. Economies were being effected; even Ambrogio was receiving a little less in terms of smaller candles than he had done in recent years.[59]

The accounts for 1384 show that a decision had evidently been taken to privilege Ambrogio definitively above his fellows. Ansanus was now receiving only four *doppieri*, but was still distinguished from Pier Pettinaio and the rest by the larger number of small candles sent to his *festa*.[60] The new rates at which the chamberlain and the four *provisores* of the Biccherna were to make the accustomed offerings were sanctioned, and extended to Ambrogio, by one of the ordinances issued by Giangaleazzo Visconti's lieutenant in Siena in November/December 1400. The offering was to be of four *doppieri* of six pounds each; the offering for the Feast of the Assumption was specifically excluded, and was to be made 'in accordance with the custom hitherto observed' [*secundum consuetudinem hactenus observatam*]. It was stated that Ansanus and Ambrogio were both to receive the new rate; but Ambrogio could in addition have up to twenty-five candles of one-pound weight each.[61]

Both theory and practice, then, accorded Ambrogio a degree of preferential treatment over Ansanus and the rest, but to judge from the accounts for the crisis year of 1402, practice, as so often, did not conform exactly to what had been laid down. Despite the political circumstances, the Sienese continued to send to Florence for the cloth for Ambrogio's *palio*, and he received, over and above his *doppieri*, twenty-nine one-pound candles, four more than the prescribed allowance.[62] Joachim and Agostino Novello,[63] Nicholas and Pier Pettinaio duly received just their four *doppieri*, but Ansanus was offered twelve candles in addition.[64]

Early in 1412 the Sienese government made another effort to economize on holy expenditures, and a list was produced of the feasts to which offerings were to be sent, at a reduced rate, for a period of ten years. The only offerings which were to continue at the existing rate were those for the Feast of the Assumption and the recently instituted celebration of San Pietro Alessandrino in November, which commemorated the uprising in November 1403 which had led to the overthrow of the regime of the Twelve.[65] Of the six saints who had occupied a privileged position since the 1330s, Agostino Novello dropped completely out of sight; Joachim, Nicholas and Pier Pettinaio were permitted two *doppieri* each; Ansanus, two *doppieri* plus fifteen one-pound candles; and Ambrogio Sansedoni, four *doppieri* and fifteen candles. In addition, offerings for St Laurence[66] and Saints Fabian and Sebastian[67] were prescribed. One *doppierium* was to be supplied for the celebration of Pentecost at the church of Santo Spirito. Twelve *doppieria* were to be sent to the Feast of the Annunciation at the chapel in the Campo, but they were all to be returned to the Biccherna; similarly, twelve were to be offered at Corpus Christi, of which all but two were to be returned. In addition, it was stipulated that for a period of ten years none of the officials was to be given *ceri* for the feast, and there were also reductions, for the same period, in the grants made to the *Opera* of the cathedral.

The bishop's saints, in the new age, may not have inspired much popular enthusiasm, but as public figures they profited modestly from the urban authorities' self-identification with the cathedral and with the religious traditions of the diocese. The *Liber Censuum* of 1400, which listed the tributes due at the Feast of the Assumption from Siena's subject communities, accorded Ansanus and his three companions the title 'patrons and defenders of the [Sienese] community and people' [*patroni et defensori de la sua comunità et populo*].[68] On May 14 1413 it was resolved that

> out of reverence for almighty God and for the blessed martyrs Ansanus, Savinus, Crescentius and Victor, patrons and especial protectors and advocates of the magnificent city of Siena, henceforth the feast-days of the said martyrs and each and every one of them shall be kept and celebrated as the days of the Lord and solemn days are kept and celebrated in the said city.

A chronicler noted that the feasts of the 'Advocates of the cathedral' [*Avvocati del duomo*], as he rather significantly called them, were henceforth to be kept like Sundays [*come la domenica*].[69] As an individual, Ansanus could not outrank, or even quite equal, the patrician Ambrogio Sansedoni in the competition for official honours, but he kept ahead of the other mendicant *beati*, and collectively he and his fellow now enjoyed in law the position in which Duccio and Simone Martini had depicted them a century before.

It might with reason be contended that Siena entered the fifteenth century already well equipped with saints, even if one or two of them were losing some of their lustre. The insecurity of the *contado* in the opening years of the century brought yet another saint to town, when San Galgano's relics were deposited for safekeeping under lock and key in the hospital of Santa Maria della Scala.[70] If fortune did not intend to visit the city in the years to come with either internal peace and stability or power in the outside world, it was at least prepared to endow it lavishly with intercessors in the court of heaven. The Sienese were increasingly conscious of their need for them, as well as their unceasing need for the services of the Virgin who had saved them at Montaperti.

Notes

1. The contributors to *I Santi Patroni Senesi* are concerned principally with the early evidence for the identity and cults of these four saints, but in 'L'iconografia dei santi patroni Ansanus, Crescenzio, Savino e Vittore' (pp. 84–115) F. Argenziano and F. Bisogni discuss representations of them as a group and individually, with useful lists and illustrations. See also the individual entries in *BS* and in Kaftal, *Tuscan Painting*.

2. Barcellona, 'Un martire locale: Ansanus', *I Santi Patroni*, pp. 10–33. For the dispute with Arezzo and the translation of 1107, see above pp. 37–9, 62–4.

3. Consolino, 'Un martire 'romano': Crescenzio', *I Santi Patroni*, pp. 34–48. For the possible source of his relics, see pp. 45–7 and cf. above, n.14, p. 55. Odericus several times mentions his altar in the cathedral, where his translation was celebrated as well as his main feast-day (*Ordo*, pp. 147, 363–4, 371–2).

4. E. Giannarelli, 'Savino, Bartolomeo e l'alternanza dei patroni', *I Santi Patroni*, pp. 64–83.

5. M.F. Patrucco, 'Un santo "milanese": Vittore', ibid., pp. 49–63.

6. Odericus uses the word *corpus* only in connection with these four saints, speaking of the *reliquiae*, *patrocinia* or *vocabulum* of others.

7. *Ordo*, p. 357. The altar is also identified as the location of the cults of Fabian and Sebastian (p. 288) and Severinus (pp. 374–5) in the cathedral.

8. Ibid., pp. 325, 376. Relics of 'the Seven Brothers' and their mother St Felicitas (p. 337) and the *patrocinia* of St Luke (p. 373) were also located in this altar.

9. Victor's feast in the early thirteenth century was evidently celebrated with less solemnity than those of a number of other saints, including Ansanus, Crescentius and Savinus (*Ordo*, p. 393). In the second half of the century the bishops began – though not consistently – to name him with the other three as their special patrons. The four are apparently first named together in 1257 in a text containing ordinances for the cathedral chapter, promulgated by Cardinal Ubaldini and later confirmed by Alexander IV (Patrucco, *Santi Patroni*, p. 48). In 1267 and 1272 the bishops did *not* name Victor when they confirmed the statute of the confraternity of *laudesi* (Meersseman, 'Le Congregazioni della Vergine', pp. 1030, 1039), but in 1274 bishop Bernardo Gallerani did so when he proclaimed an indulgence for those who visited the tomb of his brother, the *beatus* Andrea (Patrucco, p. 148; *Acta S* Martii 3, p. 49). On 10 August 1287 Bishop Rinaldo, granting an indulgence for contributions to the building of a

chapel for Ambrogio Sansedoni, also named all four saints as his patrons (*Acta S* Martii 3, p. 242). The presence of Victor's relics, together with his auspicious name, doubtless helped to promote him, but the fact that Lippo Memmi depicted him bearing both the palm of martyrdom and the bays of victory suggests an association, possibly a supposed or fictitious one, with some specific military triumph: Frugoni, *A Distant City*, p. 152 and ill. 89; Kaftal, *Tuscan Painting*, col. 1012, fig. 1137. It seems to have been believed that the victory in question was one at Sarteano which Gigli dated to 1229 (*Diario Sanese*, 1, p. 161). The *Anonimo* records the event without mentioning a specific date or Victor's feast (*Cronache senesi*, p. 48). In the seventeenth century, however, Tommasi (p. 233) said that the Sienese defeated the Orvietans at Montepulciano on 15 May 1229, which he called (wrongly but suggestively) the day of S. *Vito* (*recte* 15 June) and pursued the fugitives to Sarteano, which they took.

10. Bisogni, 'L'iconografia', *Santi Patroni*, n.124, pp. 107–8, lists images with and without the *balzana*.

11. For these commissions, see Argenziano and Bisogni, 'L'Iconografia'. In 1335 the government paid for a translation of the story of San Savino, for Pietro Lorenzetti to work from when he painted his *tavola*; and in 1339 Ambrogio Lorenzetti was commissioned to execute the altarpiece for Crescenzio. An altarpiece was painted for Victor's chapel between 1351 and 1361.

12. Detail illustrated in D'Urso, *Beato Ambrogio*, pl. 12.

13. ASS CG 103, fols 94v–97. The proposal was approved by a vote of 197 for and 10 against; the final vote, giving it the force of law, improved to 201 to 6. This enactment was made during the term of office of Pietro Randolfo of Rome, the first vicar of Charles of Calabria as perpetual *podestà*.

14. The statute of 1337 stated that the offerings to Ansanus were to be the property of the *Opera*; see below p. 286.

15. See above, esp. pp. 159–60, 165.

16. *Vitae*, miracles and documentation of the cult in *Acta S* Martii 3; iconography in D'Urso, *Beato Ambrogio*; for Ambrogio's standing in public life, Waley, *Siena*, pp. 142–6. On the city model as a saintly attribute, see above, pp. 237–8.

17. *Purgatorio* XIII, 128; A. Vauchez, 'Pier Pettinaio', in *BS* 10, cols 719–22.

18. Martindale, *Simone Martini*, pp. 211–14. In 1310, the year after Agostino's death, nine *contrade* of the *terzo di Città* decided to celebrate a *festa* for him, dressing up, playing games and running a *palio*, but the press of people who flocked to the celebrations aroused fears in the great rival families of the Tolomei and the Salimbeni that each was trying to organize 'to raise the people' to drive the other from Siena (*Cronache senesi*, p. 234). For Simone's miracles for children, and also Joachim's and Ambrogio

Sansedoni's, see D.M. Webb, 'Friends of the Family'.

19. *Vita ac legenda Beati Joachimi Senensis*, ed. P.M. Soulier, *AB* 13 (1894), pp. 386–97.

20. Ibid., pp. 391–2. San Galgano was believed, on somewhat uncertain evidence, to have been canonized in the late twelfth century. See now E. Susi, *L'Eeremita cortese: San Galgano fra mito e storia nell' agiogragia toscana del XII secolo* (Spoleto 1993). The fact that monks of San Galgano served as chamberlains of the Biccherna helped to ensure the saint a place in Sienese public iconography; he is represented on a Biccherna cover for January–June 1320 (*Le Biccherne*, n.19, pp. 78–9). In October 1330 the abbot of San Galgano passed through Siena on his way to the consecration of the abbey of Quarto, bearing the head of San Galgano and other relics. When the procession came to the *palazzo*, the *signori* came out and kissed the relic (*Cronache senesi* 143, pp. 498–9).

21. Siena 1309–10, 1, p. 385. Cf. above p. 267.

22. ASS CG 93, fol. 88v (modern numeration); ibid., 100, fol. 10.

23. ASS Biccherna 148, fol. 132 (modern).

24. Ibid., 149, fol. 127v.

25. In December 1321 the offering for Pier Pettinaio had amounted to one hundred and six pounds of wax, and the scribe recorded that the Nine attended; the expenditure was authorized by a chit without any specific reference to the Council (Biccherna 142, fol. 146v). In December 1327 only the amount spent was recorded (Biccherna 155, fol. 51v). In December 1323 the Consiglio Generale approved the expenditure on Pier Pettinaio as part of a package which included the expenses laid out by the commune 'in festivitate & commemoratione Sancti Tommassi de Aquino', presumably on the occasion of his canonisation (CG 98, fol. 151v).

26. Vauchez, 'La Commune de Sienne', ASS CG 106, fols 87v–93.

27. Ibid., fols 114–16.

28. Ibid., fol. 90v. Vauchez mistakenly read this as the vote on the proposal to ban the Nine from attendance at *festivitates*, but it is clearly the vote only on the first proposal.

29. Ibid., fols 92v, 93.

30. The Dominican petition is in CG 107, fols 33r–v (voting figures, fols. 35v, 36v); it is printed in *Acta S* Martii 3, pp. 242–3. The prior's rendering of the objectionable law was 'quod officium dominorum novem & ali officiales dicti comunis non possint ire ad aliquod festum nisi per formam statuti, quod vere fuit & est contra mentem & intentionem vestram & eorum qui dictum ordinamentum fecerunt & quasi omnium beneficium pro eo, scilicet, quod nullum est communis senensis statutum loquens quod officiales debeant ire ad aliquod festum.'

31. CG 107, fol. 33v. The voting figures are on fol. 35v. Printed by F. Cristofani, 'Memorie del B. Pietro Pettinaio', *Miscellanea Francescana* 5 (1890), pp. 37–8.

32. CG 107, fols 39v–40; printed by Vauchez, 'La Commune', pp. 765–6. An inscription extant in the nineteenth century recorded that the altar where Simone's image of Agostino stood had been 'genti Ptholomeae attributa', although it is not known who the patron of the altarpiece was (Martindale, p. 214). The Duke of Calabria had had to 'pacify' the Tolomei and the Salimbeni yet again in the summer of 1326 as vicar for his father Robert of Naples; despite fears that the *grandi* might offer him *libera signoria*, he took good advice and espoused the popular cause (*Cronache senesi*, pp. 438–40).

33. CG 107, fols. 72v–73. The final voting figures were (Nicholas) 192 to 21, (Joachim) 180 to 33 (fol. 74). Later in the century the Sienese Carmelites were associated with the wool guild in the celebration of Corpus Christi: see below p. 288.

34. Biccherna 163, fols. 63r–v. The *camarlingo* often made up his accounts at the end of December and the end of June for wax purchased for all purposes, including lighting and sealing documents, in the previous six months. Wax purchased for the Assumption would therefore appear in the December account. The wax intended for religious purposes included the candles for the altar of the Nine in the palace itself. Other expenditures, such as payments for porters and provisions, would usually be recorded at the end of the relevant month. Interestingly, rather more (a total of £38 9s.) was spent on Nicholas than on either Ansanus or Pier, who merited just over £29 each.

35. Ibid., 165, fol. 55v. £46 6s. had been laid out on 140 pounds of wax in *doppieri* and *ceri* offered at the feast of St Ambrogio, and on the decoration of the *doppieri*; £42 8s. was expended on a smaller quantity of wax for the feast of Agostino Novello. The wax cost 6s. 6d. a pound. A separate payment had been made on 23 March to the three servants who had carried the *doppieri* 'a la festa di Santo Ambruogio quando andò l'uficio', as well as for Ambrogio's *palio* (fol. 23). That is to say, Ambrogio was back roughly where he had been in March 1328, before the government's attempted economy drive, when, however, a little more (£48 8s.) had been spent on him (Biccherna 157, fol. 66).

36. The Feast of the Assumption was hardly over when, on 18 August 1329, 'Misser Urlimbacho chonistabile del comune di Siena' was paid £3289 14s. for the hire of 49 horse for two months (Biccherna 163, fol. 16). The total spent on wax for the three December saints, Ansanus (£29 2s. 8d.), Nicholas (£47) and Pier Pettinaio (£29 7s.) was £105 9s. 8d., while wax for the Assumption accounted for another £65 6s. 8d.; the total spent on almsgiving was £1766 10s.

37. Biccherna 163, fols 63r–v; 167, fol. 74. Ambrogio Sansedoni and Pier Pettinaio had in fact received *doppieri* when the magistrates honoured their feasts before 1329.

38. Ibid., 174, fols 67r–v. £25 was spent on Ansanus, a total of £85 2s.

on Pier and Nicholas.

39. Ibid., 181, fol. 50v. Ansanus's offering cost £46 16s. 4d., the others £25 5s. 10d. each.

40. Martindale, pp. 188–90. The 1335 account is in Biccherna 183, fol. 79v; in 1336 almost twice as much (£60 7s.) was expended on Ansanus as on his rivals (£30 12s. 6d. each) (ibid., 185, fol. 141).

41. In March 1333 Ambrogio, Agostino and Joachim were still receiving four *doppieri*. A bemused scribe surnamed them all 'Novello' (Biccherna 176, fols 41, 60, 80). The 1336 records show them receiving six, with considerably more (£57 14s.) spent on Ambrogio than on Agostino (£31 6s. 6d.) and Joachim (£26 2s.) (ibid. 184, fol. 180v).

42. Bowsky, *A Medieval Italian Commune*, p. 58 and n.112.

43. ASS *Statuti* 26, fol. 205r.

44. Printed by Cecchini, *Il Palio*, p. 147. For the regulations of 1274, see above, pp. 257–8.

45. See above, p. 284.

46. Biccherna 187, fol. 133. A year later the figures varied slightly, because for some reason the *doppieri* were made of unequal amounts of wax, but the basic pattern was the same (ibid., 198, fol. 57v); and in spring 1338 Ambrogio Sansedoni had demonstrated his superiority over Agostino Novello and Joachim by a similar margin (ibid., 194, fols 58r–v).

47. Vauchez, 'La Commune de Sienne', p. 760.

48. Cecchini, *Il Palio*, pp. 24, 145–7 (the accounts of August 1326).

49. For example, two large *doppieri* in painted holders, accompanied by wine and foodstuffs, were often sent to the nuns of St Barnabas on the saint's day (e.g. on 22 June 1336, Biccherna 184, f. 180v; 19 June 1341, Biccherna 207, f. 138), and this continued into the second half of the century. While enlarging the city walls in 1326 the commune had purchased land from the convent on which to build the Porta Nova (*Cronache*, p. 454).

50. CG 114, fol. 41r–v; 140, fol. 42r–v.

51. *Cronache senesi*, pp. 557, 570.

52. *Cronache senesi*, p. 590. See above, pp. 226–7.

53. E.g. 1354 (Biccherna f. 185v), 1357 (Biccherna 236, f. 112) etc.

54. Biccherna 236, f. 112; 243, f. 148v.

55. *Cronache senesi*, p. 159.

56. *Cronache senesi*, p. 634: 'E' frati del Carmino di Siena concedero all' Arte de la Lana di Siena che facessero le loro festa del Corpo di Cristo.'

57. The churches of St Onofrio and Santa Maria della Grazie in Camollia were among those erected in the wake of the Black Death, as well as 'molti altri oratori e luoghi divoti' (*Cronache senesi*, p. 558).

58. Biccherna 382, f. 183v. All of this wax was paid for together, and cost £58 11s. 4d.; another payment of £48 1s. 4d. went to the *custos* of the Biccherna for candle-holders, porterage and provisions.

59. Ibid., fol. 166v. Ambrogio's expenses amounted to £37 8s. 8d. Joachim's appeared on the same day, but were paid together with the offerings for the *capella del campo* and for the exhibition of the relics at the hospital; the total was £28 8s. Eight *doppieri* for Agostino Novello and for Pentecost were paid for together on 16 June (fol. 184). Five years earlier, when the offerings for Agostino and for Pentecost were also paid for on the same day, both had included six *doppieri* painted with the arms of the commune, plus a total of eight two-pound candles and sixty-eight of one pound (Biccherna 258, 30 June 1377, fol. 196). The difference in cost was considerable. In 1377, £106 3s. was expended on the wax (which weighed a total of 193 pounds) plus a total of £6 5s. for the holders, £1 10s. for porterage, and £1 17s. 10d. for bread and wine 'per esse feste'. In 1382 eight *doppieri* and forty lesser candles, amounting to eighty-eight pounds of wax, cost £42 11s. 4d. No other expenses seem to be recorded. In 1377 Joachim too was still receiving his six *doppieri* plus thirty-nine *ceri*, but his costs were grossed up with those of the *doppieri* that were borne to Santa Maria della Scala for the exhibition of the relics at the Feast of the Annunciation. The total was £102 5s. 10d. Ambrogio, who received ten two-pound candles and sixty-four of one pound over and above his *doppieri*, cost a round £81 (Biccherna 258, 20 May, ff. 170v–171).

60. The relative showings of the saints in terms of cost are as follows: Ambrogio £43, Joachim £22 (Biccherna 268, f. 53). The amount spent on Agostino cannot be distinguished within a total of £120 4s. laid out on various offerings and other things. The accounts for the second semester give more detail, and show that Pier Pettinaio was permitted twenty *ceri* in addition to his four *doppieri* and cost £26 16s. 4d.; Nicholas (also + twenty *ceri*) £25 8s. 0d.; Ansanus (+ forty *ceri*) £30 8s. (ibid., 270, f. 194v). Ansanus, however, was receiving other tributes at this time: in May 1382 the city's bell-founder made a bell for the Duomo which was named 'Santo Sano', and the following year a silver figure of him was placed in the cathedral: *Cronache senesi*, pp. 696, 701.

61. *Statuti* 32, f. 152. Just under five years later, the Feast of the Assumption was again exempted from any economy drive when it was agreed that the *signori* should have the power to approve whatever expenses seemed appropriate, notwithstanding any statutes to the contrary; this was to apply only to the expenses for the Assumption (ibid., 38, f. 33, 10 July 1405).

62. Biccherna 287, f. 58.

63. Ibid., ff.59, 64.

64. Biccherna 288, f. 41.

65. *Statuti* 39, ff. 15v–16. For the *palio* of Pietro Alessandrino, instituted in 1413, see Heywood, *Palio and Ponte*, pp. 81–4. Adopted as patron of the Arte degli Speziali, he was portrayed on a Gabella cover in 1440 (*Le Biccherne*, pp. 144–5), and Sano di Pietro depicted him, holding a model of

the city, in a fresco with Ambrogio Sansedoni and Andrea Gallerani in the Palazzo Pubblico (D'Urso, *Beato Ambrogio*, pl. 3).

66. Under the year 1401, the Montauri chronicler (pp. 760–61) tells how a cobbler of Siena who insisted on working on St Laurence's Day said, when reproved by a neighbour, 'St Laurence can do what he likes, I want to work and earn my bread.' Instantly stuck by paralysis, he died some months later, 'e così santo Lorenzo per farsi beffe della sua festa lo punì'. The anecdote suggests that the saint was in the news. An offering to Laurence is recorded in 1364: Biccherna 245, f. 54. Rondoni, *Tradizioni popolari*, p. 148, remarks on his cult in the region of Siena; he was patron of the cathedral of Grosseto, which was subject to the Sienese.

67. This was one of the important feasts of the year at the cathedral early in the thirteenth century: Odericus, *Ordo*, pp. 288–92. Fabian and Sebastian were also important plague saints.

68. Nardi, 'Il territorio', p. 92; the opening folio of the Liber is illustrated, pl. 2 (also, in colour, by Burckhardt, *Siena*, p. 63). The four are depicted on a painted ballot-box [*cofano*], now in the Museo Civico, made in the first decade of the century (Argenziano and Bisogni, in *I Santi Patroni*, pp. 88, 110 and figs 13, 14, 15).

69. CG 206, fol. 27; *Cronache senesi*, p. 774. For works of art commissioned by the cathedral authorities in honour of the four saints between the Black Death and the early fifteenth century, see Lusini, *Duomo*, esp. ch. 7 *passim*.

70. *Statuti* 38, f. 5v (5 December 1403). Two citizens were appointed to co-operate with the prior of San Galgano in the inventorying and 'conservation' of the monastery's property. The prior of the monastery was to retain the keys in his own possession, so that when the current unrest was over, the relics might be restored. Galgano makes frequent appearances in fifteenth-century Sienese art.

CHAPTER 8

ADVOCATES OF ORDER

In April 1457 the Sienese humanist Agostino Dati was rewarded by the government of the republic for the account he had just written of the city's recent history.[1] His *Historia Senensis* is in fact concerned only with the events of the years 1446–56, during which time the city's ruling clique, his friends and employers, had managed to weather the storms of subversion and conspiracy that had been aroused, in part, by their shift to a pro-Florentine policy.[2]

The trigger had been the death of Filippo Maria Visconti of Milan in 1447. Claiming that he had been designated Filippo's heir, Alfonso V of Naples, who had only recently consolidated his grip on the mainland half of his southern kingdom, embarked on a prolonged career of mischief-making in southern Tuscany which had dangerous implications for Siena. His target was Florence, the long-standing enemy of the Aragonese claim to the south, and now the friend (under Cosimo de' Medici) of Filippo Maria's effective successor, Francesco Sforza; under pressure to grant passage to Alfonso's troops, the Sienese clung, though not without vacillation, to a policy of 'good-neighbourliness' towards their old enemy which was not at all acceptable to certain elements in Sienese political society. Notable among the anti-Florentines was the clique around Antonio Petrucci, the soldier-politician who in 1430 had played a large part in inducing the Sienese to enter an alliance with Filippo Maria Visconti, and to go openly to war against the Florentines.[3]

Siena's diplomatic difficulties in the middle years of the century were increased by the ambivalent policy of Venice, which for a while exerted pressure on her to comply with Alfonso's wishes.

The relief created by the conclusion of a general Italian peace at Lodi in 1454 was, for the Sienese, short-lived. The *condottiere* Jacopo Piccinino, son of the Niccolò who had played a large part in liberating the Lucchese from the Florentine threat in 1431, appeared in southern Tuscany and renewed the pressure on Siena, to all appearances with the blessing of Alfonso, and the malcontents at Siena rapidly established communication with him. At this point the Sienese secured the patronage of the elderly Catalan Pope Calixtus III; but even when, thanks to his diplomatic good offices, Alfonso was prevailed upon to order Piccinino's withdrawal, the malcontents would not give up hope, and conspired to engineer a coup at Siena with Piccinino's assistance. The conspiracy was discovered and punished in the summer of 1456; Antonio Petrucci was among those condemned to exile. Agostino Dati's *Historia*, as originally written, was relentlessly hostile to Petrucci and the other *factiosi*, as he termed the party which opposed peace with Florence.[4]

In the prologue to the *Historia*, Dati explained that Siena had survived all these perils above all because of her exemplary piety. At the beginning of the third book he spelled out more exactly how and why the city had been preserved by heavenly agency:

> For although in so many centuries Siena had never acknowledged a lord, she has never lacked a prince, who truly rules this city, nor has she been without her help. I mean the most glorious Virgin and unconquered Mother of God, into whose hands once, in a time of great danger from war, the care of the whole republic was committed, and the safety and liberty of the city given in tribute into her hand. On that occasion, leaning out from heaven, she appeared to the people as they offered their vows and prayers, and so manifested herself to their eyes that she seemed to accept the protectorate of the city, not to refuse its proffered keys, and finally to assent to the people's vows.

Dati shows a little humanistic reluctance to tell so fantastic a tale if it were not amply vouched for, and proceeds:

> Furthermore, I think that the Queen of Heaven and prince of this city has never been absent from its senate and has frequently participated in its councils; she has kept vigilant guard; she has inspired the minds of good citizens; she has never neglected the salvation or dignity of her principality; not that she has fought against the enemy with white

horses or drawn sword, as the Romans boast the sons of Tindaris did for them, but [has fought] with her unconquered right hand and her virtue, she who bore the Redeemer of the whole world.

For 'good citizens' we may – not too unfairly – read Dati's political friends. He goes on to observe that had it not been for such celestial protection, Siena could scarcely have survived the machinations of the *scelerati* and *improbi* (criminals and scoundrels), which are among the epithets he customarily applies to their opponents.[5]

The period of political emergency chronicled by Agostino Dati was also a time of notable marks of papal favour and accretions to the city's spiritual prestige and self-image. On a visit to Siena in 1443, Eugenius IV – who, as Gabriele Condulmerio, had been bishop of the city from 1407 to 1431 – gave official approval to the cult of Ambrogio Sansedoni.[6] The next two decades witnessed the death of the Franciscan Bernardino degli Albizzeschi, his canonization by Nicholas V, the extension of patronage and protection to Siena by Calixtus III, the accession of a Sienese pope in the person of Pius II, and his canonization of Catherine in 1461. The regime must surely have interpreted these evident signs of divine favour, all the more welcome given the harshness of political reality, as opportunities to affirm its authority in the eyes of all beholders. In May 1448, also, the celebrations of Corpus Christi were by papal decree removed to the cathedral, 'as in all the world', and thereby became more than ever an affair of the city's government and the city's church.[7] Between 1456 and 1466, as we shall see below, the regulations for the feasts of Bernardino, Corpus Christi, Catherine and Pentecost were drafted and redrafted in a manner which betrays a conscious awareness of the common character of these festivities as demonstrations of civic *pietas* and the internal discipline of the community.

The news of Bernardino's death at L'Aquila on 20 May 1444 was marked, on 16 June, by a solemn procession at Siena, while the commune made immediate moves, which proved unavailing, to obtain possession of the saint's corpse.[8] In the following year, 20 May was kept as a public holiday by order of the *magnifici signori*, who attended the solemnities. Meanwhile, the canonization of Nicholas of Tolentino at Pentecost in 1446 was marked at Siena by *una bella festa* in the piazza in front of Sant' Agostino. This canonization was a major incentive, to the Sienese government and the other orders of friars alike, to promote their own saints. Only a few days later, on 5 June, the feast of St Catherine (who, of course, was not as yet canonized) was celebrated at San Domenico, again in the presence of the magistrates. It was estimated that more than 20,000 people were present at a spectacle of unprecedented splendour.[9] The campaigns that would result in Siena's acquisition of two canonized saints were under way.

The fact that the Aquilani had possession of Bernardino's remains sharpened the anxiety of the Sienese that they should be seen to do all they could in the cause. With Bernardino's disciple Fra Giovanni da Capistrano acting as intermediary, it was agreed that the two cities would each find 2000 ducats for the necessary expenses. Success was all but achieved by 1449. The canonization was supposed to be proclaimed in August of that year, but plague drove the curia from Rome and forced a postponement. On 12 April 1450, the six Sienese citizens who had been deputed to attend to the business reported that it was now the Pope's intention to proclaim the canonization at Pentecost. Nothing, they pointed out, could do the city more honour, given that it was a Jubilee year and the Franciscans were holding their General Chapter in Rome. It was all the more important that the Sienese should produce their share of the money; they had good information that the Aquilani were ready with theirs. In a further, still more urgent, memorandum on 3 May, the Sienese deputies were more specific: the Aquilani had part of the sum to hand (*in punto*), part ready to be drawn on the bank of Cosimo de' Medici at Rome.[10]

The financing of the campaign may have presented problems, but members and servants of the regime were personally involved in it, and have left evidence of their private devotion to the saint. Leonardo Benvoglienti, a correspondent of Aeneas Silvius Piccolomini who later fell out with him, is mentioned several times in Dati's *Historia* as an opponent of the anti-Florentine *factiosi*; he served from time to time as ambassador and as chancellor of the *balìa*.[11] He had been an adherent of Bernardino as a young man at the *studio*, and he was an important witness at the canonization process held at Siena in 1448, as was Battista Bellanti, doctor of law and another member of the same political grouping.[12]

Benvoglienti's involvement with the promotion of the cult went further, however. In 1446, at the instance of Giovanni da

Capistrano, he composed the second life of Bernardino to be written, in which he identified the saint as a product of a specifically Sienese fount of piety which had in earlier times produced, among others, Andrea Gallerani and Giovanni Colombini, founder of the Gesuati.[13] In this emphasis on the native religious traditions of Siena he was evidently at one with Agostino Dati, another devotee. In an oration in praise of Bernardino – written some time after 1464, to judge by the fact that he refers to Pius II in the past tense – Dati recites a long list of Sienese holy men going back to San Galgano, and including not only those Benvoglienti had mentioned but Pier Pettinaio and Ambrogio Sansedoni.[14] He composed several prayers to Bernardino, and in the *Historia* he relates how his brother, a monk, had had a badly injured hand healed by the saint's intercession.[15]

All was well that ended well. In the *Historia* Dati described the rejoicing with which the canonization was proclaimed at Rome on 24 May 1450.[16] According to the chronicler Fecini, the news reached Siena on the 27th. At once the shops shut, bells and trumpets sounded, and in the evening there were *gran fuochi*.[17] The Consiglio Generale met and resolved (by the intriguing vote of 172 to 1) that Bernardino should in perpetuity be invoked and celebrated as the 'fifth advocate and protector of the magnificent commune and people of the city of Siena' [*quintus advocatus et protector magnifici communis et populi Civitatis Senarum*]. A committee of citizens was to be appointed to draw up regulations for the celebration of his feast.[18] It had already been resolved, on 13 May, that a prisoner should be released in his honour; on 5 June safe-conduct was proclaimed for the 14th and 15th of the month, and for the five days preceding and following.[19] On the 15th a *festa* took place in the Campo which was described by Fecini and later by Dati.[20] There were trees and arches everywhere, all the guilds paraded, and altars were set up all over Siena; the bishop celebrated mass at the foot of the *palazzo*. Above the chapel and at the windows of the *podestà* a wooden 'paradise' was constructed, adorned with hangings and a wheel of lights, and an actor representing Bernardino ascended into it.

Proposals for the future shape of the *festa* were submitted to the Consiglio Generale on 3 May 1452.[21] As in the past, the *signori*, *capitano*, *podestà* and other officials were to attend at San Francesco with an offering of eight *doppieri* and forty *ceri*; they were to be followed by the guild officials with offerings to be determined by nine citizens to be appointed by the *signori*. Of the total offering two-thirds were to go to the church of San Francesco and one-third to the church of San Bernardino in Capriuola, on condition that the brethren of that church attended the *festa* 'collegialmente'. It was restated that a prisoner should be released in Bernardino's honour, and safe-conduct granted as if for the feast of St Mary of August. The men of San Pietro Ovile were to be responsible for cleaning the *contrada*, as was customary on similar occasions.

These regulations were not the last word. Four years later, on 17 May 1456, reference was once again made to the nine citizens who had been supposed to make regulations with permanent effect [*ordines perpetuo durandos*] for the feast.[22] Particularly at issue was the manner in which the guild officials were to accompany the *signori* to the solemn offering on the morning of the feast. The committee of nine had been appointed, but had not reported, and in the meantime arguments about precedence had frequently arisen among the guilds, which impaired the 'honour and reverence' due to the occasion. The same, regrettably, also happened at Corpus Christi, which was contrary to the honour of God and the intentions of the regime. It was therefore necessary that the committee should be empowered to make binding regulations for both solemnities, 'and the required honour exhibited to God and the said festivities'.

At this moment, the finishing diplomatic touches were being put, under the Pope's auspices, to a settlement which promised to deliver Siena from the depredations of the condottiere Jacopo Piccinino and, behind him, the hostility of the King of Naples. The conclusion of peace would leave the pro-Naples and pro-Piccinino faction in the city with no alternative except outright conspiracy to overthrow the regime, and this conspiracy was unmasked and punished in the later summer and autumn of 1456.[23] It was against this background that the committee appointed to produce revised regulations for Bernardino's feast and Corpus Christi reported on 19 May. The scribe who copied the new regulations on 8 June noted that he was writing 'in the time of the most holy Father in Christ Calixtus III Pope by divine providence, protector and defender of the liberty and status of the city of Siena'.[24]

The determination of precedence as between the guilds in the processional order was, as expected, a central concern, and the amount of their several offerings was laid down, but other aspects of the solemnities were also comprehensively dealt with. The conventual and observantine friars were to set out from San Francesco with the *gonfalone* of Bernardino and his cowl under a *baldacchino* carried by four of the 'most honoured' young men of the *compagnia* of San Francesco. Arriving by a prescribed route in the Campo, they collected the *signori* and officials and the guilds, and returned with them to San Francesco. The rector of the *studio*, the guild of *scolares* and the doctors, the consuls of the judges and notaries and of the bankers, and the prior of the consuls of the *Arte della Lana* were collectively given first place, and their respective positions at the head of the procession were minutely regulated. Then the order of the remaining guilds, represented by a prescribed number of 'principal masters' [*capo maestri*], was prescribed.[25] As had been envisaged in 1452 already, the rear of the procession was to be brought up by the second-hand-clothes dealers [*ligrittieri*], who were to bring what *doppieri* they thought fit; the whole membership of the guild attended and brought their trumpets, with which, evidently, they customarily enlivened festivities.

Other provisions made by the committee concerned the ringing of the bells of the commune as a signal to the guilds to assemble and accompany the *signori*; the proclamation of the order to clear, clean and decorate the streets, and of penalties for dirtying or obstructing them; and arrangements for the *Camarlingo* to take inventory of the offerings and fine defaulters. Six persons, two for each of the *Monti*, the political groupings which currently participated in government (the Nine, the Twelve and the *Riformatori*), were to be elected annually to make arrangements for the *festa*. The officials of the *mercantia* were to see that the regulations were copied into the guild books. A prisoner was to be offered every year by the four chief officials of the Biccherna. The master of the *Camera* was to have a wooden litter, resembling that which was used to carry the Body of Christ, made at communal expense to carry Bernardino's cowl in the procession.

The arrangements for Corpus Christi began with the departure of the consuls of the wool guild from their residence with all the guild members, their trumpets and their *baldacchino*. They made their way to the *palazzo* and accompanied the *signori* to the duomo, as they had been accustomed to do in the past. The other citizens and guilds went directly to the *duomo* at the sound of the bell, and there formed the due processional order. The procession was headed by the Flagellant confraternities, followed by the orders of friars and other religious. The *Arte della Lana* headed the guilds, which (as honour in this context was determined by proximity to the Sacrament) followed in the reverse of the order laid down for Bernardino. Following the *baldacchino* with the *corpo di Cristo* came the *signori*, *capitano* and other senior officials; the *signori* might, if they wished, be accompanied by other 'honourable persons' such as ambassadors. They were to offer ten 'torches' of four pounds of wax each, which were to be carried, lighted, around the Sacrament by their servants. Half of this offering remained in the cathedral and the other half went, 'for the love of God', to the Carmelites, a memento of the time when the public celebration of Corpus Christi in Siena had been the preserve of that order. It was further provided that any 'person, religious, order or company' who was accustomed to receive salt in alms from the commune, but failed to attend the feast of Corpus Christi, should forfeit their allowance. Penalties for non-performance were otherwise to be identical with those prescribed for the feast of Bernardino; and similarly, six citizens were to be annually appointed eight days before the feast to make the necessary arrangements. It was, finally, the responsibility of the *operaio* of the cathedral to assign positions to those waiting to make their offerings, so as to avert confusion.[26]

A strongly marked concern with the decorum of public religious ceremonial was certainly not peculiar to Siena in the fifteenth century. Siena's circumstances, however, were such that the rulers of the city were particularly anxious to ensure that such ceremonial should display a conspicuous gratitude for God's many graces visited on Siena, on the part of a cohesive, disciplined social order, obedient to the directives of its government. They had especially good reason to emphasize the city's gratitude to Calixtus III. As a graceful gesture to the Pope, the city fathers decreed that the feast of St Calixtus, 14 October 1455, should for the first time be kept as a public holiday at Siena. Agostino Dati was called upon to deliver an address in praise of the martyr-pope from the pulpit of the cathedral, in which he praised in turn the three popes who had ruled under the name of Calixtus. The current Calixtus was to be acclaimed for his crusading plans; as to what he had already achieved, Siena was a prime witness, for he had spared no expense or labour to undertake the defence of its unjustly wounded liberty, in a spirit of true affection and fervent piety.[27]

A further compliment was ultimately to be paid to Calixtus in the form of a chapel and altar dedicated to his name-saint. In 1454 it had been agreed that the *operaio* of the cathedral, Mariano Bargagli, should undertake the decoration of a chapel dedicated to St Boniface, whose name recalled the victory of Montaperti that had been won on his feast-day. Mariano was to have the patronage of the chapel and appoint the priest in consultation with the bishop and the *Opera*; but unfortunately, he was among the conspirators who were disgraced in the summer of 1456. According to Agostino Dati, in a passage omitted from the printed edition of the *Historia*, the conspirators used to meet in the cathedral itself. This outraged the right-minded, who moved to safeguard the honour of the Virgin, whose church was thus polluted. Mariano was dismissed from his post and called to account for alleged misappropriations; the rules governing the appointment of the *operaio* were changed. The altar in question was in due course dedicated to St Calixtus, a cult which was unquestionably closely identified, at least at its inception, with the victorious regime of 1456.[28] At the Feast of the Annunciation, 1457, when by custom the relics were exhibited to the people, Dati was again in the pulpit to proclaim to them an indulgence granted by Calixtus for those who should devoutly visit the 'old and holy image of the Virgin' when it was exhibited 'at stated times' in the cathedral. Here again was an affirmation of tradition, for this was the image that was believed (wrongly) to have been on the high altar when the people of Siena made their supplication to the Queen of Heaven on the eve of Montaperti.[29] With this happy event, Dati piously brought his *Historia* to an end.

The elevation of Aeneas Silvius Piccolomini to be cardinal and then, in 1458, Pope was, of course, a feather in the Sienese cap; but it also meant increased pressure to readmit the *gentiluomini*, from whom the new Pope originated, to a share in the regime. In 1459, with Pius ensconced in the city and making it plain that he expected only one answer to his polite request that the nobles should be restored to a share in political power, the Sienese gave at least some ground. Pius, for his part, well understood that granting his fellow-citizens spiritual as well as worldly favours made it all the more difficult for them to resist him. The spiritual series began with his elevation of the see of Siena to archiepiscopal rank, and the grant of a plenary Pentecostal indulgence. It culminated in the canonization of Catherine, and ended in 1463 with the gift of the arm of St John the Baptist.[30]

On 16 May 1460 the Consiglio Generale declared that the election of a Sienese as Pope was to be numbered among recent proofs of God's grace conceded to the city through the intercession of Mary, its advocate and protectress. Under the protection of the apostolic see, Siena, having been gravely vexed by many persecutions, had been preserved 'in its sweet liberty and lordship' from all those who had been disturbing the peace; now the Pope had granted his native city a surpassing spiritual treasure, a plenary indulgence for all those who devoutly visited the cathedral between vespers on the day before Pentecost and vespers on the second day following. To ensure the continued favour of God and His Mother, to avoid the sin of ingratitude, and to commemorate Pius, new regulations for the celebration of Pentecost were now decreed.

These regulations bore the mark of Pius's activities in a number of their details. The committee of citizens that was to be appointed annually eight days before Pentecost to make arrangements for the feast was to consist of only four members, one for each *Monte*; now the nobles constituted the fourth, alongside the Nine, the Twelve and the *Riformatori*. The solemn procession that was to mark the third day of the festivity was to be arranged in consultation with 'Monsignore Arcivescovo', who owed his newly exalted title to the Pope. The *operaio* was to be bound to decorate the piazza before the cathedral as he did for the celebration of the Annunciation, and to adorn the church itself 'in a manner which will uphold and increase the honour of the public authorities and of the aforesaid church' [*in modo che lo honore publico & de la decta chiesa si mantenghi & accresca*].[31]

News of Pius's canonization of Catherine was received at Siena on 1 July 1461. A chronicler noted that 'the house where she was born has been made into a beautiful chapel, with offerings from the *sigroria* and all the guilds, very honourably'.[32] However, a compulsory offering of the kind which had been awarded to Bernardino was not immediately instituted for Catherine. On 19 March 1462 the Consiglio Generale expressed the city's complacent recognition that it had 'laboured worthily' to obtain the canonization, and resolved that Catherine should be numbered among Siena's advocates, 'so that she may always intercede with Almighty God for the well-being of our liberty and our government'. The magistrates were to attend at her solemnity at San Domenico with the same offering that they made at San Francesco for Bernardino, and in general the same mode of celebration was to obtain, but the guilds were not to be burdened with an offering or expenses greater than they wished.[33]

Significant as it may be of popular resistance to the multiplication of enforced offerings, it was hardly likely that this softly-softly approach would produce results acceptable to the Dominicans – nor did it. On 12 May 1466 the brethren of San Domenico duly petitioned the government for the imposition of penalties for failure to make a proper offering. They recalled that Catherine had been canonized first and foremost because of her own merits, but also as a result of 'the industry, effort and no small expense of our community'. They recalled also that the fame of her sanctity had been so widely diffused that her feast-day had been celebrated in many places even before her canonization, 'as is well known'. They recapitulated the government's original resolution that the same should be done for Catherine as for Bernardino: the same offering by the *signori*, the same participation by the guilds, the same release of a prisoner. The *signori*, they said, had fulfilled their obligations, and so too had the major guilds, but because no penalty had been prescribed for failure to perform, the other, lower, guilds had begun to neglect 'this new custom' in a somewhat devious manner. They presented themselves to the magistrates in the Campo, and then 'took another path' and failed to offer. The brethren were now, inevitably, asking for the imposition of the same penalties that were incurred by failure to offer to Bernardino. Their wish was granted, on 16 May, by a vote of 187 to 19, and the logic of the regime's nomination of Catherine as yet another 'advocate' of the city was at last spelled out.[34]

The official designation of Bernardino and Catherine as 'advocates' of Siena, and the explicit statement that Bernardino was the *fifth* advocate, revealed a continuing mindfulness of the rank that had been awarded earlier in the century to Ansanus and his three companions. Delivering an oration in praise of Catherine, Dati had the concept clearly in mind.[35] As an individual, Catherine was Siena's representative of the class of holy women in whom so many nations rejoiced; she had been 'raised within these walls within the memory of our fathers and dwelled with our own kin'. She also simply added to the number of Siena's patrons. The city of the Virgin rejoiced in the name of the mother of God and queen of angels, and then there were the 'illustrious martyrs' Crescentius, Ansanus, Savinus and Victor, Bernardino the 'preacher of the truth' [*predicator veritatis*] and now the virgin Catherine, 'so that now, with so many intercessors, we receive benefits which confer the utmost splendour and the utmost dignity on this people'.

Ansanus and his associates made frequent appearances in artistic commissions of the mid-century, often in company with other members of the pantheon.[36] They were present on the altarpiece commissioned by the *Arte della Lana* from Sassetta for their chapel in the church of the Carmelites, which was intended for display at Corpus Christi.[37] The chronicler Fecini noted the consecration of the church of Sant' Ansanus in Castelvecchio in May 1448 and the 'furnishing' of the chapel of San Crescenzio in the cathedral early the following year, at the expense of the late bishop of Siena, Carlo d'Agnolino, who died in 1444 and was buried at the foot of the saint's altar. The 'bell of St Victor' was made in 1442 and the 'bell of St Crescentius' in 1453.[38] In 1445 the painter Vecchietta compiled the most comprehensive visual inventory of the Sienese pantheon in the form of the reliquary cupboard doors, the 'Arliquiera', which he painted for the Ospedale di Santa Maria della Scala and which depict all the important Sienese saints, from the cathedral's martyrs and Galgano to Bernardino and Catherine, neither of them yet formally canonized.[39] Around 1450, depicting the Articles of Faith in the vaults of the Baptistery, the same artist showed Ansanus and company together with Bernardino in the foreground of the Coronation of the Virgin, an up-to-the-minute portrayal of the city's official 'advocates'.[40]

In the 1450s Vecchietta and Antonio Federighi executed statues of Ansanus, Victor and Savinus (for some reason Crescentius was never completed), together with Peter and Paul, for the Loggia dei Mercanti. A particular interest attaches to the splendid figure of Victor executed by Federighi in 1457. Here the saint has become beardless, a truculent 'Roman warrior' whose mien strongly suggests a reference to the perils recently confronted and, as they would have wished to believe, surmounted by the Sienese.[41] Savinus was sometimes accorded a special position as protector of the *popolo*; in October 1482, after the seeming victory of the *Monte del Popolo* in their struggle against the *Noveschi*, the diarist Cristoforo Cantoni recorded that it was resolved to run a *palio* for Savinus, 'one of the advocates of the city of Siena and especially of the *popolo*'.[42]

The city needed all its advocates; but it is no surprise that the patronage which was claimed, invoked and competed for was supremely that of the Virgin. The continued resistance of the 'popular' party to the participation of the nobles in government, given that the Piccolomini were now well entrenched at the curia, was a source of endless tension in Siena's political life in the latter part of the century. In June 1483 an attempt was made to use the Virgin to defuse tensions which were felt to have become insupportable. According to Cantoni, it was acknowledged that the people and the city of Siena had always received infinite gifts and favours from their advocate the Virgin, and that the *Madre della Misericordia* had liberated them from innumerable perils. Knowing this, all the officials went to the cathedral with the Cardinal, where the *Madonna della Grazie*, who was normally seen only on her feast-days and at vespers on Saturday, was ready. Under the influence of the preaching of the Augustinian Fra Mariano da Ghivizzano, the government of the city was 'again' given over to the Virgin in the hope that she would once more 'liberate' the Sienese in their hour of need. The reference to what was believed to have happened on the eve of Montaperti is clear; and the ceremony of resubmission was represented on the painted cover of the Biccherna volume for the year.[43] This, however, was not enough to save the Sienese from themselves. On 22 July 1487, the feast of Mary Magdalen, Pandolfo Petrucci, a younger kinsman of the Antonio who had suffered exile in 1456 for conspiracy against the then regime, entered the city with fellow-*Noveschi* exiles. In the time-honoured manner a *palio* was instituted on the feast of the Magdalen, Petrucci's patron, to commemorate this happy turn of events.[44] In due course Petrucci established a quasi-seigneurial control of Siena which, with some interruptions, lasted until his death in 1512.

Meanwhile, the pressures of an Italian situation transformed by Hapsburg and Valois intervention bore ever more heavily on states which could not resolve their internal tensions. That Florence should obtain Hapsburg backing for its Tuscan expansionism was the last straw. There were further ceremonies of self-surrender to the Virgin at Siena, in 1525, 1550 and 1555.[45] In 1545 the last statute of the independent Sienese republic systematically enumerated the offerings the government was to make, month by month.[46] Of the saints who had been awarded honours in the 1320s, only Agostino Novello was missing (as he had been already in the list produced in February 1412); the Augustinians were compensated by an offering for the greater Augustine. Catherine and Bernardino, of course, were present, and so too was Andrea Gallerani and, from further back in Siena's sacred history, Galgano. The minimum offering was £12; Ambrogio Sansedoni, Nicholas of Bari and Pier Pettinaio merited £16 and Joachim and Andrea Gallerani £14, but Bernardino and Ansanus received £58. They were, however, outclassed by Catherine, whose solemnity at San Domenico attracted an offering of £80. James and Christopher received a joint offering of £24 and had a *palio* run in their honour, ostensibly in recognition of the fact that God, 'Virgine semper intercedente', had on their day liberated Siena from Florentine siege.[47] In honour of the popes to whom Siena was bound by historic ties of gratitude, St Pius, Pope and martyr, was honoured on 11 July and St Calixtus on 14 October.

The Virgin was, of course, in a class by herself. Apart from the arrangements for the Assumption, a special clause of the statute laid it down that the image of the Virgin which was kept in its ancient chapel in the cathedral was not to be brought forth or carried around the city for any cause without specific governmental approval, and if permission was so given, it was not to be moved without the escort of all the clergy and officials and 'the whole city'. Until the image was restored to its original place, every bell in the city was to sound continuously.[48] This image represented the utmost force at the city's disposal with which to invoke the intervention of the deity; therefore the laymen who ruled the city laid claim to the power to decide when and whether that force was to be used.

The communal commitment to the processional celebration of Corpus Christi was also affirmed and strengthened. Forty pounds of wax in white candles were to be borne by the *familiares Palatii* around the 'canopy under which the most holy Body of Christ is borne'. A new description of the processional order for Corpus Cristi made it plain that all orders of society were to attend; the rear of the procession was to be brought up by 'the rest of the citizens, the hired troops with their captain, the scholars and the whole people'. The statute strengthened earlier sanctions against those confraternities and religious persons who failed to attend the Corpus Christi procession; they now stood to lose not merely any communal allocation of salt to which they might be entitled, but all alms and offerings of any description.[49]

One glorious chapter in Siena's history remained to be written: its final resistance to a Florentine conquest backed by Hapsburg arms. In 1555, however, the city succumbed to its fate and became part of a Tuscan state based on Florence. There is a splendid irony in the fact that the last upholders of the Sienese republic took refuge at Montalcino, which, by flirting with the Florentines, had helped to precipitate the Battle of Montaperti, and thereby caused the Sienese, as they believed, to confer the government of their city upon the Virgin nearly three centuries before.[50]

Notes

1. Some account of Dati is given in his son's preface to his *Opera* (Siena 1503), and in G.N. Bandiera, *De Augustino Dato libri duo* (Rome 1733). He died, according to his son, in 1479. Another edition of the *Opera* was published at Venice in 1516. Dati has been little noticed by modern historians, but see E. Rice, Jr, *Saint Jerome in the Renaissance* (Baltimore, MD 1985), pp. 95, 234 n.33.

2. The fundamental account of Siena's predicament in these years remains that of L. Banchi: 'La guerra de' Senesi', 'Il Piccinino nello Stato di Siena', 'Ultime relazioni dei Senesi col Papa Callisto III'. Cf. A. Ryder,

Alfonso the Magnanimous (Oxford 1990), esp. pp. 273-90.

3. See above, pp. 252-3, p. 275 n.69. Pope Pius II returned an unflattering verdict on Petrucci, and suggested that the comparison between him and Bernardino, as Sienese contemporaries, was not to his advantage: *I Commentarii*, 1, pp. 996, 998.

4. The *Historia Senensis* was published incomplete and bowdlerized in the *Opera*, clearly for fear of Pandolfo Petrucci, ruler of Siena since 1487, who was the son of one of the conspirators of 1456 and related to others. Niccolò Dati in fact admitted, in veiled language, that he had censored the text, and headed each of the three books 'Fragmenta'. It is possible to reconstruct a more or less complete text with the help of two manuscripts: Siena, Biblioteca Comunale C. I.19, a collection of Sienese historical writings copied in 1571; and British Library Add. 8799, which, though copied in the 1460s, is incomplete, containing only a third of Book III. Most of the passages quoted here, however, were politically neutral and were not censored. The present writer hopes to publish an account of the *Historia*.

5. *Opera*, pp. 230v-231.

6. According to an account of this event, translated into Latin from the Italian found *in antiquissimo libro memoriali*, Eugenius, asked 'by our city' to canonize Ambrogio, said he would do so as soon as he returned to Rome; for the time being he authorized the saint's solemn celebration in the Roman province of the order, and especially at San Domenico in Siena: 'velut si Sanctus esset canonizatus; idque vel officio proprio vel ex communi Confessoris accepto' (*Acta S* Martii 3, p. 245).

7. *Cronache senesi*, p. 859. The same chronicler noted how in these years a number of Siena's dependent communes had *padiglioni* made for the carrying of the Sacrament in procession: Montorsaio in 1439, Paganico and Campagnatico in 1440, Casole in 1444, Roccastrada in 1451 (pp. 851, 852, 856, 862).

8. *Cronache senesi*, pp. 856; A. Liberati, 'Le prime manifestazioni'.

9. *Cronache senesi*, pp. 856-7.

10. CG 225, fols 17 (12 April), 32 (3 May). The *deputati* had realized that the Sienese seemed to have no available source of revenue from which the required sum could be obtained, and proposed a loan from the chamberlain of the Monte, secured against the revenues of the *gabella del mosto*. On 7 April one of the envoys had written asking for money with which to purchase wax for the dignitaries who would be present at the canonization ceremony: Liberati, n.2, p. 148.

11. The *balìa* was a commission with supreme executive powers, appointed in times of emergency, but a potential instrument of party rule. For Benvoglienti, see C. Piana, 'I processi di canonizazzione', n.2, p. 126. As governor of Città di Castello he promoted the cult of Bernardino there. Pius II sarcastically described him as 'cognomento non aequo

Benevolentum': *I Commentarii* 1, p. 171. Dati's references to him in the *Historia* are to be found in *Opera*, pp. 234v, 235, 235v, and also in a 'censored' passage in Siena, Biblioteca Comunale C.I.XIX, fol. 272. He is described as 'orator vehemens' and one of the principal opponents of war against Florence.

12. Piana, n.6, p. 127. On 1 November 1446 Bellanti wrote to the guardian of the Observant convent at L'Aquila not only attesting, as requested, to a cure received by a Frenchman, but relating how he himself had been cured of a severe fever through Bernardino's merits. Dati refers to him as *civis et iurisconsultus egregius* in the 'censored' passage of the *Historia* cited above, n.11.

13. 'La vie de S. Bernardin de Sienne par Leonard Benvoglienti', ed. F. Van Ortroy, *AB* 21 (1902), pp. 53–80. The first had been the work of another friend, Barnabà da Siena, who dedicated his more humanistic *Vita* to Alfonso of Aragon in April 1445 (*Acta S* Maii 4, pp. 739–46). For both these lives, see D.M. Webb, 'Eloquence and Education: A Humanist Approach to Hagiography', *Journal of Ecclesiastical History* 31 (1980), pp. 19–39.

14. *Opera*, pp. LXv–LXII. Dati claims also to have composed an oration in praise of Sansedoni, but it is not among the printed *Opera*.

15. Ibid., pp. LXVIIr–v (the prayers); p. CCXXV (the miracles).

16. Ibid., p. CCXXVIv. The passage is quoted by D. Arasse, '*Fervebat pietate populus*: art, dévotion et société autour de la glorification de Saint Bernardin de Sienne', *MEFRM* 89 (1977) pp. 227–8.

17. *Cronache senesi*, p. 861.

18. ASS CG 225, fol. 39v.

19. Ibid., ff. 39, 41.

20. *Cronache senesi*, p. 861; Dati, *Opera*, pp. CCXXVIv–CCXXVII.

21. CG 225, ff. 307v–308.

22. Ibid., 227, f. 180.

23. Banchi, 'Il Piccinino', pp. 243–5; 'Ultime relazioni', pp. 427–30. The relevant portion of Dati's *Historia* was heavily censored by his son.

24. ASS *Statuti* 39, ff. 76–8.

25. The *setaiuoli* were given a prominent position, but this was more an expression of hope than of fact; the position was reserved for them against the day when the silk guild should be sufficiently 'multiplied' in Siena to take its proper place. In May 1416 measures had been taken to create a silk industry in Siena, since it had been observed how much was being spent on the import of linens and silks: *Statuti* 39, f. 47v.

26. Ibid., ff. 78–9. This collection also included a revised, but undated, order for Corpus Christi, which did not alter the order of precedence as between the guilds, but distanced them from the *baldacchino*. They were, according to this order, to follow the *padiglione* at the head of the procession; then came the companies and the clergy, and then the musicians;

behind them, and immediately in front of the *corpo di Cristo*, came the canons of the cathedral. The place of honour immediately behind the *baldacchino* was allotted to 'il Cardinale co veschovi'; then came the *signori*, the graduates and officials, with the *Arte della Lana* bringing up the rear. Whether these orders were drawn up with a particular occasion or the presence of a particular cardinal in mind is not made clear.

27. *Opera*, pp. LXIIIv–LXIIIIv, CCXXXIIIIv; Banchi, 'Il Piccinino', pp. 234–5. To this context belongs Sano di Pietro's panel showing the Virgin consigning Siena to the care of the Pope (Banchi, p. 225n.; cf. above p. 265). The printed version of Dati's account of the institution of this celebration in the *Historia* (*Opera*, p. 234v) omits a passage which is to be found in Siena Comunale C.I. XIX, fol. 333: 'Civitas tum primum per eam diem feriari coepit; in maiori ecclesia solennia sacra in Calisti martiris nomen acta sunt, xv. viris ita imperantibus, cum Magistratus omnes ac frequens populus interessent.'

28. Ibid., fols 340v–41. For the chapel and altar, see Kempers, 'Art and Ritual', n.111, p. 132.

29. *Opera* p. CCXXXVIv. For 'the virgin of Montaperti', see above Chapter 6. Calixtus's indulgence was granted on 23 December 1456 (Banchi, 'Ultime relazioni', p. 430; however, in 'Il Piccinino' pp. 234–5 he implies that it was granted on 23 December 1455).

30. *Cronache senesi*, p. 869; Christiansen, *Painting*, p. 217. Pius had first carried the relic in procession at Rome, imploring aid against the Turk.

31. These regulations were copied into the same collection as those for Bernardino, Corpus Christi and Catherine: *Statuti* 39, ff. 80–81v.

32. *Cronache senesi*, p. 869.

33. CG 229, fol. 188v; copied into *Statuti* 39, fol. 79v.

34. CG 231, fol. 124.

35. *Opera*, pp. LXII–LXIIv.

36. In general, Argenzano and Bisogni, 'L'Iconografia', in *I Santi Patroni*. Note especially the list (n.13, pp. 86–7) of works of art in which all or several of the four appear. See also Kempers, 'Art and Ritual'.

37. Christiansen, *Painting*, pp. 64–7.

38. *Cronache senesi*, pp. 860–61, 856, 866.

39. H. Van Os, *Vecchietta and the Sacristy of the Siena Hospital Church*, esp. pp. 18–22.

40. Not in Argenzano and Bisogni. Most of Siena's other saints are to be found elsewhere in the fresco decoration of the Baptistery. Later in the century, massive gilded statues of all six official advocates were placed at the angles under the cupola of the cathedral.

41. Cf. the remarks of Argenziano, pp. 94–5: 'qui chiaramente l'abbigliamento e l'atteggiamento di Vittore sono quelli di un difensore della libertà repubblicana cui allude la parole "libertas" incisa sullo scudo sostenuto da un putto il quale tiene anche un ramo d'ulivo'. In a short

address to the *signori*, Agostino Dati invoked the four martyrs together with Peter and Paul (*Opera*, p. CXVv).

42. *Cronache senesi*, p. 924. Argenziano, pp. 91–2, comments on the fifteenth-century variant in Savinus's Sienese iconography which shows him holding a standard bearing the emblem of the *popolo*, a lion on a red field, instead of his pastoral staff. The earliest known example is Sassetta's *Arte della Lana* altarpiece of 1423–24, and Vecchietta also so represented him on the *Arliquiera* for the Ospedale della Scala. On the frontispiece of the *Liber Censuum* of 1400, however, it is Victor who carries the popular standard (see the illustration in Burckhardt, *Siena*, p. 63).

43. *Cronache senesi*, p. 900; *Le Biccherne*, pp. 184–5 (also in Burckhardt, *Siena*, p. 113).

44. Cecchini and Neri, *Il Palio*, pp. 64–74, 160–61. The *palio* of the Magdalen survived the death of Pandolfo Petrucci but is last mentioned in 1526, in which year the convent of La Maddalena, which was closely identified with the Petrucci, was destroyed. The Magdalen and the Virgin and Child are shown presiding over the return of the Noveschi in a Biccherna cover of 1488 (*Le Biccherne*, pp. 192–3).

45. W. Heywood summarizes these events in *Palio and Ponte*, pp. 44–54 (previously, *Our Lady of August and the Palio of Siena* [Siena 1899], pp. 74–92), drawing on A. Toti, *Atti di Votazione della Città di Siena a del Senese alla SS. Vergine Madre di Gesu Cristo* (Siena 1870).

46. Siena 1545, pp. 366–70. The regulations for the Assumption are also published by Cecchini, *Il Palio*, pp. 162–3.

47. Ibid., pp. 374–5. Cecchini (p. 74) believed this *palio* to have been a substitute, instituted in 1528, for the recently abolished *palio* of the Magdalen.

48. Ibid., pp. 372–3.

49. Ibid., pp. 371–2, 373–4.

50. For a recent account, see F. Landi, *Gli Ultimi Anni della Republica di Siena* (Siena 1994).

CONCLUSION

It would be otiose to list the transformations which, in a series of stages since the sixteenth century, have deprived the patronal festivals of Italy of their overt political content as it would previously have been understood. A study of the *feste* between the sixteenth and the twentieth centuries would have its own fascination. Girolamo Gigli's *Diario Sanese* records how, in the eighteenth century, the public authorities sent an offering, on one saint's day after another, to the appropriate church. Did these genuflections retain a 'political' meaning? Can the celebration of the saints be said still to have any political significance in the modern age?

The sixth heavenly advocate of Siena has come a long way since 1461. The visitor to Siena at the end of April will see the young men of the *contrade* parade in Catherine's honour in their *palio* costumes, accompanied by the equally picturesque trumpeters of the commune, as the *sindaco* and other dignitaries process to make their offering at the elaborate *Santuario Cateriniano* into which the Benincasa house has long since been transformed. The onlooker will note the presence of representatives of the Vatican and the Italian state, and observe that by custom the oil for the perpetual lamp of the *Santuario* is provided by another Italian commune, whose *sindaco* heads a delegation to make formal delivery of it on this occasion.

Already in her lifetime Catherine, through her writing and counselling, had become more than a merely Sienese figure. Six centuries after her death, five centuries after her canonization, further recognition of her spiritual gifts was forthcoming at the highest level. In 1939 she was proclaimed a patron saint of Italy, and in 1970 a Doctor of the Church. There might seem little left for her to achieve, but changing times even now perhaps offer new opportunities. A saint with so high a political profile can expect to be appealed to for guidance in the midst of present discontents, not least a patron of Italy at a time when the future of the Italian constitution, if not of the Italian state itself, is in doubt. In 1992 the President of the Republic, Francesco Cossiga, resigned the day before Catherine's festivity; his last official act was to celebrate Liberation Day, 25 April, a secular festivity whose continuing value was being questioned by press and politicians. The speeches of the dignitaries at the *Santuario* not unnaturally reflected these concerns. The *sindaco* of Lecce, presenting the oil on behalf of his commune, took the opportunity to refer to the problems of the south. The archbishop of Siena reminded his audience that Catherine had always been mindful of the need for institutional change, and suggested that the time was ripe for her to be proclaimed a co-patron of Europe. At mass in San Domenico afterwards further dimensions of her presumed relevance to the modern world were rehearsed by Cardinal Pio Laghi. She was, for one thing, a woman. She had been a loyal daughter of the church in difficult times, like the present, and she had called the church back to its one and only destined home, for at Avignon it had lacked a *centro di gravità*.

Three months later, and a little further south, a humbler saint received the homage of his commune. Handbills advertised the festivities for Rufinus of Assisi on 10 and 11 August. The martyr-bishop, historically a shadowy figure, shares his feast-day, 11 August, with the less shadowy Clare, and the celebrations have to be so arranged as to accommodate the *pietas* due both to the ancient saint of the cathedral and to the more charismatic disciple of St Francis. Here too the trumpeters, in medieval garb, precede the *sindaco* to mass at the cathedral, and long wax tapers, beribboned in the colours of the commune, are borne in homage to Rufinus. At the mass a bevy of bishops commemorate the saint who, as a bishop himself, provides the pretext for a discourse on the pastoral role of the church. In 1994, Clare's centenary year, the faithful were urged to consider her and Francis as the finest flowers of the soil of Christianity that had been tended in Assisi by Rufinus. In the neighbouring Marche, the citizens of Ascoli Piceno were being asked to remember how, on St Emidio's feast-day (5 August) fifty years before, prayers had been offered to the saint that Ascoli should be a city of postwar reconciliation, spared the horrors and divisions that might follow in the wake of liberation.

Particularly clear in this instance was the appeal to the saint as a link between his people and their collective social and cultural past. The church has its own reasons for wishing to prevent modern man from becoming what J.R. Hale once termed a 'social amnesiac', ignorant of and indifferent to his history. The rulers of the medieval Italian cities (as indeed of other medieval societies) appealed to a not altogether dissimilar sense of linkage. A saint's developing legend, like that of Petronius at Bologna, might be intimately bound up with the history of his city. The stories of the saints that were recited liturgically, expounded orally to the people and embodied in urban chronicles, represented a body of historical folklore, like secular myths of Roman or Trojan origins. The martyrs who had, perhaps, evangelized and suffered in the locality of the city established the city's Christian pedigree and the continued, or rediscovered, presence of their relics should strengthen the people in their Christian identity, as Ambrose evidently felt when he revealed Gervasius and Protasius to his Milanese congregation. Eleventh- and twelfth-century bishops, whether confronted with outright heresy or simple unruliness on the part of the prominent laymen who were moving up alongside them to take control of the city, could be similarly motivated. The latter, in their turn, had every reason to connect themselves with a source of power and authority which, both spiritually and temporally, transcended the here and now. Even if their preference was for their own patron, no disrespect could be intended to the saints whose presence was enshrined in the mother church of the city.

The fresh emphasis laid in certain fourteenth-century Tuscan cities on the festivities of old episcopal patrons may express the desire of lay elites to stress both their influence over the local church and the spiritual aspect of the public authority which they sought to monopolize. That authority, after all, was rarely uncontested, from within the city or without. Whether the victory went to one man or to a syndicate, a balance had to be struck between emphasizing, with appropriate symbols, the unique and particular character of the regime in power, and maintaining essential continuities with the civic past. The newly instituted commemorative celebration, the cult associated with an individual or a family, however spectacular, could not simply supersede the rituals of the old-established patron who, as the recipient for generations of offerings from town and country, expressed the city's identity and its authority over a dependent territory. A *signore* might well in fact seek to identify himself, by means of his coinage, by artistic commissions or by ostentatious benefactions to the patronal festivity, with this time-honoured fount of 'authority and honour'.

These observations must suffice to indicate one possible way of approach to a question which I have not treated as central in this book. My emphasis has tended to be on continuities, on a core of observance and the accretions to it, and I have not subjected changes of emphasis after, let us say, 1400 to the close scrutiny they might well warrant. There has been a strong tendency in much recent scholarship to minimize the differences between the so-called 'republics' and the seigneurial regimes which had replaced them in most cities by the end of the fourteenth century, particularly in view of the social and political elitism increasingly to be observed also in the 'republics'. It may be thought that I subscribe too obviously and too thoughtlessly to that tendency. It can certainly be observed that the age of the *signori* (or, if it is preferred, the age of elitism) was also the age of Corpus Christi and of the ever more irresistible advance of the Virgin. These (whoever deployed them) were the symbols of universal royalty, as well as having an affective appeal to the mass of Christians.

Meanwhile, the invention of tradition, in the form of civic ceremonial in honour of the saints, continued and has flourished into our own times. For Verdi and the nineteenth century, the Battle of Legnano could be presented as a secular patriotic legend. For the twelfth century its secular significance was clear enough, though hardly national in a nineteenth-century sense. The heavenly credit for the defeat of Barbarossa went, under God, to St Peter and/or St Ambrose, depending on the standpoint of the narrator. The story that three white doves flew from the shrine of the martyrs of Trent, Martirius, Sisinnius and Alexander, in the church of San Simpliciano in Milan, to rest inspirationally on the Milanese *carroccio* on the battlefield, was not told by contemporaries, and seems to have become current only in the sixteenth century. The day of the battle (29 May) was the feast-day of these martyrs, whose relics were presented to Simplicianus, Ambrose's successor as bishop of Milan. This story was of a type which, as we have seen, became familiar in and after the later thirteenth century. Today the *festa patronale del carroccio* is celebrated annually at San Simpliciano. In a parish newsletter distributed in May 1991 the *parroco* reminded his flock that 'parishes too have a protector, who is usually the saint whose name they bear. The patronal festival takes place every year to render homage to that saint...' Unfortunately, San Simpliciano's own day falls on 16 August, 'when Milan is deserted'; for this reason, among others, the feast of the martyrs of Trent and of the *carroccio* fills the place of the parish patronal festival. The programme for 1991 envisaged that on 26 May, the Sunday nearest to 29 May, a historical pageant with *gonfaloni* representing the ancient *porte* of Milan would take place in the piazza in front of the church; the 'civil and military authorities of Milan' would then be present at mass, and either the *sindaco* or his delegate would present a *cera*. The very old and the relatively new join together in an accommodation with the seasonal patterns of life in the modern city.

Such changes in the patterns of social life – and, still more, changes in the relationship between church and state, and in the shape and content of modern piety – have, quite obviously, radically altered and attenuated the celebrations of the saints of the city-states. Above all, there cannot now be any legally enforceable compulsion on the citizen-body in general to attend. Yet a virtual compulsion – for at least a few people in exposed positions, office-holders and members of the local establishment – clearly remains, whether in individual cases it is felt as a pleasure or a burden. An English mayor who conscientiously objected to attending a Remembrance Day parade would court grave disapproval.

There are long-term continuities here which it is easier to sense than to demonstrate. From their beginnings in what might once have been called a less polite age, the *feste* always combined a medley of elements: the exaction from the people of demonstrations of obedience to authority, a public demonstration of piety and status by the rulers of society, a spectacle and a holiday (whether individuals welcomed it or saw it as interference with making a living), the supplication of divine power on behalf of the whole community. Those who took the initiative in organizing this collective supplication did so because they exercised power in society, and their power in society was in principle reinforced by their visible enactment of that role. This was true of the bishops in the beginning, and it was equally true of the various secular rulers who succeeded them. As a result, the public space might be appropriated (rather than privatized) by the elite, in a double sense. On the one hand they ostentatiously monopolized the management of ceremonies, like the patronal festival and also the processions for Corpus Christi, which were the concern of the whole city; on the other they employed the urban space as the theatre for their own festivals, their own ceremonial (including their funerals), while (as has been argued for Florence) the lowly retired into the parish.

Complex questions of the relationships between public and private, and between 'church' and 'state', in fact lie at the heart of the subject. The performance of the civic cult required the professional co-operation of the clergy. There were political and personal relationships, which certainly cannot be comprehended in one formulaic description, between prominent laymen and the bishops, cathedral clergy, monks and friars, who also helped to make up urban society. The Sienese laymen who voted for an offering to Ansanus, to Ambrogio Sansedoni and Pier Pettinaio, or Ser Parmigiano Pucci, *operaio* of San Zeno of Pistoia, who urged an annual procession and offering for his saint, presumably saw themselves as serving the saint's, the public and their own interest by so doing. Every phase of European history has been marked by accommodations between the lay and clerical elements in the social elite, which have never been as clearly distinguished from one another as some of the Gregorian reformers thought they should be. The story told in this book is in large part the story of such accommodations.

SELECT BIBLIOGRAPHY

NB. The works included here are for the most part those cited more than once or in more than one section of the work, or for other reasons regarded as important. Works cited in only one place or context will be found in the appropriate Note.

List of Abbreviations

AB	*Analecta Bollandiana*
Acta S	*Acta Sanctorum* (Antwerp 1643–Brussels 1925; anastatic reprint of January–October, Brussels 1965–70)
AFH	*Archivum Franciscanum Historicum*
ASF	Archivio di Stato, Florence
ASI	*Archivio Storico Italiano*
ASL	Archivio di Stato, Lucca
ASP	Archivio di Stato, Pistoia
ASS	Archivio di Stato, Siena
BS	*Biblioteca Sanctorum*
BSP	*Bollettino Storico Pistoiese*
BSSP	*Bollettino Senese di Storia Patria*
BSUSP	*Bollettino della Società Umbra di Storia Patria*
CG	Consiglio Generale
CNI	*Corpus Nummorum Italorum*
DBI	*Dizionario biografico degli italiani*
FSI	*Fonti per la Storia d'Italia*
JEH	*Journal of Ecclesiastical History*
MEFRM	*Mélanges de l'Ecole Française de Rome*
MGH	*Monumenta Germaniae Historiae*
MGH SS	*Monumenta Germaniae Historiae, Scriptores*
Muratori	L.A. Muratori (ed.), *Rerum Italicarum Scriptores*, 25 vols, Milan 1723–52

PL   *Patrologia Latina*, ed. J.P. Migne
RIS   *Rerum Italicarum Scriptores*, n. ed.
RSCI   *Rivista Storica della Chiesa in Italia*
Villani   Giovanni Villani, *Nuova Cronica*, ed. G. Porta, 3 vols, Florence 1991

1. Primary Sources

A. Published Statute Collections

NB: These are listed alphabetically by city and then by date of recension or publication.

AREZZO, 1327: *Statuto di Arezzo (1327)*, ed. G. Camerani (Florence 1946)

ASCOLI PICENO 1377: *Statuti di Ascoli Piceno dell' anno MCCCLXXVII*, ed. L. Zdekauer and P. Sella (Rome 1910)

BOLOGNA 1245–67: *Statuti di Bologna dell' anno 1245 all' anno 1267*, ed. L. Frati (3 vols, Bologna 1869–77)

BOLOGNA 1288: *Statuti di Bologna dell' anno 1288*, ed. G. Fasoli and P. Sella (2 vols, Città del Vaticano 1937–39)

CAMERINO 1424: *Statuta Comunis et Populi Civitatis Camerini (1424)*, ed. F. Ciapparoni (Camerino 1977)

COMO 1335: *Statuti del Como del 1355 Volumen Magnum*, ed. G. Manganelli (2 vols, Como 1939–45)

CREMONA 1485: *Statuta civitatis Cremonae* (Brescia 1485)

FAENZA 1415: *Statuta Faventiae*, ed. G. Rossini with an introduction by G. Ballardini, *RIS* 28.v.

FAENZA 1527: *Magnifice Civitatis Faventie Ordinamenta novissime recognita & reformata* (Faenza 1527)

FERRARA 1476: *Statuta Civitatis Ferrarae* [no title page] (Ferrara 1476)

FERRARA 1567: *Statuta Urbis Ferrariae reformata anno Domini MDLXVII* (Ferrara 1567)

FLORENCE 1322–25: *Statuti della Repubblica Fiorentina*, ed. R. Caggese (2 vols, Florence 1910–21), 1, *Statuto del Capitano del Popolo degli Anni 1322–25*; 2, *Statuto del Podestà dell' Anno 1325*

FLORENCE 1415: *Statuti Populi et Comunis Florentiae collecta castigata & praeposita anno salutis MCCCCXV* (3 vols, Fribourg [*recte* Florence] 1778–83)

FOLIGNO C14: *Statuta Communis Fulginei*, ed. A Messini and F. Baldaccini (2 vols, Perugia 1969)

FORLÌ 1359: *Statuto di Forlì dell' anno MCCCLIX, con le modificazioni del MCCCLXII*, ed. E. Rinaldi (Rome 1913)

LUCCA 1308: *Statuto del Comune di Lucca dell' anno 1308*, ed. S. Bongi and L. del Prete (Lucca 1867) (*Memorie e documenti per servire all storia di Lucca*, 3.iii)

LUCCA 1376: *Lo Statuto della Corte dei Mercanti in Lucca del 1376*, ed. A. Mancini, V. Dorini and E. Lazzareschi (Florence 1927)
LUCCA 1490: *Statuta Lucensia* (Lucca 1490)
LUCCA 1539: *Lucensis Civitatis Statuta nuperrime castigata et quam accuratissime impressa* (Lucca 1539)
MODENA 1306–7: *Respublica Mutinensis (1306–7)*, ed. E.P. Vicini (2 vols, Milan 1929–32)
MODENA 1327: *Statuta Civitatis Mutine (anno 1327 reformata)*, 2 vols (Parma 1864)
MODENA C15: [*Statuta inclyte civitatis mutine*] [no title page] (Modena 1488)
OSIMO C14: *Il Codice Osimiano degli Statuti del Secolo XIV*, ed. D. Cecchi (2 vols, Osimo 1991)
PADUA C13: *Statuti del Comune di Padova dal secolo XII all' anno 1285*, ed. A. Gloria (Padua 1873)
PARMA 1255: *Statuta Comunis Parmae digesta anno 1255*, ed. A. Ronchini (Parma 1856)
PARMA 1266–1304: *Statuta Comunis Parmae ab anno 1266 ad annum circiter 1304*, ed. A. Ronchini (Parma 1857)
PARMA 1316–25: *Statuta Communis Parmae ab anno MCCCXVI ad MCCCXXV*, ed. A. Ronchini (Parma 1859)
PARMA 1347: *Statuta Comunis Parmae anni MCCCXLVII, accedunt leges Viceomitum Parmae imperantium usque ad annum MCCCLXXIV* (Parma 1860)
PERUGIA 1343: *Statuti di Perugia dell' Anno MCCCXLIII*, ed. G. degli Azzi (2 vols, Rome 1913–16)
PERUGIA 1526: *Primum volumen statutorum Auguste Perusie magistratuum ordines & auctoritatem aliaque egregia civitatis ordinamenta continens* (Perugia 1526)
PIACENZA C14: *Statuta Varia Civitatis Placentiae*, ed. G. Bonora (Parma 1860)
PISA C12–C14: *Statuti inediti della Città di Pisa dal XII al XIV secolo*, ed. F. Bonaini (3 vols, Florence 1854–57)
PISTOIA C12: *Lo Statuto dei Consoli del Comune di Pistoia*, ed. N. Rauty and G. Savino (Pistoia 1977)
PISTOIA 1284 : *Breve et ordinamenta Populi Pistoresi anni MCCLXXXIIII*, ed. L. Zdekauer (Milan 1891)
PISTOIA 1296: *Statutum Potestatis Comunis Pistorii anni MCCXXXXVI*, ed. L. Zdekauer (Milan 1888)
PISTOIA 1313: *Statuti dell' Opera di S. Jacopo di Pistoia volgarizzati l'anno MCCCXIII*, ed. S. Ciampi (Pisa 1814)
PISTOIA 1546: *Statuta Civitatis Pistorie* (Florence 1546)
RAVENNA C13: *Statuto del secolo XIII del comune di Ravenna*, ed. A. Zerli and S. Bernicoli (Ravenna 1904)
RAVENNA 1471: *Statuti del Comune di Ravenna*, ed. A. Tarlazzi (Ravenna 1886)
REGGIO C13: *Consuetudini e Statuti Reggiani del Secolo XIII*, ed. A. Cerlini, I (Reggio Emilia 1933)
REGGIO 1582: *Statuta Magnificae Comunitatis Regii* (Reggio 1582)

SIENA 1262 (a): *Il Constituto del Comune di Siena*, ed. L. Zdekauer (Milan 1897)
SIENA 1262 (b): L. Zdekauer, 'Il frammento degli ultimi due libri del più antico constituto senese', *BSSP* 2nd ser. 2 1 (1894), pp. 131–54, 271–84; 2 (1895), pp. 137–44, 315–22; 3 (1896), pp. 79–92
SIENA 1309–10: *Il Costituto del comune di Siena volgarizzato nel MCCCIX–MCCCX*, ed. A. Lisini (2 vols, Siena 1905)
SIENA C13–C14: *Statuti Senesi scritti in volgare ne' secoli XIII & XIV*, ed. F.-L. Polidori (3 vols, Bologna 1863–77)
SIENA 1545: *L'ultimo Statuto della Repubblica di Siena (1545)*, ed. M. Ascheri (Siena 1993)
SPOLETO 1296: *Statuti di Spoleto del 1296*, ed. G. Antonelli (Florence 1962)
TODI 1275: *Statuto di Todi del 1275*, ed. G. Ceci and G. Pensi (Todi 1897)
TODI 1551: *Statuta Civitatis Tudertine* (Todi 1551)
TREVISO C13: *Gli Statuti del Comune di Treviso*, ed. G. Liberali (3 vols, Venice 1950–55)
TREVISO C14: *Gli Statuti del Comune di Treviso (sec. XIII–XIV)*, ed. B. Betto (2 vols, Rome 1984–86) [= FSI 109, 111]
TREVISO 1574: *Statuta Provisionesque Ducales Civitatis Tarvisii cum additione tertii voluminis constitutionum & literarum ducalium* (Venice 1574)
VERONA 1276: *Gli Statuti Veronesi del 1276 colle correzioni e le aggiunte fino al 1323*, ed. G. Sandri (2 vols, Venice 1940–59)
VERONA 1475: *Leges et statuta civitatis Verone* (Vicenza 1475)
VICENZA 1264: *Statuti del Comune di Vicenza 1264*, ed. F. Lampertico (Venice 1886)

B. Other Primary Sources

Alle Bocche della Piazza: Diario di Anonimo Fiorentino (1382–1401) (BNF, Panciatichiano 158), ed. A. Molho and F. Sznura, Florence 1986
Allegretti, A., *Diario Sanese*, Muratori 23, cols 763–860
Andrea da Strumi, *Vita Sancti Arialdi*, ed F. Baethgen, *MGH SS* 30, ii, pp. 1047–75
Anonymi Ticinensis liber de laudibus civitatis ticinensis, ed. R. Maiocchi and F. Quintavalle, *RIS* 11.i
Bongi, S. (ed.), *Bandi Lucchesi del secolo decimoquarto, tratte dai registri del R. Archivio di Stato in Lucca*, Bologna 1923
———— *Inventario del R. Archivio di Stato*, 4 vols, Lucca 1872–78
Il Caleffo Vecchio del Commune di Siena, vols 1–3 ed. G. Cecchini, Siena 1931–40; vol. 4, ed M. Ascheri, Siena 1984; vol. 5 (Introduction by P. Cammarosano), Siena 1991
Chronica Breviora aliaque monumenta faventina a Bernardino Azzurinio collecta, ed. A. Messeri, *RIS* 28.iii

Chronica Parmensia a sec. XI ad exitum sec. XIV, ed. A. Barbieri, Parma 1858
Chronicon Parmense, ed. G. Bonazzi, *RIS* 9.ix.
Corazza, Bartolomeo del, *Diario Fiorentino (1405/9)*, ed. R. Gentile, Florence 1991
Corpus Chronicorum Bononiensium, ed. A. Sorbelli, 3 vols, *RIS* 18.ii
Cronache e storie della Città di Perugia dal MCL al MLXIII, ed. F. Bonaini, A. Fabretti and F.-L. Polidori, *ASI* 16.i (1850)
Cronache senesi, ed. A. Lisini and F. Iacometti, *RIS* 15.vi
'Cronica Perugina inedita di Pietro Angelo di Govanni in continuazione di quella di Antonio del Guarneglie, già dette del Graziane', ed. O. Scalvanti, *BSUSP* 4 (1898), pp. 57–136, 303–400; 9 (1903), pp. 33–113, 141–380
Cronica volgare di anonimo fiorentino, dall' anno 1385 al 1409, già attribuita a Piero di Giovanni Minerbetti, ed. E. Bellondi, *RIS* 27.ii
Damian, St Peter, *Sermones*, ed. G. Lucchesi, Turnhout 1983 (*Corpus Christianorum, Continuatio Medievalis* 57)
Dati, Agostino, *Opera*, Siena 1503
Dati, Gregorio, *L'Istoria di Firenze dal 1380 al 1405*, ed. L. Pratesi, Norcia 1902
Dei, Benedetto, *La Cronica*, ed. R. Barducci, Florence 1985
Diario d'anonimo fiorentino dall' anno 1358 al 1389, ed. A. Gherardi, in *Cronache dei secoli XIII & XIV* (= *Documenti di Storia Italiana* 6), Florence 1876, pp. 207–588
Diario Ferrarese 1409–52, ed. G. Pardi, *RIS* 24.vii, pt 1
Dominici, Ser Luca, *Cronache*, ed. G.C. Gigliotti (2 vols, *Rerum Pistoriensium Scriptores*, 1, 3) 1933–39
Finzi, V. 'Di un inedito poema sincrono sull' asssedio di Lucca dell' anno 1430', *Zeitschrift für romanische Philologie* 20 (1896), pp. 219–76
Fonti sui Comuni Rurali Toscani, ed. N. Rodolico, Florence 1961–
Ghirardacci, C., *Della Historia di Bologna, parte prima* (Bologna 1605); *parte seconda* (Bologna 1657); *parte terza*, ed. A. Sorbelli, *RIS* 33.i
Johannes Ferrariensis, *Ex Annalium libris Marchionum Estensium excerpta*, ed. L. Simeoni, *RIS* 20.ii
Landucci, L., *A Florentine Diary*, trans. A. de R. Jervis, London 1927
Le Biccherne; Tavole Dipinte della Magistrature Senesi (secoli XIII–XVIII), ed. L. Borgia *et al.*, Rome 1984
Le "Vite" dei Quattro Santi Protettori della Città di Faenza', in *Chronica Breviora aliaque monumenta faventina*, pp. 337–84
Memorie e documenti per servire alla storia del Principato Lucchese, 16 vols, Lucca 1813–1925
Mercati, A., *Miracula B. Prosperi Episcopi et Confessoris*, *AB* 15 (1898), pp. 161–256
Nardi, L. et al., 'Il territorio per la festa dell' Assunta: patti e censi di Signori e Comunità dello Stato', in *Siena e il suo Territorio nel Rinascimento*,

ed. M. Ascheri and D. Ciampoli (2 vols, Siena 1986), 1, pp. 81–249
Ordinarium Ecclesiae Parmensis e vetustioribus excerptum reformatum a. MCCCCXVII, ed. A. Barbieri, Parma 1866
Ordo Officiorum Ecclesia Senensis ab Oderico ejusdem ecclesiae canonico anno MCCXIII compositus, ed. J. C. Trombelli, Bologna 1766
Pasqui, U., *Documenti per la Storia della Città di Arezzo*, 3 vols, Florence 1899–1937 (*Documenti di Storia Italiana* 11, 13, 14)
Pellegrini, A., 'Il Piccinino', *Zeitschrift für romanische Philologie* 23 (1899), pp. 382–409; 24 (1900), pp. 329–57; 25 (1901), pp. 230–43, 686–96; 26 (1902), pp. 301–13
Pius II, *I Commentarii*, ed. L. Totaro, 2 vols, Milan 1894
Regesto del Capitolo di Lucca, ed. P. Guidi and O. Parenti, 3 vols, Rome 1910–39
Reid, P., *Complete Works of Rather of Verona*, Binghamton, NY 1991
Relatio Translationis Corporis Sancti Geminiani, ed. G. Bertoni, *RIS* 6.i, pp. 3–8
Salimbene di Adam, *Cronica*, ed. G. Scalia, 2 vols, Bari 1966
Spicilegium Ravennatis Historiae sive Monumenta Historica ad Ecclesiam Ravennatem Spectantia, Muratori I.ii, cols 525–83
Stefani, Marchionne di Coppo, *Cronica Fiorentina*, ed. N. Rodolico, *RIS* 30.i
Tolosanus, Magister, *Chronicon Faventinum*, ed. G. Rossini, *RIS* 28.i
Tommasi, G. *Dell' Istoria di Siena*, 2 vols, Venice 1625–26
Il Tumulto dei Ciompi, ed. G. Scaramella, *RIS* 18.iii
Ughelli, F., *Italia Sacra*, 2nd edn ed. N. Colet, 10 vols, Venice 1717–22
Villani, Matteo and Filippo, *Cronica*, ed. F. Dragomanni, 2 vols, Florence 1846
Zaccaria, F.A., *Anecdotorum Medii Aevi maximam partem ex archivis pistoriensibus collectio*, Turin 1755
Zambotti, B. *Diario Ferrarese 1476–1504*, ed. G. Pardi, *RIS* 24.vii, pt 2

2. Secondary Works

Affò, I., *Storia della Città di Parma*, 4 vols, Parma 1792–95
Altieri-Magliozzi, E., *L'Archivio di Pistoia conservato nell' Archivio di Stato*, Florence 1985 (*Inventari e Cataloghi Toscani*, 16)
Argenziano, R. and F. Bisogni, 'L'iconografia dei santi patroni Ansano, Crescenzio, Savino e Vittore', in *I Santi Patroni Senesi*, ed. Consolino, pp. 84–115
Avogari, R. degli Azzoni, *Memorie del Beato Enrico, morto in Trivigi l'anno MCCCXV corredate di documenti, con una dissertazione sopra San Liberale e sopra gli altri Santi de' quali riposano i Sacri Corpi nella Chiesa della già detta Città*, Venice 1760

Banchi, L., 'La guerra de' Senesi col Conte di Pitigliano (1454/5)', *ASI* 4th ser. 3 (1878), pp. 184–97
────── 'Il Piccinino nello Stato di Siena e la Lega Italica (1455/6), ibid., 4 (1879), pp. 44–58
────── 'Ultime relazioni dei Senesi col Papa Callisto III', ibid., 5 (1880), pp. 427–40
Benati, A. and A. Samaritani, *La Chiesa di Ferrara nella Storia della Città e del suo territorio: secoli IV–XIV*, Ferrara 1989
Bertagna, M., 'Note storiche e documenti intorno a S. Lucchese', *AFH* 62 (1969), pp. 3–114, 449–502
Bovero, A., *L'opera completa del Crivelli*, Milan 1975
Bowsky, W., *A Medieval Italian Commune: Siena under the Nine, 1287–1355*, Berkeley, CA 1981
Burckhardt, T., *Siena the City of the Virgin*, trans. M.M. Brown, London 1960
Cecchini, G. and D. Neri, *Il Palio di Siena*, Siena 1958 (published in both Italian and English)
Chiappelli, A., 'Note Storiche della Onoranze e del Culto di S. Agata in Pistoia', *BSP* 28 (1926), pp. 112–16
────── 'Storie e costumanze delle antiche feste patronali di S. Jacopo in Pistoia', *BSP* 21 (1919), pp. 1–34, 67–95, 157–86; 22 (1920), pp. 65–87, 134–44
Chittolini, G., 'Civic Religion and the Countryside in Late Medieval Italy', in *City and Countryside in Late Medieval & Renaissance Italy: Essays presented to Philip Jones*, ed. T. Dean and C. Wickham, London 1990
Christiansen, K., *Painting in Renaissance Siena 1420–1500*, New York 1988
Compagnoni, P. *Memorie Istorico-Critiche della Chiesa e de' Vescovi di Osimo, Opera Postuma continuata da Filippo Vecchietti*, 5 vols, Rome 1782–83
Cristofani, A., *Delle Storie di Assisi libri sei*, Assisi 1902
D' Urso, P.G., *Beato Ambrogio Sansedoni 1220–1287*, Siena 1986
Fanti, M., *La Fabbrica di S. Petronio in Bologna dal XIV al XX secolo: storia di una istituzione*, Rome 1980 (*Italia Sacra*, 32)
Fasoli, G., 'La composizione del falso diploma Teodosiano', in *Scritti di Storia Medievale*, ed F. Bocchi et al., Bologna 1974, pp. 583–608
Ferrali, S., *L'Apostolo S. Jacopo il Maggiore e il Suo Culto a Pistoia*, Pistoia 1979
Fioravanti, J.M., *Memorie storiche della Città di Pistoia*, Lucca 1758
Frugoni, C., *A Distant City: Images of Urban Experience in the Medieval World*, trans. W. McCuaig, Princeton, NJ 1991
Gai, L., *L' altare argenteo di San Jacopo del Duomo di Pistoia*, Pistoia 1984
────── 'Testimonianze jacobee e riferimenti compostellani nella storia di Pistoia dei secoli XII–XIII', in (ed.), *Pistoia e il cammino di Santiago: una dimensione europea nella Toscana medioevale, Atti del Convegno Internazionale di Studi, Pistoia, 29-29-30 settembre 1984*, Perugia 1987, pp. 119–230

Garrison, E.B., 'Sienese Historical Writings and the Dates 1260, 1221, 1262, applied to Sienese Paintings', in *Studies in the History of Medieval Painting*, 4 vols, Florence 1960–62, 4, pp. 23–58
────── 'Towards a New History of the Siena Cathedral Madonnas', in ibid., pp. 5–22
Gigli, G., *Diario Sanese*, 2 vols, Lucca 1723
Golinelli, P., 'Culto dei santi e monasteri nella politica dei Canossa nella pianura padana' in *Studi Matildici: Atti e memorie del III Convegno di Studi Matildici*, Modena 1978, pp. 427–44; reprinted, slightly revised, in *Indiscreta Sanctitas*, pp. 9–29
────── *Culto dei santi e vita cittadina a Reggio Emilia (secoli IX–XII)*, Modena 1980
────── 'Istituzioni cittadine e culti episcopali in area matildica avanti il sorgere dei comuni', in *Culto dei santi, istituzioni e classi sociali in età preindustriale*, ed. S. Boesch Gajano and L. Sebastiano, L'Aquila-Rome 1984, pp. 141–97; reprinted, slightly revised, in *Indiscreta Sanctitas*, pp. 55–101
────── *Indiscreta Sanctitas: studi sui rapporti tra Culti Poteri e Società nel Pieno Medioevo*, Rome 1988
────── *Città e culto dei santi nel medioevo italiano*, Bologna 1991
Guidi, P., 'Per la Storia della Cattedrale e del Volto Santo: note critiche', *Bollettino Storico Lucchese* 4 (1932), pp. 169–86
Heywood, W., *Palio and Ponte*, London 1904
Janson, H., *The Sculpture of Donatello*, Princeton, NJ 1963
Kaftal, G., *Iconography of the Saints in Tuscan Painting*, Florence 1952
────── *Iconography of the Saints in the Painting of North East Italy*, Florence 1978
Kempers, B., 'Art and Ritual in Siena Cathedral', in *City and Spectacle in Medieval Europe*, ed. B.A. Hanawalt and K.L. Reyerson, Minneapolis, MN 1994, pp. 89–136
Kern, L., 'A propos du mouvement des flagellants de 1260: S. Bevignate de Perouse', in *Studien aus dem Gebiete von Kirche und Kultur: Festshrift für Gustav Schnürer*, Paderborn 1930, pp. 39–53
Lanzoni, F., *San Petronio Vescovo di Bologna nella storia e nella leggenda*, Rome 1907
────── *Le Origini delle Diocesi Antiche d' Italia*, Rome 1923
Liberati, A., 'Le prime manifestazioni di devozione a S. Bernardino dopo la sua morte da parte del comune di Siena', *BSSP* n.s. 6, 1935, pp. 143–61
Lilii, Camillo, *Dell' Historia di Camerino*, pt 1 (all published), Camerino 1652
Lusini, V., *Il Duomo di Siena*, Siena 1911 (first part only; all published)
Marchesan, A., *Treviso Medievale*, 2 vols, Treviso 1923
Martindale, A., *Simone Martini, complete edition*, Oxford 1988
Miller, M., *The Formation of a Medieval Church: Ecclesiastical Change in Verona 950–1150*, Ithaca, NY 1993

Mittarelli, G.B., *Annales Ordinis Camaldulensis*, 9 vols, Venice 1755–73; facsimile reprint, Farnborough 1970

Orselli, A.M., *L'idea e il culto del santo patrono cittadino nella letteratura latina christiana*, Bologna 1965; reprinted in *L'immaginario religioso*, pp. 3–182

——— 'Spirito cittadino e temi politico-culturali nel culto di San Petronio', in *La coscienza cittadina nei Comuni Italiani del Duecento (Atti dell' XI Convegno Storico Internazionale dell' Accademia Tudertina)*, Todi 1972, pp. 283–343; reprinted in *L'immaginario religioso*, pp. 183–241

——— *L'immaginario religioso della città medievale*, Ravenna 1985

Papi, A.M., *Pastori di Popolo: Storie e leggende di Vescovi e di Città nell' Italia Medievale*, Florence 1988

——— 'San Zanobi: Memorie Episcopali, tradizioni civiche e dignità familiari', in *I ceti dirigenti nella Toscana del Quattrocento*, Florence 1986, reprinted in *Pastori di Popolo*, pp. 127–76

Pellini, P., *Dell' Historia di Perugia*, 3 vols, Venice 1664, photographic reprint Perugia 1970 (= *Fonti per la Storia dell' Umbria* 15)

Peyer, H.C., *Stadt und Stadtpatron im mittelalterlichen Italien*, Zurich 1953

Pezzana, A., *Storia di Parma*, 4 vols, Parma 1837–39

Piana, C., 'I processi di canonizazzione di San Bernardino', *AFH* 44 (1951)

Ricci, E., 'La leggenda di Santa Mustiola e il Furto del Sant' Anello', *BSUSP* 24 (1918), pp. 133–55

Rodolico, N., *Dal comune alla Signoria: saggio sul governo di Taddeo Pepoli in Bologna*, Bologna 1898

Rondoni, G., *Tradizioni popolari e Leggende di un Comune Medioevale e del suo Contado*, Florence 1886

Rossi, F., *Italian Jeweled Arts*, Engl. trans., London 1957

Rubin, M., *Corpus Christi: The Eucharist in Late Medieval Culture*, Cambridge 1991

I Santi Patroni Senesi, ed. F.E. Consolino, Siena 1991

Sorbelli, A., *La Signoria di Giovanni Visconti a Bologna e le sue Relazioni con la Toscana*, Bologna 1901

Spicciani, A., 'Scopi politici degli interventi fiorentini nelle istituzioni ecclesiastiche e nella tradizione liturgica della Valdinievole', in *Itinerari di ricerca nelle fonti archivistiche della Valdinievole*, ed. R. Tolu, Pistoia 1987

Trexler, R.C., 'Florentine Religious Experience: the Sacred Image', *Studies in the Renaissance* 19 (1972), pp. 7–41

——— 'The Magi Enter Florence. The Ubriachi of Florence and Venice', *Studies in Medieval and Renaissance History* 1 (old series 11), 1978, pp. 129–218

——— *Public Life in Renaissance Florence*, Ithaca, NY 1980 (republished 1991)

Van Os, H., *Vecchietta and the Sacristy of the Siena Hospital Church: A Study in Renaissance Religious Symbolism*, The Hague 1974

Vauchez, A., 'La commune di Sienne, les Ordres Mendiants et le Culte des Saints. Histoire et renseignements d'une Crise (novembre 1328–avril 1329)', *MEFRM* 89 (1977), pp. 758–67

———— *La Sainteté en Occident aux derniers siècles du moyen âge*, Rome 1981
———— 'Patronage des saints et religion civique', in *Patronage and Public in the Trecento*, ed. V. Moleta, Florence 1986, pp. 59–80
Waley, D.P., *Siena and the Sienese in the Thirteenth Century*, Cambridge 1991
Webb, D.M., 'Friends of the Family: Some Miracles for Children by Italian Friars', in *The Church and Childhood: Studies in Church History* 31, ed. D. Wood, Oxford 1994, pp. 183–95
———— 'The Holy Face of Lucca', in *Anglo-Norman Studies* 9 (*Proceedings of the Battle Conference 1986*), ed. R.A. Brown, Woodbridge 1987, pp. 227–37
———— 'The Pope and the Cities: Heresy and Anticlericalism in Innocent III's Italy', in *The Church and Sovereignty c. 590–1918 : Essays in Honour of Michael Wilks*, ed. D. Wood, Oxford 1991, pp. 135–52
———— 'Saints and Pilgrims in Dante's Italy', in *Dante and the Middle Ages: Literary and Historical Essays*, ed. J.C. Barnes and C.O. Cuilleanáin, Dublin 1995, pp. 33–55
White, J., *Duccio: Tuscan Art and the Medieval Workshop*, London 1979

INDEX

For the names of individual saints, see under 'saints and *beati*'. No effort has been made to achieve complete consistency of nomenclature. Saints are usually indexed under the commonly used English form of their names where one exists, e.g. 'John, the Baptist'. Otherwise the Latin or Italian form may be used, depending which has been more commonly used in the text.

Abraham, feast of 72
Albergati, Cardinal Niccolo 231
Alberto, Bishop of Vercelli 83
Albornoz, Cardinal Gil 224–5
Alfonso V, King of Aragon and Naples 215, 298–9, 303, 314 n.13
All Saints' Day 107, 133 n.132, 214, 229
almsgiving, communal 139, 198, 294 n.36
Altopascio, battle of (1325) 161, 192 n.86
Ambrose *see under* saints and *beati*
Ammirato, Scipione 224
Ancona 146
   coinage, 235
Andrea of Strumi 50–51, 54
Angevin kings of Naples 10–11, 24, 153
   Charles I 10, 151, 206, 235
   Louis, 167
   Robert 158, 189 n.64, 294 n.32
Antipopes, 71
   Clement III (Guibert of Ravenna) 60, 65
Ansfridus, Bishop of Siena 37, 276
Antognolla 225
Apostles, feasts of the 98, 107, 109, 204
   see also individual saints under saints and *beati*
L'Aquila 300–301
Arezzo 2, 7, 9, 14, 37–9, 62, 66–8, 105, 114, 116, 136, 152, 166, 167, 203, 222–4, 252, 260
   coinage 224
   statutes 118, 122, 222, 223

Arras, Congress of 231
Ascension Day 19, 102, 106, 150, 169
Ascoli Piceno 103, 237, 318–19
   coinage 235
   statutes 1109, 116, 118, 123
Assisi 48–9, 83–5, 138, 224, 229, 318
Athens, Walter Duke of 116, 165, 203, 206, 222
Attila the Hun 219
Atto, Bishop of Pistoia *see under* saints and *beati*
Augustine *see under* saints and *beati*
Augustinian Hermits *see under* friars, orders of
Azario, Pietro 201–2

Baglioni, Alberto de' 229
Bargagli, Mariano 306
Barnaba da Siena 314 n.13
Bastia 224
Batoni 81
Bellanti, Battista 301
Benevento, battle of 279
Bentivoglio, Giovanni 212, 216, 233
Benvoglienti, Leonardo 301–2
Berceto 42–3
Bergamo 12
Bernard, Cardinal-bishop of Praeneste 147
Bettona 224, 244 n.115
bishops, as relic-acquirers, 4–5, 35–6, 42–3, 64–6, 69, 78–80, 86
   as saints 4, 6, 25, 106, 136, 147–8, 154–5, 233
blasphemy 125–6, 219

333

Bologna 2, 7, 11 12, 36, 77–8, 81, 84, 136, 149, 170, 173–80, 182, 204, 212, 216, 217, 220, 230, 236, 239 n.28, 249, 319
  coinage 197 n.168, 233
  statutes 96, 107, 114, 176, 177, 179–80
Bonifazio, Count 44
Borgo San Lorenzo 103
Botticelli, Sandro 167, 246 n.168
Braganza, Bartolomeo da, Bishop of Vicenza 150
bravium *see palio*; races and games
Brescia 12
Brisighella 173
Brunelleschi, Filippo 167
Buondelmonti family, of Florence 181
Buonsenior, Bishop of Reggio 61, 82

Calabria, dukes of
  Alfonso 230
  Charles 287, 292 n.13, 294 n.32
Camerino coinage, 235
  statutes, 125, 126
Camino, da, family of Treviso 8
  Gerardo 98, 141, 150
  Guecellone 141, 142, 210
Campaldino, battle of (1289) 124, 152, 247 n.168
Cancellieri, Riccardo 1
canonization, episcopal, 82, 141
  papal, 83, 85–6, 98–9, 101, 107, 110, 141, 142, 144, 145–8, 216, 250, 293 n.25, 300–302, 307–8
Canossa, house of 43, 44, 65
Capistrano, Giovanni da 301–2
Cardona, Raimondo 172
Carmelites *see under* friars, orders of
Carnival 212
Carrara 113
Carrara, lords of Padua 8, 110, 119, 233
carroccio 257, 320–21
Castelli, counts of 141
Castiglione degli Ubertini 105
Castiglione, Francesco 193 n.106, 237
Castracani, Castruccio 9, 96, 113, 155–6, 161, 162
Cavalcanti
  Giovanni, Florentine priest at Pescia 157
  Lamberto, *podestà* of Osimo, 147

cense payments 3, 67, 80, 88 n.24
Charles I of Naples *see under* Angevin kings of Naples
Chiusi 227–9
Christmas 76, 106, 118, 119, 200
Cimabue 274 n.53, 276
Cino da Pistoia 161
Ciompi revolt 165, 168, 206–7
Città di Castello 313
city models, as saintly attribute 180, 233, 235, 237–8, 277, 296–7 n.65
coinage 25, 231–6
  see also under individual cities
Colle di Val d'Elsa, battle of (1269) 152, 251, 255–6
Como coinage, 234
  statutes, 122
Compostela 17, 75, 78–9
confraternities 183, 230, 260–61, 264, 278, 312
Conradin, grandson of Frederick II 10, 148, 256
Constantinople 176, 215, 227
contado obligations at festivals 2, 18, 76, 81, 111–17, 118, 120, 132 n.115, 162, 179–80, 222, 256, 257, 262, 290
Contarinus of Pistoia 78, 80
Corpus Christi 16, 21, 25, 116, 119, 121, 183–4, 204, 212, 215, 236, 250, 288, 289, 300, 303, 304–5, 309, 312, 314 n.26, 322
Correggio, Giberto da 119, 151
Corsagno 76
Cortona 12
Cosenza, Archbishop of 229
Cossa, Cardinal Baldassare 180, 245 n.146
Cossiga, Francesco 318
Cremona 13, 82, 85–6, 138
  coinage 185 n.7, 234
  statutes 103, 138–9
Crivelli, Carlo 235, 237
Cross, Feast of the 108, 113, 133 n.141, 192 n.85, 204, 241 n.71
  see also Volto Santo
Crown of Thorns 106, 150, 169–70, 183, 231

Damian, Peter *see under* saints and *beati*

INDEX

Dandolo, Andrea 100
Dante Alighieri 122, 161, 229
Dati
   Agostino, humanist of Siena 24, 244 n.122, 261, 264, 265, 298, 300, 301–2, 305–6, 309
   Gregorio, chronicler of Florence 2, 212
Dei, Benedetto 152, 212, 240 n.33
Diego del Gelmírez 79, 91 n.57
Dominici, Ser Luca, notary and chronicler of Pistoia 1–2, 24
Donatello 168, 224
Duccio 264, 274 n.53, 290

Easter 106–7, 118, 199–200, 211, 212, 229
Eleanora of Aragon (wife of Borso d'Este) 211
Emperors Charlemagne 38, 56 n.14
   Charles the Bald 38
   Charles IV 96, 114, 154
   Constantine 19, 227
   Constantine IV 66
   Frederick Barbarossa 71, 320
   Frederick II 9, 10, 24, 148, 151, 152, 205, 237, 264
   Henry III 44
   Henry IV 66
   Henry V 66, 87–8 n.18
   Henry VI 77, 188 n.54
   Henry VII 11, 152 155
   Honorius 168
   Louis of Bavaria 11, 155, 161, 287
   Louis the Pious 39
   Otto I 40
   Otto II 43
   Otto IV 232
   Phocas 270 n.24
   Theodosius I 174, 176
   Theodosius II 174, 176
   Wenceslas 11
Epiphany 107, 119
Erlembald, follower of Ariald of Milan 51
Esdras, Bible of 230
Este family of Ferrara 8, 11, 12, 98, 119, 177, 219
   Azzo VIII 177, 217–19
   Borso 211, 221–2, 231
   Ercole 231, 233

   Leonello 215–16
   Niccolò 125, 185 n.10, 231

Faenza 81, 112, 150, 170, 171–4
   coinage 195 n.138, 236
   Four Holy Protectors, 111, 171–3
   statutes 107, 108, 111, 117, 122, 123
Faggiuola, Uguccione della 113–14, 155–6
fairs and markets 25, 43, 97, 108, 189 n.61, 213, 219
Faitinelli family of Lucca 139–40, 185 n.13
Fasoli, Raniero da 145
Federighi, Antonio, sculptor 310
Feltre, Bernardino da 229
ferie, dies feriati, see holidays
Ferrara 8, 64–6, 139, 211–12, 215, 229, 231
   coinage 231
   statutes 66, 107, 109, 125
   see also Este
Fiadoni, Tolomeo, *see* Ptolemy of Lucca
Figline 109
Flagellants of 1260 145, 217
Flaminio, Giovanni Antonio 3, 172, 225
Florence 1–2, 7, 8, 12–13, 18, 23, 35, 45, 50, 53, 79, 82–3, 105, 114, 136, 140, 152–68 *passim*, 171, 181–2, 183, 204–7, 208, 211, 212, 213–14, 216, 222–4, 226, 236–7, 249, 250, 251 n.3, 255, 258–68 *passim*, 277, 278, 289, 298–9, 311–12, 322
   churches
      Baptistery (San Giovanni) 7, 83, 121, 124, 167, 181, 205
      Cathedral (Santa Reparata, later Santa Maria dei Fiori) 166–7, 181, 207, 249
      Or San Michele 168, 181
      San Lorenzo 36, 167
      San Miniato al Monte 45, 181
      Santa Maria Novella 183, 264
   guilds
      Arte della Lana 167; Calimala 110
      Parte Guelfa 152, 165, 166, 168
   statutes 104, 110, 112, 121, 124, 168

336 PATRONS AND DEFENDERS

Zecca Altarpiece, 164, 168, 236, 237
Foix, Gaston de 172
Foligno 84, 103
   statutes 97, 103, 104, 115–16
Fondulo, lords of Cremona 234
Forli 150, 225
   statutes 118
Forlimpopoli 225
France 74, 75, 117, 194 n.114
Franciscans *see under* friars, orders of
friars, orders of 9–20, 24, 26, 85, 137–8, 139, 142, 148, 181, 229, 249, 278, 280 ff.
   Augustinian Hermits 279, 283, 313
   Carmelites 183, 203, 283, 288, 305, 309
   Franciscans 117, 141, 149, 227, 264, 279, 282–3, 301, 303, 304
   Dominicans 139, 149, 150, 176, 183, 197 n.179, 264, 277–8, 281–2, 308
   Servites 99, 194 n.123, 255, 279, 283
Fusignano 173, 225

Garfagnana 81
Genoa 117
Gente, Giberto da 208
Geremei, faction of Bologna 174
Gerolamo di Giovanni, painter 246 n.159
Ghibellines, ghibellinism 9, 153–4, 161, 166, 251, 255–6, 267
Ghiberti, Lorenzo 167
Ghivazzano, Mariano da 310
Giotto 276
glossators 175
Gonzaga family of Mantua 12, 214, 236, 237
   Federigo 212
Good Friday 98, 118, 119
Gozzoli, Benozzo 246 n.167
Gozzolini, Jacopo, of Osimo 146–7
Gradenigo, Giovanni 99–100
Gratioli, Gratiolo, of Bologna 182
Gregory of Tours 4
Gregory the Great *see under* saints and beati
Grosseto 297 n.66
Guala, cardinal-legate 153–4

Gualdo (Tuscany) 64
Gualfredus, Bishop of Siena 39
Guelf, guelfs 10, 23, 147, 152–4, 156, 160, 165, 166, 175, 205–7, 251, 256
Guibert of Ravenna *see under* antipopes
Guido da Siena 264
Guido, cardinal legate 70–71
guild participation in festivals 102, 105, 112, 116, 120, 121, 126, 142, 151, 171, 178, 183–4, 187 nn. 42 & 45, 200, 202, 205–8, 219, 303–5, 308
Guinigi, Paolo 1, 97, 114, 136, 156, 232, 275 n.39
Guy of Spoleto, King of Italy 56 n.29

Heisterbach, Caesarius of 263
Henry VI, King of England 231
Hildebrand, papal legate 69
holidays, *feries, dies feriati* 97, 100, 103, 106–11, 121, 147, 147, 158, 172, 183, 196 n.157, 229, 240 n.33
Holy Cross, feast of 108, 113 n.141, 192 n.85, 204, 241 n.71
   see also Lucca, Volto Santo
Holy Trinity 212
Hugh of Provence, King of Italy 40
Hungarian invasions 39, 40, 42

images 16, 20, 124–5, 150, 218
   of the Virgin, *see under* Mary, the Virgin
Imola 81, 174, 179
inventiones, see under relics

Jacopo della Quercia 179
Jacopo di Cione, painter 164, 236, 238
Jerusalem 17, 19, 83
   heavenly 19, 47
Jews 125
John, King of Bohemia 96, 154, 162, 238 n.3
jousting 111, 123, 214, 216
Judas Maccabeus 279
Justina, Empress 35

knighting, ceremonies of 123

Laghi, Cardinal Pio 318
Lambert, King of Italy 174
Lambertazzi, faction of Bologna 150

Lamporecchio 81
Lancia, count Federigo 115
Landucci, Luca 109, 212, 214, 215
Landulf, follower of Ariald of Milan 51
Landulf Senior, chronicler of Milan 52, 174
Lanfranc, master-mason 60–62
Larciano 2
Latini, Brunetto 122
laudi 181, 260
Lecce 318
Legnano, battle of 320
Legnano, Giovanni da 179
Lent 123, 211
Litanies, Major and Minor 19, 20, 53, 75
Liutprand, King of the Lombards 37–8, 42
Livorno 12
Lodi 13
  peace of 299
Lorenzetti, Ambrogio and Pietro, 292 n.11
Louis IX, King of France 10, 150
Lucari, Buonaguida 261
Lucca 1, 7, 8, 11, 12, 53, 64, 71–6, 78, 83, 105, 136, 139–40, 153–5, 156–7, 161–4, 167, 198–9, 209, 210, 213, 214, 216, 252, 275 n.69, 299
  coinage 192 n.86, 232–3
  statutes 96–7, 105, 112, 113–14, 114–15, 117, 122, 136, 139, 154, 162, 202, 203, 204, 213
  Volto Santo 7, 64, 72–6, 78, 81, 90 n.41, 105, 113, 136, 154, 162, 163, 192 n.86, 210, 213
Luni, Bishop of 113

Maiano, Giuliano and Benedetto da 173
Mamertus, Bishop of Vienne 19
Manfred, King of Sicily 10, 148, 235, 251, 255, 261, 261, 275 n.63, 279
Manfredi family, lords of Faenza 171, 173, 195 n.138, 214, 236
Mantua 53
  coinage 236
  Holy Blood, cult of 44–5, 57 n.37, 236
  see also Gonzaga

markets *see under* fairs and markets
Markward of Anweiler 85
Mary, the Virgin 6, 7, 9, 18, 24, 40, 98–9, 104, 105, 106, 107, 109, 116, 119, 123, 136, 138, 140, 142, 145, 149, 150, 151, 164, 169, 170, 171, 176, 181, 184, 204, 211, 217–19, 237, 249–75 *passim*, 276–7, 270, 282, 287, 291, 299–300, 306, 307, 310, 311–12
  Annunciation, Feast of the 227, 237, 245 n.130, 287, 289, 296 n.59, 306, 307
  Assumption, Feast of the 21, 22, 98, 102, 103, 113, 115, 118, 122, 138, 171–2, 202, 203, 204, 208, 210, 211, 212, 215, 221, 229, 232, 241 n.57, 256, 282, 284, 285–6, 289, 290, 294 n.34, 296 n.61, 311
  Betrothal of 229–30
  Coronation of 164, 309
  images of 124–5, 143, 166, 181–2, 204, 230, 253, 263–5, 270 n.24, 276, 310, 311–12
  Nativity of 162, 165, 221, 271
  Purification of 20, 21, 211
  robe of 263–5
  St Mary of the Snows 221
  Visitation 132 n.126
  wedding ring of 227–30
Massa (Marittima) 281
Massa Trabaria 68
Matelica 146
Matilda, Countess 44, 57 n.37, 60–62, 65
Mazza, Clemente 167
Medici, of Florence 167, 232, 237, 239 n.30
  Cosimo, *pater patriae* 193 n.106, 237, 298, 301
  Lorenzo 193, n.107, 215
Medicina 76
Memmi, Lippo 274 n.49, 292 n.9
mendicant orders *see* friars, orders of
Michelangelo 179
Milan 6, 12, 35–6, 45, 50–52, 53, 136, 152, 174, 221, 319, 320–21
  coinage 234–5
  see also saints and *beati*, Ambrose; Visconti

Modena 6, 7, 11, 42, 46–7, 60, 82, 136, 167, 216–19, 221
  coinage 233
  statutes 104, 124, 125
Monselice 77
Montagnana 78
Montagutolo 109
Montalcino 115, 251, 258, 259–60, 286, 312
Montaperti, battle of (1260) 18, 26, 152, 249, 250, 251–75 *passim*, 291, 306, 310, 312
Montefalco 214
Montepulciano 259, 292 n.9
Montopoli 105

Naples, rulers of *see* Alfonso V, Angevins; *see also* Calabria, dukes of
Nazarius, moneyer of Milan 50–51
Niccolò, sculptor 62
Nonantola, Abbey of 42

Occimiano 200
Odericus, canon of Siena 20–21, 63, 270 n.24, 277
Opicino de Canistris 199–202
Ordelaffi, lords of Forlì 223
Orvieto 83, 249, 274 n.49, 275 n.63, 288, 292 n.9
Osimo 146–7
  statutes 104, 106, 120–21, 125
Otto of Freising 66

Padua 8, 77–8, 110, 138
  coinage 233
  statutes 97
Paganus, priest of Lucca, 187 n.49
palio, pallium (also *bravium*) 2, 68, 81, 115–16, 198 n.179, 200, 203, 210, 213, 214, 220, 289
  see also races and games
Pallavacino, Oberto da 148
Palm Sunday 19, 150
Pandulf, Cardinal 77
Paris 79
Parma 6, 7, 8, 11, 13, 42–4, 49, 82, 136, 151–2, 174, 183–4, 203, 207–8, 210, 221, 237, 249, 264, 247 n.170
  coinage 132 n.125, 234
  Societas Cruxatorum 151
  statutes 112, 113, 117, 119, 121, 123, 187 n.41, 202
patronage, concept of 3–4
  terminology of 103–6, 223, 259–60
Pavia 154, 199–202
  coinage 234
Pazzi conspiracy 211
Pecci, Jacomo di Rainaldo 214
Pellegrue, Arnaut de, Cardinal 152
Pentecost 76, 196–7, 120, 201, 212, 289, 296 n.59, 300, 301, 307
Pepoli family, of Bologna 175
  Taddeo da 197, 204, 233, 239 n.28
Perugia 11, 12, 83, 112, 115, 145–6, 183, 214, 216, 224–6, 227, 229–30
  coinage 245 n.135
  statutes 100–103, 109, 110, 124, 146, 202–3
Perugino 230
Pescia 156
Peter Damian *see under* saints and *beati*
Petrucci
  Antonio 252, 275 n.69, 298–9
  Pandolfo 310–11, 313 n.4
Piacenza 36, 43, 82, 85, 220
  statutes 103–4, 118
Piccinino
  Jacopo 299, 303
  Niccolo 188 n.57, 299
Piccolomini family, of Siena 267
  Aeneas Silvius *see* popes, Pius II
pilgrims, pilgrimage 16–18, 22, 44, 62–3, 75, 78–80, 84, 85, 172, 177, 181, 185 n.10, 230
Pisa 1, 2, 9, 96, 114, 115, 116, 154, 155, 161, 165, 181, 183, 185 n.11, 198, 204, 210, 213, 224, 249, 252, 267
  statutes 106, 109–10, 117, 125
Pistoia 1–2, 7, 9, 12, 78–81, 113, 114, 116, 120, 135, 136, 155–6, 157–61, 163, 164, 208, 210, 214, 238, 240 n.47, 278, 322
  Opera di San Jacopo 7, 80, 114, 116, 126, 158, 160, 189 n.65
  statutes 107, 108–9, 110, 114, 116
plague 1, 110, 210–11, 229, 236, 250, 262, 287
Poggibonsi 140
Polenton, Sicco 185 n.11
Politi, Lanceloto 265

popes
  Alexander II 39, 67, 74, 90 n.45
  Alexander III 66, 72, 89 n.36
  Alexander IV 150, 291 n.9
  Anastasius II 90 n.38
  Benedict VIII 44
  Benedict XII 202
  Calixtus II 39, 76
  Celestine I 175
  Calixtus III 262, 299, 303, 305–6
  Celestine III 72
  Celestine V *see* saints and *beati*, Peter Celestine
  Clement IV 235
  Clement V 152
  Eugenius III 72, 80, 90 nn.38, 39
  Eugenius IV 167, 233, 235, 300
  Gregory the Great *see under* saints and *beati*
  Gregory X 278
  Honorius II 39
  Honorius III 37
  Innocent II 89–90 n.38
  Innocent III 67, 83, 85
  Innocent IV 88 n.23, 176, 187 n.40, 264
  Leo IX 44
  Leo X 186 n.13, 189 n.60, 235
  Lucius II 90 n.38
  Martin IV *see under* saints and *beati*
  Martin V 102
  Nicholas V 300
  Paschal II 61, 71, 74, 82
  Pius II 274 n.54, 300, 301, 306–7
  Sixtus IV 227, 229, 235, 237
  Stephen II 37–8, 276
  Urban IV 10, 146, 151
  Urban VI 232–3
  Vitalian 66
Portiuncula, Indulgence of the 229
Postignano 85
Poujet, Bertrand de, Cardinal 195 n.128
Prato 214
prisoners, release of 99, 102, 118–19, 142–3, 144, 163, 199, 204, 262, 302–3
processions 14–22 *passim*, 158–9, 182–4, 199–200, 202–3, 210, 213, 304–5, 208, 312
  see also relics, processional use of

Provence 117
Ptolemy of Lucca (Tolomeo Fiadoni) 153–4
Pucci, Ser Parmigiano, of Pistoia 159–60, 278, 322
Pungilupo, Armanno, heretic of Ferrara 139

races and games 81, 111, 115, 121–4, 152–3, 162–3, 167–8, 171, 180, 191 n.73, 192 n.97, 199, 200–201, 203, 207, 210–12, 213, 214–16, 220–21, 240 n.50, 258, 280, 282, 292 n.18, 310
Radagasius 168
Rainerius of Pistoia 78–9, 92 n.57
Rangerius of Lucca 64, 73, 90 n.45
Rather of Verona 40–41, 45
Ravenna 42, 47–8, 68–9, 154, 171
  statutes 88 n.30, 120
Reggio Emilia 11, 42, 45–6, 69–71, 82, 221–2
  statutes 71, 111, 112–13, 122
relics
  acquisition of 5, 15, 25, 60, 109–10, 226–7
  exhibition of 66, 217, 218, 223, 227, 228, 229, 287
  inventiones and *translationes* 14–15, 34–6, 38–9, 43–4, 60–62, 62–6, 69, 70, 72, 77–9, 82–3, 84, 86, 106, 143–4, 153–4, 157, 165, 173, 174, 179, 224, 225, 228, 231
  processional use of 15–16, 63, 166, 178, 181, 216, 217,223, 226, 230–31
  'recognition' (*expositio, revelatio*) of 61–2, 154, 226, 231
  theft of 15, 41, 227
  translations of *see under inventiones and translationes*
Ricci, Brancaleone 141
Rocca Ceneta 98, 100
Romano, Ezzelino and Alberico da 8, 97, 98, 125, 138, 148, 149, 150–51, 169, 210
Rome 17, 19, 42, 47–8, 63, 65, 66, 67, 301–2
Roseto, Jacopo, goldsmith 178
Rossi, Marsilio de' 238 n.3
Rusca, lords of Como 234

saints and *beati*
  Abdon and Sennen 156
  Abbundius 122, 233
  Agatha 20, 158, 201
  Agnes 107
  Agostino Novello 279–89, 311
  Agricola *see under* Vitalis and Agricola
  Alberto di San Georgio 231
  Alberto di Villa d' Ogna 138, 185 n.4
  Alluccio 157
  Ambrogio Sansedoni 238, 266–7, 277, 278–86, 288–9, 290, 292 n.9, 300, 311, 322
  Ambrose 7, 25, 35–6, 52, 152, 174–7, 179, 193 n.106, 221, 234–5, 272 n.33, 319
  Andrea Gallerani 287, 291 n.9, 302, 311
  Andrew 119, 120
  Anne 105, 110, 164–5, 205, 215, 231, 238, 287
  Ansanus 26, 37–9, 57 n.35, 62, 276–8, 280, 283–6, 288–9, 290, 296 n.60, 309–10, 322
  Anselm of Lucca 53, 57 n.37, 73
  Ansovinus 126, 235
  Antoninus of Piacenza 36, 103, 118, 220
  Antonio, hermit of Lucca 188 n.54
  Antony Abbot (Antony of Vienne) 33, 120, 125, 164–5, 185 n.10, 207
  Antony of Padua 97–8, 110, 137, 138, 139, 186 n.15, 233
  Antony the Pilgrim of Padua 139, 186 n.15
  Apollinaris of Ravenna 47–8, 68–9, 120, 122, 154–5, 226
  Archelaus 85
  Ariald of Milan 45, 50
  Atto of Pistoia 78–80, 160–61
  Augustine 35–6, 162, 168, 196 n.157, 200, 202, 311
  Barbatianus 120
  Barnabas 105, 110, 124, 152–3, 155, 164–5, 167, 194 n.110, 236, 288, 295 n.49
  Bartholomew 98–9, 108, 151, 210, 277
  Benedict 164
  Benvenuto Scottivoli of Osimo 104, 125, 146–7
  Bernard of Parma 82
  Bernardino 24, 26, 107, 110, 132 n.126, 216, 300–305, 308, 309, 311, 313 n.3
  Bevignate 101, 110, 145–6
  Blaise 110, 201
  Boniface 258, 259, 270 n.24, 286, 306
  Bovo 120, 121
  Brizio 243 n.115
  Calixtus, pope and martyr 305–6, 311
  Catherine of Alexandria 107, 164, 1988
  Catherine of Siena 26, 119, 300, 301, 307–9, 311, 317–18
  Cecilia 230
  Christopher 105, 124–5, 150, 31
  Ciriacus 42, 235
  Clare 138, 318
  Colomba of Reate 226
  Columbanus 220
  Corrado 224
  Cosmas and Damian 232, 236–7
  Costanzo of Perugia 102, 103, 197 n.179
  Crescentius 55 n.14, 276–7, 290, 309–10
  Crispolto 224, 244 n.115
  Daniel, hermit, of Padua 233
  Davino of Lucca 164
  Dionisus 168
  Dominic 16, 109, 120, 137, 139, 176, 178–9, 198, 230
  Donatus 7, 14, 38–9, 67, 118, 122, 167, 193 n.102, 203, 222–4, 238 nn. 3 & 5, 260
  Donninus 43
  Dorothy 156
  Efisus and Potitus 109–10
  Eligius (Eloi, 'San Lo') 271
  Emidio 103, 116, 123, 235, 237, 319
  Emilianus 103, 130 n.72, 172–3
  Ercolano of Perugia 101, 102, 119, 124, 183, 197 n.179, 214, 224, 225–6
  Eulalia 158, 161, 237
  Fabian 105, 289

INDEX

Fazio of Cremona 138
Felicola 43
Felicianus of Foligno 103, 115
Felix of Bologna 178
Felix and Fortunatus of Vicenza 106, 150, 169
Floriano 177, 178, 196 n.158, 230
Fortunatus of Todi 106
Francis 84, 98–9, 137, 138, 151, 176, 177, 318
Frediano 24, 71–3, 136, 154, 192 n.85, 198
Galgano 290, 302, 309, 311
Gallus 221
Geminianus 6, 7, 15, 16, 25, 42, 46–7, 68, 104, 124, 125, 167, 186 n.22, 216–19, 221, 238
George 65–6, 120, 185 n.10, 211–12, 215, 231, 265–7, 275 n.69
Gervasius and Protasius 35–6, 49, 234, 319
Giovanni Calybita 42
Giovanni Colombini 302
Giovanni Gualberto 45
Gregory the Great 4, 19, 244 n.115, 270 n.24
Henry of Bolzano 99, 141–5, 185 n.5
Hilary 8, 121, 151–2, 155, 174, 207, 234, 247 n.170
Himerius 85, 103, 138, 185 n.7, 234
Homobonus of Cremona 85, 103, 110, 138, 185 n.7
Isidore 231
James the Greater 2, 7, 78–81, 108, 114, 123, 135, 136, 158, 160–61, 163, 210, 240 n.47, 311
Joachim, father of the Virgin 110, 287
Joachim of Siena 279–89
John the Baptist 2, 14, 83, 104, 105, 109, 111, 112, 124, 130 n.67, 136, 164, 165, 171, 204, 205–7, 208, 211, 212, 214, 215, 222, 223–4, 226, 232, 236, 307
John the Evangelist 120, 164
Joseph 110, 132 n.126, 229–30
Julian the Hospitaller 168, 207, 240 n.39
Justina of Padua 77, 138, 233

Laurence 107, 140, 164, 289, 297 n.66
Laurentinus and Pergentinus 222
Leo of Voghenza 65
Leonard 189 n.61
Leopardus of Osimo 104, 106, 147
Liberalis of Treviso 100, 104, 126, 144, 170
Louis of Toulouse 102, 110, 137, 156, 168
Lucchesius of Poggibonsi 140
Lucy 107, 119, 121, 143, 238 n.3
Luke 77, 182, 207
Magi, Three 237, 247 n.10
Marcus, Pope 193 n.106
Marinus 201
Mark 7, 99–100, 119
Martin of Tours 22, 72–3, 75–6, 90 n.41, 105, 136, 158–9, 161, 162–4, 167, 194 n.110, 195 n.128, 209, 210, 232, 238 n.3
Martin IV, Pope 110
Martini, Simone 262, 264, 273 n.44, 277, 279, 284, 290
Martyrs of Trent 320
Mary, the Virgin *see* Mary, the Virgin
Mary Magdalen 107, 198, 310–11
Matthew 164
Matthias 77
Maurelius 87 n.18, 231
Mercurialis 118
Metro of Verona 40–41
Michael the Archangel 105, 150, 164, 169, 204
Moderannus 42–3
Mustiola 227–9
Nazarius and Celsus 36, 52, 55 n.7
Nevolone of Faenza 173
Nicolas of Bari 121, 283, 284, 286, 289, 311
Nicolas of Tolentino 110, 300
Nicomedes 43
Onofrio 206–7, 240 n.33, 288
Parisius of Treviso 98–9, 141
Paul 48, 104, 105, 123, 164, 171, 176, 220
Paulinus of Lucca 24, 25, 77, 105, 136, 153–4, 163, 189 n.62, 226, 232
Peter 7, 46–7, 57 n.37, 81, 98–100,

104, 105, 122, 123, 125, 136,
  144, 149, 150, 153–4, 164, 170,
  171, 173–4, 176, 220, 232, 233,
  235, 236, 244 n.115
Peter Celestine (Pope Celestine V) 111
Peter Damian 45, 47–50, 88 n.28,
  110, 172, 172
Peter Martyr 107, 132 n.126, 137,
  149, 198
Peter Parenzo 83
Petronella 288
Petronius 7, 16, 25, 77, 107, 136,
  174–80, 216, 220, 230, 233, 238
Philip 82–3, 121, 124, 166, 167, 181
Pier Pettinaio 279–89, 311, 322
Pietro Alessandrino 289, 296 n.65
Pius, pope and martyr 311
Policronio 156
Proculus 107, 179, 231
Prosdocimus 110, 138, 233
Prosper of Reggio 42, 46, 69–71,
  82, 111, 221–2
Raimondo Palmario of Piacenza 85
Ranerius of Pisa 106, 224
Regulus of Lucca 64, 75, 76, 90
  n.41, 115, 12, 136, 162–3, 164,
  210, 213
Remigius 43
Reparata 105, 124, 136, 164, 167–8,
  215, 226, 269 n.6
Rigo, s.v. Henry of Bolzano
Rocco, Roche 111
Romanus 65–6, 231
Romuald 45, 88 n.28
Rophilus 225
Rossore 224
Rufinus of Assisi 48–9, 68, 84–5,
  138, 186 n.22, 318
Savinus 110, 172–3, 225, 276–7,
  290, 309–10
Savinus of Piacenza 36
Sebastian 105, 201, 211, 289
Severus 77
Sigismund 110
Simeon of Polirone 44
Simplicianus of Milan 321
Stephen 101, 102, 105, 107, 109,
  129 n.39, 164, 177, 202
Syrus of Pavia 154–5, 200, 226, 234

Theobald 77
Theodore 120
Theodore of Lucca 136, 238
Terentius 130 n.72, 171–3
Thomas Aquinas 110, 137, 139, 293 n.25
Thomas Becket 196 n.158
Tiziano of Rocca Ceneta 98–100
Torpete 188 m. 54, 224
Ubaldo of Gubbio 82
Ursicinus 120, 176
Ursula 169
Valerianus 118
Venantius 125, 126, 235
Victor, pope and martyr 105, 124,
  164–5, 166, 207, 214, 215
Victor the African 276–7, 290, 291
  n.9, 309–10
Victor of Osimo 147
Vincent 169
Vincent Ferrer 110, 132 n.126
Vitalianus 104, 147
Vitalis 48, 120, 122, 170
Vitalis and Agricola 36, 107, 174
Vitus 100
Zeno 7, 25, 40, 41, 58 n.41, 106,
  107, 120, 123, 136, 149, 159–60,
  163, 167, 208, 234, 278, 322
Zenobius 16, 105, 136, 164–5, 167,
  168, 181, 207, 212, 236, 238,
  269 n.6, 278
Zita 139–40, 164, 185 n.5, 192
  n.85, 198
Salimbene of Parma 137, 138, 149,
  208, 237
Salimbeni family, of Siena 292 n.18,
  294 n.32
Salimbene 252
Ventura, painter 277
Salvani, Provenzano 251, 255, 261
San Benedetto Polirone, monastery
  44, 70
San Baronto 79
San Gimignano 140, 238
San Quirico in Venere 76
San Vito all' Incisa 109
Sano di Pietro 265, 296 n.59, 315 n.27
Sardinia 110
Sarzana 113
Sassetta 309, 316 n.42

Scala, lords of Verona, 8, 11, 234
   Mastino 120, 156
Serravalle Pistoiese 2, 156
Servites *see under* friars, orders of
Sforza, Ascanio 212
   Francesco 156, 221, 234, 298
   Galeazzo Maria 235
Sicard of Cremona 18–19, 85, 138
Sicily 10, 11
Siena 1, 6, 8, 9, 12, 13, 18, 23, 24, 25–6, 37–9, 110, 115, 136, 152, 153, 166, 173, 181, 182, 183, 203, 204, 210–11, 215, 216, 226, 227–9, 236, 238, 245 n.130, 249–316 *passim*, 317–18, 322
   Arte della Lana 288, 305, 309
   Biccherna covers
   hospital of Santa Maria della Scala 110, 257, 288, 290, 296, 309
   Nine Governors and Defenders 204, 210, 258, 260, 262, 278, 280–87
   seals 255
   statutes 97, 107, 111, 114, 132 n.115, 204, 256, 311–12
Sinibaldo, priest of Pescia 157
Sovicille (Siena) 105
Spello 26, 126
Spoleto 224, 249
   statutes 112, 115
statutes, urban 95–127 *passim*
   see also under individual cities
Stefani, Marchionne di Coppo 206
Streghi, Alessandro 24, 154, 164

Taddeo di Bartolo 238, 278
Teano, Abbey of 167
Tempesta, Guecellone 119
Templars, Order of 145
Terni 179
Thessalonica 174
Todi 106, 126
Tolomei family, of Siena 255, 292 n.18, 294 n.32
   Pia 279
Tolosanus, Magister, of Faenza 81
Totila 226
Tours 22
Treviso 8, 12, 119, 141–5, 150–51, 170, 249
   statutes 98–100, 104, 110, 116, 141, 150, 170, 210
Tunis 117

Uberti, Farinata degli 251
Urbino, Duke of 214

Varano, counts of, lords of Camerino 235
Vasari, Giorgio 273 n.44
Vecchietta, Lorenzo di Pietro 309, 316 n.42
Velletri, Giovanni da, Bishop of Florence 83
Veneziano, Domenico 167, 246 n.167
Venice 7, 8, 12, 13, 23, 99–100, 117, 119, 170, 186 n.13, 216, 226, 274 n.56, 298
Verona 6, 7, 8, 12, 40–41, 45, 57 n.40, 62, 78, 122–3, 136
   coinage 234
   statutes 106, 107, 109, 123, 124–5, 149, 211
Vicenza 8, 12, 150, 169
   statutes 106, 120, 124–5, 150, 169
Villani, Filippo 165, 210
   Giovanni 112, 116, 124, 152, 154, 161, 165, 167, 181, 205–6, 213
   Matteo 167, 181
Virgil 236
Visconti, lords of Milan, 11
   Azzo 234
   Bernabo 120, 221, 235
   Filippo Maria 12, 152, 188 n.57, 210, 214, 221, 233, 234, 253, 298
   Galeazzo 220, 235
   Giangaleazzo 1, 11–12, 166, 168, 169, 179, 220, 221, 234, 289
   Giovanni, Archbishop of Milan 220
Vittoria, 151
Voghenza 65, 88 n.18
Volterra 116, 161
Volto Santo *see under* Lucca

Wadding, Luke 156
William Rufus, King of England 73
Winchester 79, 92 n.57

Zenobius, 'centurion' of Arezzo 39

www.ingramcontent.com/pod-product-compliance
Lightning Source LLC
Chambersburg PA
CBHW070012010526
44117CB00011B/1527